IMAGES AND IDEAS IN MODERN FRENCH PIANO MUSIC

The Extra-Musical Subtext in Piano
Worksby Ravel, Debussy, and Messiaen

To my parents,
Ernst Bruhn (1911-1992) and Leonore Bruhn (1924-1995).
Your deaths, sadly, framed my work on this book.
To you I owe the seeds of everything I am and know.

IMAGES AND IDEAS IN MODERN FRENCH PIANO MUSIC

The Extra-Musical Subtext in Piano Worksby Ravel, Debussy, and Messiaen

by

Siglind Bruhn

AESTHETICS IN MUSIC No. 6

Edward Lippman, General Editor

PENDRAGON PRESS

STUYVESANT, NY

Other Titles in the Series AESTHETICS IN MUSIC

No. 1 *Analysis and Value Judgment* by Carl Dahlhaus, translated by Siegmund Levarie (1983) ISBN 0-918728-20-7

No.2 *Arts, Science/Alloys: The thesis defense for his doctorate d'Etat* by Iannis Xenakis (1985) ISBN 0-918728-22-3

No. 4 *Musical Aesthetics: A Historical Reader* (3 volumes), by Edward A. Lippman; Vol. I: *From Antiquity to the Eighteenth Century* (1986) ISBN 0-918728-41-X; Vol. II: *The Nineteenth Century* (1988) ISBN 0-918728-90-8; Vol. III: *The Twentieth Century* (1991) ISBN 0-945193-10-6

No. 5 *Contemplating Music: Source Readings in the Aesthetics of Music* (4 Volumes) by Ruth Katz and Carl Dahlhaus; Vol. I: *Substance* (1987) ISBN 0-918728-60-6 Vol. II: *Import* (1989) ISBN 0-918728-68-1 [PP368]; Vol. III: *Essence* (1992) ISBN 0-945193-04-1; Vol. IV: *Community of Discourse* (1994) ISBN 0-945193-16-5

Library of Congress Cataloging-in-Publication Data
    Bruhn, Siglind
        Images and ideas in modern French piano music: the extramusical subtext in piano works by Debussy, Ravel, and Messiaen / Siglind Bruhn.
        p. cm. -- (Aesthetics in music ; no. 6)
        Includes bibliographic references and index.
        ISBN 0-945193-95-5
        1. Piano music -- Interpretation (Phrasing, dynamics, etc.)
        2. Performance practice (Music)--France--20th century. 3. Music--Philosophy and aesthetics. 4. Music--Semiotics. 5. Music and language. 6. Debussy, Claude, 1862-1918. Piano music. 7. Ravel, Maurice, 1875-1937. Piano music. 8. Messiaen, Olivier, 1908- Piano music. I. Series.
        ML724.B78 1997
        786.2'156'0944--dc21   97-40215
                                                                        CIP
                                                                        MN

CONTENTS

CONTENTS

CONTENTS

LIST OF PLATES

The music examples from
Olivier Messiaen's *Vingt regards sur l'Enfant-Jésus*
were set after the score published by Éditions Durand, Paris (© 1947)
with kind permission of the editor.

The music examples from Claude Debussy's *Préludes*
were set after the scores published by Günter Henle, Munich (© 1986)
with kind permission of the publishing director.

The music examples from Maurice Ravel's *Miroirs*
were created after consultation of the scores by Lafond, Paris and Schott, Mainz;
those from Ravel's *Gaspard de la nuit* are based on the editions published by
Durand, Paris and Peters, London and New York.

ACKNOWLEDGMENTS

It is with great pleasure that I acknowledge the many sources of help that shaped this book. My special thanks go to fellow interpreters in many parts of the world who have generously given their time to read parts of the manuscript in various stages of its development, enriching both my (non-native) English style and my thoughts with a wealth of suggestions. I am especially grateful to Beryl Chempin, Peter Gilroy Bevan, and Nils Holger Petersen in Europe, Gerhold Becker in Hong Kong, and Daniel Albright, Father Thomas O'Meara, and Budd Udell in the United States. I owe particular debts to Yvonne Loriod Messiaen, who answered my many letters with great patience. Finally, my cherished friend and former assistant at the University of Hong Kong, Viven Chan Chuk Wan, has been of invaluable help in proof-reading all music examples and, in more than one case, prevented me from making a fool of myself.

As to the silent helpers who, mostly unbeknownst to themselves, significantly shaped my thoughts and prepared me for the task at hand, I want to extend particular thanks to Diether de la Motte, singularly inspiring teacher of music analysis during my undergraduate years, who laid a firm basis for my continued interest in the field, and whose *Musikanalyse* encouraged me to "look and listen for myself rather than apply a system." The late Carl Dahlhaus significantly influenced the direction of my research, particularly with his *Musikalische Hermeneutik*. More recently, Lawrence Kramer's works on musical representation and Theo Hirsbrunner's thoughtful studies on the music of Debussy, Ravel and Messiaen have had impact that any reader familiar with these works will recognize.

Preliminary versions of chapters appeared in the journals *20th Century Music*, *The Michigan Academician*, *Symmetry: Culture and Science*, and *Studia Musicologica Norvegica,* and in the volume *Interart Studies: New Perspectives* (Amsterdam: Editions Rodopi, 1997); I am grateful to the editors of these publications for permission to reuse the material. A German-language monograph devoted exclusively to Messiaen's cycle *Vingt regards sur l'Enfant-Jésus*, which it investigates under the angle of spiritual structuring, appeared almost simultaneously with this book in Frankfurt (Siglind Bruhn, *Musikalische Symbolik in Olivier Messiaens Weihnachtsvignetten*, Peter Lang 1997).

ACKNOWLEDGMENTS

Several of the chapters have also benefited, in their earlier versions, from the helpful comments of colleagues who heard them at conferences, lectures or seminars, particularly in Eugene, Oregon and Miami, Florida (regional meetings of the Society for Music Theory), Savannah, Georgia (Annual Meeting of the College Music Society), Santa Barbara, California (Annual Meeting of the Semiotic Society of Maerica), Baton Rouge, Louisiana (Annual Meeting of the Society for Music Theory), The University of Rochester (National Endowment for the Humanities Seminar on "Modernism in Music and Literature"), Ferris State University, Michigan (Annual Meeting of the Michigan Academy of Arts and Sciences), and The University of Lund, Sweden (INTERART Conference). I very much appreciate the input; I have learned much from all of you.

Among many wonderful friends, I wish to single out ten who have been instrumental in making me feel at home and welcome during my first three years in Ann Arbor, and have witnessed the growth of this book, shaping it in many a secret way. Frances Trix, Near-Eastern scholar and dedicated lifelong student of a venerated Sufi master, was of great help in understanding some of the mystical aspects with which I was dealing. Fred Bookstein, morphometrist and polymath, lent his beautiful baritone to chamber music sessions and his insatiable curiosity about music to much-needed clarifications of my text. Jim Cogswell, painter of images and words and philosopher of Eastern and Western thoughts, invariably contributed novel perspectives. Mary Anne Perrone, devoted teacher and defender of the less privileged, Ricardo Bartelme, physician and anthroposophist, and Kate Moore, professor of nursing, were reliable sources of boundless warmth. Teresa Schulz, planetary scientist and video artist of that which matters in everyday life, reminded me of "seeing" when I was in danger of getting lost in speculation. Rosamund Bartlett, scholar of Russian culture specializing on the connections between literature and music, was a perfect sounding board for many of my ideas. Susan Walton, ethnomusicologist and student of Buddhism and yoga, gave generous affirmation for my inner resources. Very importantly, Kendall Walton, philosopher, aesthetician, and cellist, was always there to share my enthusiasm, while quietly making sure that I stayed connected to "the rest of the thinkers about art and music out there." Bless you all!

PREFACE

Visual images, whether realistic or fantastic, represent objects that are not defined solely by their visual attributes. Conveying far more than colors, shapes and structures, they may capture characters and moods, interactions and conflicts, symbols and concepts. Similarly, literary works not only portray people and situations, emotions and thoughts, but can just as easily speak of music—describing a work, probing the reactions it elicits, and even imagining the processes of its creator's mind—or of visual art.

Music, by contrast, has often been called a closed system; it does not represent, it _is_. While the discussion of how and to what degree music can be said to express emotions is still ongoing, the suggestion that this unique language might be capable of "portraying" anything other than musical components and structures, musical conflict and beauty, is often considered controversial and easily conjures up simplistic notions of "program music."[1]

This study undertakes to show that some music can be understood as portraying and nuancing, commenting on and interpreting a non-musical stimulus, and to elaborate in detail just how this is achieved in a number of small musical works. The result reveals that there is a wealth of possible relationships between musical components and the extra-musical stimuli that presumably brought them into being. Readers will necessarily take exception with one or another interpretation, and they are heartily encouraged to do so! More perhaps than complacent consent, the urge to disagree with, or modify, a proposed interpretation will further the main purpose of this study: to heighten our sense of excitement at exploring just how composers express images of their mind's eye, impressions from nature and daily life, images gleaned from visual or poetic sources, as well as more complex ideas and spiritual concepts in musical language.

[1] The much-disputed distinction between music's capacity to rouse emotions and its ostensible inability to express very specific sentiments flanks the realm of discussion at one end; its known ability to portray by imitating the sounds connected with objects of primarily non-musical reality—from cuckoo's calls to hunting-horn fanfares—indicates the other end of the spectrum. Neither approach touches the larger issue: whether music is capable of 'representing' anything non-musical by means of its own language.

xi

My case studies, all of piano music, are intended to bring together two interest groups who, unfortunately, often work separately: solo performers and interpretive music analysts. Among practicing musicians who approach a piece from the physico-sensual experience, soloists are the ones who retain the largest degree of individual responsibility for interpretation. Among the more intellectually inclined music lovers, analysts are the ones most likely to want to—and are often skilled enough on the piano to be able to—attempt to render their insights from the hermeneutic analysis and search for hidden messages at the instrument.

I am writing, then, for three overlapping groups of readers:

1   pianists who wish better to understand the pieces they study,
2   music scholars with interdisciplinary interests in general,
    and a love for hermeneutic readings based on thorough
    analysis in particular,
3   interdisciplinary scholars with an interest in artistic representation.

Each piece is discussed in its entirety. This approach was chosen in order to avoid the temptation to interpret only choice passages of a given piece without making sense of the entire compositional *gestalt*—a procedure frequently encountered in studies organized around a methodological question, but ultimately frustrating for performer-interpreters and potentially unsatisfactory even for readers mainly interested in the interpretive analysis.

Finally, the attempt to keep the number of footnotes to a minimum reflects my personal preference. By and large, footnotes will only be inserted to extend the position exposed in the main text into a degree of detail or depth that might not be of interest to every reader, and without which the argument stands independently. I have largely refrained from backing my statements with references to the existing secondary literature or distancing my views from those of other scholars, and have instead decided to express my gratitude to particularly helpful texts up front while leaving references for further reading for the appendix.

Jean Honoré Fragonard (1732-1806), *La balançoire (The Swing)*
Wallace Collection, London. Reprinted with permission

INTRODUCTION

How she swings into the air in the space
between the flutter of her indiscreet skirts
and the quivering grove! What flashes
of half-seen legs, what else is not seen
by him who leans back in his indiscreet
pleasure of showing himself from where he is hiding!
What glances! Her air-borne shoe
in light suffused like a burning cloud
of visceral throbbing in the leaves!
How this garden is seeded with voluptuousness
entwined around the trees and the poses
and the pointing fingers and shadows!
How many skirts remain and constrain
the sex and breasts, swelling prisoners
divined by his sharp cattiness!
How statues and walls are swinging
in this vertigo of which the ropes are
so horny a grace of a happy husband!
O how she swings and flutters! How fashionable
the lover and his pose — and his obscene
delight in only looking!
How his eyes undress her, and how she resists
with a cutting and wry glance,
knowing how much lace there is to tear!
How nothing else in the world matters more!

Jorge de Sena (1919-1978): Fragonard's *Swing*[2]

[2]From: Jorge de Sena, *Metamorphoses*. Trans. Francisco Cota Fagundes and James Houlihan (Providence, RI: Copper Beech Press, 1991). With emendations by Claus Clüver (as introduced in a paper presented at the conference Interart Studies: New Perspectives, Lund (June 1995).

Word and Image

The poem reprinted above is my current favorite within a genre known by the German term *Bildgedicht*, literally "picture poem" or "poem on a painting" but usually rendered in English by a term that sounds much more intimidating to all but literary scholars, namely "ekphrastic poem." The long-forgotten Greek term *ekphrasis* is best defined as "the verbal representation of visual representation";[3] a more encompassing definition declares ekphrasis "the verbal representation of a real or fictitious text composed in a non-verbal sign system."[4]

What must be present in a *Bildgedicht* is a three-tiered structure of reality and its artful recreation: a scene—imagined or real; a visual representation of that scene—in a painting or drawing, photograph, carving, or sculpture; and a poetic rendering of that visual representation. The poetic rendering can and should do more than merely describe the visual image. Characteristically, it evokes interpretations or additional layers of meaning, changes the viewers' focus, or guides our eyes towards details and contexts we may otherwise have overlooked.

While the terms *Bildgedicht* and *ekphrasis* are normally restricted to the word-image relationship, a similar case has been made by recent scholarship for literary recreations or representations of musical compositions and ballets. Evocative descriptions of and narrations on texts belonging to any non-verbal sign system actually serve the same function as the traditional *Bildgedicht*, follow the same conventions and make the same demands on the readers as verbal texts evoking paintings and sculptures.

While ekphrasis in the strictest sense thus refers to a representation in one medium of something that has been previously represented in another, two adjacent phenomena also fall into the wieder category. On the one hand, there are lyrical depictions of actual images or scenes. In this case, the secondary representation refers to that which it describes as though it had been depicted by an artist, thus bestowing on a natural scene a heightened beauty or perfection. On the other hand, the existence of a primary text is given, but the reference the secondary text makes to it is indirect. This occurs particularly in lyrical reflections which, while

---

[3]James A. W. Heffernan, *Museum of Words: The Poetics of Ekphrasis from Homer to Ashbery* (Chicago: The University of Chicago Press, 1993), p. 3.

[4]Claus Clüver, "On Representation in concrete and semiotic poetry"; paper given at the 3rd International Conference on Word and Image, Ottawa (Aug. 1993).

triggered by an image, may focus on the mental or spiritual aspect of reality as captured, with only scarce reference to the concrete nature of the object or scene. Put another way, there is a scale that leads from the unmediated depiction of objects (real or imagined, particular or generic, of "natural" or seemingly random design) through the renewed representation of something previously depicted (in concise plots with possibly allegorical figures, sophisticated structure, and texture) to the portrayal of, or meditation on, an image's mental or spiritual significance, the concepts and thoughts associated with it.

Music and Word, Music and Image

This book is concerned with something like an inverse equivalent of the tri-partite scale of poetic reference to images. At its midpoint, as an analogue to ekphrastic poetry, I discuss pieces that can be described as musical representations of something first represented, or alluded to, in words. On the side closer to the reality of the image, I investigate works that depict actual images or scenes without explicitly referring to a particular previous representation in another artistic medium. On the side that is furthest removed from a mere portrayal of objects and scenes, I discuss musical portrayals of and reflections on religious attributes—be they defined as doctrinal symbols or rooted in mystically-individual inspirations and insights.

The development from pictoriality to interiority begins in the figurative realm, with vignettes evoking visual and auditory images of ecstasy: Delphic columns, Etruscan urns, French fireworks, Christmas chimes, and the inebriated dance of the Spirit of Joy. It moves on through emotional memories or fantasies linked to enchanted places: the cathedral sunken in the lake, the gate of a Moorish palace, the moon-lit terrace of an Indian palace, a valley filled with bell sound, and the hills on an Italian island. From there, we turn to impressions associated with wind and weather, and to flowers, insects and birds—general images accessible to all yet captured in a unique way. A final group in this first category unites performers on various kinds of stages: minstrels and comedians, pathetic gentlemen, and nocturnal serenaders.

More precise non-musical stimuli in prior poetic representation are found in pieces referring to fictional creatures in tales (nymphs, fairies, and sprites) that carry with them a characterization as well as a context given in the plot or story from which they are known, and which their mere names evoke. One step further are musical pieces whose title or caption refers to particular poetic works, albeit in a general and perhaps largely atmospheric way; this is the case with Debussy's preludes inspired by poems of Charles Baudelaire, Lecomte de Lisle, and Gabriel Mourey. Finally, this second category subsumes the three "musical poems" by Ravel explicitly based on poems from Aloysius Bertrand's *Gaspard de la nuit.*

The third part of the study deals exclusively with those among the twenty scenes Messiaen imagined in the context of Nativity that transcend the realm of impression or representation. While the collective title of the cycle, *Vingt Regards sur l'Enfant-Jésus,* suggests a series of vignettes on the Birth at Bethlehem and thus clearly emphasizes the visual, the composer's prefacing remarks point the listener far beyond the depictable.

Music's Representational Capacities

In view of the goal and the subject matter delineated above, my study falls into the field of musical hermeneutics—the reading of a musical text as carrying a message from another realm, and the interpretation of the details of the musical language as expressing, if not representing, something outside its supposedly closed semantic system.

According to Lawrence Kramer's very helpful outline of musical hermeneutics, music may be read with the aim of discovering its discursive meaning if at least one of three conditions is met:

(1) if the composer has provided us with verbal clues,

(2) if either the musical or the verbal texts (or both) include quotations or allusions that furnish a context beyond that which is presupposed in the piece itself,

(3) if the musical structure itself speaks in "pictures" or "symbols" that, within the given historical framework and among interpreters embedded in a certain cultural context, elicit universally shared responses and understandings.[5]

[5]For Lawrence Kramer's illuminating discussion of "hermeneutic windows" see the initial chapter, "Tropes and Windows," (pages 1-20) in his book *Music as Cultural Practice* (Berkeley: University of California Press, 1993). An equally commendable investigation into the subject is Edward Lippman's chapter "The Problem of Musical Hermeneutics: A Protest and Analysis" in *Art and Philosophy: A Symposium* (New York: New York University Press, 1966).

In order to limit the scope of the present study, I selected as case studies only musical works that carry some kind of textual inclusion.[6] The textual inclusions determine a primary orientation in the interpretation of the compositional components. This reading of the musical elements, which may be enhanced or focused, nuanced or modified by the identification of musical citations and structural tropes, in turn casts its own light back on the text, exploring its depth, favoring one possible nuance over another, sometimes adding nuances that may not be evident in the verbal message as such but that the composer regarded as implied. The interpretive process of shifting one's attention back and forth from a work's contextual aspects to its components, allowing for the two aspects to comment mutually on one another and thus enhance one's understanding, and of continually revising one's "expectation of meaning" during the interplay with the text, is what Gadamer described as the "hermeneutic circle."[7]

Among the ways in which words can inform our access to and understanding of music, we can distinguish various categories.

(1)   Descriptive titles constitute, of course, the most common category. For the purpose of this study, I considered only titles with wordings pointing outside the world of music itself—i.e. titles not specifying musical structure, texture, genre etc.. These realities may refer to the physical, emotional, mental or spiritual realm; they may contain single words, half sentences, complete phrases, proper names, or any other semantic structure; and they may cover, in principle, the entire spectrum that is found in literature or the visual arts.

(2)   Captions are titles placed under the final bars of a composition (Debussy's miniatures provide the best-known example). In that position, the titles are reminiscent of descriptive labels attached to paintings or

---

[6]The main body of this book thus does not include the only piece in the two books of Debussy's *Préludes* that, in the composer's revised version, carries a non-allusive, abstract title. An analysis of the musical text without any hermeneutic purpose is given in appendix 1, in the interest of providing pianists with a complete set of in-depth studies of all twenty-four preludes. It is, however, important to remember that Debussy originally intended to compose for this spot a prelude with the title / caption "Toomai des éléphants," i.e. a piece named after the protagonist in one of Rudyard Kipling's stories from *The Jungle Book.*

[7]For more details see Hans-Georg Gadamer, *Wahrheit und Methode* (Tübingen: J. C. B. Mohr, 1960); translated as *Truth and Method* by Joel Weinsheimer and Donald Marshall (New York: Crossroads, 1989). The discussion of the hermeneutic circle can be found on pages 291-294 of the English translation.

printed underneath illustrations. Captions typically invite the viewer/ reader into a circular process of reception: in approaching the work, the entire impression is usually taken in, if only cursorily, before the "meaning" proposed by the artist is known. Once the verbal explanation is read, this reading is inflected and enriched by the impressions gained beforehand. In turn, the enriched understanding of the artist's intention stimulates and focuses the viewer's next, longer look at the work of art. Captions can allude to generic impressions (a kind of flower or bird, a weather condition, etc.), to specific, widely-known fictive or real persons (protagonists of famous literary works, renowned actors, etc.), or to artifacts and objects of beauty considered the shared heritage in the composer's culture (a temple, an exquisite part of landscape, etc.).

   (3)   *Epigrams*, i.e. excerpts from poems or prose texts, appear above or, in Debussy, below a composition. They may or may not be identified by the composer; they may precede or follow the musical work itself or another verbal stimulus on which the musical work is based, such as a poem (as in Ravel's *Gaspard de la nuit*) or a meditative thought (as in Messiaen).

   (4)   *Poems* may appear implicitly or explicitly. The range spans from the musical heading citing the collective title of a group of poems, through the quotation of the title or any other line of a poem, to the explicit and purposeful juxtaposition of a complete literary poem with its musical counterpart.

   (5)   *Subheading remarks*, used typically by Messiaen underneath the title proper, consist predominantly of incomplete phrases. They cha- racteristically end in an ellipsis, and express something akin to glimpses of meditative insights.

   (6)   *Prefacing remarks* ("Author's Note") may appear, as they do particularly in Messiaen, on the pages preceding the actual musical text in the score. These remarks may offer further explicit hints at the intended spiritual content. They may even point to further texts, as when a single expression draws in an entire biblical context, or when a work of art by which the composer declares to have been influenced opens our eyes to a text associated with it, etc.

   Some further categories have been omitted here, particularly those where the verbal input forms part of the actual musical performance, as in vocal compositions on the one hand, stage and film music and other interart arrangements on the other hand.

At this point I would like to address briefly a question that arises frequently. It regards the validity of interpreting a particular musical detail or trope as expressive of a particular extra-musical stimulus. Given that a composer's music is characteristically based on one idiom and vocabulary, one may wonder whether any details mentioned in an analysis are not merely the building blocks of that idiom, rather than carriers of any (extramusical or other) meaning. A comparison of the musical language with the verbal sheds light on this issue. While a particular people's system of verbal expression—say, French—is certainly based on a specific, overall syntax and wordstock, the place of a particular word in that functional context by no means predefines the "message" it carries, or the nuance it expresses, in a particular context. Thus a musical detail —a deceptive cadence, a melodic falling tritone, a rhythmic pattern— may represent one metaphor in the context of one piece while referring to an entirely different extra-musical aspect in another, just as within the French (or English, or any other) language, a half-sentence or phrasal expression often derives its meaning entirely from its context. Such discrepancies can reach a point at which the same string of words, embedded in a different referential reality, evokes strikingly different associations. Thus, while the word group "clotted blood" represents an unambiguous syntactic unit with unambiguous lexical meaning, the connotations conjured up differ dramatically if these words appear in the evening news, a biology lecture, or a love poem.

The Composers

Achille-Claude Debussy was born in St. Germaine-en-Laye on August 22, 1862, and died in Paris on March 25, 1918. His family background was modest; his father was a traveling salesman and later a clerk, his mother a seamstress. Early recognition of his musical talents was due to his piano teacher Mme. Mauté, the mother-in-law of the poet Verlaine who was to have considerable influence on the composer. Debussy was accepted into the piano and theory classes at the Paris Conservatoire at age 10, and by the age of 12 performed Chopin's F-minor Concerto. He did not, however, complete his studies in piano performance but concentrated on composition, winning the second *Prix de Rome* in 1883 and the first *Prix de Rome* a year later. The ensuing two-year stay at the Villa Medici in Rome influenced him less than the exposure to Javanese gamelan during the Paris International Exposition of 1889, which accounts for much of his very personal treatment of color and tonal language.

Debussy's main works outside the piano repertoire include the opera *Pelléas et Mélisande*, the ballet *Jeux*, which he wrote for the famous Russian choreographer Diaghilev, the orchestral pieces *Prélude à l'après-midi d'un faune*, *Nocturnes* and *La mer*, as well as a great number of songs on poems by, among others, Musset, Banville, Gautier, Verlaine, De Lisle, Bourget, Mallarmé, and Baudelaire.

* * *

Maurice Ravel, Debussy's junior by almost thirteen years, was the eldest child of a very cultured family of Swiss and Basque origin. He spent only the very first months in the little town in the Pyrenees where he was born, but lived in Paris for the remainder of his life, i.e. until the end of 1937. He began attending the Conservatoire at age 12, studying harmony with a pupil of Delibes, and two years later was also admitted to one of the piano performance classes. Having left the Conservatoire at age 20, he started composing, inspired by impressions from the Javanese gamelan music heard at the Paris International Exposition of 1889 and by concerts with works by Rimsky-Korsakov, Wagner, Chabrier and Satie but as yet without any formal education in composition. Two years later, in what seemed like a fresh start, he returned to the Conservatoire as a member of Fauré's composition class. His failure to gain the coveted *Prix de Rome* was a handicap in terms of bureaucratic recognition, but did not thwart his creativity. An early friend of Baudelaire, Poe, and Mallarmé, Ravel was also a member of a coterie known as 'Les Apaches', a circle of composers, painters and poets that provided its members with a platform upon which to share new works and a congenial environment for aesthetic discussion.

Ravel's main works outside the piano repertoire include the orchestra pieces *Bolero*, *Spanish Rhapsody,* and *La Valse*, the ballet *Daphnis and Chloé*, the operas *L'heure espagnole* and *L'enfant et les sortilèges*, as well as chamber music and many songs (among them *Shéhérazade* with orchestra and *Histoires naturelles* with piano).

* * *

Olivier Messiaen was born in Avignon in 1908, the son of Pierre Messiaen, a teacher of English who translated the complete works of Shakespeare, and the poet Cécile Sauvage. Having begun composing at the age of seven, he is said to have discovered Debussy's *Pelléas et Mélisande* when only ten years old—a discovery that confirmed his "decision to devote his life to music." He entered the Paris Conservatoire at age 11 to study harmony, counterpoint and fugue (winning a *premier prix* at age 17), piano accompaniment (*premier prix* at age 19), music history (*premier prix* at age 20), and composition (*premier prix* at age 21). Immediately thereafter he became the principal organist at the cathedral La Trinité in Paris, a position that he held for more than forty years. He was appointed professor of composition at the Paris Conservatoire in 1967 and won the coveted Erasmus Prize in 1971. Messiaen continued to compose, research, and teach until his death in 1992.

As a composer, Messiaen was completely independent of any "schools," both in his native France and elsewhere. While "La jeune France," the group he founded in 1936 together with Jean Yves Daniel-Lesur, Yves Marie Baudrier, and André Jolivet, declared themselves dedicated to a "return to the human" and opposed to the neoclassicism then prevailing in Paris, it was actually based on friendship between the four composers rather than on a shared musical aesthetics or ideology. As a teacher, on the other hand, Messiaen influenced an entire generation. Among his students were Pierre Boulez, Karlheinz Stockhausen, and Iannis Xenakis.

The Works

Debussy's twenty-four Preludes, written between 1909 and 1913, constitute a summit of piano composition comparable to the large piano cycles of the Romantic era. What makes this work so outstanding is not only the superbly varied array of sound colors and other depicting devices, but also the impressive wealth of musical thoughts, each of them unique within both the cycle and Debussy's entire compositional output.

The Preludes present us not so much with a chain of pieces linked in content and demanding to be rendered in the order in which they appear, but rather with a collection of single pieces of very different origin and character. The composer, typically critical of his own creations, remarked that they weren't all equally good—a judgment that has survived to this day especially among those who don't know the Preludes too well. This is one more reason to consider the cycle in its entirety and to juxtapose, in study as well as in performance, well-established pieces with little-known ones.

The number of pieces, twenty-four, picks up a tradition that originated with 18th-century composers' joy of being able to write pieces on all major and minor keys for the "well-tempered clavier." From the two volumes of J. S. Bach's preludes of 1722 and 1744, each of twenty-four, the incentive remains the same with those who followed:

Austrian composer Johann Nepomuk Hummel's 24 Preludes "in the major and minor keys," op. 67 (1814/15),

Frédéric Chopin's famous 24 Preludes op. 28 (1836-39),

French composer Valentin Alkan's 25 Preludes, op. 31 (1847; his collection includes two in C major),

French-Hungarian composer Stephen Heller's 24 Preludes, op. 81 (1853),

German-Italian composer Ferruccio Busoni's 24 Preludi, op. 37 (1879-80),

Russian composer Alexander Skryabin's 24 Preludes, op. 11 (1888-96), and

French-Russian composer César Cui's 25 (*sic*) Preludes, op. 64 (1903).

Debussy followed this example, yet without linking his design to the idea of twenty-four different keys in any particular order. What distinguishes his cycle significantly from its forerunners is the fact that he chose poetic titles. Here again, Debussy looked back on a tradition in his own country: the close relationship between, and mutual influence of, music and words. One could speak of the literary character of French music in general. Machaut, Jannequin, Couperin, Rameau, Berlioz, Boulez wrote their own texts, employed descriptive titles, or wrote extensively about music. As one scholar observes somewhat tongue-in-cheek: "Any educated Frenchman can make up a poem, just as any American can improvise a new 'popular' tune. The French language is heavy with old literature, as the American air is loaded with ta tá, ta ta tá."[8]

In the Paris of the late nineteenth and early twentieth centuries, composers found an atmosphere of artistic ferment, nourished primarily by the literary figures of the circle that met regularly at such places as the Chat Noir. As Paul Dukas recounts, "Verlaine, Mallarmé, Laforgue brought us new tones, new sounds. They projected heretofore unseen lights onto the words; they used methods unknown to their predecessors; they allowed the verbal substance to produce effects of a subtlety or power that one would not have thought possible. Above all, they conceived their verses or their prose like musicians...."[9]

[8]Marcel Raymond, *From Baudelaire to Surrealism* (New York: Wittenborn, Schultz, 1950), introduction.

INTRODUCTION

Debussy became involved in a number of literary circles, particularly at the Librairie de l'Art Indépendant, at the Taverne Weber, which he frequented together with his close friend Pierre Louys, and at the "Tuesdays" at Mallarmé's house.[10] A quotation from the composer's mouth, recounted again and again in the literature about him, gives a good idea of his conception of the relationship between music and word:

> I conceive a different dramatic power: of a music that begins where the expressive power of the word ends.

[9] See Robert Brussel, "Claude Debussy et Paul Dukas," in *Revue Musicale* 7 (1926), 101.

[10] Arthur B. Wenk, in his monograph *Claude Debussy and the Poets* (Berkeley: University of California Press, 1976) includes an extensive discussion of the importance of Debussy's literary associations. Among Debussy's literary acquaintances of this time Wenk mentions particularly:

- Maurice Vaucaire, whose adaptation of *As You Like It* Debussy agreed to set to music;
- Maurice Donnay, the playwright who described an occasion at the Chat Noir with "the joyous Debussy conducting our wild chorus throughout the evening";
- Adolphe Willette, who illustrated the first edition of Debussy's *Mandoline*;
- Charles Cros, inventor and poet, whose *L'Archet* Debussy tried to set to music;
- Paul Bourget, literary critic, novelist and author of *Les Aveux*, a collection of poems of which Debussy set seven to music;
- Comte Robert de Montesquieu, a wealthy poet and patron whom Debussy at one time approached for funding;
- Gabriel Vicaire, the satirical poet;
- Jules Bois, for whose play *Les Noces de Sathan* Debussy was commissioned to compose incidental music;
- Gabriel Mourey, with whom Debussy planned several operas including *La Légende de Tristan* and *L'Embarquement pour ailleurs*;
- Jean-Marie Comte de Villiers de l'Isle-Adam, author of the play *Axël*, for which Debussy composed incidental music in 1889;
- Henri de Régnier, the poet whose *Scènes au crépuscule* inspired Debussy's *Nocturnes* and influenced his *Proses Lyriques*;
- Maurice Denis, the artist and critic who illustrated *La Demoiselle élue*;
- Paul-Jean Toulet, who later planned a collaboration with Debussy on *As You Like It*;
- René Peter, who undertook a number of projects with Debussy including three comedies, and for whose play *Tragédie de la mort* Debussy composed a *Berceuse*;
- Catulle Mendès, poet, journalist and librettist who collaborated unsuccessfully with Debussy on an opera, *Rodrigue et Chimène*;
- Jules Laforgue, whose poetry Debussy admired and quoted;
- Jean Moréas, with whom Debussy discussed Schopenhauer and Goethe;
- Francis Vielé-Griffin, who published two of Debussy's poems;
- Paul Valéry, whose Monsieur Teste is the model for Debussy's Monsieur Croche;
- Charles Morice, who attempted a collaboration with Debussy based on poems of Verlaine;
- Pierre Louys, who was to become one of Debussy's closest friends; as well as Paul Verlaine, Stéphane Mallarmé, André Gide, and Marcel Proust.

Debussy's oeuvre for solo piano contains a large number of miniatures accompanied by evocative words, lines, or epigraphs. These verbal
allusions never precede the music but invariably appear beneath the final
measures of the score. This has led to suggestions that they may not be
intended to guide the imagination. It has even been held that performers
and listeners would actually appreciate the music for its absolute value
just as much without having in mind the allusion given in the caption.

While Debussy's music provides a complete aesthetic experience
even when perceived without any extramusical stimuli, there is much
more to the composer's explanatory after-titles than meets the eye.
Careful investigations into the metaphors and material components,
semantics and structure, attitude and perspectives adopted in both the
non-musical source alluded to and in the musical miniature alluding to it
reveal highly complex relationships.

One can thus read the results of the musical analysis as Debussy's
interpretation and creative re-enlivening of a poet's or artist's imagery,
or—in a few cases—of that expressed in nature. This adds a vital perspective to our appreciation of the "absolute" music, affecting both our
performance and our listening attitude.

* * *

Ravel composed the piano cycle *Miroirs* (Mirrors) in the years
1904-1905. This was the time of the "Apaches," the circle of friends of
which Ravel was the central figure. Each of the five pieces included in
Miroirs is dedicated to one of the Apaches: *Noctuelles* to the poet
Léon-Paul Fargue, *Oiseaux tristes* to the Spanish pianist Ricardo Viñes
who greatly stimulated the composers of his time and premiered many of
Debussy's and Ravel's works, *Une barque sur l'océan* to the painter Paul
Sordes in whose home the gatherings of the Apaches took place,
Alborada del gracioso to Michel D. Calvocoressi, a prolific music critic
who recognized and praised Ravel's works from the very beginning, and
La vallée des cloches to the composer Maurice Delage, with whom Ravel
maintained a vivid correspondence throughout the time of his absence
from Paris.

The title of the piano cycle, *Miroirs*, alludes to notions on several
levels. As a noun of daily language, the word means, of course,
"mirrors." In a wider sense, both the English word and its French equivalent embrace mirroring surfaces of various kinds: not only the silvered
glass but also water, one of the favorite topics of early twentieth-century
art. The title of the cycle may also call into play the very process of

reflecting and mirroring, both the "reflection" of moods in colors or sounds, and a person's mirroring in a social interaction, including feedback and criticism, affirmation and correction. Finally, a piece of music may be understood as a mirror of sorts, particularly in the case of objects and events so elusive that they may otherwise be perceived only in the subconscious, never emerging to the surface of our attention (like, for instance, the play of night moths). *Miroirs* serves as a collective heading for five works dealing with images as diverse as insects and birds, ocean and valley, dawn song and bell sound. In his biographical sketches Ravel writes the following lines, which attest to the composer's distinctly descriptive intention:

> *Le premier en date de ces morceaux - et le plus typique de tous - est, à mon sens, le second du receuil: les "Oiseaux tristes". [J'y évoque] des oiseaux perdus dans la torpeur d'une forêt très sombre aux heures les plus chaudes de l'été.*

> (The first in terms of date among these pieces—and the most typical of all—is, to my mind, the second one of the collection: "Sorrowful Birds". [Here I evoke] birds lost during the hottest summer hours in the torpor of a very dark forest.)

Beyond the merely descriptive, "mirror" was a key word of symbolist poetry. Notions of the unreal and the suggestive are often expressed through mirrored images and reflections. In Mallarmé's *Hérodiade*, "mirror" is a specifically important word, and in a letter to a friend of 1864, the same poet committed himself to the idea of "peindre non la chose, mais l'effet qu'elle produit" (to paint not the thing, but the effect it produces). A famous aphorism of Ernest Hello confirms this: "L'art a pour caractère de préparer l'harmonie qui n'est pas encore faite en nous présentant l'image dans un miroir." (The character of art is to prepare the harmony that is not yet established in presenting us with the image in a mirror.)

With *Miroirs*, Ravel thus renews a tradition of French secular music which, in stark contrast to Beethoven and generations of composers influenced by him, prefers "painting" to "expressing one's feelings." In this concept of art the idea, according to André Suarès, is to paint the object without primarily concerning oneself with the painter's feelings. The title of the cycle, *Mirrors*, might then finally be understood to denote an artistic attitude rather than a programmatic title.

* * *

Ravel's widely-read friend, the Spanish pianist Ricardo Viñes, introduced the composer to a book of poetry by Aloysius Bertrand, *Gaspard de la nuit. Fantaisies à la manière de Rembrandt et de Callot.* The wording of the title is significant. Gaspard, a male first name, is of Persian origin, where the word literally refers to the man in charge of the royal treasures. Gaspard of the Night or the treasurer of the night thus creates allusions to someone in charge of all that is jewel-like, dark, mysterious, perhaps even morose.

The subtitle, "Fantasies in the Manner of Rembrandt and Callot," seems to confirm the impression that both the more reassuring and the spookier aspects of the night are being evoked. Rembrandt's fascination with the subtle shades of darkness is well known. The further mention of Callot establishes a direct connection to E. T. A. Hoffmann (1776-1822), the German composer and poet of the supernatural and expressively distorted who, in 1815, had published fantasy pieces "in the manner of Callot." The etchings of Jacques Callot (1592-1635) depict gruesome details of war, death and destitution; he is often regarded as a Baroque predecessor of the Spaniard Francisco Goya. Callot's famous cycle *Caprice des Gueux* (Scoundrels' Whim) particularly attests to his talent for the grotesque and ludicrous and may have inspired both Hoffmann and Bertrand as well as Goya.

Bertrand, originally baptized with the first name Louis which he only later changed to Aloysius, only lived from 1807 until 1841, mostly in Paris. *Gaspard de la nuit* was published posthumously in 1842. He is considered the creator of the lyrical prose poem; a generation of poets attempted to imitate him, and lyricists like Théophile Gautier and Charles Baudelaire learned from him.

The collection of poems is divided into six books followed by a series of separate pieces, and rounded off with a number of what the author referred to as *Chroniques et proses diverses* (chronicles and various prose pieces). The poems are arranged in such a way as to suggest some kind of number mysticism: the first three books comprise incrementally decreasing numbers of poems (11, 10 and 9 poems respectively), the remaining three books similarly increasing numbers (6, 7 and 8). There are thus books with 6, 7, 8, 9, 10 and 11 poems respectively. The obvious choice for the number of poems incorporated in the "separate pieces" would seem to have been 12. But that number not being one of mystery, one is hardly surprised to discover that the section contains 13 poems—a figure reminiscent of the evil depicted in many tales and fables.

Premier livre	(First Book)	= 9 poems
Second livre	(Second Book)	= 10 poems
Troisième livre	(Third Book)	= 11 poems
Quatrième livre	(Fourth Book)	= 8 poems
Cinquième livre	(Fifth Book)	= 7 poems
Sixième livre	(Sixth Book)	= 6 poems
Pièces détachées	(Separate Pieces)	= 13 poems

Now Gothic tales and stories about ghosts, monsters and moon-lit cemeteries do not constitute a characteristic component of French literature. It was only since E. T. A. Hoffmann's unexpectedly far-reaching influence on the French literary scene that people in the "land of clarity" showed a surprising willingness to be taught by their German neighbors to enjoy frightening horror scenes.

Ravel seems to have had a keen sense of this. In a letter of 17 July 1908 to his friend Ida Godebska about his three-months of intense work on three poems from Bertrand's collection, he wrote that he felt as if inspired by the devil, "... no wonder, since he [the devil] is in fact the author of these poems." Another source of inspiration for the composer may have been the treatment of language. While Bertrand's "rhythmic prose" is not entirely without predecessors—Fénelon, Senancour and Chateaubriand had made attempts in this genre—it truly flowered only with the symbolists. Significantly, it was in 1908 that the *Mercure de France* brought out a new edition of these prose poems. Just as poets strove to free themselves from regular verses with rhymed endings, so also did musicians like Wagner, Liszt, and Debussy pass beyond regular phrase structure and metric order. The resulting "musical prose" may usefully be seen as an equivalent to the development in lyrical composition. Ravel's subtitle "3 Poèmes pour piano d'après Aloysius Bertrand" confirms this close connection.

* * *

Whereas Debussy's two volumes of *Preludes* constitute a collection of miniatures with a wealth of never-repeated musical invention, and Ravel's *Miroirs* and *Gaspard de la nuit* are not characterized by shared motivic material, Olivier Messiaen's *Vingt Regards sur l'Enfant-Jésus* is cyclical in many respects. Most extraordinary about its cyclical nature is the fact that the cross-refentiality is not restricted to musical parameters, but extends to concepts—and that these concepts, along with certain facets of their concomitant musical expression, are cyclical in the

composers entire oeuvre. (For a more extensive discussion of the particu-
larities of Messiaen's musical language, see appendix I.)

In terms of ideas expressed, Messiaen's music can be subsumed
under three themes: the glorification of God and His divine love (including both music for religious purposes and secular music on religious
themes), the myth of Tristan and Isolde, and bird song.[11] On a higher
plane, however, all three themes merge into one: the praise of God who,
out of unconditional love, gave mankind His Son; the praise of idealized
human love which, even in its most exemplary form, is only a poor and
blurred reflection of Divine love;[12] and the praise of God's creation, the
infinite beauty of nature—the epitome of which Messiaen saw in bird
song.

Messiaen's religious background goes back to his father, Pierre, a
devout Catholic who felt that "It is a grace to be born into a Catholic
family. What light for the understanding." Pierre took his children to
church and commented that they showed real passion for religious music
and the ceremonies of the liturgy. The composer's mother, the poet
Cécile Sauvage, was not religious. She describes humankind in her poetry
as "ephemeral mosquitoes" who are "running in infinity without hearing
the rabble" or "roaring strangely on life and death."[13] Later, the composer
would define his life's goal, confessing that the principal idea informing
all his creative work was the truth and reality of the world view of the
Catholic faith. Messiaen called this the noblest, most valuable, most
useful aspect of his work.

Since the beginning of Christian sacred music, composers have created musical symbols to express transcendental ideas. These symbols
include the use of certain keys and modes, the choice of specific intervals
perceived as connected to religious concepts (from the chromaticism in
laments over human sinfulness to God's perfection in the octave), the
shaping of pitch lines for special images of visual symbols (see, for
instance, the many melodic outlines tracing the shape of the Cross), and
the translation of Christian terms into their numerological equivalents
embodied in rhythmic, metric or otherwise countable units. This develop-

---

[11]"Il y a dans ma musique cette juxtaposition de la foi catholique, du mythe de Tristan et
Yseult et l'utilisation excessivement poussée des chants d'oiseaux." (Claude Samuel,
Entretiens avec Olivier Messiaen, Paris: Éditions Pierre Belfond, 1967, p. 12)

[12]"...un très grand amour est un reflet, un pâle reflet mains néanmoins un reflet du seul
véritable amour, l'amour divin". (Claude Samuel, ibid., 1967, p. 22)

[13]Pierre Messiaen, *Images*. Paris, 1944, p. 129.

ment peaked in the sixteenth and early seventeenth centuries as an already very elaborate musical rhetoric coincided with a heightened desire for mystical expression.

Messiaen was deeply familiar with this tradition. In over forty years as organist at La Trinité in Paris, he perpetuated a legacy handed down to him through compatriots and predecessors like César Franck, Marcel Dupré, Maurice Emmanuel, and Paul Dukas. Regarding music as "an act of faith" that, according to his treatise *La technique de mon langage musical*, aims above all "to express with a lasting power our darkness struggling with the Holy Spirit", he developed a unique musical language that includes a wealth of symbolism. His piano cycle *Vingt Regards sur l'Enfant-Jésus*, composed between March and September of 1944 and premiered in the following year by his wife, pianist Yvonne Loriod, is one of many pieces in which Messiaen explored what one might refer to as "musical representations of the attributes of the Divine."

As his primary inspiration, the composer names the Gospels, the Missal, as well as the texts of a group of exemplary Christians spanning five countries and seven centuries: the Italian Dominican friar Saint Thomas Aquinas (1225?-74), the Spanish mystic Saint John of the Cross (1542-91), the French theologian Ernest Hello (1828-1885), the great poet and writer of Catholicism Paul Claudel (1868-1955), the Belgian Benedictine abbot Dom Columba Marmion (1858-1923), the French mystic Saint Theresa of Lisieux (1873-97), and the American trappist monk Thomas Merton (1915-1968). Reading through his biblical quotations not only in this cycle but also in *Nativité du Seigneur*, it becomes clear that his favorite sources of inspiration were the Apocalypse, the Gospel of John and the Letters of Paul.

Besides these various religious sources, the influence that emerges from Messiaen's comments most powerfully is visual art. There are four references to works of art in the *Vingt Regards sur l'Enfant-Jésus*. Outside this cycle, we can identify the impression created by Chagall's and Bosch's paintings (in *Cinq rechants)*, and the transformation into music of a surrealist painting by Penrose (in *Harawi*). In his public talk known as the Notre-Dame conference, we find Messiaen mentioning Fra Angelico, Grünewald, Michelangelo, Tintoretto, Rembrandt, and Chagall as well as, perhaps particularly important for the cycle under consideration, the medieval stained-glass windows which, as he says, tell us the life of Christ, of the holy virgin, of the prophets and the saints and thus serves as a "catechism through images."

The writer who undoubtedly had the single greatest influence on Messiaen's religious thinking was Columba Marmion. His major works, *Le Christ, Vie de l'âme* and *Le Christ dans ses Mystères* appeared in 1918 and 1919 respectively.[14] In the latter book, this Belgian priest of Irish descent speaks about the various *regards* falling upon the infant Jesus in the manger—from the highest, those of the Father and the Holy Spirit, to the lowliest, those of the angels, the shepherds and the Magi. In the Author's Note that prefaces the score of the *Vingt Regards sur l'Enfant-Jésus*, Messiaen mentions that he has seized this idea and expanded it to twenty "looks" (or "perspectives").

As it now stands, Messiaen's cycle with its *Twenty Contemplations of the Infant Jesus* includes a number of very different agents looking down upon the Child in the manger. Some are "persons" (like the Father, the Virgin, the angels, the prophets, shepherds, and Magi); others are described by the composer as "immaterial or symbolic beings" (such as Time, the Heights, Silence, the Star, and the Cross). A third group occupies a realm between these two, encompassing the *The Church of Love* and *The Spirit of Joy Contemplating the Infant Jesus*, as well as more problematic agents such as those in *The Son Contemplating the Son* and *The Awesome Unction Contemplating the Infant Jesus*. Then there are a number of pieces whose titles do not explicitly allude to a look upon the Child in the manger, but quote instead concepts of the Catholic faith perceived or reinterpreted by Messiaen as *regard*-ing Jesus. These include concepts related to God's power (*Through Him all things are Made* and *The Almighty Word*), to the birth of the Son on earth (*The first communion of the Virgin* and *Christmas*), and concepts expressing the Christ's loving attitude towards His human brothers and sisters (*The Kiss of the Jesus-Child* and *I Sleep but my Heart Wakes*). Finally, there is one piece whose wording refers specifically to the relationship between the Divine and the human, *The Exchange*.

The word "regards" is commonly translated as "look" or "gaze" or "glance".[15] Unfortunately, the English word "look" is ambiguous (cf. "in which way does a person *look* at me" vs. "what does the person *look like*" —an ambiguity not found in the French *regard* or the German *Blick*). The word "gaze" has been so strongly linked, in recent discourse, with notions

---

[14] For what seems to be the only English translation to date see Columba Marmion, *Christ, the Life of the Soul* (London and Edinburgh: Sands & Co.; St. Louis: B. Herder Book Co., 1928).

[15] In fact, only thirteen of the twenty *regards* feature the word "regard" in their heading.

of gendered seeing that it seems equally inappropriate here, while a "glance" is simply too short. I have decided to use the English equivalent to the term Messiaen himself uses elsewhere in his preface: *contemplation*. In his "Author's Note," which prefaces the score, the composer speaks of the "contemplation of the Infant-God of the manger, upon whom many eyes are laid."[16] This wording takes into account not only the persons featured looking upon the Child in the manger, whom we would imagine deep in thought rather than cursorily looking (*The Father's Contemplation, The Virgin's Contemplation*). As a concept, contemplation also works better than any of the other terms in the case of, as Messiaen calls them, "immaterial or symbolic beings," and especially with those "agents" in connection with whom the idea of a perception with the visual sense alone would seem highly inappropriate—where an inner "seeing" is being alluded to (*The Heights' Contemplation, Time's Contemplation, Silence's Contemplation; The Church of Love Contemplating the Infant Jesus*, etc. This is particularly true for such difficult concepts as "the Awesome Unction" which Messiaen imagines laying eyes upon the Jesus Child.

(For a summary overview of the musical symbols and their occurrence throughout the cycle, please refer to appendix II.)

[16]The precedent for the English usage of "contemplation" stems from the liner notes to Peter Serkin's recording of the *Vingt regards* (RCA-Red Seal CRL 3-0759); notes by Olivier Messiaen, translated by Cathérine de Montmarin and Peter Serkin.

It is important to stress here that beyond the linguistic difficulty of translating *regard*, there is also the question of the broader meaning of the French word. I owe thanks to Larry Peterson, who generously shared with me many insights gained in private conversations with Olivier Messiaen. He recalls that the composer used the word "regard" in a wider sense, a sense that encompasses the notion of twenty different "perspectives" of the Jesus-Child. (Larry Peterson, private correspondence, September 1994.)

Part I

IMAGES AND IMPRESSIONS

The Representation of Fictitious Images

Thou still unravish'd bride of quietness,
  Thou foster-child of silence and slow time,
Sylvan historian, who canst thus express
  A flowery tale more sweetly than our rhyme:
What leaf-fring'd legend haunts about thy shape
  Of deities or mortals, or of both,
    In Tempe or the dales of Arcady?
  What men or gods are these? What maidens loth?
What mad pursuit? What struggle to escape?
  What pipes and timbrels? What wild ecstasy?
(...)

Who are these coming to the sacrifice?
  To what green altar, O mysterious priest,
Lead'st thou that heifer lowing at the skies,
  And all her silken flanks with garlands drest?
What little town by river or sea shore,
  Or mountain-built with peaceful citadel,
Is emptied of this folk, this pious morn?
  And, little town, thy streets for evermore
Will silent be; and not a soul to tell
  Why thou art desolate, can e'er return.
(...)

from John Keats (1795-1821), "Ode on a Grecian Urn"[17]

The Grecian urn described here, Keats scholars and art historians inform us, does not exist. The beautiful depictions evoked so emphatically by Keats represent motifs seen on several different vases but, for the lyrical purpose, attributed to a single object;[18] this technique is referred to as cumulative ekphrasis. Taking this a small step further, we find poetic descriptions of visual depictions that do not exist at all but are presented as though they did; this is called fictional ekphrasis.

[17]John Keats, *Odes, Lyrics and Sonnets*, Oxford: Clarendon Press, 1916, p. 45

[18]Keats wrote his 1819 ode after seeing an exhibit at the British Museum which, in 1816, had complemented its treasures of classical vases by acquiring the Elgin marbles.

Finally, there are lyrical portrayals of objects (flowers and animals, landscapes and architectural creations) that are "seen" with an artistic eye before being translated into a verbal homage. Shelley's West Wind, for example, is so much more than a gust of air from a certain direction!

The first part of this study deals with musical representations of images and impressions that may or may not have been previously depicted in art or poetry. The captions and titles suggest scenes or framed pictures rather than direct, unmediated experiences, but, as the contextual analyses will show, verification is not the main issue here. It seems to matter neither to the composer nor to music lovers whether the Delphic sculptures evoked in Debussy's first prelude were in fact meant to represent dancers—whether he remembered correctly what he had seen in the Louvre. The convincing atmosphere of South-Italian island folklore does not lose any of its charm even if research reveals that accessible records do not contain exactly these tunes, heard in the context of Debussy's *Les collines d'Anacapri* as though they were real-life quotations. *Footprints in the Snow* may not exist as a painting, but the composer strongly insinuates that it could; and the music of *Sorrowful Birds* and of *The Valley of the Bells* makes us wonder about, and long for, the poems whose musical reflections Ravel created in his *Miroirs*.

The factual absence of a particular, identifiable Grecian urn having the properties specified by Keats does not generally seem to prompt lovers of poetry to think of the ode as a betrayal. Quite to the contrary, most readers probably go to great lengths to picture the artifact in their minds, and it is this interaction between the verbally suggested image and the listener's attempt to recreate its alleged source in the mind's eye that opens paths to a particularly reinforced or refocused aesthetic experience.

The following five chapters aim at a similar experience. It will be shown how the musical miniatures, appraised in all their detail in light of the descriptive wording that sets their extra-musical frame of reference, evoke in the listener's mind vivid and luminous pictures or scenes.

TIMES OF ABSORPTION

Danseuses de Delphes   (Debussy, *Préludes*, vol. I, no. 1)

The title of this short piece, *Dancers of Delphi*, is very telling. Debussy is known to have seen the column with three bacchantes in the *Louvre*. Their dance evokes absorption, and is thus a symbol for the designation of the Greek temple site of Delphi.

The temple at Delphi, dedicated to the god Apollo (the god of music, poetry and prophecy, and leader of the Muses), was famous throughout Greek antiquity for its oracle. The Pythia, a priestess with extrasensory powers, sat on a three-legged stool (a tripod) over a fissure in a rock from which vapors emanated. Under the influence of these probably slightly drugging gases, she would gradually enter into a trance. Pilgrims to the temple then asked her to predict events in their future, to help with decisions, and to suggest auspicious days. Her often obscure recommendations (obscure no doubt in great part because of the slightly intoxicating effect of the gases) were interpreted by another Apollonian priest as the voice of the god himself.

While attention is often drawn to Debussy's allusion to the dancers' cymbal sounds (see the double seconds F/G in bars 3/4, 8/9, 27/28 and C/D + G/A in bars 16/17), what is much more intriguing is how Debussy's tonal language and texture seem to reflect the gradual clouding of the mind, and subsequent entry into trance, of the priestess at Delphi.

In a tempo marked *Lent et grave* (slow and solemn) and a mood indicated as *doux et soutenu* (sweet, or soft, and held back), the first phrase evolves with two distinctly different components. (For a melodic excerpt of these phrases, please refer to the music example on the following page.) Bars 1-4,[19] are in compound three-part texture. One strand is made up of bass octaves in regular quarter-notes, a second strand of right-hand chords also in regular quarter-notes, and the third strand,

---

[19] I use subscripted numbers to refer to the beat in a bar; thus bar 4_1 indicates the first beat in bar 4. Wherever it might appear more appropriate, I may speak of bar 4d for the downbeat of bar 4 (which may not include all of beat 1). Correspondingly, 4m designates the middle of bar 4 in tables and other abbreviated references.

evolving from these stately surroundings, is an almost hidden melody: buried inside the right-hand chords in bars 1/2, the tune only emerges in bar 3. The bass strand begins with steps strongly supportive of the B♭-major tonality indicated in the key signature (tonic on the downbeats, dominant on the third beats), and even the chromatic ascent from the first to the third degree in bars 3/4 does not weaken but rather serves to enhance the tonal feeling. Similarly, the right-hand chords endorse the tonal center with tonic chords on the downbeats of bars 1 and 2 and on the second beat of bar 4, as well as a slightly tainted tonic on bar 3d. Neither the augmented chords on the weak beats in the two initial bars nor the chromatic—and thus not tonally centered—melodic ascent in these bars can camouflage the feeling that this piece begins in a clear B♭ major.

The shorter component that complements the first phrase until the end of bar 5 displays a simple texture in parallel chords while being even more strongly tonal. (Its chord sequence—B♭ / d / g / C / d / B♭ / C / F— represents a fairly traditional I-iii-vi-V/V-iii-I-V/V-V progression.) Both the half-note notation for the bass octave in bar 4_2 and the *pp diminuendo* under unbroken *portato* marks distinguishes this "tail" as something like a background to the preceding main part of the phrase.

The second phrase (bars 6-10) is an enhanced repetition of the first. Over an unchanged bass, the melody is now doubled in octaves, and the right-hand chords, considerably thickened, not only reach into a much higher register but also fill the quiet after-beat eighth-notes with a much more urgent motion. The urgency expresses itself also in the complementing "tail" of the phrase that, although previously a mere background progression in very soft shades, now begins in *mf*—i.e. louder than anything heard so far. (Have the vapors, gentle and almost unnoticed, taken over? The additional beat at the end of bar 10, easily overlooked, allows time to think this over.)

The third phrase displays a very subtle further development with regard to texture and tonality. The bass gives up its independence and gets locked into an octave pedal on F. The second-strand chords, still kept in the very much thickened version adopted in the previous phrase, constitute not so much a logical harmonic progression but an ascending sequence of root-position chords. While in bars 11/12 the tonal context is still mainly that of the B♭-major scale, bars 13/14 represent a fairly tainted A♭ major, concluding with squarely cross-related chords (see the B/B♭ in the consecutive G major / B♭ major chords on bar 14_3). Melodically, the simple ascent in the chords is countered, *doux mais en dehors* (soft but standing out) in an equally simple descent. (Personality and complex reasoning seem thus noticeably reduced in favor of mood).

The fourth phrase continues the trend of gradual simplification and loss of independence. Only two layers remain: a triple-octave melody and the second-strand chords. Both strands begin locked in parallels whereby all melodic notes constitute the fifths degree in chords of an all-major progression (see bars $15-16_1$). The melody then gets caught in a repetitious D-G-C, and its rhythm gradually loses all its momentum until it finally comes to a standstill, with caesura and *fermata*, in bar 20. While still loosely referring to F major as the dominant of B♭, the phrase contains several cross-related chords (see bar 15: C major / A major, bars 17/18 C major / A♭ major). Dynamically, this is the most exposed moment within the piece, launched from *mf* into a *f* climax and diminishing—against off-beat chords in *pp*—*only* towards the end.[20]

---

[20]Note that the *pp* indications clearly refer to the off-beat, off-center chords. The triple-octave melody is still somewhat like *mf* in bar 18, *p-mp* in bar 19, and reaches the softness of *pp* only on the final C—always against the backdrop of considerably softer chords.

The fifth phrase seems to complete the process of disintegration. Melody and chords appear again locked in parallels. The melodic notes now constitute the thirds of an all-major chord progression that is characterized by almost continuous crossrelationship.[21] Dynamically, the phrase begins in *p* and recedes first, only to return to *p* at the last chord with what sounds like an unearthly sigh. (This phrase can probably be read as the musical equivalent of what, after some time of inhaling toxic vapors, would amount to a floating sensation with a loss of any frame of reference to reality.)

The final phrase of the piece seems to indicate that the entire process could now start all over again. Tonally, bars 25/26 have returned to a solidly established B♭ major; melodically, the tune of the opening bars is quoted, and each note set here in the augmented chords that were previously confined to the accompanying strand. In bars 27/28, a sense of eeriness is once more created by strangely clashing chords in diminishing volume. But the final bars return to earth with four octaves of untainted B♭ major, spanning the entire dynamic spectrum used in this piece.

Canope   (Debussy, *Préludes*, vol. II, no. 10)

The caption of this prelude, and the nature of its reference to the musical content, are often regarded as a riddle. A "canope" is an Etruscan burial urn, typically one with a lid bearing a likeness of the head of Osiris, the ancient Egyptian God ruling over the realm of the dead. Debussy is known to have had two such urns on his writing desk. The connotations are thus threefold: first, a vase—a solid object very unlike the waters and weathers, dances and moods, fairies and pixies whose lightness and ambiguity the composer usually favors; second, times long past—the Egyptian period with its worship of Osiris dates back to the third millennium B.C., and the Etruscan period is dated to the 9th or 8th centuries B.C.; finally, a solemn occasion, a funeral.

The indications for tempo and mood confirm this notion: Debussy requests *très calme et doucement triste* (very calm and softly sad). The opening theme (see bars 1-4d, extended up to the downbeat of bar 7) may be perceived as depicting the slow pace of an ancient funeral procession.

---

[21] Here is a short overview over the tonal structure within this phrase. The second line gives the reigning chord, the third indicates the pitch that effects the cross-relationship.

bar	21				22		23			24				25
chord	B♭		D♭	A♭	C♭		E♭	B♭	D♭	F	A	C	E	B♭
notes		D♮/D♭		C♮/C♭	G♭/G♮			D♮/D♭	A♭/A♮	C♯/C♯	C♯/C♯	G♮/G♯	B♮/B♭	

8

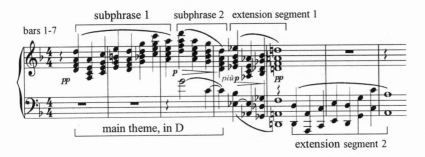

The tonality in the main phrase fluctuates, owing to the B♮/B♭ alternation, between the minor and the Dorian scales on D. The melody, while in itself pentatonic (employing only the pitches D E G A C), clearly confirms D as the tonal root: it begins and ends on D, while its first subphrase also emphasizes A. All melodic notes except for the C are supported by minor-mode triads, thus giving this phrase a very unified mood—were it not for the middle-strand notes which, accompanying the shorter second subphrase (see bar 3), throw a light of doubt on the simple tonality.

The extension consists of two segments. The four chords in bar 4-5d convey three impressions simultaneously:

- they continue the solemn pace and conclude in a D-minor chord, thus confirming both the ceremonious occasion and the tonality;
- they temporarily slow down the tempo (*cédez - - - // mouvement* = give way up to the sign //, then resume the previous tempo), thus underscoring the basic mood;
- their three consecutive major-mode chords contrast with the use of minor-mode triads prevailing so far, thus striking a different emotional string, one that is often perceived as more direct, warmer and thereby more touching.

The second extension, while retaining the rhythmic pace and returning to the original tempo, differs in texture—it presents a unison melody under the sustained D-minor chord. Its melody is an exact recurrence of the theme's first subphrase.

The following four bars can be imagined as a kind of religious chant, first sung by the priest alone (bars 7/8) and repeated by the congregation (see the doubling in octaves in bars 9/10). Both utterances are accompanied by protracted D-major seventh chords.

9

bars 7-10

A subtle effect of bitonality is created here. While the downbeat A, enhanced both by its separate entrance before the remainder of the chord and by the dash and subsequent p - pp hush, clearly serves as the fifth in a D-major harmony, it also provides the root for an A major triad whose third and fifth (see the C♯ in its prominent position at the beginning of the chant's two lines and the E♮, additionally emphasized with an *acciaccatura*, at the first climax) are filled with mournful chromatic steps.

In the following phrase, the lamenting becomes increasingly poignant. The melodic rhythm appears more impassioned; the harmony is less poised and, with changes in very bar, more high-strung than before. Even the phrase structure reflects the state of heightened urgency with its significant elision (the D in bar 14 is both the final note of a phrase—compare the melodies in bars 11/12 and 13/14—and the beginning of the new development in bars 14/15).

bars 11-14

The central segment of the prelude, while still in soft hues, conveys a sense of agitation. Bars 14/15 simultaneously embody three tonal areas: D minor in the melodic treble and E♭ major in the middle-strand counterpoint sound before C-F as a harmonic backdrop. The B♭ major / G minor of bars 17 and 19 seems to answer the call of the harmonic strand, but the resolution into an enharmonically notated A^9 (bar 18) thwarts any sense of an even momentary tonal commitment (see the music example on the following page). In a slightly increased tempo (*animez un peu*), the triplet patterns on A recall the rhythmic pattern of the chant. The actual chant recurs in bars 20/21 and 22/23, albeit over a new bitonal pillar that includes a G^7 chord besides the A-major triad.

The subsequent tonal shift, from A major to an implicit A♭ major (bars 24/25), is conspicuous for the unusual symmetric pitch arrangement in the descending run. In an invention worthy of Scriabin and Messiaen's

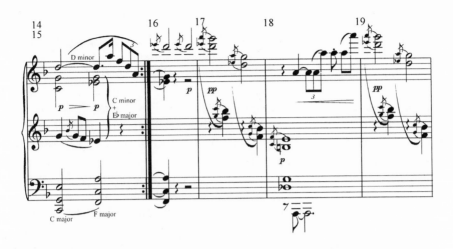

artificial scales, Debussy devises a highly idiosyncratic combination of steps which, with 1/2 + 1/2, 3/2 + 1/2 + 3/2, 1/2 + 1/2, is perfectly mirror-symmetrical, but does not confirm the underlying A♭-major tonality.

The evocation of an ancient funeral ceremony is completed by a recapitulation of several components. The procession theme is heard once again with an identical first subphrase, reinforced with parallels in the left hand (bars 26-28d). Its second subphrase is transposed up one semitone and thus abandons the relationship to D as a tonic (bars 28-29d). The first extension also begins in semitone transposition but then deviates even more and concludes, harmonically ambiguous, on the chord that supported the most agitated phrase (compare the chord in bars 30-33 with that in bar 14d and 15d). The treble recalls the lament in its original pitch pattern (compare upper strand bars 30-31 with bars 11-12). The tempo slows down more and more (from *retenu* = held back in bar 29 via *plus lent* = slower in bar 30 to *très lent* = very slow in bar 32). Correspondingly, the intensity decreases from the earlier *pp* through *très doux et très expressif* (very soft and very expressive) to *encore plus doux* (even softer).

To complete the impression of sounds of mourning retreating, the melody omits its final note, the very clearly anticipated D, and the work thus closes as if hanging in the air, in deep absorption.

Feux d'artifice   (Debussy, *Préludes*, vol. II, no. 12)

Debussy's final prelude, called *Fireworks*, refers to the annual mid-July celebrations on Bastille Day, commemorating the beginning of the French Revolution. On 14 July 1789, the Bastille, a fortress that served as a state prison and was regarded by many as the symbol of the despotic monarchy, was stormed and its prisoners freed. The famous Eiffel Tower was built in 1889, on the centenary of this crucial event in French history. Each summer, the Parisians celebrate the birth of the concepts of liberty, fraternity and equality with glamorous fireworks.

Just as in a fireworks production for public entertainment the design is finely orchestrated yet presented in such a way as to appear improvised and dreamlike, so also in Debussy's musical depiction. The visual display typically contains an almost continuous sequence of slighter sparkling explosions as a backdrop for the more carefully spaced-out glorious cones of color, all different from one another yet basically variations of the same "blossoming-flower" event. While this applies to all fireworks, an additional treat of the Parisian event is its climax, the "bomb". Not surprisingly, there are very close correspondences to all these events in the music.

- As a backdrop, we hear an almost uninterrupted "sparkling" motion in very fast values of usually very light color, including rippling clusters (bars 1-16), pentatonic groups (bars 25-29 etc.), wide *arpeggios* (bars 35-38 etc., 57-69), *glissandi* on the black and the white keys (bars 17, 61-64 and 87) and *tremoli* (bars 71-78, 90-98). The only interruption of this constantly scintillating flow occurs in bars 47-56, i.e. strategically placed in the very center of the piece.
- The "glorious cones" are musically represented by a theme that is heard in six versions, all recognizably variations of the same substance, but not ever the same in timing, spacing, interval pattern, texture etc.
- The "bomb" explodes at the climax, on the downbeat of bar 87.

The musical excerpt on the following page juxtaposes the six versions of the theme for easier comparison.

Notice, for example, that
- the theme's initial component begins in four different ways:
with an upbeat to the middle of the bar, a double-*acciaccatura* preceding the downbeat, on the downbeat, or on the middle beat;

12

bars 27-31
bars 35-38
bars 42-45
bars 65-67 + 68-70
bars 79-81 + 82-84
bars 93-96

- the same short component can also end in five different note values and with different distances to the following component;
- its interval can change from perfect fifth to tritone to perfect fourth.

And yet, behind all this highly improvisatory-seeming detail there is indeed a fundamental scheme that helps a performer's orientation. One can detect three large sections followed by a coda.

Section A is designed in bridge form:
- bars 1/2 introduce rippling clusters, built on the six chromatic notes between F and B♭;
- bars 3-6 add a quasi-melodic tritone curve in double octaves (D-A♭-D-A♭);
- bars 7-10, the center piece, use the same two pitches as well as an additional C, in now more extreme registers and with some accents and *marqué* (emphasized);
- bars 11-14 recall bars 3-6 but in contracted and therefore redoubled curves;
- bars 15/16 are an enhanced version of bars 1/2.

Section A is followed by a transition based on a diatonic cluster that progresses in four ways:

- the ascent of a three-pitch group
  (1) stepwise (see bars 18/19: B♭+C♭/D♭; bars 20/21: B+C/D♭, C+D♭/E♭),
  (2) through several octaves;
- the decreasing time intervals
  (3) between ascending steps
      (bars 18/19 = 2 bars in the first cluster position,
      bar 20 = one beat each in the second and third cluster position,
   bar 21 = two cluster positions in each beat) and
  (4) between octave displacements
      (bars 18-21 = four bars in the central octave,
      bars 22/23 = two bars in the next higher octave,
      bar 24 = half a bar each in ascending octaves).

This transition thus serves as a something like a multimedia *crescendo* that plays with the excitement of the fireworks audience.

Section B contains three "stanzas" of the theme, each preceded by short introductions in the form of the particular form of sparkling arabesque that will accompany it.

- Bars 25/26 present waves built on the pentatonic scale G-B♭-C-D-E (which, on another level of harmonic listening, may be heard as C-E-G-B♭-D, a belated dominant-ninth chord of F, the central tone of the accompaniment ripple in section A).
- Bars 27-31 introduce the theme in its first version. Interestingly, what in bar 30 is perceived by many listeners as a chromatic shift in the tune, causes the accompaniment to shift as well, not merely in pitch but even in quality: from the pentatonic scale to the whole-tone scale on B in the first half of bar 30, and on to the whole-tone scale on C in the second half-bar. In bar 31, the earlier pentatonic pitch contents is restored.
- Bars 32-34 serve as a preparation for the second stanza, expanding the scope of the waves and adding both weak-beat bass-notes (see the C in bars 33/34) and pitch alterations (see the oscillation between C♮ and C♯ in these bars).
- Bars 35-38 contain the second version of the theme, accompanied by waves built on a five-note excerpt of the whole-tone scale: C♭-D♭-E♭-F-G.
- Bars 39-41 act as a third preparation. Beginning in *ff* but decreasing thereafter, short whole-tone scale excerpts are posited against

14

pentatonic excerpts, before giving way (in bar 41) to a figure based on the A♭ major scale.

- Bars 42-44 (with a possible inclusion of the first melodic beat of bar 45) contribute the third version of the theme that is characterized, among other features, by its fanfare-like insertions (see the final beats of bars 42 and 43).

Section C, longer and more dramatic than the two preceding sections, presents a hybrid form: part development section, part fantasy.

- Bars 45/46 combine a variation of the theme's final ascending interval (C-A♭) with development of an earlier component. (The melodic line B-A-D♯, first heard in the second half of bar 45, is derived from G-F-B in bars 44.)

- Bars 47-53m develop the latter component further, leading in *molto crescendo* to an abrupt halt. The final segment, derived from the accompaniment in the preceding bar (see bar 53, beat 1, which stems from the left-hand part in bar 52), then gives rise to further development (see bars 53-56).

- Bars 57-64 introduce what appears as the first "fantasy" episode: the first four bars, in *mouvement, plus à l'aise* ([back to] tempo, [but] more at ease), are distinguished by a color and melodic line unrelated to anything that was heard so far. The following four bars, in *pp rubato*, stand out primarily through their wide-spaced downbeat chords, *glissando* effects, and cross-related chords (see bars 61/62: C major / F♯ major, E major / B♭ major; bars 63/64: E♭ major / A major, G major / C♯ major—all of which are paired in tritone distance).

- Bars 65-70 present us with a first development of the thematic material, in ternary form with a cadenza as the center piece. As in the first occurrence of the theme, the accompanying *arpeggios* are based on a pentatonic scale. They are, however, dramatically suspended during the second half of each thematic bar. The metric position of the theme's initial component also recalls the original version (compare bars 65/66 with bars 27/28) but the previously introduced tritone interval is added in the bass (see the repeated E♯-B, discontinued only during the cadenza). The tempo is *molto rubato*, the dynamic expression very passionate.

- Bars 71-78 follow with further development derived from the longest component of the theme and enveloped in continuing *tremolo/trill* motion.

- Bars 79-84 constitute a second and even more extended development of the theme, in *mouvement élargi* (enlarged tempo), as before with internal repetition (compare bars 79-81m with bars 82-84m), a *cadenza*-like insertion in the middle (the second half of bar 81, in a *p subito* that surprises in the neighborhood of the *f crescendo* and *éclatant* [garish]). An ascending sequence serves as a transition to the short final phrase. During this section, the accompanying *arpeggios* are based on the diatonic cluster B♭-C-D (and thus reminiscent of the transition after section A).
- Finally, bars 85-87 conclude this largest section of the prelude with a climax in a rich, multi-voiced texture. The ascent in four chromatic steps is an extension of the last-heard version of the theme (See bars 84-86: bar 84 concludes the theme proper with C-A-G-B♭-A♭-D♭; this is followed by the sequence D-B-A-C-B♭-E♭ and leads in the subsequent two bars through the partial sequences C-B♭-E♭, C♯-B-E, D-C-F, D♯-C♯-F♯ to the outburst of the "bomb," a bass attack on the lowest key of the keyboard. The after-effect of the bomb explosion manifests itself in a parallel of black-key and white-key *glissando*.

A pause at the end of bar 87, though not written against rests, clearly brings the music to a metrically free halt. The coda then sets in with a spelled-out *diminuendo* (*mf, p, più p, pp*). This recapitulates the tonal content of the prelude's opening bars before linking in a chromatic descent (B-B♭-A-A♭) into the final *tremolo*. Concurrently, an equally spelled-out *ritardando* progresses from *plus lent* (slower) through *très retenu* (very much held back = much slower) to *encore plus lent* (even slower).

Quite unexpectedly then, we hear a quotation from the *Marseillaise*, the French national anthem, sounding *de très loin* (from far way; see the upper strand, bars 91-96). The anthem tune receives an immediate answer with the final version of the fireworks theme. The C-major contexts of both the *Marseillaise* and the fireworks theme clash with the D♭-A♭ of the *tremolo*. However, the fireworks theme "gives in," the *Marseillaise* breaks off, and the prelude concludes in an untainted D♭ major.

David Lewin, in his analytical essay on this piece, captures the effect of this musical quotation beautifully when he writes:

In the fireworks proper we have just witnessed a brilliant display of design, color, transformation, and organized motif. We might imagine ourselves standing somewhere around the Trocadéro or the Eiffel Tower, surrounded by other brilliant symbols

16

of modern French design and civilization. Suddenly we are re-minded, by music from somewhere else, far away, out of tune, that the display is meant to celebrate some "old" and "remote" ideas of a republic based upon liberty, equality, and fraternity.[22]

Noël   (Messiaen, *Vingt regards*, XIII)

(Les cloches de Noël disent avec nous les doux noms de Jésus, Marie, Joseph...)

"The Christmas bells speak with us the sweet names of Jesus, Mary, Joseph," says Messiaen of the piece that, within a cycle dedicated to vignettes centering on the Child in the manger, carries the simple title *Christmas*. Just as his title seems intent on capturing the untroubled, exuberant expression of joy, so also does his music.

The piece is laid out as a very regular rondo. The different sections are clearly distinguished on every level, i.e. in texture, complexity of material, modal organization, tempo, dynamic inflections etc., making the simple form easily accessible to listeners.

refrain	bars 1-5
codetta	bars 6/7
episode 1	bars 8-20
refrain	bars 21-25
episode 2	bars 26-52
refrain	bars 53-57
episode 1 (var)	bars 58-64
refrain	bars 65-69
coda	bars 70-80

The refrain, marked by the composer as *comme des cloches* (like bells) and *Très vif, joyeux* (very lively, joyous), consists of three strands spread out over almost the entire keyboard. In the middle strand, a middle-register attack on downbeats guarantees metric simplicity. The upper strand features a quick alternation of a four-note chord and its transposition a whole-tone lower. The rhythm is irregular within the bar

---

[22]David Lewin, Debussy's "Feux d'artifice" in *Musical Form and Transformation: 4 Analytic Essays*, New Haven/London: Yale University Press, 1993, p.158. Lewin also draws our attention to the CD dyad in bars 7-10 that he reads as "C.D.", i.e. Debussy's signature —the signature under the entire collection of twenty-four preludes, given in a piece which, both by its title and more particularly through the use of the anthem snippet, is declaredly nationalistic. In Lewin's words: "The signature is «*CD, musicien français*»", and with this explicit comment distances the twenty-four preludes from their German ancestors, identifying their author as a determinedly French composer.

itself (short-short-*long-long-long*-short). Since the last attack in the bar is a repetition rather than a transposition, there is an inversion of the order in every other bar, thus causing an alternation on the level of bars, as if in augmentation of the alternation of chords. In the third strand we hear a chromatic cluster made up of the three lowest keys (A/B♭/B♮), attacked "off beat," as it were, on the sixth eighth-note in a nine-eight measure. All chords are marked as accented *ff* and are to be collected by a continuous pedal into a single sound. After four bars in which this material is heard without any inflection in volume, articulation, or tempo, the fifth bar wraps the refrain up by extending the strand-1 pair with a third chord, moving the strand-2 chord in contrary motion along, and suspending the cluster chord in the low bass register—still, however, within the same pedal and its protracted voluminous sound.

There are, then, merely three chords: the strand-1 four-note chord and its transpositions, the strand-2 three-note chord (and its transpositions in bar 5),[23] and the strand-3 cluster. The interval structure in all three strands is dominated by the semitone—either in chromatic proximity as in the lowest register, or in the form of the augmented octave as in the framing intervals of the other two chords. The total tonal context is that of the twelve-tone scale, and there is no discernible tonal center.

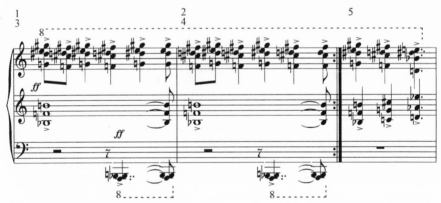

[23]There is, literally, a slight irregularity in the final attack of bar 5. Note, however, that the three-chord contrary-motion here is reminiscent of two earlier instances in the cycle of a very similar progression. The second piece, *Regard de l'étoile*, ends with a coda that features a three-chord contrary motion unrelated to anything heard in the piece itself. The rhythmic shape—eighth-note, eighth-note, eighth-note with *fermata*—resembles the sequence quarter-note, quarter note, dotted quarter-note in bar 5 here. The tonal material cast in a different rhythmic format also serves as the theme of eternity in Messiaen's piece IX, *Regard du temps*.

The entire five-bar refrain recurs unchanged in bars 21-25, 53-57 and 65-69. Its first instance is followed by a two-bar codetta, its final instance by a longer coda. The codetta, surprisingly, introduces important material for the episodes. The nine-note chord that marks its beginning and rings throughout it is built from a transposition of mode 4.[24] This is the mode that, having been symbolically defined in V, *The Son Contemplating the Son*, represents the *Word Incarnate* throughout Messiaen's entire cycle, and thus suggests that what is celebrated here is not only the birth of a child, but also the birth of hope, and of God's promise towards humankind. The second element in the codetta, consisting of two eight-note chords, presents the building-block on which draws the first episode of the rondo. Finally, the codetta's third element is developed from the bass cluster of the refrain. Bar 7 features the fifth attack (the one that was omitted in the refrain's fifth bar), off beat as before but allowed to ring much longer, and followed by a shake that doubles the lowest pitch in the octave. This shake will recur in the coda and close the piece.

In the rondo's first episode, the tempo is slowed down to *Modéré, un peu vif*, i.e. to about three quarters of the former pace. The dynamic level is reduced to *f* and less, while both the rhythmic and the expressive complexity are increased. In terms of structure, interestingly, the section is itself designed like a small-scale rondo, with the following building blocks:

miniature refrain	bars 8/9
miniature episode 1	bars 10-12
miniature refrain	bars 13/14
miniature episode 2	bars 15-17
miniature refrain	bars 18-20

The refrain within episode 1 is launched from a four-note chord preceded by the unusual phenomenon of five whole-tone *acciaccaturas*. The group is repeated on the downbeat of the second bar. Both the model and its repetition are complemented on the after-beat by a surprisingly soft augmented-octave attack in the bass register. The melodic part, marked "like a xylophone," is dominated by a repeated D♯ characterized by a powerful *crescendo*. After an ornamental flourish at the point of climax, the melody returns once more to D♯ and concludes with descending whole-tone steps. The second bar does not revive the melody but instead closes early with a single four-note attack in the high register. Thissmall-

---

[24]The notes are C♯ D E♭ E, G A♭ A B♭. For details on Messiaen's modes and a preview on other occurrence of this mode in the cycle, see, respectively, the account of Messiaen's musical language and the brief overview of the cycle in the appendices.

refrain, bars 8/9, 13/14 etc.

episode 1, developed from the codetta chord pair, bars 10-12

episode 2, bars15-17

refrain recurs unchanged the first time but is considerably expanded the second time; see the repetition of its first bar in bars 18/19, the extended flourishes on the climax, the more elaborate descent at the end of the melodic line, and the substitution of the simple four-note attack at the end with a brilliant polyrhythmic figure in bar 20.[25]

[25]Note that the metric notation is somewhat odd here. The initial nine-eight bar of the miniature refrain (bar 8) corresponds with bar 18 and the almost identical repetition—except for a more elaborate descent—in bar 19. The recurrence of bar 9 begins here on the last quarter-note of bar 19 and extends through bar 20, expanding in duration from the original four-eight extension to five eighth-notes.

The small-scale episode 1 (the first episode within the rondo form of the piece's first episode) derives the pitches in its two upper strands from the chord pair in the codetta. This material, split into four attacks, is heard five times, the last two times in changing rhythmic shape. The basically regular metric design of the initial group is expanded, by a conspicuous bass attack in *sfz*, to nine thirty-seconds, thus creating a tie to the nine-eighth scope of the original refrain bar.[26]

The three bars of the miniature episode 2 each begin with a soft flourish and continue even more mutedly with strings of repeated major seconds, thus retaining the whole-tone interval so predominant in this section.

The rondo's second episode is very different in character from both the first episode and, certainly, from the boisterous refrain. Marked *Très modéré* (and slowed down to only half the tempo of the first episode) and *tendre*, with a *rubato* upbeat at the beginning and a *rallentando molto / au mouvement* at the entry of the "recapitulation," this section is much more pensive than the other two components. In terms of layout, this episode resembles a small-scale sonata movement:

miniature exposition	bars 26-30
repeat of exposition	bars 30-35
miniature development section	bars 36-41
miniature recapitulation	bars 42-47
mini coda (with second development)	bars 48-52

Note that apart from the small-scale exposition and its repetition, all inner sections are set off by a whole-bar rest. These silences add considerably to the extraordinarily gentle atmosphere of the section.

Messiaen's symbolic play with modes, rhythmic values and small-scale shapes is beautiful here, very subtle while creating a strongly soothing impression on the listener. The mode on which this section is predominantly built is mode 3. This mode is used only once elsewhere in the *Vingt regards sur l'Enfant-Jésus*, but that second occurrence is most conspicuous. In XVII, *Regard du silence*, modes 3 and 4 appear vertically juxtaposed in a rhythmic pattern that stems directly from V, *The Son Contemplating the Son*. In this latter piece, the titling makes it clear that Messiaen sought to portray two aspects of Jesus in the guise of two

---

[26]The rhythmic organization of both figures is very similar indeed. Counting bar 1 in eighth-notes and each of the three figures in bar 10 in thirty-seconds, one gets a pattern of [2+2+2] + 3, where the "3" at the end is clearly an extended 2-beat unit. Thus the Trinitarian "3" is essential here. It helps to think of both figures counted as "1 - 2 - 3 - 1 2 3."

different modes (and in rhythmic forms that are, fittingly, derivations of one another). This leads one to suspect that the modes correspondingly juxtaposed in XVII, modes 4 and 3, were chosen with a similar intent in mind, and that mode 3 is therefore symbolic for an aspect of the Child Jesus. Since the piece presently discussed, *Christmas*, appears very direct and pictorial in its celebration of the birth of the Child among Mary and Joseph, mode 3 can safely be interpreted as representing the CHILD IN THE MANGER.

The mode consists of THREE groups of THREE pitches. In the melodic part of the episode's thematic phrase, the composer uses THREE occurrences of a characteristic six-note chord built from mode 3. Almost not surprisingly, the number of silent bars within the section is THREE, and each rest extends for exactly THREE beats. Furthermore, there are THREE instances of a closing component—at the end of the mini exposition, recapitulation, and coda respectively—each consisting of THREE notes. Finally, mirroring plays a major role, with regard to both pitches and rhythmic patterns, as indicated with arrows in the example below.

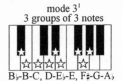

mode 3¹
3 groups of 3 notes

B♭-B-C, D-E♭-E, F♯-G-A♭

The miniature development section within this sonata-shaped second episode is related to the exposition mainly through its rhythmic design (compare particularly the rhythm in bars 36-38₃ with that in bars 26-28₃).

Tonally, Messiaen makes an important statement that asks us to shift our attitude from a mere joyous celebration of a human birth to the awareness that this birth is an act of GOD'S LOVE.[27] The section is characterized by the pitting against one another of two modes: transpositions of mode 3 for the descending three-note chords in the upper strand of the initial phrase, the repeated chords in the second phrase, and the pre-beat attacks in the lower strands of the second phrase, and a transposition of mode 2 for the thematic passage of the first phrase in the two lower strands.[28] The CHILD IN THE MANGER is clearly supported by GOD'S LOVE, in a very similar way as the difficult duality of the *Son of God* and the *Son of Man,* the shadow of the SUFFERING ON THE CROSS over the INCARNATION OF THE WORD (see mode 6 over mode 4 in piece V, *The Son Contemplating the Son*) is supported in the lowest strand by the theme (and mode) of GOD'S LOVE.[29]

In the miniature coda, fragments of mode 3^4-mode 2^2 superimposition (as in the small-scale development) alternate with fragments in mode 3^1. Soon enough, these quotations of modal basis appear in a format closer and closer to the thematic phrase. The characteristic six-note chord is re-instated in bar 50 and descends through several inversions in bars 51/52. The closing component leads in *attacca*-style back to the refrain (*sans attendre*, i.e. without waiting).

Finally, the rondo's own (large-scale) coda plays with the refrain's fifth bar (see bar 69) by extending it further and further at the head (see bars 70-73) before returning it to its original pitch extension, albeit in rhythmic augmentation (see bar 74). The remainder is reminiscent of the codetta (bar 75 = bar 6, bar 76 = bar 7, picked up in bar 80). Within the powerful dynamic increase from *mf* (bar 70) through *ff* (bars 74-76) to *fff* (bar 80), a fragmented insertion from the second episode—in the original slow tempo and in *p tendre*—reminds us of the gentle and pensive perspective of the Christmas celebration.

---

[27] The musical symbols representing GOD'S LOVE, are discussed more fully at the beginning of part III of this book (see, within the section GOD'S LOVE, the first chapter on *The Father's Contemplation.* For a brief overview at this point, readers may want to refer to the overview in Appendix III.

[28] The chain of descending chords is taken from mode 3^4 in phrase 1 of the mini development section, and from mode 3^1 or 3^3 in phrase 2 (beginning with the repeated chords at the end of bar 38). The strand-2+3 pitches represent mode 2^2 in the first phrase but then switch to mode 3^2 for the second phrase. One could thus argue that mode 3, the symbol for the CHILD IN THE MANGER, is present in all its manifestations, launched by GOD'S LOVE.

[29] This is analyzed at length in part III, chapter 2.

Regard de l'Esprit de joie

(Messiaen, *Vingt regards*, X)

(Danse véhémente; ton ivre des cors, transport du Saint-Esprit... la joie d'amour du Dieu bienheureux dans l'âme de Jésus-Christ...)

When Messiaen talks about a "fervent dance" and the "drunken sound of horns," one is strongly reminded of Psalm 150: 3-5. In the Catholic Bible version, it reads: "Give praise with blasts upon the horn, praise him with harp and lyre./ Give praise with tambourine and dance, praise him with flutes and strings./ Give praise with crashing cymbals, praise him with sounding cymbals." These characterizations, suggesting an almost unlimited extent of exuberance, are linked with another concept of the composer's, that of "the joy of the blissful God's love in the soul of Jesus Christ." As Messiaen confesses in his Author's Note, he "was always very much intrigued by the fact" that God is *bien-heureux* (a word that means happy and cheerful as well as blissful) and that this ineffable and continuous joy lived also in the soul of Christ. This kind of joy, Messiaen says, seems to him like ecstasy or rapture—and he wants rapture or ecstasy to be understood "in the most delirious sense of the term" —probably in the sense of the "prophetic frenzy" so prominently evoked in the Books of Samuel. Hence his surrealist terminology in the subheading, recalling the "ecstasy of the Holy Spirit."

The piece is laid out in seven clearly marked sections. They are juxtaposed in tempo and character, in material and gesture, and in tonal organization. The combination of choices on each level weaves a highly symbolic web. Here is a first overview:

I	bars 1-32	*Presque vif* f, unison with "violent" clashes	*Thème de danse orientale et plain-chantesque* (Oriental dance theme, in the mode of plain chant)
II	bars 33-40	*Modéré, expressif*	with *Thème de joie* (Theme of Joy) - 3 variations
III	bars 41-53	*Un peu plus vif*	a pattern undergoing asymmetric growth (13 variations + codetta)
IV	bars 54-131	*Bien modéré*	"like a hunting song, like horns" - 3 long variations
V	bars 132-184	*Très modéré / Modéré*	*Thème de joie* framing *Thème de Dieu* (varied); ternary layout
VI	bars 185-216	*Presque vif*, chordal, different crashes	*Thème de danse orientale et plain-chantesque*
VII	bars 217-231	*Très lent / Modéré / Bien modéré / Vif*	Coda; various thematic reminiscences

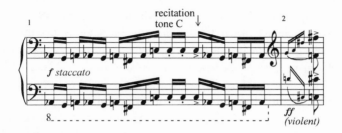

The framing dance in Messiaen's *Contemplation of the Spirit of Joy* provides a stunning example of a musical expression of rapture, all the while brimming with theological symbolism. In its original form, it consists of a frantically paced *unison*, evolving, in constant *staccato,* at the simple distance of an octave in the bass register. Any metric sense is purposefully avoided; each of the sixteen segments differs in length and rhythmic grouping. The only scansion of the ecstatic motion occurs in the form of irregularly interspersed 'crashes' which, one is tempted to interpret very programmaftically, may represent cymbals or other strongly disssonant instruments. These crashes interrupt the frantic simplicity of the *unison*, producing a contrast in every parameter. Texturally and tonally, the practically simultaneous attack of nine notes comprising eight different pitches comes as a shock after the extensive octave parallel that it interrupts, and the polyrhythmic *acciaccatura* groups followed by two augmented octaves are about as far as one can get from a *unison* setting. Rhythmically, the accented eighth-note attack suspends the otherwise almost constant motion in sixteenth-notes. Dynamically, the crash is marked *ff* and *violent*, thus standing out from the continuous *f* around it. Finally, the original bar and its fifteen identical repetitions are also set off from the remainder of the section in terms of register; they reach two octaves higher than the *unison* ever ventures.

The rhythmically almost monotonous *unison* and particularly the prominence of recitation tones create what Messiaen wants us to hear as an allusion to plain chant. The recitation tone, enhanced either by multiple repetition, or by explicit accents, or by a combination of both, centers on C. From there it rises repeatedly to D♭ and D but finally returns, supported from below by the cadential notes F♯ and G, to C. The notes of the chant span a single octave and are taken from one of Messiaen's modes. Mode 4^2, i.e. the transposition to the second semitone of mode 4, contains the pitches F♯ G A♭ A, C D♭ D E♭. (Messiaen omits the eighth note E♭ and

25

jumps instead to the octave F♯, as seen in bars 18, 24, 28.) The mode symbolizes one of Christ's aspects: that of the WORD INCARNATE.

In two instances, an extended *unison* passage is ornamented with *acciaccatura* groups without interrupting its motion. These ornamental groups appear in (perfect or near) parallels and in the register and dynamic level of the *unison*, thus differing distinctly from the contrary-motion, dissonant crashes in elevated register described above.[30]

There are, then, the sixteen lines in the chant with their respective recitation tones, the main crashing chords—also exactly sixteen, albeit distributed somewhat irregularly—and the ornamental *acciaccaturas*. Noticing these patterns of departure and return, of increasing and slackening intensity, helps a performer to trace the excitement within the ostensible monotony of the rapturous dance. The table below shows the patterns, the distribution of the crashes, and the movements of the recitation tone.

line	(rhythmic notation)	chordal clash	recitation tone
1	♪♪♪♪♪♪♪♪♪♪♪♪♪♪♪♪♪	1	C
2	♪♪♪♪♪♪♪♪ ♪♪	2	C
3	♪♪♪♪♪♪♪ ♪♪♪♪ ♪♪♪♪	3,4	C-D♭-C
4	♪♪♪♪♪♪♪♪♪ ♪ ♪ ♪♪♪♪♪♪♪♪♪♪♪ ♪♪♪♪♪ ♪ ♪		D♭-D-C
5	♪♪♪♪♪♪♪♪♪♪♪♪	5	C
6	♪♪♪♪♪♪♪♪♪♪	6	C-D♭
7	♪♪♪♪♪♪♪♪♪♪♪♪ ♪♪	7	D♭
8	♪♪♪♪♪♪♪♪	8	D♭
9	♪♪♪♪♪♪♪♪♪♪♪♪♪♪♪♪♪♪♪♪♪♪♪♪♪♪♪♪♪	9	D♭-D
10	♪ ♪♪♪♪♪	10	C-D♭
11	♪ ♪♪♪	11	C-D♭
12	♪ ♪♪♪♪ ♪ ♪♪♪♪	12	G-D♭-D
13	♪ ♪♪♪♪♪♪♪♪♪♪	13	D♭
14	♪♪ ♪♪♪♪♪♪♪♪♪♪♪ ♪♪♪♪♪♪♪♪♪♪♪ ♪ ♪♪♪♪♪ ♪ ♪		C-D♭-C
15	♪♪ ♪♪♪♪♪♪♪♪♪♪♪♪♪♪♪♪	14,15	F
16	♪ ♪♪♪♪♪♪♪♪♪♪ ♪♪ ♪♪ ♪ ♪♪ ♪	16	G♯-C

[30]In the context of multiple occurrences of these gentle ornaments, the regular crash is rendered somewhat redundant. The crash is not lost, however, but made up for. Towards the beginning of the "fervent dance," the ornamented passage is preceded by a double crash, while towards the end of the section, the same two-fold crash occurs in the phrase following the ornamented one.

The second section of *The Spirit of Joy Contemplating the Infant Jesus* reflects prominently the divine number THREE. It is laid out in THREE segments and contains THREE components. The processes occurring with regard to these components are also THREE; these processes both confirm and question the relationship between the segments, as they mingle repetition with transposition and internal extensions.

- The first segment spans THREE bars (see bars 33-35). The initial bar contains a rocking figure characterized in the right-hand part by extremely large melodic leaps and a prevalence of THREE interval combinations: the augmented octave, the semitone, and the semitone over fourth and tritone (a chord that includes a three-note cluster with octave displacement). The left-hand part, in triads, is determined by ascending lines that are mostly but not entirely chromatic in the two lowest parts. This component recurs in bar 36, transposed six semitones up, and in bar 39, transposed three semitones up. The first transposition features an internal extension (see the 10th to 13th sixteenths in bar 36), thus resulting in a transposition of an extra THREE semitones for the remainder of the component. The second transposition retains the same extension but inserts another addition just before it, this time by way of a partial repetition (see bar 39: the 3rd to 7th sixteenths are repeated).

- The second component, introduced in the second bar of the section, is identified as the *Thème de joie* (Theme of Joy). It presents a  seven-note ascent built from the Mixolydian scale, with a rhythmic acceleration in the run-up to the octave.[31] This theme recurs in bar 37, transposed THREE semitones down (i.e. on G) and in octave doubling. The second transposition in bar 40, another THREE semitones lower (i.e. on E) and also in octaves, is extended by way of internal repetition. The initial notes of the ascent, E-F♯-A-B, are repeated as the two outermost voices of ten-part chords; these chords are then themselves repeated an octave higher and extended, thus reaching the fifth and sixth notes of the *Theme of Joy*. The final note E, however, is omitted—a fact that will prove very important later on.

[31] The Mixolydian scale on B♭ is: B♭ C D E♭ F G A♭ B♭.

- The third component consists of THREE flourishes. The first, heard in the high treble register at the beginning of bar 34 and leading to a cluster *tremolo*, recurs in each of the two other segments (see bars 37 and 40). The second and third follow the final note of the *Theme of Joy* and thus recur only once, since the third statement of the theme remains incomplete. The highly-pitched second flourish remains unaltered (cf. the end of bar 34 with the end of bar 37), while the third flourish is more independent, more extensive, and more volatile. In contrary motion with a *crescendo* from *p* to *ff*, it confirms the tonal center of the preceding *Theme-of-Joy* phrase. Where the theme is on B♭ (as in bar 34), it is followed by a two-part flourish launched from B♭s at a distance of four octaves and contracting to a *unison* B♭; where the theme is centered in G (as in bar 37), the subsequent flourish begins on Gs at a distance of six octaves and contracts, in even more extensive waves, to a *unison* G. The two-part flourish on E is, of course, thwarted by the incomplete third transposition of the *Theme of Joy*.

If we had any doubts that Messiaen's "Spirit of Joy" is indeed the Holy Spirit of the Trinity, the highly conspicuous usage of the number THREE alone could serve as an affirmation. There are THREE segments in this section, THREE bars to each segment, and THREE components on which the section is based. The structuring principle rests on THREE simultaneous processes that, normally, establish different forms: identical repetition, transposition (by THIRDS, for that matter), and internal extension.

Section III, while certainly an entity of its own, is at the same time conceived as a complement to the preceding section. What holds the components of this section together is the pitch E—i.e. precisely that final note of the third *Theme-of-Joy* statement that would have served as a hinge for the gigantic contrary-motion flourish, but was omitted from the previous section. This pitch E now assumes primary importance. The only notes untouched by the fantastic contortions of Messiaen's "asymmetric growth" in bars 41-53 are the two E's at which the hands meet on the last beat of each bar. In the bar that, after the twelfth alteration, is dedicated to descending, *toccata*-style clusters, the note that remains unchanged is the repeated E in the left hand. Next, in the midst of the alternation of two contrary-motion crash chords in bars 55-58, the note that stays invariably the same is E (along with D, here). And as if the point were not yet made, the final bar of the section contains nothing but

E's: they descend in three-part *unison* over five octaves, thus covering all E's on the keyboard!

Aside from the idiosyncrasy of this immutable pitch, two phenomena invite closer investigation: the number play that Messiaen has hidden within this section, and the process of asymmetric growth. This latter requires some explanation, both in general and in this particular instance. When Messiaen subjects a figure to asymmetric growth, he repeats it several times while moving individual notes or note groups by chromatic increments—some upwards, others downwards. The process resembles that of an object being mirrored in an uneven reflecting surface; it involves both extravagant stretches and instances of implosion or collapse, where pitches originally at a good distance from one another approach, crash, and eventually fold over one another. The typical number of repetitions associated with this device is twelve; with that, all pitch combinations will have been exhausted. Thirteen versions of the figure, as we have here, also occur throughout Messiaen's work; in this case, the original pitches are restored in the end, albeit in an entirely different octave allocation.

In this passage in the third section of *The Spirit of Joy Contemplating the Infant Jesus*, Messiaen fills a FIVE-beat bar with, in the right-hand part, four groups of wildly zigzagging triplets concluding in a longer note E, pitted against FIVE trilled notes in the left-hand part, the last of which is equally E. (This E is the lowest E on the keyboard and thus particularly prominent.) In each of the right-hand triplets, the first note falls, bar by bar and step by chromatic step, until it reaches the next lower octave in bar 53. Meanwhile, the other two notes rise in the same way to the next higher octave. Only the E remains what it is, and in the same register. In the left-hand part, the first and fourth trilled notes ascend gradually while the second and third notes descend. As a result of these simultaneous alterations, each part goes through a crash and collapse phase, often with different points leveling at different moments, and even the two parts create an implosion towards the end of the thirteen-bar process.[32]

In the bar that follows the dramatic *crescendo accelerando* of the growth process, Messiaen prolongs the immutable right-hand E in TENfold

[32] In the right-hand part, the triplets collapse (i.e. level out their original intervals) at different moments: triplet 1 in bar 45, triplet 2 in bar 46, triplet 3 in bar 50, triplet 4 in bar 51. In the left-hand part, the initial interval is annulled in bars 44/45, the one between the third and fourth trill notes in bar 46. In subsequent groups, the original shapes are thus completely altered. The right and left hands begin clashing in bar 47; their initial pitches are in cross-over position ever thereafter.

repetition while contrasting it in the higher register with a FIVEfold group based on something like a reinforced turn-figure. These contain their own tonal symbolism. The chords that fall on the FIVE beats of the bar take their pitches from the black keys of the piano, while the intermittent double-notes contribute all the white keys. This black-against-white oscillation in extremely fast tempo (see bar 54, *au mouvement plus vif*) refers back to the similarly swift figure at the beginning of *Regard des Hauteurs* (see VIII, bar 1, *vif*), and thus brings to this later piece the allusions created in the earlier one.

Continuing his play with the figure FIVE, Messiaen concludes the section with FIVE more bars. All retain the constantly repeated E as a unifying feature. Four of them (bars 55-58) consist of *acciaccatura* chords (with FIVE notes in each hand), and the final bar, as was mentioned earlier, features an impressive FIVE-octave *unison* descent.

We can, then, observe at least four symbols in this section: one is structural (asymmetric growth), one tonal (a wavy figure made from a black-key cluster over a white-key cluster), one is a pitch (E) and one a number (5). An interpretation of these symbols in perspective to the religious context would be based on the following observations.

- "Growth" that develops in a manner beyond our immediate grasp stands, in all of Messiaen's oeuvre, for the transition to another dimension. The piece within the *Vingt regards sur l'Enfant-Jésus* that is almost entirely built on this process of asymmetric growth is *L'échange*, the exchange of natures in Christ, the prototypical transition that transcends human comprehension.

- Messiaen uses the twelve-tone context in the relaxed form of black keys above white keys with the symbolic connotation of natural sounds: all-encompassing, but not harsh. *The Heights Contemplating the Infant Jesus*, his prototypical bird piece within this cycle, can be understood to stand for nature's rejoicing at the birth of Christ. By extension, the same meaning attaches itself also to the derived bar in the *Contemplation of the Spirit of Joy*.

- The immutable pitch E has a forerunner within *Vingt regards*, in the piece that also establishes the symbolic meaning of "growth." III, *The Exchange*, features E as the hinge for the bifurcation in the three-note (Trinitarian) *component b*, and as the single constant pitch and thus anchor in the twelvefold growth process to which *component d* is being subjected. In the theological context of the exchange of natures, in which the Son of God, born as the

30

Son of Man, returns to divine nature, and in which Man is invited to imitate Christ while God reaches down to meet human fallibility, the only immutable entity is God. The immutable pitch thus takes on the function of a musical representative of the Divine.

- The number FIVE, in the context of Christian symbolism, is often understood as a reminder of the co-existence of the christological with the Trinitarian aspect, and thus as a compound of 2 and 3. Christian art knows depictions in which the five fingers of a hand are prominently shown with three fingers extended and two folded in. (See, e.g., Carlo Maderna's marble sculpture *Santa Cecilia* in the Roman church S. Cecilia in Trastevere.) Another interpretation, possibly more relevant in this context seeing how Messiaen groups elements within the compound 5, is to understand the symbolic number as consisting of repeated (and repeated then stands for "various") manifestations of TWO, the symbol of the duality of Jesus, complemented by a powerful manifestation of ONE, the symbol for the one and only God. As laid out in detail above, Messiaen works on various levels with groups of TWO leading to a prominent ONE. The bar undergoing growth with its prominently recurring fifth beat E (in *unison*, a further confirmation of ONEness) may represent the many other examples. Finally, FIVE is also the number of Jesus; one is reminded of His FIVE wounds on the Cross, the FIVE secrets connected with Him (incarnation, suffering, resurrection, ascension and last judgment), and also of the FIVE initials of the Greek words for *Jesus Christ God's Son Savior* that build the acronym ΙΧΘΥΣ, i.e. the word for fish, a mystical symbol for Christ.

Section IV of *The Spirit of Joy Contemplating the Infant Jesus* is based on a thematic idea of its own, unique in the entire cycle of *Vingt regards*. Messiaen designates it, in the score under bar 60 and in the preface, as *comme un air de chasse, comme des cors* (like a hunting song, like horns), and his subheading remark also contains the mention of the drunken sound of horns ("ton ivre des cors").

The section is conceived as three stanzas of a song, in which the second and third are variations of the first. Each stanza consists again of three segments: a phrase, its varied transposition, and a development.

31

	stanzas 1	stanza 2	stanza 3
	(bars 60-83)	(bars 84-107)	(bars 108-113)
phrase	bars 60-65	bars 84-89	bars 108-113
variation	bars 66-71	bars 90-95	bars 114-119
development	bars 72-83	bars 96-107	bars 120-131

The tonal organization of this section is based on Messiaen's mode 2. This is the most regular of his modes,[33] consisting of alternating whole-tone and semitone steps and thus existing in merely three transpositions. This mode with its complete, threefold appearance is established in the initial piece of the *Vingt regards*, *The Father's Contemplation*, as the tonal symbol for GOD'S LOVE. It will be worth exploring in some detail how completely the threefold appearance of mode 2 is used in this section of *The Spirit of Joy Contemplating the Infant Jesus.*

However, before turning to the modal analysis, another tonal symbol in the context of GOD'S LOVE should be mentioned. This is the F♯-major key signature with F♯ as the tonal center. As a key signature it is highly significant since Messiaen's musical language mostly relies on local acci-dentals. The unexpected use of a key signature (in a modal piece at that, which then requires a wealth of additional accidentals) must therefore be taken as an emphatic statement. Messiaen scholars concur that the over-whelming number of musical sections the composer notated with a key signature carry that of F♯ major. This is also the case in the *Vingt regards*. Leafing through the score we find key signatures in the following pieces or sections:

I	*The Father's Contemplation*	entire piece	6 sharps, *Theme of God*
VI	*Through Him All Was Made*	bars 205-end	6 sharps, from Th. of God
X	*Spirit of Joy Contemplating*	bars 60-143 etc.	(various)
XV	*The Kiss of the Infant Jesus*	bars 1-72/95-	6 sharps, from *Th. of God*
XIX	*I Sleep, But My Heart Wakes*	entire piece	6 sharps *Theme of Love*
XX	*Church of Love Contemplating*	bars 161-end	6 sharps, from *Th. of God*

Five of the six pieces that are notated with key signatures in the cycle *Vingt regards* thus refer (albeit modally) to F♯ major. They do this not only through their six sharps but also through additional indications of tonal centered ness. This sheds a particular light on the piece investiga-ted here, and on the composer's decision to write key signatures for the

---

[33]Mode 2 is the most regular of the modes the composer actually employs. The first mode, identical with the whole-tone scale, surpasses mode 2, of course; however, Messiaen hardly ever uses it.

entire section IV as well as for several later phrases. True to the link between F♯-major and mode 2 in *The Father's Contemplation*, I shall examine these key signatures in connection with the mode-2 organization of *The Spirit of Joy Contemplating the Infant Jesus*.

The initial phrase of the hunting song is suggested by the signature with three sharps as in A major, and based on the first transposition of mode 2 (A B♭ C C♯ D♯ E F♯ G). The melody is in the left-hand part, where it evolves in four-part chords strongly reminiscent in texture of those in the initial piece of the cycle, *The Father's Contemplation*. The theme sets out from the ambiguous third of A (C♮ in the upper part, C♯ in the lowest) from where it descends to an A-major triad. Its characteristic material concludes in bar 61 with the (horizontal) interval C-A leading to a (vertical) A major chord. In bar 62 follows a four-chord figure that superimposes a melodic gesture over nothing but A-major chords. The accompaniment in the right-hand part consists of a five-sixteenths figure launched in A minor but continuing in A major. This accompaniment continues unchanged throughout the phrase, interrupted only for the sudden *fff* insert in bar 63. The insert, consisting of three descending eight-part chords, derives from the second transposition of mode 2 (C♯ D E F G G♯ A♯ B). So does the broken-chord figure of the left hand, whose *f legato* overrides the *mf staccato* of the accompaniment in the final two bars of the phrase (see bars 64/65, where the right hand now accommodates the modal change and thus sounds oriented more towards E). The phrase thus ends on the equivalent to a dominant of the original A.

Mode 2^2 now serves as a basis for the transposition of the phrase. Bars 66-68 present the initial two bars of the hunting song, followed by the four-chord figure described above, in mode 2^2 with a strong tonal tendency towards E. The three eight-part chords of the insert and the broken-chord figure that concludes the phrase revert the modal translation by reestablishing the first transposition of mode 2. The third, developmental phrase of the stanza (bars 72-83) sets out in mode 2^3, on what amounts to the subdominant D (D E♭ F F♯ G♯ A B [C], with prominent D-major chords in the leading left-hand part), but reverts immediately to the tonic. After a sidestep in bar 75, featuring in the left-hand part a chord not derived from any transposition of mode 2 and juxtaposed by pure F♯ major in the right hand, the section concludes with a perfect cadence: dominant (bar 76) followed by extensive tonic (bars 77-83).

The individual stanza of the hunting song retraces, then, the essential steps that characterize the tonal argument of *The Father's*

Contemplation.[34] In symbolic understanding, they therefore refer to that which the opening piece expressed: GOD'S LOVE. It is this strong inner relationship to the key symbols of the cycle that explains Messiaen's use of explicit key signatures in a tonal context that is, for once, *not* F♯ major.

The second and third stanzas of the hunting song are varied transpositions of the first. The transpositions take us—we will hardly be surprised—to mode 2^2 or the dominant in the second stanza (with D♭ as the tonal center and a corresponding key signature of five flats) and to mode 2^3 or the modal subdominant in the third stanza (centered in F and marked with one flat). Messiaen thus recreates in the three stanzas of the song the same "complete" appearance of GOD'S LOVE as he did in the three segments of the individual stanza: GOD'S LOVE shows itself in all its three, and only three, faces.

How, one may wish to ask, does Messiaen draw a link between the serenity of GOD'S LOVE as epitomized in the extremely slow initial piece of the cycle and this exuberant song? A remark from the preface (*Note de l'auteur*) helps here. Messiaen writes that he has always been struck by the fact that God is happy, and that this ineffable and continuous joy dwelt in Christ's soul. As he qualifies, this is "a joy that for me is an ecstasy, a drunkenness, in the most *delirious* sense of the word."[35]

Beyond all this, there is yet another very interesting interpretive background for the hunting song; in this case, we focus on the initial melodic gesture. In the midst of his "Creation" piece (VI, *Through Him All Was Made*), Messiaen introduces a four-chord group that he marks *Theme of Love* and that is quite literally generated from the end of the second stanza in *The Father's Contemplation* (cf. VI, bar 170 etc. with I, bar 15). This theme is explicitly taken up only in the two final pieces of the cycle. In bars 24-27 etc. of no. XIX, *I Sleep, But My Heart Wakes*, Messiaen labels as *Theme of Love* a two-bar gesture that substitutes the first two

---

[34]For a detailed discussion of the tonal layout in *The Father's Contemplation*, refer to the first chapter in part II of this book. Here is, however, a short comparison of the tonal layout in that piece dedicated to *God's Love* and in the hunting-song stanza of *The Spirit of Joy Contemplating the Infant Jesus*:

I — *The Father's Contemplation*		X — hunting song stanza	
section I	tonic to dominant	phrase 1	tonic to dominant
section II	dominant to tonic	phrase 2	dominant to tonic
coda	T-D-T-S-D-?-T	development	S-T-?-D-T

[35]J'ai toujours été frappé par ce fait que Dieu est heureux—et que cette joie ineffable et continue habitait l'âme du Christ. Joie qui est pour moi un transport, une ivresse, dans le sense le plus *fou* du terme. (The italics are Messiaen's.)

chords of the original shape with a three-note figure and its repetition before concluding in the syncopated descending fourth (example b). In bars 31-38 of XX, *The Church of Love Contemplating the Infant Jesus*, this more extensive version recurs, albeit with an additional interval change that is 'corrected' as of bar 39. Towards the end of the segment based on the *Theme of Love* there is, intriguingly, a development that substitutes two sequences for the repetition (see ex. c). It is this version which, in turn, serves as a direct albeit somewhat ana-

a) *Theme of Love*, VI: bar 170

b) *Theme of Love*, XIX: bars 24/25

c) *Theme of Love*, XX: bars 47-50

d) Hunting Song, X: bars 60/61

chronistic forerunner of the gesture in the hunting song (ex. d).

All these details invite further speculation as to their symbolic message, as does the very prominence of this section—with its central position not only in the tenth piece itself but also in the entire cycle (as the tenth of twenty pieces), its protracted modal coloring and the thematic relationship to the *Theme of Love*. Why did Messiaen choose the metaphor of the hunt to cast this important section? Aloyse Michaely[36] finds a convincing inspiration in medieval art and its frequent juxtaposition of Christ's birth and the hunt of the mystical unicorn. The unicorn which, according to legend, can only be trapped when confronted by a pure virgin on whose lap it then jumps, figures in visual art as a symbol for Christ's incarnation in the womb of the Virgin. Beginning with the 12th century, the motif of the unicorn appears in depictions both of the nativity itself and of the Annunciation. Growing out of this, the hunt of the mystical unicorn as an allegory of the Annunciation developed in the 15th century. Mary is shown sitting in an enclosed garden (a symbol mentioned

---

[36]Aloyse Michaely, "Verbum Caro: Die Darstellung des Mysteriums der Inkarnation in Olivier Messiaens *Vingt regards sur l'Enfant-Jésus*," (Hamburg: *Hamburger Jahrbuch für Musikwissenschaft*, vol. 6, 1984), 241.

by Messiaen himself in the comments to piece XV, *The Kiss of the Infant Jesus*). The archangel Gabriel, disguised as a hunter and sounding a hunting horn, chases the unicorn with his four hunting dogs (see the four horns needed for the four-part chords in the hunting song). The four dogs are named after the four divine qualities that have brought about the Incarnation of the Son: Compassion, Truth, Justice, and Peace (see psalm 85, verse 11). The dogs chase the unicorn, which has taken refuge in the garden, into the Virgin's lap. With this art-historical background, which was certainly familiar to Messiaen in mind, the composer's choice to call his theme "hunting song" gains deep meaning as an emblem expressing the joy over the birth of Christ.

Lastly, returning to the immediate context in which section IV of *The Spirit of Joy Contemplating the Infant Jesus* appears, it should be observed that this section is related to the preceding section III in two interesting ways. In its tonal layout based on the three transpositions of mode 2 and, thus, its symbolic link to GOD'S LOVE, the section acts as a realization of that which was prepared: the presence of God in the immutable pitch E, realized in His Love. In its metric layout, the fourth section follows the numerological arrangement based on the figure FIVE. The accompaniment figure of the initial stanza contains FIVE sixteenths, and there are FIVE bars with this figure in each of the thematic sections of the stanza (owing to the fact that the accompaniment is interrupted for the inserted bar). In fact, the entire hunting song, with the exception of these little inserts, is based on metric groups of FIVE sixteenths.

Moving on, section V presents, structurally, an irregular ternary form, and thematically, a combination of the *Theme of Joy* with the *Theme of God* in various realizations of the mode of GOD'S LOVE. The layout allows us to distinguish a frame (bars 132-143 and bars 175-184) around a contrasting middle segment (bars 144-174). The initial segment can itself be read as conceived in ternary form (4 bars with the *Theme of Joy*, 4 bars of development, 4 bars of *Theme of Joy* transposed). A somewhat different view and interpretation are, however, probably more relevant here. The *Theme of Joy*, expanded to a four-bar phrase, is contrasted with two bars that are only remotely related to the thematic gesture. Subsequently, these two bars are transposed three semitones up and followed by the expanded *Theme-of-Joy* phrase in the same transposition. (Both segments, by the way, are built on pedal-note chords. In bars 132-135, the rooting pitches Eb/F/Ab appear repeated every half bar in the bass, while bars 136/137 contain two of the three pitches as inner pedals: Ab in the

36

left and E♭ in the right hand. These pedal-notes strengthen a sense of tonality that is otherwise challenged to the extreme by fierce crashes.)

The contrasting middle segment of the fifth section falls into two roughly equal halves, bars 144-158 and 159-174. The initial gesture derives directly from the *Theme of God*; the original chords, characteristic melodic intervals and strict use of mode 2 are retained, while rhythm, meter and phrase length are freely modified. (Cf., e.g., *Vingt regards,* no. I, *The Father's Contemplation,* bar 1, with no. X, *The Spirit of Joy Contemplating the Infant Jesus*, bars 144/145.) The tonality is instead moored in the subdominant, i.e. mode 2^3 (centered in B in bars 144-149 and in D in bars 159-164), a transposition that also informs the flourishes ornamenting these phrases. The remainder of the segment contains such a wealth of signifiers that a glimpse must suffice here. In bars 152/3, a triadic ascent in the left-hand part built from mode 2^3 is juxtaposed with a triadic descent in the right derived from mode 3^1. The latter mode, as the discussion of piece XIII, *Noël*, has shown in detail, symbolizes the CHILD IN THE MANGER. Messiaen thus unites two images, as though proposed by the "Spirit of Joy": GOD'S LOVE is rising as the *Child* is descending.

At the reentry of the framing *Theme of Joy* in bar 175, the four-bar phrase is expanded through three more bars and intensified with *crescendo* and insistently increasing tempo. This mad rush suddenly breaks off, only to allow the development, from the lowest register of the keyboard, of a new explosion of speed and intensity that surpasses the preceding one by far. Using the four initial notes of the *Theme of Joy*, Messiaen begins in single-voiced texture that he then quickly increases. The four-note group thus ascends through seven octaves, gaining ever-greater volume, and hardly can a last-minute *rallentando* and *caesura* prevent us from tumbling head over heels into the return of the fervent oriental dance.

The recurrence of the *Thème de danse orientale et plain-chantesque* in bars 185-216, melodically as well as structurally identical with bars 1-32, brings two consequential surprises. The first concerns the texture. The original *unison* with both hands in the bass register is completely abandoned here. The oriental tune appears only in the right-hand part, in parallel fourths four octaves above the earlier register. The left hand adds a contrast, a palindromic *ostinato* figure of FIVE different dyads and three-note chords rooted in the two lowest white keys of the keyboard. The bilaterally symmetrical figure with its ascent-descent of whole-tones and perfect fourths is complete after 9 beats or, respectively, $9 + 8 = 17$, $9 + 8 + 8 = 25$, $9 + 8 + 8 + 8 = 33$ beats. As can be expected in the course of a dance

37

with irregular phrase structure, this *ostinato* accompaniment often does not reach completion. The abridged form highlights the irregularity and exacerbates the impression of wildness and pious frenzy.

The second "surprise" in this reprise is of an entirely different nature. As one will recall, the initial "oriental dance" is interspersed with violent crashes that consist of polyrhythmic *acciaccatura* groups followed by two augmented octaves. Here, significantly, the crashes are replaced by consonant chords (preceded by homorhythmic *acciaccaturas*). What is more, these chords constitute inversions of the F♯-major triad with added sixth. This is a chord that, by the time the listener of Messiaen's cycle arrives at *The Spirit of Joy Contemplating the Infant Jesus,* is securely established as one of the symbols for GOD'S LOVE. Introduced very prominently in the opening piece, *The Father's Contemplation,* the triad with added sixth recurs indicatively in the *Theme of Love* first presented in no. VI, *Through Him All Was Made.* The substitution of the dissonant crashes with the "chord of love" is, then, another powerful statement of Messiaen's musical message. This transformation seems to invite us to recognize GOD'S LOVE even in the wildest outbursts of elation—or: even the cymbals that provide scansion in the otherwise seemingly uncontrolled, ecstatic dance movement are expressive of GOD'S LOVE![37]

The coda, as mentioned earlier, sets out in the key signature of GOD'S LOVE, with the six sharps of F♯ major. In this notational context, the basic gesture of the *Theme of Joy* is quoted one last time, with two partial extensions that take it almost to the highest pitches on our keyboard.

---

[37]This is certainly in keeping the Muslim understanding of Allah who is very much present in delirious joy and ecstatic dances, as the famous Whirling Dervishes demonstrate so powerfully. One wonders whether Messiaen's reading in mysticism may have included any Sufi poetry. The "oriental dance" of the "Spirit of Joy," conceived in the context of the birth of Jesus, suggests this connection. (See Javad Nurbakhsh, *Jesus in the Eyes of the Sufis,* London: Khaniqahi-Nimatullah Publications, 1983.) Another possible source for Messiaen's image of the celebratory dance may go back to Jewish ritual dances. See also 2 Samuel 6:5 and 6:14, verses that depict David "dancing before the Lord with abandon."

The second segment (bars 220-228), although without the suggestive key signature, confirms F♯ major as the essential frame of reference (see the broken F♯-major chord in the left hand). At the same time, there is a clear reminiscence of section III. This manifests first in the juxtaposition of longer trilled notes with wildly zigzagging treble figures, then also in the "bird" figure (cf. bar 221/222 with bar 54) and in the contrary-motion crush chords over an immutable pitch (compare bars 223-228 with bars 55-58). The coda's final segment recalls section IV with the beginning of the hunting song (now in F♯, the key of GOD'S LOVE!). Finally, an enormous plunge in increasing tempo brings the piece to an abrupt, dry end on the two lowest white keys on our keyboard and their octaves.

Tonally, sections VI/VII together, or the recurrence of the oriental dance in conjunction with the coda, can then be said to rely on two hinges. One is the low double note A/B that roots the *ostinato* accompaniment of the dance in bars 85-216 and closes the piece; the other is the F♯-major triad with added sixth that interrupts the dance with sixteen inserts, underlies the final quotation of the *Theme of Joy*, remains present all through the section-III reminiscences (see e.g. left hand, bars 223-228, second beats), and informs the final appearance of the hunting song.

To sum up, Messiaen depicts the presence at the manger of the "Spirit of Joy" in a number of symbols that reinforce one another.

Symbols of God's joy	sections	Symbol's of God's love	sections
Theme of Joy	II, V, VII	*Theme of God*	V
hunting song	IV, VII	mode 2 as $2^1, 2^2, 2^3$	IV
fervent dance	I and VI	F♯-major triad + sixth	VI, VII
birds/nature rejoicing	III	F♯-major key signature	VII
number play with FIVE	III, IV		

Other symbols of God's presence	section
number play with THREE	II
immutable pitch E (section III)	
asymmetric growth—as a manifestation of the incomprehensibility of God's Incarnation and the "exchange of natures"	III
key signatures—other than F♯ major, and thus all the more unusual in Messiaen's language explained in retrospect when bars 217-219, quoting the beginning of section V, and bar 229, quoting the beginning of the fourth section, are both transposed to F♯ major.	IV, V

According to his perception of the "ecstasy of the Holy Spirit" and, by extension, the exuberance of the Divine joy at the birth of the Son, the composer unites in this piece representations of rapture with emblems of GOD'S LOVE.[38] "La joie d'amour du Dieu bienheureux" is what he sets out to express: God is blissful (if we resort to poetic language) or simply, God is happy—happy to the degree of dancing wild dances and singing a hunting song to the sound of drunken horns.[39]

[38]As established in the opening piece of the cycle, *God's Love* is represented through six musical symbols. These are

(1)	the *Theme of God* as a thematic phrase,
(2)	the F♯-major key signature as the "divine signature" used by Messiaen throughout his work,
(3)	mode 2 as the most "perfect" mode, with three transpositions (the figure three standing both for complete and for the trinity),
(4)	the F♯-major triad with added sixth as the "chord of love," endorsed as such in the *Theme of Love* later in the cycle, and
(5)	the prominent melodic pitch A♯ as the "note of love," confirmed in several instances, the most prominent among them in *The Virgin's Contemplation*.

[39]It is worth mentioning that this cheerful aspect of *God's Love* recurs later, in a different context. Bars 21-41 of *First Communion of the Virgin* present a development of the *Theme of God* in mode 2^2 in the rhythmic shape of the hunting song suggesting, presumably, Mary's happiness and bliss at the thought of the heavenly child in her womb.

ENCHANTED PLACES

La cathédrale engloutie   (Debussy, *Préludes*, vol. I, no. 10)

The title of this prelude, which translates as *The Engulfed Cathedral* or *The Submerged Cathedral*, goes back to an old Breton legend. In the fourth of fifth century, the town of Ys in the province of Marmorique was engulfed by the sea, supposedly because of the impiety of the inhabitants, punished like a French counterpart to the biblical Sodom. Its cathedral, epitomizing the pious part of the population, is said to have been allowed to rise sometimes and be seen at sunrise. People whisper about having discerned the cathedral spires, and even heard monks' chanting emerging from the sea on misty mornings.[40] The piece thus contains a catalogue of Debussy's preferred images: water, including reflections seen or imagined on its surface; bells, and chant.

The calm and depth of the water seem depicted in the framing bars of the first section (bars 1-5 and 14-15). *Profondément calme, dans une brume doucement sonore* (profoundly calm, in a softly reverberating haze) indicates the composer, and *pp, sans nuances* (very soft, without nuances [of melodic intensity, of dynamic increases or decreases, of any kind of enhancement]). The background pitches (see G-D, right hand: bars 1, 3 and 5, and left hand: bars 1-2, and E-B, left hand: bar 5 and both hands: bars 14-15) together with the slow, gently expanding ripples (portrayed in the ascending doubled parallels in bars 1, 3 and 5) stem from the pentatonic scale G A B D E and allow two bars to be played each in a single collective pedal. (This remains true even when, in bars 3-4, the

---

[40]See also the extensive account given by Gustave Flaubert in his "Par Champs et Par Greves," (in *Voyages*, ed. R. Dumesnil, vol. 1, Paris: les Belles Lettres, 1948, pp. 312/313, 324, 355): ". . . restes d'une belle église des templiers, pure, sobre, niches charmantes . . . La nef n'a qu'un côté latéral, pas de transept. Autel en pierre. . . . Il reste une tour sur le côté droit du portail, nous sommes montés. Campagne plate, la mer, les moulins qui tournaient, vent. - Conversation avec les marins.- Un vieux nous a dit qu'il avait vu dire la messe en mer (un autre nous avait dit le contraire) sur les ruines d'Ys, car ils placent Ys ici. Les gens nous ont prétendu qu'on voyait encore des pierres taillées comme s'il y avait eu une ville." Edouard Lalo adapted and expanded this legend for operatic purposes in *Le Roi d'Ys.*

passing notes F-C in the descending bass temporarily complement the pentatonic context to a full diatonic range on the white keys; the haze, created not so much by the low-registered notes themselves but much more by their overtones, is very much in keeping with the atmosphere suggested in the heading.)

As the ripples subside for a while, giving way to an eerie calm, we hear soft suggestions of bells and what could be monks' chant in Lydian mode on E. Although Debussy continues to write bar lines, in the ambiguous six-four/three-two time chosen for this piece, the two archaic musical elements appear actually free from metric structuring.

bars 5-13

The first vision of the submerged church—a glimpse of detached spires, as it were—is insinuated by a melodic gesture introduced in bar 16. Supported by full chords in *sempre pp*, there appears what could be described as a melodic drawing of a steeple: F♯-G♯-D♯-G♯-F♯. As the distance between the enchanted onlooker and the submerged cathedral lessens (in reality or only in imagination), the spire motif is transposed higher and higher (see bars 19 and 22), as if gradually rising from the water. The change of perspective focuses the eye on only one slope of the steeple (the motif is shortened to its ascent only), and the slope sometimes appears slightly less steep (see bars 19/20 etc. where the second melodic interval is reduced from a perfect fifth to a fourth). The tonal context is still pentatonic: B C♯ D♯ F♯ G♯ in bars 16-18 and E♭ F G B♭ C in bars 19-21 are transpositions by four semitones each of the original pentatonic mode, while bars 22/23 present a different five-tone mode on G: G A C D F.

Two further devices assist in emphasizing the gradual rise of the cathedral into view. First, there is a dynamic increase from *pp* (bars 16-18) through *p* (bar 19) and the very specific request *augmentez progressivement, sans presser* (increase gradually, without rushing) to *f* (bars 22-24), *più f* (bars 25-27) and *ff* (bar 28 onwards). Secondly, the gently moving

42

water, depicted from bar 16 onwards with undulating triplets in the low register, is pierced, as it were, by the tip of the highest spire: little figures appear, indicated *marqué* (enhanced, see bars 19-21), taken from a tonal context (B♭ C D E♭ F) foreign to the surrounding pentatonic mode, and in a rhythmic organization based on the regular eighth-note and its division —and thus in contrast to the surrounding triplet murmur.[41] Finally, from bar 23 onwards, the music seems to suggest that traces of the cathedral's nave can now be discerned. Two largely sweeping lines in Dorian mode on D outline its dimensions.

The most glorious moment for any witness of the legendary event is reached when the cathedral is perceived in its entirety. Debussy chooses C major, a key otherwise rarely used in his compositions, for this occasion. Over a resonant double octave on the Cs of the lowest register[42],

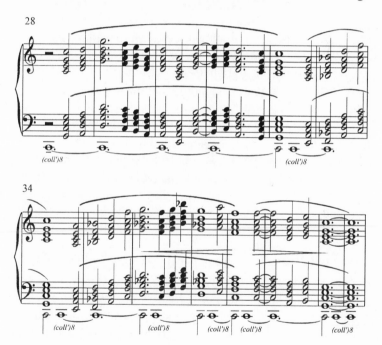

[41] It seems vital to execute this duplet-based rhythm very precisely; the B♭ in bar 19m and the C in bar 20, beat 1 are often played too early, thus appearing as if on the second of three triplet quavers. This loses a subtle dimension Debussy obviously very consciously desired.

[42] The *coll'octava* (= with octave) is certainly a more likely reading of the composer's intention than the simple *octava* (= an octave lower).

parallel triads recalling the triumphant sound of a full orchestra delineate the engulfed house of God in all its magnificence. But not for long! After a further *crescendo* in bars 36-37, the image seems to fade again. Single accented notes repeat the spire motif (see bars 40-41) while the body of the church is once again swallowed by the waters, indicated by a sudden hush to soft shades (bars 39-40) and a return to chords based on fourths, fifths and double seconds.

In bars 47-53, the chant of the monks is heard once again. The melodic line is set in a lower register and the former bell is replaced by a pedal-note G♯, thus redefining the earlier Lydian mode as G♯ minor. And it is now that the onlooker is granted another quick glimpse of what was thought lost until the next magic dawn. Unexpectedly, the dynamic level rises again, bringing with it several statements of the second half of the spire motif (see bar 57: G♯-D♯-C♯, bars 59 and 61: C♯-G♯-F♯). But the image disappears very swiftly, this time with a gesture of dominant-seventh chords descending in whole-tone steps (bars 62/63) and concluding with several quasi-cadential chord pairs (bars 63/64 heard as plagal, bars 64/65 as authentic, and bars 65/66 again as plagal).

After a transition, as the enchanted onlooker muses on the experience, the entire cathedral rises once more from the waters, this time clearly before the mind's eye—Debussy specifies *comme un écho de la phrase entendue précédemment* (like an echo of the phrase heard previously) and *flottant et sourd* (floating and muffled). A bridging bar (see bar 83) returns us to the resonance of the beginning (*dans la sonorité du début*), but the image of the cathedral lingers in the mind in a continuing pedal-note C and a conclusion on a soft but widely registered C-major chord.

La Puerta del Vino   (Debussy, *Préludes*, vol. II, no. 3)

This prelude is one of three pieces that Debussy wrote under the inspiration of the Alhambra, the thirteenth-century Moorish palace close to Granada in southern Spain. (The other pieces are *Lindaraja* for two pianos and *Soirée dans Grenade* from the cycle *Estampes* for piano solo.) *La Puerta del Vino*, or *The Wine Gate*, is the name of one of the palace gates. Debussy is said to have received a postcard with a picture of this gate from the Spanish composer Manuel de Falla. (Another story credits the postcard to the pianist Ricardo Viñes, but the identity of the sender has little to do with the source of the inspiration.)

Two features immediately strike anybody who sees a picture of the monument under the gleaming Spanish sun. On the one hand, the decoratively colored reliefs, while slightly faded through the centuries, are still impressive and bear witness to an extended period of Arabic supremacy on European soil. On the other hand, the gate creates a very stark contrast of light and shadow: the darkened medieval arch throws deep shadows onto the sand-colored, sunlit path that leads through it.

In addition to its beautiful Islamic mosques (one thinks of those in Cordoba and Seville) and other architectural treasures from the time of Moorish occupation, the province of Andalusia also retains a unique musical heritage from the same origin. The *flamenco*, a characteristic Andalusian type of light-hearted, often wild song and dance with guitar accompaniment, is traced back by some scholars[43] to North African origins from where it was said to have been picked up by the gypsies who had come to Spain from Flanders (*flamenco* being Spanish for Flemish). Similarly, the *tango*, a song and dance type known in both Latin America and southern Spain, seems to have etymological roots in northern Africa[44]. Both the *flamenco* and the *tango* are passionate in character, with special emphasis on contrasts between an almost rude expression of fervor (in less enlightened times commonly recognized as the "male" component) and a sweet and languishing "female" element.

Debussy succeeds in capturing these multi-layered contrasts—Moorish/Spanish, light/dark, male/female, rude/sweet—with the allusion to the Andalusian "Wine Gate." The tempo indication, *mouvement de Habanera*, sets the stage for the tango rhythm that is a distinctive feature of the piece (see example). The *Habanera*, named after Havana, the capital of Cuba, is a popular Cuban and Latin-American version of the tango.

The rhythm, prepared in two introductory bars that do not yet contain the characteristic dotted-note figure, is fully established in bar 3. Firmly rooted on D♭ and its fifth A♭, it persists throughout the entire first section of the prelude (see bars 3-41). Suspended for what amounts to a new introduction at the beginning of the development section (bars 42/43), the same rhythm then supports—though less pervasively—the temporary second tonal center B♭/F (see bars 44-49 and 55/56), before it tonally returns to D♭/A♭ for the recapitulation (see bars 66-82 and 85/86).

[43] See A. Chottin, *Chants arabes d'Andalousie*. Paris, 1939

[44] See e.g. Fernando Ortiz, *Hampa afro-cubana: glosario de afronegrismos*. (Havana, 1924), who attributes to the word *tango* the generic meaning "African dance."

In exposition and recapitulation, the perfect fifth is complemented by the major third F to form an open-position triad on D♭ (see bars 6-20, 23/24, 66-78, 81/82 and 85-90). It is countered, however, by two elements supporting rivaling tonal centers: the perfect fifths E-A and A-D in bars 1-4, and the tune that is launched, in bar 5, from B♮. This tune is built on the notes B C D E F (G) A♭ B and has a very special flavor—particularly in those bars where the semitone / minor-third combination prevails (see bars 11, 13/14, 16), interval sequences regarded as distinguishing features of both Gypsy and Arabic scales.

Like many tunes of this origin, this one is also the heavily embellished version of an extremely simple line. Syncopated anticipations of a melodic step, *appoggiatura*-resolution pairs as "sighs" (especially preceded by two upbeat anticipations of the *appoggiatura* pitch) and swift flourishes that return to the note that triggered them, are the most characteristic features. Here, then, is the "Arabic tune" and, for comparison underneath, the simple line from which it derives.

The descent E-D-C-B with pitches from the same scale also informs a transitional motif in bars 25-30 (see example) as well as a second short motif, in the middle voice of bars 31-34, seems drawn from a transposition of the scale to E. (Because of the further tonal development in this piece, it helps to imagine this transposition as the subdominant over B).

bars 25-27

The final melodic component of the exposition (see bars 35-41), still in tonal rivalry with the underlying D♭ major, seems conceived as an elaborately and passionately ornamented version of a (dynamically increasing) diatonic ascent G-A-B(=C♭) followed by a (dynamically decreasing) chromatic descent B♭-A♮-A♭. And it is only here, at the very end of this section, that the two layers: *tango* accompaniment and melodic line, harmonically merge into a D♭ major chord.

bars 35-41

Going over the entire exposition once again, we find that Debussy creates a similarly consistent contrast with regard to rhythm. On the one hand, the *tango* accompaniment is very strongly metrical; as the dynamic markings in bars 3/4 indicate, he envisions the one-bar figure under a single slur and with a single *diminuendo*. On the other hand, the languishing tune emphasizes syncopations, avoids most strong beats by either rest or tie or by a *crescendo* towards the weak second beat in many bars; it also sets triplets against the *tango*'s dotted figure or, later (bars 33-40), against the regular eighth-notes. As a unifying feature, the Spanish flavor of the *tango* is enhanced through additional *couleur locale*, created by emulations of castanets and guitar sounds, noticeably in the *acciaccaturas* (bars 1-4), flourishes (bars 13-16), and arpeggiated chords (bars 21, 25-30).

The development section (see bars 42-65) explores variations of the introductory bars 1/2 and new adaptations of the Gypsy/Arabic scale before it turns to a short retransition. Here are the details:

- The prelude's introductory bars recur unchanged in bars 42/43.
- By bar 44, however, the figure adopts a harmonic format—with a falling augmented fifth (D-G♭) preceding the perfect fifth in the bass—which becomes the basis for much that is to happen in this section.
- Bars 50/51 and 53/54 build directly on this new model.
- Bar 58 superimposes perfect fifth (right hand) and tritone (left hand) with an additional passing note in each *arpeggio*.
- Other bars show further development: bar 52 sets the superimposed augmented and perfect fifths in a melodic context reminiscent of bar 17; bar 57 picks this up while simplifying the left-hand part and displacing two of the right-hand intervals (here notated as minor sixths) an octave up; bar 59, still based on the same melodic outline, derives from the preceding bar 58, chromatically descending in right-hand perfect fifths superimposed over left-hand tritones—a harmonic pattern that is then continued, without any melodic reference, throughout bars 60/61; finally, bars 55/56 retain the melodic gesture from the introductory bars but enrich the harmonic setting and add new chromatic slides as *acciaccaturas*.
- The scale, transposed now to F♯ (the dominant of B on which it first occurred) provides the tonal basis for the passionate melodic gesture in bars 44-49, which in its outline is remotely reminiscent of bars 35/36 while retaining the syncopations from the first tune.

In the retransitional bars 62-65, further echoes of the main tune fade above a dominant bass—this time the dominant A♭ of the original pedal D♭—and thus prepare for a hushed beginning of the recapitulation. This section remains close to the exposition that it quotes in part (compare bars 66-73 with bars 5-12, and bars 75-84 with bars 17-26).

The coda (bars 85-90) presents a last and very powerful embodiment of the stark contrast that is the emotional source for this prelude. The *rubato* motif of bars 25-30, only just begun and in *pp lointain* (very soft, far away) and *un peu retardé* (held back a little) even more dreamy than in its first appearance, is brutally interrupted by a *ff molto crescendo* outburst, which in turn immediately reverts to softer shades and fades— both dynamically and in terms of tempo, with what seems like a composed closing *ritardando*.

La terrasse des audiences du clair de lune

(Debussy, *Préludes*, vol. II, no. 7)

The Terrace for Consultations in the Moonlight is one of three moon pieces written by Debussy for the piano. Probably the best known is *Claire de lune* from the *Suite Bergamasque*. More important in this context is *Et la lune descend sur le temple qui fut* in the second book of the *Images*, a piece that, in many respects, can be regarded as a counterpart to this prelude.

In search of possible sources for the wording of this caption we are directed to two contemporary publications. Pierre Loti's *L'Inde sans les Anglais* (India without the English), published in 1903, contains a reference to "des terrasses pour tenir conseil au clair de lune" (terraces where to consult with one another in the moonlight). Even more likely is the suggestion that Debussy might have taken the wording from René Puaux' *Lettres des Indes,* which appeared in the newspaper *Le Temps.* In an issue of December 1912 we read the sentence: "La salle de la victoire, la salle du plaisir, les jardins des sultanes, la terrasse des audiences au [sic] clair de lune." (The hall of victory, the hall of pleasure, the gardens of the sultans, the terrace of the moonlight audiences.) Contemporary readers would have perceived these lines in the context of the festivities surrounding the coronation of King George V as Emperor of India, which received much comment at the time.

These remarks, however, are not intended to imply that the prelude contains any distinct element that could be isolated as conveying the flavor of the Indian subcontinent. Definite traces of Indian music are absent. This should not surprise us because, in contrast to Indonesian gamelan music and examples of Chinese and Japanese art that had been introduced to the West so successfully by the time Debussy was writing his Preludes, substantial knowledge of Indian art and music was probably not available to the composer. The choice of the particular wording for the caption of this prelude rather attests to two topics frequently recurring in Debussy's music. One regards his preoccupation with hazy light and the evocation of mysterious coloring, taken up again and again in so many of his pieces. The other is an enchantment with the India described by Rudyard Kipling. Characteristically, the eleventh piece in the second book of preludes, now known under its revised title *Les tièrces alternées*, was originally to be called *Toomai des éléphants* (Toomai of the Elephants), after the youthful hero in Kipling's first *Jungle Book.* We are thus dealing here not with India as it is or might have been, but with an idealized image, created by a very skillful and popular author; a country in which the human relationship with nature and the spiritual in nature were said to be both more mysterious and more immediate than in the West.

The particular color of the prelude is achieved through various devices that, while not unusual within Debussy's musical language, are here combined in characteristic ways. These include, above all, competing tonal centers, a very consistent choice of chords, and a technique of structural overlap and associative development that seems to express some dreamlike (or moon-inspired?) quality.

On first inspection, the prelude's initial section (bars 1-8d) seems firmly rooted in the tonality of F♯ major, which is established visually by the prescribed key signature (six sharps), and audibly by the prevalent pedal note, the dominant root C♯. The opening chord, an inverted vii^7 of F♯ major, further endorses this notion, as do the $C♯^7$ (= V^7 of F♯) chords on all strong beats from bar 3 to bar 5d. Conflict with this tonality arises when, tied into bar 2 and persisting throughout this bar, the lower-strand chord as well as the subsequent double-octave melody clearly represent the dominant-seven chord of C major—a key that could not be further remote from F♯ major. The same polar chord recurs in bar 5; it is also implicitly expressed in the hazy arabesque which, in the high treble register, intersperses its chromatic meandering with the falling intervals F-D and B-A♭, i.e. with notes that will inevitably be heard as reinforcing the underlying G-B-D-F chord.

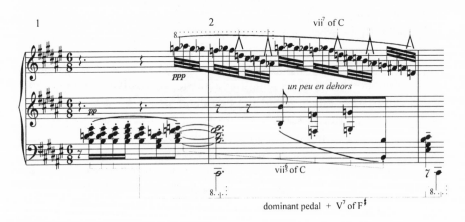

As if this gentle conflict between two tonalities at tritone distance were not enough, the remaining accented chords of this passage support another pair of tonalities. On the fourth eighth-note of bar 1, the chord that links the initial vii^7 of F♯ with the tied V^7 of C is a V^7 of A. In bar 3, the chords on beats 3 and 6 represent the V^7 of E♭, a chord that also dominates the right-hand part of bar 4, in the midst of all kinds of other dominant-seventh chords.

As the figure shows, the four tonalities abundantly supported here by their res- pective leading-note chords represent one of the axes in the circle of fifths. On the main plain, F♯ major as a home key of sorts is opposed by its antipode C major; on a secondary plane, E♭ and A serve to com- plete the cross.

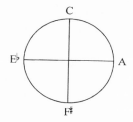

Further analysis reveals that this use of axis tonalities is no coinci- dence. In bars 28 and 30, the salient and harmonically untainted G-major seventh chords point towards C as an (at least temporary) tonal center. The chords in bars 29 and 31, by contrast, refer (as G^7-B♭^{7}-C♯^{7}-E^7) to C, E♭, F♯ and A respectively—i.e. to the same tonal axis that was established in the initial bars of the prelude.

In the rudimentary recapitulation as well as in the final line of the coda, the idea is taken up once again: bar 36 (launched with a tie from the final sixteenth-note of bar 35) affirms the dominant-seventh chord of C major, prolonged as in the prelude's initial bars in the prominent intervals within the arabesque (see bars 37 and 38). At the same time, bars 37/38 make a strong case for F♯ as the primary tonal center, presenting the complete perfect cadence with the subdominant B in the bass, a nine-part dominant-seventh chord in the upper strand, and the tonic F♯ again in the bass. In bar 42, the strong-beat F♯-C♯ interval is immediately followed by its antipole C-G.

Besides this play with tonalities, the play with texture is significantly responsible for the color of the piece. The prelude's first section retains a single texture, consisting of the arabesque discussed above in the high register, a melody supported with dominant-seventh chords or their deriv- atives in the middle strand, and repeated pedal-notes in the very low register. By contrast, the middle section (bars 13-35) is characterized by subtle and ever new variants of this texture:

- Bars 13-14 feature two melodic voices in mirror image (see the chromatic descent from D♯ to B♯ and back, in double octaves in the right hand, and in the left hand the chromatic ascent-descent from D♯ to F♯). Chords support the strong beats. Bar 15 serves as a transition in that both melodic voices appear in double octaves (see G♯-F♯ and B♮-B♯). They thus lead smoothly into the some-what submerged double-octave melody and into the double-octave pedal on C♯ of the next bars.

- Bars 16-18 comprise four layers: The melody—in double octaves and in chromatic curves as before—is countered by a second voice that is only partially chromatic and much more independent. The rhythmically supporting notes cover here a five-octave range, with four C♯s and one B representing a protracted V^7 of G♯ (see the example on the following page).

- Bars 19/20 appear again as a transition. In bar 19, the double-octave C♯ in the upper register is emancipated from its pedal-note lock and anticipates the next bar. Bar 20 contrasts the double-oc-tave melody in the treble, now enriched with parallel sixths, with a complementary accompaniment pattern in the lower strands.

bars 16-18

- Bars 21-24 retain the enriched octave + sixth parallel in the upper voice. The texture is further thickened in that the chromatically ascending counterpoint in the middle strand now also appears in three-part parallels (predominantly representing the crucial chord of this piece, the dominant-seventh). Off-beat pedal-notes in the bass are reminiscent of the preceding phrase.

- Bars 25-27 intensify the texture even further. The melody moves in seven-part parallels in the extremely high and very low registers, while the counterpart in the keyboard's middle range comes in six-part chords with acciaccaturas. The following bars expand the melodic strand to ten-part chords (see bars 28m-31) and, for the first time in the prelude, the repeatedly attempted dynamic increases are not immediately hushed but allowed a powerful *crescendo* to a point beyond forte. Only then, when the actual limit of what a pianist's two hands can play at any one time has been reached, does Debussy concede to a short recapitulation within the middle section: bars 32-34 are a varied version of bars 13-15, and bars 34/35 also contain a transposition of bars 16/17.

Structurallye, this prelude is the musical equivalent of a light conversation that wanders from one topic to another in free association—as one would expect from an encounter in the moonlight. It is probably not until the coda figure in bars 39-41 that we suddenly notice the relationship between the ever-changing, always-similar melodic curves in the middle section and the prelude's initial motif in the middle strand of bar 1. Hindsight only reveals the inner connection of some of the topics—as is often the case with particularly enchanted conversations.

La vallée des cloches   (Ravel, *Miroirs*, no. 5)

The rather unusual combination of words in this title, *The Valley of the Bells*, evokes two images: one geographical, the other musical. One way of picturing what Ravel may have had in mind when composing this piece is to imagine a journey from one end of a valley to the other and back. During such a trip, the traveler might pass by locations each characterized by their own bells, which are distinguished by pitch, frequency of stroke, loudness and sound quality. Each of these bells (or sets of bells) would continue to be audible for a certain distance, but most probably not to the other end of the valley. The sound might greet travelers, then trail off once they have passed. Finally, one might even envision that, like certain sounds we encounter in modern travel (ambulance sirens, for example), the same sound would hit the ear in a slightly different way depending on the direction from which it emanates, and might thus give the impression of existing in two different pitch appearances. Or else, different communities in the valley might emulate each others' bell sounds or have a shared idea, but come up with slightly different pitches.

Geographically, the valley can be pictured as housing three distinct settlements. The community from which the musical journey is launched is musically depicted in bars 1-6 and 49-54; the settlement one envisions in the central part of the valley would then be represented first by bars 12-18, then, returning, by bars 42-47; and the sounds of the community at the other end of the valley would be heard in bars 19m-34d.

Following this conjectured setting, one may imagine the journey beginning at the far end of the valley, with a set of two bells in G♯. (The fact that the piano texture requests octaves for each bell—see bars 1/2 etc.—is almost certainly owing to the ringing quality Ravel had in mind, and not to the idea of two bells sounding in *unison*.) The two bells evoked here. have irregular strokes, both in the distance between the lower and the upper bell and in the amount of time passing before the double bell stroke is repeated. After bar 9, this first set of bells is no longer audible. It will be heard again during the very last leg of the journey, in bars 49 and 51.

The second set of bells contains five pitches tuned in a pentatonic scale (G♯ B C♯ E F♯) and arranged in superimposed perfect fourths (see G♯-C♯-F♯ and B-E). The lowest note G♯ guarantees a pleasant harmony with the first set and thus probably belongs to the same community. Rhythm and loudness are absolutely even: the jingle is in continuous sixteenth-notes, which are demanded *très doux et sans accentuation*, i.e. very soft and without accents (neither at the beginning of each recurring four-sixteenth group nor on the highest pitches). Shortly before the middle of bar 6, however, something happens: while the bells responsible for the pitches G♯, B and C♯ continue without wavering, the highest pitch F♯ is no longer heard, and E is moved to its spot. (From here onwards, the pitch contents of this set is thus identical with that of bell set 3.) After an uninterrupted jingle up to the end of bar 9, the motion breaks off, resumes for a fragment of two patterns, and falls silent—only to be resumed at what may be the traveler's return to this end of the valley, in bars 49-52.

The third bell sound is again tuned in with the earlier two sets. Like the two others it is rooted in G♯; it repeats four of the five pitches making up bell set 2 in a lower octave (G♯ B C♯ E), and also picks up the combination in perfect fourths (see bell set 2: G♯-C♯-F♯/B-E; bell set 3: B-E/G♯-C♯). As in the initial set of bells, the pattern is that of a double stroke—here with steady distance between the two strokes but varying time lapses before each recurrence. Beginning later (see from bar 4) and louder (*p un peu marqué* = soft, somewhat accented), these bells are heard until the end of bar 12. What is more: the community at the other end of the valley seems to share the same aesthetic values and employ a very similar set of bells; see from bar 24. Two sets of superimposed perfect fourths are encountered here, as well as ascending motion where the other was descending; but otherwise the two bell sounds appear very closely related (cf. bars 4-14 = B-E/G♯-C♯ with bars 24-33 = B♭-E♭-A♭/ C-F-B♭). This variation of bell set 3 seems to fade away at some point; see bars 28-30 where the lowest pitches are taken over by a new motion in parallel major thirds, and bar 31 where only the uppermost part A♭-B♭ remains. The full three-part bell set resumes its strokes in bars 32/33, after which it undergoes various distortions, incorporating the major-third motion that had interfered before (see in bars 34-36: E♭-G/F-A), and a combination of superimposed fourths and a major triad in bar 37. Restored once more to its original form in bars 38-41, its uppermost fourths (enharmonically redefined as D♯-G♯/E♯-A♯) are heard for some more time while the traveler is already on the way back through the valley (see bars 42-44), and almost without interruption lead to the first recurrence of the original set of parallel fourths that musically indicates the approach to that side of the valley, where the journey began (see bars 45-47; also bars 50-52).

A fourth bell, heard for only a short while (see bars 6-11), is very low and heard in single strokes marked *p* but with an accent. Its G♮ clashes distinctly with the pentatonic tonality prevailing so far and might thus indicate, in terms of our story, the point of leaving the first community. Upon returning to the point of departure, this bell is not heard again. Instead, the final bars of the piece feature a much more harmonious stroke of five bells. Based on the G♯ in the same low register, an *arpeggio* like sound blends in with the pitches of the jingling second bell set, thus concluding the journey through the valley of bells on a very pleasant note.

Returning once more to the point of departure from the first community, there is a fifth bell. With a distinct three-fold triple stroke in accented *mf* on E♯—another pitch that is incompatible with the pentatonic set of the first three bell sets—this bell seems to represent the lingering between the different settlements. It is interesting to observe that its threefold triple bell stroke occurs first on the path between the community of departure and the settlement in the central portion of the valley (see bars 6/7, 8/9, 10/11). The same pattern of 3 x 3 strokes is heard again, on a different pitch (B♭), during those bars that lead from this part of the valley to the community at the other end (see bars 16, 17, 18). Even during the first steps of entering this community, already enthralled by its particularly beautiful chant, the traveler hears another version of this fifth bell motive (see in bars 20, 21, 22 the double seconds in two octaves, as well as the variation in bar 23). When the traveler gets ready to embark on the return trip, the threefold triple bell stroke is heard once again, this time on E♭ (see bars 34, 35, 37).[45]

There are, however, other musical landmarks besides the bells that characterize the settlements in this valley. The community in the center is distinguished by a very solemn and somewhat sad chordal gesture. Remotely reminiscent of the bell set in perfect fourths, it sets out with a descending step in full homophonic texture (see bar 12, first and third of the four strands) that is repeated twice (bars 13 and 14), sequenced (bar 14), repeated again (bar 15), and concluded with a final chord (bars 16, 17, 18).

Much more eloquent is the community at the far end of the valley. Its chant (thus called by Ravel, see the indication in bars 19/20) presents itself as a little ternary form with coda:

a	=	bars 19m - 23m
b	=	bars 23m - 27m
a'	=	bars 27m - 31m
(varied sequence	=	bars 31m - 34)
(coda/transition	=	bars 36m - 41)

Both the central settlement and the community at the far end have idiosyncratic bass motions to support their musical gestures. In bars 12-14 and 42-44, falling steps in double octaves sustain not only the harmony but also the metric order, by complementing the otherwise heavily syncopated motions with strong beats. Bars 14/15 and bars 44/45, 45/46 enhance this even more by ascending steps from upbeat to downbeat. The chant, by contrast, is supported by a string of pedal-point fifths interrupted by occasional octaves:

bars	20-22	24-25	26-27 /	28-30 /	32-33	34-36	37-40
	F	D♭	C	F	A♭	C	B♭
	B♭	G♭	F	B♭	D♭	F	E♭

The following music examples identify the bells heard in this valley. The diagram below attempts a possible visualization of the journey as narrated in the music.

---

[45]One could even go so far as to detect an augmented version of this "bell of transition" and its characteristic triple stroke in the bass of bars 16-19.

The bells heard at one end of the valley

The chant heard at the other end of the valley

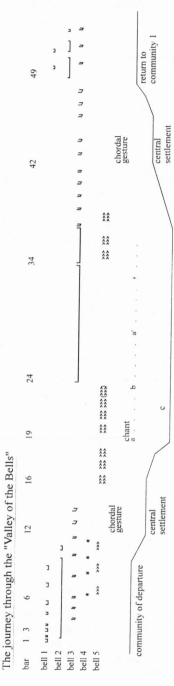

The journey through the "Valley of the Bells"

Les collines d'Anacapri   (Debussy, *Préludes*, vol. I, no. 5)

In southern Italy, set scenically in the bay of Naples with a view of the Vesuvius volcano on clear days, is the island of Capri. Benefiting from a strategic location as well as a climate that provides a welcome relief from the hot Neapolitan summers, the island has been popular with the upper classes of the various peoples that have inhabited Italy for the past 2500 years. Founded as a Greek colony circa 400 B.C., Capri later fell successively into the hands of the Romans, Lombards, Normans, Austrians, Spaniards, French, English, and Italians.

Today, ferries land at the slightly larger of the two small towns, Capri, the capital of the island. 1600 feet up on one of the many hills, lies Anacapri, its smaller sister. Still sleepy and remote from modern life in the 1990s, how much more must it have represented seclusion, unspoiled nature and equally unspoiled *joie de vivre* for a composer at the beginning of the century!

The composition *The Hills of Anacapri* begins with a motif of penta-tonically tuned bells.[46] The bells, struck *très modéré* (in a very moderate tempo) and allowed to ring for an extra measure of six strokes (longer than most performers find the patience to hold!), suddenly break off to make way for a snatch of lively *tarantella* (see bars 3/4),[47] followed by a spirited tambourine clash. The bells repeat their subdued statement, pro-longed here and fading (with an effect, in bar 6, that should sound almost like the passively rebounding after-strokes of bells). The tambourine does not enter with a sudden tempo contrast as before. Instead, its clashes con-nect the calm of the bells with the liveliness of the *tarantella* by an

---

[46]In 1992 when this author visited Anacapri, neither of the church bells could be found to ring in quite the same way. However, the effect of the actual bells is at odds with the effect Debussy seems to create. In the quiet of the village air, the modest bells struggle for atten-tion without the additional resonance often granted to the smaller bells of village churches situated in a valley; their sound seems to hang in the air in a manner that blends with the secular sounds of village life, rather than solemnly demanding respect for the sacred. Another possible explanation, offered by an inhabitant of the island, is that Debussy's bell sounds may want to suggest cowbells.

[47]A tarantella was originally a kind of ritual dance thought to cure the bite of the tarantula, a poisonous spider. Later on, tarantellas became courtship dances in which the women traditionally carry tambourines. In terms of rhythm, the Italian tarantella is related to the French Gigue. Typical meters are six-eight and twelve-eight, or four-four time with trip-lets. Debussy chooses the ambiguous meter "twelve-sixteen equals two-four" to accommo-date both the compound *and* the simple time without complicating the score with triple indications.

extremely powerful *accelerando* (see Debussy's indication *en serrant*) that speeds the tempo up about 100% in the space of less than three bars. Another snatch of a *tarantella* melody (see bars 10/11), and finally an accompaniment is established that presents the actual *tarantella* tune from its beginning (see bars 14-20), rounded off once more with the short snatch heard twice before (see left hand bars 21-24).

bars 14-18

A second theme provides a passionate contrast with the lighthearted dance (see the slower note values, the indication *p expressif*, and the high degree of chromaticism: bars 24-31). This is followed by a genuine folk tune (see the example above, and in the score, bars 31-35/35-39 in the lower register, bars 40-43 in the higher register, bars 43-45 in the middle register, with extension until bar 48).[48] This folk tune is very free in tempo. Debussy's instructions (*avec la liberté d'une chanson populaire*: with the freedom of a folk song) say this very clearly. So do his agogic indications which, intriguingly, try to recreate a South European flavor by requesting a lingering not at the end of the phrase (as is more typical for Northern European folklore) but in the middle, followed by a sudden pick-up with *crescendo* towards the closure (see particularly bars 33/34 + 34/35, bars 37/38 + 38/39). The section is rounded off by almost imperceptible quotations of the bell motif that is here wrapped into the accompaniment figure (see right hand bar 42 first half and bar 43 second half).

bars   32-39
        40-47

[48]It is interesting to observe (and to bring out, as a performer!) that the ambiguous *tarantella* meter remains valid throughout the passionate phrase and the first complete statement of the folk tune (see the tremolo figure in bars 11-17, 21-29, 32-38)—with two-four time in the melodic part against an effective six-eight (rather than the 12/16 Debussy indicates) in the accompaniment. Only from the restatement of the folk tune in the higher and middle registers onwards are texture and metric structure changed, now including accented bass notes (B alternating with F♯), fragments of a secondary line (see bars 40-43 the ascent from F♯ to D♯ and from G♯ to B) and clear two-four time.

The middle section is completely free of the lively triplet figure. In the manner of a Neapolitan love song, characteristically sung by a tenor, a three-line stanza with two extensions is presented. The rhythm is anything but simple; while the tune of the love song is in six-eight time, supported on the heavy beats by most of the surrounding voices, there is one voice that counters with a *hemiola*, setting a three-four against the six-eight (see the repeated F♯ in bars 49/50, 55/56, 59/60, 62). Another inner voice creates a small-scale "two against three" (see bar 51), and finally the entire chorus changes from six-eight to four-eight in the second halves of bars 53, 55, 55, 57 and 59 (see the example below). The final bars, again with reminiscences of the bell motif, continue both the gradual slowing down and the alternation of 6/8 and 3/4 time.

bars 49-54

With the return to the lively tempo, the chiming of the bells and the tunes of the villagers appear inseparably mingled. Bells accompany in bars 66/67, 73/74, 75, 76, 82, 83, 84, 86, 88, 90-93); the *tarantella* tune is heard first in the highest register from which it plunges (having "lost its way" in bars 71/72) with heavy accents into the lowest regions. It is then repeated in its full shape and original register (bars 74-80). The popular tune is quoted, albeit not quite completely (see bars 80-84 in the highest register, bars 84/85 in the middle register). The coda (from bar 86 onwards) features cymbal seconds A-B in all octaves and snatches from the *tarantella*. The conclusion, marked *lumineux* (luminous) by the composer and reaching into the highest octave of the modern keyboard, should be read (and performed) as a pure expression of *joie de vivre*.

60

This piece is fairly tonal. Sections in B major (the folk tune and the love song) are interspersed with passages where B major seems tainted by its relative G♯ minor (as in the *tarantella* whose melody alone—but not the accompaniment—could be heard as G♯ minor). B frames the bell motif, while the tambourines accent both G♯ (see the middle register) and B (low and high registers). B is present as a pedal note in bars 10, 40, 45-48, 85-96, but G♯ provides the root for bars 66-72.

WIND AND WATER, FOG AND SNOW

Le vent dans la plaine   (Debussy, *Préludes*, vol. I, no. 3)

In the search for a possible extra-musical source for the title we do not have to look far. Debussy himself, in his songs *Ariettes oubliées*, uses the words attributed to the French composer and poet Favart as an epigram to the poems by Paul Verlaine. What is significant here is that this epigram is longer than that used in the Préludeand contains a crucial piece of information. Its second line specifies the lightness and subdued nature of this wind:

> *Le vent dans la plaine*
> *suspend son haleine*

The wind in the plane is holding its breath! —and not blowing with untrammeled force, as one might have expected after reading only the first line.

This is the third piece in a row built on a B♭ pedal-note. While the composer thus ties three consecutive preludes together musically, the question whether the intoxicating vapors of *Danseuses de Delphes* (no. 1, refer back to pp. 5-8, the gently billowing sails or passion-concealing veils of *Voiles* (no. 2, see pp. 74-77), and the winds in this piece reflect any common imagery must be left to the interpretative fantasies of the individual performer or listener.

When comparing the tonal aspects of the three preludes one finds that the first, despite some considerable deviations, is firmly rooted in B♭ major. The second piece explores the whole-tone context over the same root, a context that is interrupted for a short spell of pentatonics but then regained. The third piece suggests yet another alternative built on the same pitch; it begins with—and regains later, after an excursion—what amounts to a five-note excerpt from the Phrygian mode on B♭,[49] intersper-

---

[49] The Phrygian scale on B♭ is B♭ C♭ D♭ E♭ F G♭ A♭ B♭. The "wind" pattern does not encompass F and A♭ here, although F appears (albeit in company of a foreign E♭♭) as a grace-note in bars 5 and 6.

sed with tonally related passages on a similar excerpt of the Dorian mode on E♭.[50]

It is interesting to observe how a composer expresses "wind holding its breath" in the parameters of rhythm, dynamics, and tonal language. Debussy chose for his rhythm a number of very regular patterns which, combined, determine the mood of the piece in such a way that the occasional deviations are truly startling. The constant flow of softly murmuring sixteenth-note sextuplets, established at the very outset of the prelude, constitutes the dominating feature. This flow is suspended in bars 9-12 and 50/51, 52/53 in favor of much slower but equally regular values. This motion, however, is not as steady as the previous murmur.

When first encountered in bars 9-12, it draws almost to a standstill—see the concluding notes of each two-bar subphrase as well as, perhaps more importantly, the accompanying *cédez* (give way / release). At its recurrence, the recession in tempo occurs slightly earlier and is suddenly interrupted by spells of the regular breeze—see in bars 51 and 53 where the sextuplet rhythm cuts into a *cédez*.

Other interruptions of the rhythmic regularity are even more unexpected. In bar 28 and, derived from the same pattern, in bars 30/31 and 33/34, a sudden short-short-long rhythm in *f crescendo*, followed by an accented syncopation in *subito p*, breaks in as a real surprise. (One may imagine some abrupt gusts.) At the very end of the piece (see bars 54/55), a reminder of these gusts is heard in a very much softened version: the short-short-long has been leveled to a regular triplet, and the dynamic increase now leads gently into a syncopated chord which, here, appears without particular dynamic emphasis, neither as a climax nor as an anti-climax. Finally, in the next-to-last bar, the *crescendo* is abandoned altogether and the syncopation is swallowed by the third note of the triplet, bringing about the special kind of stillness well-known on breezy days that a poetic mind might well perceive as "the wind holding its breath."

Blending with the suggestions of these rhythmic choices, Debussy's dynamics also depict a gentle, somewhat volatile but always playful zephyr (see particularly the off-beat intensifications in bars 5/6, 16/17 and 48/49, as well as the stopped increase at the end of bars 8, 16, 20 and in bar 24). The general tone color is indicated as *aussi légèrement que possible* (as lightly as possible), and the realm of *p* is only abandoned for the sudden, short gusts in *f crescendo* mentioned above.

---

[50]The complete scale here is E♭ F G♭ A♭ B♭ C D♭ E♭. F, however, is not used, and A♭ only in passing towards the end of bars 10 and 12.

In terms of tonal organization, the pedal-notes are particularly intriguing. The following table gives an overview:

```
bars 1        9       13 15   21        28      33 34      44      50 54
     B♭       B♭      B♭ B♭♭ =A (G A♭) G♭      G G♯ (E) B♭        B♭ B♭
     E♭                                                           E♭
              (falling B♭ to G♭,   rising G♭ to G♯)
```

The design of the prelude is simple. After the introductory murmuring of the wind in a B♭/C♭ "trill with octave displacement" (bars 1/2), the main theme with its characteristic double-dotted rhythm is presented.

bars 3-6

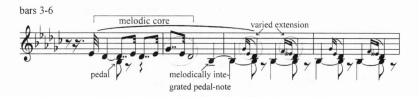

The soft murmur resumes in bars 7/8, followed this time by four slower-paced bars. These are built mainly on the E♭ six-five chord, representing the Dorian mode on E♭.

bars 9/10

A third time the murmur sets in (bars 13), this time with more triggering force (see the beginning with a lower bass note and with dynamic emphasis). The dotted-note theme with the flattened pedal-note now sounds in what appears (due to the absence of the fifth degree in bars 15-17) as Lydian mode. It is shortened by one bar and intensified with additional chromatic ascents (bar 17).

The fourth phrase is even more compressed and enhanced. A one-bar "murmur" (bar 18) launches a version of the theme in an artificial scale (B♭♭ C♭ D♭ E♭ F G♭ A♭ B♭♭) which, to the relief of the performer's eyes

65

that may by now be weary of double-flats, is at last enharmonically redefined (B♭♭-C♭ becoming A-B).

Bars 22-24 bring the first contrast: a three-bar unit whose twelve beats are grouped—rhythmically, but above all tonally—as 5+3+4. Beginning in a whole-tone context over G with a 5/4 unit, the remaining beats of the three-bar phrase introduce foreign notes (see bar 23: C, D and bar 24: E). The phrase is then sequenced a semitone higher (bars 25-27). The following two phrases, different as they may appear on brief inspection, are actually variations of this pattern (compare bars 28-34 with bars 22-27). The phrase length of three bars and the underlying rhythmic pattern are the same. However,

- the tonal context, previously from the whole-tone scale, is now G♭ major;
- the foreign notes, earlier in parallel fifths within the left hand, are here cross-related chords[51] in the right hand;
- the trill, which previously started off with shifts across the keyboard before it settled, is now a *tremolo*—which is steady to start with but then moving in contrary motion to the chords;
- the chromatic shift, occurring earlier from the model (bars 22-24) to its sequence (bars 25-27), is repeated here at the very end of the second phrase (bar 33) and is extended through G to G♯ (bar 34).

It is as if Debussy were consciously attempting to explore all possibilities of variation on a given material with very few parameters.

The subsequent prolonged phrase serves as a retransition. It begins on G♯ with the murmur followed by the dotted-note theme, then moves down two whole tones, repeats the theme, and in bar 44 returns to the original B♭ pedal. Without further introduction, the main theme is now recalled twice in different registers (see bars 44/45 and 46/47). The following bars derive from the third phrase of the piece (compare bars 48-53 with bars 7-12) but contain more disquiet than before.

The coda, while based on the pitches of the murmuring breeze, nonetheless picks up not only the gust rhythm but also the chromatic shifts from the contrasting section. The C♭-major chord, which is integrated in the basic mode, forming part of the Lydian scale on B♭, slides up through C major and D♭ major to D major and remains unresolved. Meanwhile, both the dynamics (*p - pp - più pp - ppp)* and the tempo (*un peu retenu = poco ritenuto*) are receding and bring the prelude to a whispering close. The *laissez vibrer* (allow to vibrate) in the final bar suggests that, after

---

[51]For cross-related chords see bar 29: F♭ minor, D♭ major, F♭ minor, with A♭♭/A♭ and F♭/F.

the pedal has cleared the C♭ on the arpeggiated octave and has then released the octave on the downbeat of the last bar, the low B♭ should be left to ring until it fades on its own. If struck in true *ppp*, this should not require undue patience from either the performer or the audience and is a very beautiful way of concluding this prelude. It conveys an eerie quality of loneliness—as if it were now nature's turn to hold its breath.

Ce qu'a vu le vent d'ouest   (Debussy, *Préludes*, vol. I, no. 7)

This is Debussy's third prelude on the subject of *wind*. After the indirect impact of gently moving air on sails or veils in *Voiles* (vol. I, no. 2, see pp. 74-77) and the more real but still mainly whispering wind in *Le vent dans la plaine* (vol. I, no. 3, refer back to pp. 63-67), the indication *Animé et tumultueux* announces stronger forces of nature this time.

When taking a closer look at the music Debussy has created to depict "what the west wind has seen," we may wish to try to distinguish both those features that this prelude has in common with the two earlier wind preludes, and those which are specific here. There are two features that attract immediate attention: the pedal-notes and the use of scales.

In *Voiles*, the bass pedal B♭ is actually present or at least implied throughout all but seven of the prelude's sixty-four bars (leaving out only short passages at the opening and close). The same pedal-note in *Le vent dans la plaine* governs thirty-one of fifty-nine bars or roughly half the piece, this time firmly established in the outer sections but suspended in the middle of the piece. Finally in the tale of the West Wind now under consideration, the pedal-note F♯ can be found in the bass register of bars 1-24, 54-58 and 62-71 (implied in bars 6, 58 and 69). In addition, this pitch appears as the central melodic note in bars 26-29, after another interruption with a bass sonority F♯ still implied (see bar 25). This pedal-note thus determines forty-four bars, as in *Le vent dans la plaine*, grouped together in the outer sections of these preludes.

In this case, however, secondary pedal-notes make powerful contributions. As dynamics and tempo have reached what sounds like the force of a considerable storm, the bass register is characterized by a repeated after-beat B in doubled octave and *ff*, while the right hand contributes a wildly whirling figure on three octaves of C♯ (see bars 35-41). Within the framework of traditional tonal language, these two pitches represent the subdominant and dominant respectively of the primary pedal-note F♯. Yet a new color in the piece, with *ff* — *p* contrast and *toccata* patterns, is built over a pedal D♯ (see bars 42-46) in ascending octaves of the lowest voice, bars 47-51 in sudden gusts of high-pitched tremolo, interrupted and concluded by after-beat double-octave strokes and a final whirl in the lowest register (see bars 49-52). Considered once again in terms of a hidden tonal framework, this D♯ represents the relative of F♯. In conjunction, these various pedal-notes, each firmly established in their own right, support all but two short passages: bars 30-34 and bars 59-61. The first passage presents a chromatic ascent from the strident trill on C (see the pattern in alternating hands, bars 24-30) to the new pedal C♯; the other represents the insertion of a component transposed at the tritone (compare bars 59-61 with bars 7-9).

In terms of scales, *Voiles* is predominantly built on the whole-tone scale, with only its short middle section in a pentatonic mode over the same root. *Le vent dans la plaine* begins and ends in only slightly tainted five-note excerpts of the Phrygian and Dorian scales respectively, while featuring some (equally tainted) whole-tone bars in its middle (bars 22-27). In the third wind piece, the five-pitch groups are not so prominent, although one could identify short passages at the beginning and end of the prelude built on a similar pitch content, this time probably not taken from any particular mode (see F♯ A C D E♭ in bars 1-4, tainted with grace-note A♭ in the latter bar, and expanded in bars 5/6 by the fully integrated A♭ to a six-note figure).

More convincing in this prelude are the whole-tone passages.[52] In bars 10-14, the whole-tone context on G (C♯ D♯ F G A B) is tainted by a foreign note, the pedal-note F♯ (see the upper note of the left-hand *tremolo* as well as the right-hand pitches). Bars 19/20 and 23-27m are erected on the whole-tone scale over F♯ (C D E F♯ G♯ B♭), and even bars 27-30 continue this pattern with the exception of additional chromatic neighbors of B♭ in the melody. The chromatic ascent that begins on the final quarter-note of bar 32 can be read as (and actually sounds very much like) an alternating pattern of excerpts from the two whole-tone scales. Bars 35-38d and bars 39-42d are pure realizations of the whole-tone scale on B (C♯ D♯ F G A B), and the concluding chords of this section once again present alternations of excerpts from the two whole-tone scales (see bars 51-53). Finally in the coda, the melodic left-hand line is

[52]One must, of course, be careful not to overstate this point, since Debussy has used the whole-tone scale elsewhere. There are, however, not too many pieces where the scale is used with such consistency, and that all three should be linked to the image (or metaphor) of gentle or playful wind seems at least significant.

taken from the whole-tone scale on C (see bars 63-68), followed by one homophonic bar on the whole-tone scale on C♯ before giving way to the two final diatonic bars.

As is well known, Debussy has taken his title *What the West Wind Has Seen* from one of the fairy tales of the Danish poet Hans Christian Andersen. In his story *The Garden of Paradise*, Andersen tells of a prince who, wandering the world in search of the Garden of Eden, meets the "mother of the winds." While he is talking to her and questioning her, the four winds who are her sons return home one after the other, each giving accounts of what they have done and seen. Here is the excerpt comprising the tale of the West Wind (a wind that, for the Danish just as much as for the French, is the wind that comes from across the Atlantic Ocean):

> *(North Wind):* - *"...there's my brother from the West. I like him best of all—he smacks of the sea and brings a heavenly chill along with him."*
>
> *"Is that little Zephyrus?" asked the prince. "Yes, that's Zephyrus, all right!" said the old woman [= the mother of the winds]. "But he's not so little after all. In the old days he was a handsome boy, but that's over now!"*
>
> *He looked like a wild man, but he had on a baby's cap so as not to hurt himself. In his hand he carried a mahogany club, chopped down in the mahogany forests of America. It could be no less!*
>
> *"Where do you come from?" asked his mother.*
>
> *"From the forest wilderness," he said, "where the thorny lianas make a fence between each tree, where the water snake lies in the grass and mankind seems to be unnecessary."*
>
> *"What were you doing there?"*
>
> *"I was looking at the deep river and saw how it plunged down from the cliff, turned to spray, and flew up to the clouds to carry the rainbow. I was watching the wild buffalo swimming in the river, but the current dragged him along with it, and he drifted with a flock of wild ducks that flew in the air where the water went over the edge. The buffalo had to go over. I liked that, so I blew up a storm so the ancient trees went sailing and were dashed to shavings."*
>
> *"And you haven't done anything else?" asked the old woman.*
>
> *"I've been turning somersaults in the savannahs, and I've been patting the wild horse and shaking down coconuts. Oh, yes, I've got stories to tell, but one shouldn't tell everything one knows. You're well aware of that, old lady!" And then he gave his mother such a that she almost fell over backward. He was really a wild boy*[53].

[53]Hans Christian Andersen, *The Garden of Paradise*; from *Hans Andersen's Fairy Tales: A Selection*, trans. L. W. Kingsland (Oxford: Oxford University Press, 1959).

This wind thus tells of nature: forest wilderness untouched by human beings, rivers, clouds and rainbows. He also shows his mischievous nature when talking about the delight he took in seeing the buffalo go over the brink—such delight that he blew up a mighty storm that caused even more havoc. His playful mood expresses itself in wild whirls in open fields and in the childlike fun at the scattering of coconuts. Even when hugging his mother, Andersen's West Wind is indeed an unruly fellow.

The prelude's musical structure can roughly be described as A B B' A' coda. The A sections contain two components, neither of them melodically determined, while the B sections encompass several melodic elements.

In the initial A section, a basic windy whirl is established in bars 1/2. Harmonically an inverted dominant-seven chord (appearing as a six-five chord over F♯), it rhythmically depicts sudden short gusts by lingering on the lowest pitch before embarking on a swift arpeggiated flourish through two and a half octaves. In bars 3/4, accented peak notes are added, every other time ornamented by grace notes. Harmonically, these constitute one more six-five chord, appearing as a transposition to the tritone of the previous one (compare F♯ A C D with C E♭ G♭ A♭). The melodic element thus introduces a harmonic feature—the juxtaposition of original position and the transposition to the half-octave—that will play a role at other instances in the piece. Bars 5/6 expand on the previous development by alternating the two chords in a large-scale ascent/descent accompanied by a powerful *crescendo-diminuendo.*

The section's second component explores similar expressive aims by different musical means. A bass *tremolo* in perfect fifth interval, joined after one beat by the major chord over the same root, is shifted in what amounts to a parallel-motion turn figure (up through two chords, down again, up once more). The chords are harmonically incompatible[54] and realized dynamically once again in *crescendo-diminuendo* (see bars 7-9). The A' section differs in detail but not in spirit.

- In bar 54 (which structurally corresponds with bars 1/2), the bass-note F♯ appears in trill motion alternating between the minor and the major second as its auxiliary note; each change is to be expressed in a small and probably very sudden increase followed by an immediate hush.

[54]For easier comparison, it may help to re-write enharmonically the E♭ major chord as D♯ major: F♯-A♯-C♯ is followed by D♯-F×-A♯ (with a cross-relationship of F♯/F×) and leads into A-C♯-E (where A is cross-related to the preceding A♯).

- Bars 55/56 retain the varying trill in the bass. The right hand picks up the pitches from the original triad with added sixth (F♯-A-C-D), in a figure reminiscent of the accents preceded by grace-notes in the second halves of bars 3/4. Interestingly, these six-five notes are then infected by the minor-major alternations in the bass, so that every other statement alters the chord to F♯-A-C♯-D♯.

- From the second beat of bar 56 onwards, the tritone-transposed six-five chord recurs, albeit here in the enharmonic writing as (B♯)-D♯-F♯-G♯. These two bars (55/56) thus correspond with bars 3/4.

- The following two bars are identical with their model (compare bars 57/58 with bars 5/6) except for the final two notes. While the first component of the A' section is thus one bar shorter than its model in the A section, the second component is extended by one bar.

- Bars 59-61 are the transposition by a tritone of bars 7-9. Bar 62, as if to put things right after all, adds the central bar of the phrase in the original transposition (cf. bar 62 with bar 8).

Section B begins in bar 10 with the juxtaposition (already mentioned earlier) of the pedal-note F♯ and the whole-tone pitch content that does *not* include F♯. The melodic component in the right hand develops logically from the preceding phrase. It also consists of parallel shifts, this time not of major chords but of double seconds in octave doubling. What makes this element appear more melodically significant than the preceding one is its distinct rhythmic shape. Characteristically, the more accented of the two shifts constitutes a leap of a tritone, and thus confirms the predominant role played by the tritone shift in this prelude. For later reference, this element will be labeled motif *a*.

bars 10-14

Parallel shifts also determine the following four bars. Here, a major chord in second inversion (see B♯ in the bass clef, E♯-A-B♯ in the treble clef, an enharmonic writing for C + F-A-C) is transported upwards through four chromatic steps. After a rest, the process is repeated three times on the same level, three times an octave higher, and finally once a semitone higher (see bars 15-18). The melodic element in this phrase also develops from preceding material. Drawing on the strongly dotted rhythmic shape of motif *a*, motif *b* alternates an accented F♯ with gradually rising pre-beat notes, first in a single-voiced strand (see bars 15/16) and then in four-octave intensification (see bars 17/18). The dynamic realization demands only *crescendo* followed by *subito* return to the previous level; however, the intensified repetition of motif *b* departs from *p* as the dynamic center. A further increase occurs in the realm of tempo. While Debussy requests in bar 15 *commencer un peu au-dessous du movement* (to begin a bit below the tempo), he specifies a gradual return to the original animated tempo in bar 17 (*revenir progressivement au mouvement animé*). Bars 19/20 extend motif *b* by quoting it in its tritone transposition (!), in a chordal setting based on the whole-tone scale, and with each accented longer beat followed by an ascending, dynamically increasing whole-tone scale flourish[55]. The general dynamic level has now risen to *mf*.

Bars 21-24 present motif *c*. This melodic element, continuing the intensification process from *f* to *ff*, further develop the core elements of this piece. The melodic idea is based on the whole-tone scale on C (C D E F♯/G♭ A♭ B♭). Since the vertical setting of each melodic note is, however, in a major chord (right hand) and an inverted V^7 over the same root (left hand), only the voices launched from B♭ (3 octaves), D (2 octaves) and A♭ (lowest pitch) move within this whole-tone realm, while the remaining two voices (starting with F) use exclusively the pitches from the alternative whole-tone scale. The pedal-note F♯, the octave flourish on B♭, and the final chord and its repetition (B♭ C E B♭ C E A♭ C) all derive from the whole-tone scale on C. Bars 23-25 introduce a trill motion. Written in sixteenth-notes but appearing in the context of heightened tempo and intensity, the result is probably only slightly slower than the one in bars 10-14. Characteristically, this trill on C is the transposition—by a tritone, of course—of the earlier trill on F♯ (albeit with a whole-tone auxiliary).

After the strident beginning demanded by the composer for the beginning of this trill, the dynamic intensity subsides very drastically, to

---

[55]Note that the rhythmic notation is very confusing here, owing to Debussy's most unusual beaming. The four eighth-notes of each half bar consist actually of a two-hand chord on the first eighth-note, the F♯ octave and a right-hand long-short-short on the second eighth-note, a four-thirtyseconds group on the third eighth-note, and two fast notes (D-E) plus the final chord on the fourth eighth-note. (Debussy's grouping under beams seems to suggest triplet understanding, but this is not endorsed by the actual number of note values.)

reach *p* and a somewhat reduced tempo (*un peu retenu*) in bar 26 where motif *d* sets in. This melodic element is much more sketchy than any of the other three. In very close register, overlapping in its octave jump with the accompanying trill and not supported by any bass pedal, this motif is designated with the words *p mais en dehors et angoissé*, soft but clearly audible and anguished. The metrically irregular *crescendo* motions do not even allow the hush to fall on strong beats (as in motif *b*) but cross the bar-lines in such a way as to obscure the metric order temporarily. The bridging chromatic ascent of the trill begins with unexpected *f* (often overlooked by performers) and increases from there, only to fall back into *p* as the right hand continues with a free development of the motif (see bars 31-32). For the next chromatic ascent, bridging this time to the B' section, Debussy requests *en serrant beaucoup et augmentant beaucoup* (contracting very much and augmenting very much; or increasing very much in both dynamics and tempo).

Bars 35-38 and 39-42 are a free restatement of motif *a*. The rhythm is simplified, with only simple dotting and a downbeat beginning. The *tremolo*, as an accompaniment replaced by the pedal-note B and the three-octave whirl on C♯ already mentioned, is converted into a dramatic event with chordally set double trills in *toccata* pattern, following now the concluding chord in bars 38 and 42. This dramatic pattern is then explored further in a bridging passage (see bars 43-45). After another bar recalling the chromatically ascending chords of earlier transitions, motif *c* is re-stated. The texture, with pedal-note *tremolo* in the highest register, is again different, and the chordal setting of the motif appears as a series of six-five chords—of exactly the inverted dominant-seventh chord that was established at the outset of this prelude (see left hand, bars 47-50). Motifs *b* and *d* do not recur in the B' section.

In the coda, the right-hand chords also use the pitches of the original six-five chord (see bars 63-66). The little melodic gesture (bars 67-68) is equally centered on this chord. After a rudimentary but triumphantly loud and stretched-out reminiscence of motif *a* in bar 69, the final two bars conclude the piece with the major-mode version of the six-five chord already used at the beginning of the A' section, in what seems like a Debussyan adaptation of a Picardy-third ending.

The components of this composition—whirling *arpeggios*, *tremolos*, trills, *toccata* patterns, suddenly rising chromatic elements, *crescendo-/ subito pp* effects—all depict very well the mischievous but basically innocent. The same playfulness is also expressed in the dotted rhythm so

73

prominent in motifs *a, b* and *c*, while the "anguished" mood desired for motif *d* might allude to the reaction felt as a result of some of the West Wind's more destructive deeds.

Voiles   (Debussy, *Préludes*, vol. I, no. 2)

The French word "voiles" has two meanings: veils or sails. Our imagination links both to the wind; they might billow, flap, undulate softly, or even be still. They are the visible means catching the invisible, the breeze. The veil hides a woman's face from the eyes of the world and often symbolizes purity; sails, originally conceived as stark white, are often perceived with a similar connotation. Finally, emotions and impressions may be called veiled: unclear, partly hidden, perhaps detached from what might be overly real. Debussy seems to use all these images to compose an extraordinarily beautiful, airy piece of music[56].

Of the sixty-four bars of the prelude, fifty-eight are built exclusively on one of the two whole-tone scales. This choice of tonal context is significant since it means an avoidance of the semitone and its longing, yearning—or whatever passionate quality we have come to attach to it. Moreover, the entire prelude rests on the bass pedal-note B♭. This pedal-note is truly absent only in the initial four and the final three bars; in bars 31/32 and 44, it must be assumed as implied—although it is worthwhile investigating why in just these bars the composer does not even indicate sustaining ties.

The somewhat veiled quality of feelings is expressed also by several other means. Regarding thematic material, the amount of repetition is such that listeners can let go of active alertness, abandoning themselves to impressionistic day-dreaming. Melodically, there is a strong prevalence of stepwise motion. The melodic design is thus almost devoid of complexities and surprises (see particularly the two main components, the double-third figure in bars 1/2 and the octave chant beginning in bar 7). Metrically, large portions seem to be floating. This is achieved through downbeat rests (as in both components mentioned above), literal syncopations (as in the octave chant bars 8d, 10d, 11d), or dynamic concealment (as in the initial figure where both middle beats carry weight while the downbeat is light). Finally regarding rhythm, the composer indicates as a

---

[56]Edgard Varèse, who knew Debussy quite well, said the piece was really about the American dancer Louise Fuller, famous in Paris for creating flowing waves in the air with long, semitransparent veils attached to her ankles and hands.

subheading that the prelude is to be kept "in a rhythm [that is] without rigidity and caressing."

The first motif in this prelude is introduced in bars 1-6. It consists exclusively of whole-tone scale double thirds which, were it not for the octave displacement in bar 2, would represent a single stepwise descent. Downbeats, except for the slightly emphasized final one, are dynamically weak or avoided. The stronger beats that do occur are long (dotted or tied values) followed by swift motion, giving this figure a unique air of weightlessness. Tonally, the figure begins twice (see bars 1m, 3m) on G♯, a melodic center that will remain important throughout the piece.

bars 1/2

The first motif then gives way to a chant in solemnly moving octaves (see bars 7-14).

bars 7-14

| reiterated beginning | core phrase | repeated final |

It is characterized by a reiterated beginning (see bars 7/8 and 9) and a repeated final note (see bars 13 and 14). The launching as well as the final notes are A♭. Thus the chant appears centered in the same pitch that, as G♯, triggered the first figure. Again, downbeats are avoided or dynamically weak except for the slightly emphasized concluding notes. When the chant later recurs in chordal version, this feature, which would appear as an intensification in other contexts, here adds to the impression of simplicity since the whole-tone scale allows for only two different chords, both of them augmented and thus without any tension between them.

At the beginning of what is perceived as the first contrasting section of the prelude, Debussy introduces another billowing figure. Beginning with a whole-tone "turn" and also launched from, and returning to, a melodically central A♭ (see bars 22-24, 26-28, A♭/G♯), this figure picks up elements from the previous components: the augmented

bars 22/23

triad from the developed chant (see at the end of bar 24) and the double-thirds from the initial figure (see bars 25-27; the enharmonic writing of these thirds may look confusing but does not sound any different from the beginning). The development of this figure is launched, in bars 29/30, as a simple embellishment, but gives way to the first appearance of chromatic segments in bar 31, used antiphonally with inversion and diminution. This, significantly, is the moment when the B♭ bass pedal is suspended for the first time.

bars 22-24

In the accompaniment, a swaying figure centered in D (bars 22-28) later gives in to the overall prevalence of scalar motion (bars 29/30). This, in turn, is further transformed: first, still rhythmically specific, to D-E—E (see bar 31); then to a very neutral feature, much loved by Debussy, the trill with octave displacement (see from bar 32 onwards). This split-level trill accompanies the recurrence of the chant in bars 33-37, which is here further intensified both in texture (with triple octave) and in structure (appearing without any redundancy, i.e. without both the aborted opening and the repeated final note). A transition reminiscent of the figure in bars 22/23 concludes this section in bar 41, bringing with it an intensification on the emotional level, with *p crescendo* (over the previously prevalent *pp*) and the contracting tempo demanded by *serrez*.

The next section acts like the second episode in a rondo: it is set apart from its surroundings in all its parameters. Bars 42-47, while still rooted in B♭ for the bass pedal and A♭ for the melodic center (see the upbeat/downbeat groups of A♭ in bars 42, 43, 44) are built on the pentatonic scale B♭ D♭ E♭ G♭ A♭. The section is also more lively in tempo, contrasting the moderate motion of the main section with a development from *en animant* (enlivening / quickening) through *rapide* (fast) to *emporté* (carried away), before the opposite instructions *cédez* (give way / release) and *très retenu* (very much held back). As if that were not enough, the dynamics, too, are in stark contrast to the other sections of the piece. Much more explosive, they interrupt a color until then confined to the *pp-p* range with outbursts up to *f* as well as accents and a contrast of *crescendo molto* (bar 43) and *diminuendo molto* (bar 44). As in the chromatic instance within the first contrasting section, it is here again the moment of highest tension that is distinguished by a suspension of the bass pedal (see bar 44).

With bar 48, the piece returns to the whole-tone scale and, after a two-bar introduction with a new five-note *glissando*-like figure, to the chant (see bars 50-54). After an extension that alternates the *glissando* figure with chords (chords that are also based on five-note excerpts from the whole-tone scale; see bars 54-57, with ensuing overlap until bar 60m), this section is rounded off with reminiscences of the initial motif (see bars 58-62, extended to bar 64).

Structurally, this prelude loosely resembles a rondo. What distinguishes the recurring main sections or refrains from their counterparts in 18th-century music is something Alban Berg stressed strongly when discussing recapitulations: "Imagine what experiences the themes have had since they first occurred," he is quoted as exclaiming when a student tried to get away with a simple reworking of the exposition material. Debussy seems to agree with Berg; both recurrences of the main material are changed and influenced by what has happened in between. In bars 33-41, the trill with octave displacement crosses the voundaries of the contrasting section not only with its material but, perhaps more importantly, with its additional central note, D. In bars 48-64, the *glissando* figure as well as the chords derived from it are each based on five-note excerpts of the whole-tone scale, thus paying reverence to the intermittent pentatonic section.

Une barque sur l'Océan   (Ravel, *Miroirs*, no. 3)

The image here is of a boat or barge—"ship" would be *bateau*—on the ocean. Performed only once during Ravel's lifetime, the piece elicited the following comment from Gaston Carraud, music critic of *La Liberté*:

> ". . . like a succession of colors imposed on a drawing barely
> sketched. . . Unfortunately the view changes every moment. It
> is a confusing kaleidoscope and we cannot even tell what kind
> of weather prevails on this ocean."[57]

There is undoubtedly truth in Carraud's perception. The "confusing kaleidoscope" that Ravel paints does not conform to traditional images of contained wildness and a securely focused view. This small boat on the immense ocean is subject to experiences whose outcome is unknown at the time that we, the listeners, witness them. Ravel's music exposes the listeners to this disquieting unpredictability.

[57]Quoted in the English translation from Roger Nichols, *Ravel* (London: J. M. Dent & Sons Ltd, 1977), p. 44

In the main section, a swaying motion over large waves forms the backdrop of a plaintive melody that arises in the middle ground of the texture (see example, bars 4-10). The plaintive tune seems to express hope amidst sighs, while sudden changes of the waves' height and speed evoke the relentless capriciousness of the elements (see, e.g., bars 11/12 where the left-hand figure on the second beat is both half as fast and much more restricted in range than those on beats 1 and 3).

The second thematic component (see bars 38-43 etc.) features forceful outbursts that repeatedly carry a *tremolo* from *pp* to *ff* in the course of a single bar. These may be read as depictions of drama—be it that of the pathetic little vessel or that of the storms that rough up the ocean. The third thematic element suggests a human presence in the scene. During a momentary absence of any note values fast enough to paint ripples or waves, we hear a chordally supported melody marked "very expressive." An emphatic upbeat leads to a one-and-a-half-bar suspension that drops a fourth in *diminuendo*; then a sudden *sf* bursts out with what strikes the ear as an extremely distressed sigh (D♯-B♯). The entire melodic gesture can be heard as a passionate, perhaps desperate outcry.

bars 46-49

Before we observe the details of Ravels structural layout and tonal language in this piece, it is interesting to note the "fate" encountered by each of the three thematic elements listed above. The first (the swaying motion above large waves) recedes in the course of the work; its initial occurrence encompassed twenty-seven bars, with ten bars of the basic motion (bars 1-10) followed by a three-bar turbulence (bars 11-13), an incomplete repeat of the basic motion (bars 14-20), and a recurrence of the turbulence (transposed to different levels in the two hands in bars 21-23 and extended up to bar 27). When the basic motion is reestablished towards the middle of the piece, it covers only seven bars 61-67, and the very end of the work recalls mere fragments in bars 132-137.

By contrast, the human element in this picture, represented by the desperate outcry, gains more and more ground as the piece progresses, and thus captures ever more of the listener's attention. The gesture that first covered three bars without any melodic repetition is extended in bars

76-78, where the final distressed sigh (here E♯-D) is repeated—softer with regard to both dynamics and rhythmic intensity—in bar 80. Further softened and displaced two octaves up, it recurs in bar 83 (enharmonically as F-D), from where the sigh now triggers its own phrase.[58] When the outcry is heard for the last time, it is expanded in both directions. The accompaniment and the chord supporting the initial melodic note G in bar 121 are anticipated in bars 119/120—albeit with a B♮ in the chord instead of the later B♭. Even before that, the *arpeggios* in bars 117/ 118 prepare the same chord. Similarly after the phrase, its final distressed sigh (here E-C♯) is taken up in bar 126, while the closing note together with the supporting chord are extended throughout bars 128-131.

Finally, the second component, portraying the dramatic gusts, is more locally persistent than pervasive. Each time it happens it is savored thrice (see bars 38/39, 40/41, 42/43; intensified in bars 68/69, 70/71, 72/73, appeased in bars 111/112, 113/114, 115/116).

Between the three principal thematic components whose development was briefly outlined above, two contrasting sections are inserted:

- The first covers bars 28-37, thus linking the initial statement of the swaying motion with the first appearance of the dramatic gusts. A new pedal note B♭ clearly announces the structural caesura, after the prevalent pedals F♯ (in bars 1-10, 14-20) and G (concluding the section bars 23-27). The new pedal is introduced in the opening bar of the contrast, bar 28, and retained as the lowest textural layer of bars 29-35. The middle strand presents the broken chords or waves, which thus sound as if cushioned and much less out of control. On either side of these waves, i.e. immediately above the pedal-note and in the highest register, two strands consist of chordally supported melodic lines. They are intriguing in their contrary motion. While the treble descends in

---

[58]Particularly interesting here is the fact that the structure of this new phrase assumes a layout similar to that observed in the first occurrence of the swaying motion. Here is a structural comparison:

first thematic component		third thematic component	
bars 1-3	introduction of accompmt.	bars 81/82	introduction of accompmt.
bars 4/5, 6/7	two-note melodic trigger (2x)	bar 83	two-note trigger (1x)
bars 8-10	five-note extended version	bars 84/85	five-note extended version
bars 11-13	section-internal contrast	bars 86-88	section-internal contrast
bars 14/15	introduction of accompmt.	bars 88/89	introduction of accompmt.
bars 16/17	two-note melodic trigger (1x)		(two-note trigger omitted)
bars 18-20	five-note extended version	bars 90/91	five-note extended version
bars 21-23-27	contrast, transposed/expanded	bars 92-94₁-97	contrast, acc. expanded

steps that constitute a whole-tone scale with one semitone (C♭) filled in, the tenor-range chords ascend in a chromatic motion that widens towards the end of the scale. Keeping their pitch patterns, the voices then lap over and under one another as in the crests and valleys of water—an apt musical metaphor for the loss of control.

bars	29	30	31	32	33	34	35	36	37
r.h.	B♭ A♭	F♯ E	D C C♭B♭A♭	C♯D	E F G♯B	C D	E F♯G♯B♭	C D	
l.h.	B C	C♯D	E F A♭B C	F♯E	D C B B♭A♭	F♯E	D C B♭		

- The second contrasting section, much longer than the first, is inserted in bars 81-110, i.e. before the final recurrence of all three thematic components. Its accompaniment pattern develops from that which supports the preceding extension of the outcry. (Cf. the oscillating figure based on F♯-A from bar 79 onwards, which later assumes the form of a repeated mordent A-G-A, interspersed by D/G/A chords in bars 98/99 or D♭/E♭/A and C/E/A chords in bars 100-102.) The middle strand combines melodic components heard before.[59] The two-note upbeat in the first half of bar 98 is reminiscent of the initial melodic gesture (see bar 4), while the three-chord descent in the bar's second half recalls, with regard to rhythmic shape and pitch outline, the corresponding three chords of the desperate outcry. This section thus reveals the immediate relationship between the two most powerful images evoked in this piece: that of the dangerously exposed barge in the vastness of the ocean, and that of the lamenting human voice.

Having thus established a tentative table for the metaphoric value of the various thematic and structural elements, we turn to the emotional

---

[59]The further development during the following four bars seems to revert the phrase structure discussed earlier:

bars 98/99, 100/101	six-note gesture	bars 1-3, 81-82	introduction of waves
bars 102/103	two-note gesture	bars 4/5, 83-84	two-note gesture
bars 103-106	extension with waves	bars 8-10, 84/85	five-note gesture

Just as the introductory bars 1-3 and 81-82 anticipate the pitches that will accompany the melodic gesture, so do we find a continuation of the pitches that accompany the preceding measures in the extending bar 103. For details see in bars 100-102, left hand, the pitches G-D♭-E♭-B♭; also, continued throughout bars 103-106 in multiple inversions, the right-hand chord = D♭-E♭-G-A, which recurs in bars 103-106, beats 1/2. The pitch groups continue further, in a gradually more and more simplified format, in bars 107-110. Here, two statements of the two-note gesture in the middle of the texture (see bars 107, 108: B♭-E♭) are set against a new melodic line hovering over the right-hand broken chords (see bars 107-110: A-G, A-G, A-G-F).

message attached to them. In order to gain a deeper understanding of the content, a close look at the tonal language employed in this piece is necessary. Such a glance will focus both on the horizontal and on the vertical; it will ascertain how tonal reference is ordered in the course of the sections or in the course of the entire piece, and how each thematic element is set in its vertical perspective.

Regarding tonality, *A Barge on the Ocean* seems fairly traditional at first glance. Ravel establishes F♯ as a tonal center and endorses this pitch on many levels:

- The key signature with three sharps, supported by the pedal note at the beginning (bars 1-10/14-20) and end of the piece (bars 132-138), suggests F♯ as the key note of a minor mode.
- In bars 1-10 and 14-20, all notes in both hands derive from the F♯-minor ninth chord (F♯-A-C♯-E-G♯), a chord formation Ravel is known to have used throughout his work in the early years of the twentieth century.
- In the right-hand part of bars 81-97, the interval F♯-A appears as a pedal, pointing once again to F♯ minor.

While the transposition of the first thematic element to the dominant (see the C♯-minor ninth chord in bars 61-67) is entirely traditional, the pitch second in importance to F♯ in this piece is not C♯ but B♭. B♭, appearing predominantly as a pedal-note, is significant as a contrasting key not only in terms of the number of bars it covers, but also insofar as it determines the two large contrasting sections of this piece. As a pedal-note, this pitch covers twenty-nine bars (bars 28-35, 68-80, 103-110). In the first two instances, B♭ enters in a way to create a stark tonal contrast, without the least preparation during the preceding bars. In bar 28, it follows on the heels of an extended G major chord, and in bar 68, on those of a C♯-minor ninth chord. Both chords contain B♮, so that the B♭ creates a cross-relationship, suggesting thus a profound and repeatedly perceived uneasiness with the thematic achievement of these contrasting sections: a link between the swaying motion and the dramatic gusts in the first case, the swaying motion and the desperate outcry in the second. Only in the third case, when the B♭ pedal arises beneath various inversions of the ongoing E♭[11] chord (E♭-G-B♭-D♭-F-A), is there no surprise. This chord, which in bar 100 emerges in transformation from the G-minor ninth, serves as a subdominant to the second tonal center B♭; its smooth preparation of the previously disruptive pedal B♭ might be read as an attempt at integration, after much inner struggle.

Beyond these two tonal centers, the piece contains three characteristic vertical settings. While the minor chord with several superimposed thirds (i.e. with the seventh, ninth and occasionally eleventh intervals over a root) is undoubtedly a typical harmonic building block in Ravel's music and must primarily be understood as such, our interpretation of the tonal language in *Une barque sur l'océan* would miss its point if we failed to look deeper. It is above all the first thematic element, the swaying motion above large waves, that is entirely based on this chord. The minor ninth chord is here often tainted with a feature Ravel also employs elsewhere: the *sixte ajoutée* (the added sixth, in his case added not to the triad but to the seventh chord). Here is a harmonic map of the first element:

bars	1-10	11-13		14-20	21-22		23,25	24,26/27
	G	F♯	E	G	(B)	F♯	F♯	
	E	D	C	E	G♯	D	D	D
	C♯	B + C	A + B	C♯	E + F♯	B + C♯	B + C♯	B
	A	G	F	A	C♯	G	G	G
	F♯	E	D	F♯	A	(E)	(E)	

The second thematic element builds harmonically on the simple triad with added sixth;

see e.g.	bars 38, 40, 42	=	G♯-B-D♯ + E♯,
	bars 39, 41	=	B-D-F♯ + G♯,
	bar 43	=	F♯-A♯-C♯ + D♯.

In other instances, however, Ravel's musical language exploits all the colors of bitonality and cross-relationship. The most poignant example can be found in the third thematic element of the piece, the "human" component. Let us observe this in the first occurrence of what I have been calling the desperate outcry (bars 46 to bar 49, beat 1). Bars 46-48 feature in the bass an unequivocal, four-octave pedal note G♯. Against this, Ravel employs chords that, when enharmonically redefined for easier reading, represent F♯ major leading through F minor to C major. The concluding sigh knows three harmonic layers: a melodic D♯-B♯ supported by G♯s in the bass, in between a C-major six-five chord, and a C♯ in the bass!

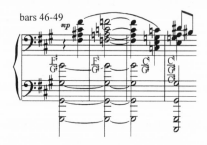

bars 46-49

82

The following overview of the layout gives also the main harmonic orientation of the components. See how they relate alternatively to the two tonal centers.

	bars			pedal note
I	1- 22	A	*first thematic element* (swaying motion over large waves),	F♯
			with inner contrasts (turbulence) in bars 11-13 and 21-23,	
			extended through bar 27	G
	28- 37	B	first contrast	B♭
	38- 43	C	*second thematic element* (dramatic exposure of the barge)	G♯
			followed by a transition in bars 44/45	
	46- 49	D	*third thematic element*	
			followed by a long transition in bars 49-60	C♯ G♯
II	61- 67	A'	*first thematic element* (abridged, transposed P4 down;	C♯
			with the inner melody but without the turbulence)	
	68- 75	C'	*second thematic element* (different harmonization)	B♭
	76- 79	D'	*third thematic element* (transposed dim3 [=M2] up)	B♭
			extended through bar 80, and with further development	B♭
			until bar 95; followed by a transition in bars 95-97	F♯
	98-110	E	second contrast	B♭
III	111-116	C"	*second thematic element*	A
	121-124	D"	*third thematic element* (on the semitone between *D* and *D'*!)	A
			preceded by a preparation in bars 117-120, and	
			followed by an extension until bar 131	
	132-139	A"	*first thematic element* (original key, fragmentary;	F♯
			without the inner melody and without any contrasts).	

Attempting to interpret the sum of the tonal metaphors in the piece, one may read along lines such as the following. What I have been calling the swaying motion above large waves, evoked in the image of the barge amidst the ocean, serves as a typical Romantic symbol for the immensity and indomitability of nature as it surrounds us. The musical component representing this image comes in the guise of chords built from consonant intervals. What I have interpretated as the desperate outcry, standing for the human component in the seascape and for the shout of individualism and subjectivity versus Romantic idealism, appears greatly troubled and torn. Correspondingly, the musical component that depicts this aspect is characterized by bitonality and cross-related chords: vertical as well as horizontal images of ambivalence.

In the transitional sections where the composer suggests a mediation between the three components and the images they depict, the overall anchoring changes drastically. Musically this is realized in form of a secondary pedal that entails a shift in the previous thought pattern.

83

Similarly (Ravel leads us to conclude), if we wish to merge Romantic notions of nature's supreme power and the relative irrelevance of human presence in it, with the human cry demanding to be heard individually, we need to do more than juxtapose the two; we need to practice shifting our basic way of thinking until (as in the third change to the B♭ pedal) the two realities become well integrated.

Brouillards   (Debussy, *Préludes*, vol. II, no. 1)

There are several possible sources for Debussy's impressions of *brouillards* or *fog*. On the one hand, the composer is known to have been inspired by Monet whose 1879 painting *Vétheuil in the Fog*, subtitled *Impression* when it was first shown in 1887, contributed significantly to giving the artistic movement of his time an identity. (Monet later said about this painting that "it would inform people about his working methods and his ideals"; a similar statement could probably be made about this piece of music and Debussy's working method and ideals.)

Another inspiration may have come from the illustrator Arthur Rackham, whom Debussy so admired as to use some of his captions as epigraphs (see e.g. *The fairies are exquisite dancers*, also in Book II of the Preludes). Rackham has given his own reading of misty weather. In a collection of his work, entitled *Arthur Rackham's Book of Pictures*[60], we find an illustration entitled *Fog*. The story behind the piece reads: "Bidden to a party at a friend's home, but imprisoned by the weather, the artist conveyed his explanations and regrets to his hostess by means of this drawing." (See the illustration on the following page).

Debussy's musical choices for capturing the haziness of that weather condition and the sense of unreality it typically conveys, rely primarily on three features: the indistinct effect achieved by a continuous use of bitonality, careful decisions regarding register and articulation, and an almost complete absence of true melodic material. The texture thus created prevails throughout most of the prelude's fifty-two bars. The few contrasting passages are not only melodically determined but actually appear in unison setting, giving, as it were, short glimpses of what the world may look like once the fog has gone. We find here a musical depiction of what might be poetically described as interweaving elements in misty air: each moment of apparent brightness turns out to be just one more illusion.

---

[60]*Arthur Rackham's Book of Pictures* (New York: The Century Co., 1914)

"Fog" from *Arthur Rackham's Book of Pictures*
(New York: The Century Co., 1914), plate 34. Reprinted with
permission of Harlan Hatcher Library, The University of Michigan.

The prelude's opening material sets white-key triads in the left hand against arpeggiating figures, mainly on black keys, in the right. As the notation indicates, the right-hand figures are *legato*, while the left-hand chords are to be played in that specially pedaled *staccato* that emphasizes lightness over sonority and impact over duration without, however, interrupting the sound flow.

C D E F G A B; recurring root = C

The pitch context of the right-hand arpeggios is that of the C♭-major scale, although the impression given in Debussy's usage points more towards a Dorian mode on D♭. A first glance at the left hand suggests C major, but the fact that the leading note B is resolved either in traditionally forbidden diminished-to-perfect-fifths parallels (see bar 1) or not at all (see bar 2) thwarts any simple notion of tonality. A sense of shifting colors within what amounts to various shades of luminous gray is created by subtle changes in mini-rhythm within a pattern of frequent repetition. The following table aims to give a sense of these mini-rhythms by listing the number of regular notes sharing a beat and the pattern of repetitions:

bars	1	2	3	4	5, 6	7, 8 etc.
	5/5/5/5	2/ 6 /2/ 6	5/5/5	6/6/6/6/6/6	2/2/5/5/2/2/5/5	5/5/5/5..
		(3+3)(3+3)				
repetitions	* = *	* = *		* = * = *	* = *	* = *

Dynamics, as requested in the subheading, alternate between the extremely even and light touch in which the left hand is given just slightly more weight than the right (*extrêmement égal et léger, la main gauche un peu en valeur sur la main droite*) and very brief intensifications (see e.g. bar 2). These short bursts strike the listener as signs of hope that the mist might lift and allow the world to reappear—a hope often dashed before it has time to develop (see bars 5, 6 etc.).

From bar 9 onwards, the left hand is locked for a while in a repeated G-major triad, countered in the right hand by a six-five chord on G^b that is later enharmonically redefined as F♯. The two chords are superimposed on one another in the central octave of the keyboard and thus create a murmur in a very restricted register and in *più pp*. Into this murmur, a third strand enters. Its two quasi-melodic voices—one slightly higher than however, they are clearly part of the overall picture: pitches from G major are used for occasional *acciaccaturas* while the main notes clearly support the F♯-major chord.

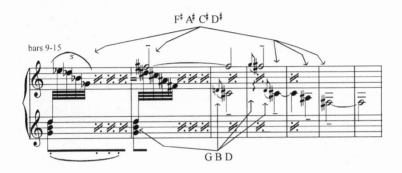

In the four bars that conclude this section, the left-hand triad gives up its steady position and once again shifts back and forth through various keys until it settles on an E minor chord. Meanwhile, the right hand stays with the F♯-major six-five chord (and its inversions) before it is reduced to a mere arpeggiated octave on C♯.

New material is presented in bars 18-20. The melodic center C♯, prepared in the course of the two preceding bars, now serves as a root for a four-part unison setting that explores the extreme ranges of the keyboard, only returning to more "earthy" spheres in the slightly accented final octaves (bar 20, beat 2). Here, a Phrygian tonality on C♯ is vaguely evoked[61]. The unison motif, reminiscent of chant or perhaps bells, is prolonged through a repetition of its concluding, contrary-motion octave jumps (see bar 21) and then complemented in a similar phrase (see bars 22-24). Once again, the final octave contraction is extended through two further repetitions that, varied this time, are to be detected in the right-hand D^bs of bar 25 (see the last bar of the example on the next page).

---

[61]The Phrygian scale on C♯ reads C♯ D E F♯ G♯ A B C♯.

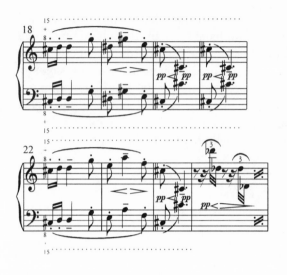

The metaphor here is certainly no coincidence. If the chant motif embodies an aspect of reality, hindsight reveals that this aspect, represented by the collapsing four-part unison C♯ or D♭, has actually been around all along. Plunging broken octaves on D♭ have been heard as early as in bar 2, and the D♭-based perfect fifths at the beginning of bars 5 and 6, as well as the implied Dorian mode on D♭ in the right-hand arpeggios, testify to this second layer of reality that, from the very outset, has led a parallel existence to the more prominent white-key presence in the left-hand triads and the indistinct murmur of the combined texture.

The effect of fog clearing provided by the contrasting texture is soon blurred, as the first material finds its way back into the picture. After two tentative fragments (bars 20 and 21), the beginning of the prelude is restated (compare bar 24, beat 3 to bar 27, beat 2 with bars 1-4). A short transition leads over to a new pattern of bitonality, based this time on the tritone distance of roots that has often been called one of Debussy's hallmarks. Bar 29 sets the F♯ against C: the F♯-major chord is created jointly by both hands before it concentrates as a G♭-major triad in the right hand; the C-major chord, during the flourish represented only by the single note G, is later confirmed as a complete chord in the left hand. Bar 30 constitutes a partial repetition and subsequent shift: the flourish remains in F♯ major with the additional G, but the accented triad with its two-chord *acciaccatura* now sets D major in the left hand against A♭ major in the right.

As happened before with the primary material of this prelude, this new bitonal pattern, one part of which is harmonically redefined, now serves as a backdrop for a very rudimentary melody. From bar 33 onwards, in *Un peu retenu* (somewhat held back = slower), the combination of D major with G♯ major establishes itself as an accompaniment from which emerge single pitches that demand some prominence but hardly form a line. This section concludes in bar 37 with a bitonal juxtaposition of G major and D♭ major.[62]

Finally, there follows a short section that recapitulates various elements in the form of a summary. The melodic component is represented first in the unison melody of the contrasting material (cf. left hand, bars 38/39, with both hands, bars 18/19), then in a rhythmically varied version (bar 41), and finally in an incomplete version disguised by enharmonic spelling (bars 47/48: D♭-D-G-E♭-A♭). Also recalled is the earlier transitional moment when fragments of the main material interweave with the tune (compare bars 43/44 and 48/49 with bars 20/21). Reminiscences of the bitonal combinations at the distance of a tritone appear in the flourish of bar 40 (not with complete triads here but only with empty fifths, on C♯ and G) and in the *arpeggio* in bar 47 (with D♭ and G as alternating single pitches).

Tonally, the recall of the secondary material seems to uphold if not outshine the ambiguity that has reigned throughout the piece. Only the first time does it conclude as previously: on the C♯ that was recognized as one of the prelude's tonal centers. The rhythmic variation closes on a very low C♮ (see bar 43, reiterated in bars 44-46), which in turn is prolonged on the middle C in bars 47/48 and then blends into the tonally vague portion dominated by primary material.

Finally, there is a small detail at the beginning of this final section that is intriguing for the eye albeit imperceptible to the ear. The simple right-hand chord is written with both enharmonic alternatives for each of its three pitches: G♯-C♯-G♯ (retained throughout bars 39 and 41/42) as well as A♭-D♭-A♭. This seems like the most compressed format possible of the enharmonic redefinition that had occurred twice in the course of the prelude: a visual reminder to the performer of the haziness intended by the composer?

Des pas sur la neige   (Debussy, *Préludes*, vol. 1, no. 6)

The title literally translates as *Steps on the Snow* but is commonly known as *Footprints in the Snow*. While the latter version undoubtedly

[62]Compare bars 30-37   with bars 9-15:

30/31	D major / A♭ major established	9	G major/ G♭ major six-five established
32-35	D major / G♯ (=A♭) major	10-14	G major / F♯ (=G♭) major six-five
35-37	shift D/G♯ to C/F♯ and G/D♭	14-15	shift G major to E minor and D minor
33-37	melodic line in middle of arpeggios	10-15	melodic lines both sides of arpeggios

sounds much smoother and more poetic in English, it might help to keep in mind that the French word "pas" does not denote merely the pattern, left in a perhaps otherwise immaculate surface and seen there by some onlooker. The word also refers to the actual step—the physical action of a living being making its way through the snow, probably freezing, perhaps lonely and exhausted.

Debussy's verbal descriptions at the beginning of the piece suggest the mood in the prelude. *Triste et lent* (sad and slow) he requests, and for the footsteps, *Ce rythme doit avoir la valeur sonore d'un fond de paysage triste et glacé* (this rhythm should have the sound value of a sad, icy landscape) and for the melody *expressif et douloureux* (expressive and sorrowful).[63]

Structure and material of the prelude appear deceivingly simple. The footsteps are conveyed in the main motif, which is heard in 24 of the 36 bars of the prelude. When first presented, the lowest note of the motif, the middle D that constitutes the keynote, serves simultaneously as a repeated pedal—as if keeping the walker glued to the ground. The ascending seconds D-E and E-F in their stumbling rhythm invite an interpretation as

the steps of the left and right foot respectively. (Not that it matters which is which. But it helps to think of these two-note groups in their very syncopated rhythm as musical embodiments of actual motions of a person walking with difficulty through the snow.) Joining the footsteps are the sorrowful melody (bars 2-4, 5-7, 17-19, 20-25) as well as various diatonic and chromatic progressions in the lower voices that are worth exploring in more detail later.

The basic layout of the prelude can be deduced from tracing the presence and absence of the footstep motif. Having halted for a short while in bar 7, the motif resumes for several bars but is suspended again in bars 12-13. The short codetta that concludes the prelude's first section in bars 14/15 contains some tentative probing of the characteristic rhythm in the lowest voice. The repeated falling tritone, however, does not seem

---

[63]It seems essential to count the rhythm precisely when first learning the piece. Only by playing the short heavy-beat note exactly—one twelfth of the half-bar duration allotted to each footstep—can the quality of faltering, imprecise movements resulting from the difficulties of walking in snow be captured. Longer values, as they are most often heard, change the composer's intention and make the steps sound languid. This comes too close to the sorrowful tone of the melodic and thus deprives the piece of one of its expressive facets.

to advance the walker. The second section is laid out similarly to the first. There is a moment of heightened emotion in bars 22-24, which feature only the motif's second half—one imagines the snow walker groping for a secure footing. But in vain; the motion stops again (bar 25). It picks up at its old level and pace in bars 26-28, yet not for long. Once more the steps are suspended (bars 29-31). In the short coda (bars 32-36), the motif, now doubled in octaves, is transferred into the higher register, as is the rooting pedal-note D.

Comparing the two sections of the prelude in more detail, we find:

Ia		IIa	
bars		bars	
1	introduction: footsteps over D pedal	16	introduction: footsteps over D pedal + bass ascent G A♭ B♭
2-4	melody + footsteps over D pedal	17-19	melody (var.) + footsteps over D pedal+ twofold bass ascent G A♭ B♭
5-7	off-beat rise + fall; footsteps over descending open triads	20-25	off-beat rise + fall, varied + extended; footsteps over descending open triads (extended)
Ib		**IIb**	
8-10	footsteps over chromatic parallel seventh + bass line establishing C♯/D♭ as new root	26-28	footsteps over chromatically descending triads
11-13	new melody in bass	29-31	melody in treble from earlier extension [compare bars. 28-31 / 21-24];
	footsteps cease over sustained chord		footsteps cease over melody in inverted triads
codetta		coda	
14/15	sustained chord of unrelated to original tonality; off-beat notes (from bars.5/6) footsteps falling in tritone C as momentary root	32-36	footsteps in high register over D pedal in higher octave off-beat falling thirds (from bars 30/31) ending in G minor (IV) + F (from I); cadential bass pattern leading in plagal D-G-D-G-D-G to final D minor

These observations completed, I wish to show that Debussy has composed footsteps on many more levels. His depiction extends far beyond the immediately obvious motivic play. Indeed, the difficulty of balancing oneself in the snow finds its expression in various subtle musical details.

The primary lens through which the increasing loss of control—and the efforts to regain it—are shown is that of tonality and pedal notes, in conjunction with varying degrees of chromaticism. The picture is completed by a number of gestures representing attempts to achieve balance and counteract instability.

- Bars 1-4 are rooted in the tonic pedal D, with for a scale an unambiguous D minor. The motivic three-note ascent *from* D (D-E-F) is balanced, in the initial melodic gesture, with a three-note ascent *towards* D (B♭-C-D). The remainder of the melodic line provides the missing pitches G and A, reached in two falling minor thirds (bars 3/4: B♭-G, C-A). The phrase ends in a D-minor chord. These falling intervals thus counter-balance the rising steps, both with regard to the complementarity of the motion (falling versus rising) and with regard to the framing interval (which, in the three-note ascents, is also a minor third).

- In bars 16-19, the motif is equally rooted in the tonic pedal D. The melodic three-note ascent appears in the lower voice, enhanced with two repetitions. As such it expresses more urge (in reiterated efforts) but at the same time less security. Not only does it not touch the anchoring note D at all; what is more, its A♭—in the scale on D the flattened fifth—seriously puts the basic tonality into question. The falling thirds in the treble also find A twice replaced by A♭ as if after a slipped step, resulting in a major instead of the minor third. The final bar of the phrase, however, drops the lower-voice gesture, resolves the A♭ and thus regains D minor in a last-minute, weak-beat conclusion.

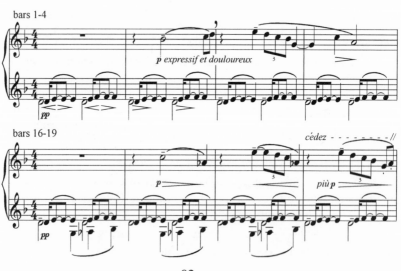

92

- Bars 5-6 find the footsteps without a
rooting pedal note. However, the open-
chord descent in the lower voices begins with D as a pitch in G major and
ends with D as the root of the final D

bars 5/6

minor chord—thus anchoring the tottering walk even more deeply. The tonal context is Dorian on D (i.e. with B♮ instead of B♭),
established in two complementary tetrachords: the treble ascent
A-B-C-D and the bass descent G-F-E-D. In bar 7, the motif is
suspended, and the treble does not resolve into the D minor chord
below it but plunges with an a[7] chord across the motif's register
into the middle-ground of the texture, from where it will not
resurface for quite a while.

- Bars 20-25 begin similarly: in a descent in parallel open triads
that seems targeted towards the secure footing in the low D. However, the two lowest voices take an unexpected augmented-second
step, as if uncontrollably slipping past the D minor they had
aimed at. In the treble, C is flattened—whether anticipating the
frightening slip in the bass or triggering it, remains open. As an
enharmonic repetition of the preceding B, this C♭ noticeably
interrupts the expected ascent. Consequently, the footsteps themselves are affected by this turn of events. Locked into the motif's
second half (the semitone E-F, see bars 21m-24), they only
recover as a left/right walking motion after a complete interruption. The prominent interval in the treble, the repeated falling
(major!) third E♭-C♭, is far removed from the relative stability of
the home key D. In increasing expressive intensity (see Debussy's
en animant surtout dans l'expression [enlivening above all in
terms of the expression]) the phrase reaches, in bar 23, the highest
pitch so far. From here, the melodic gesture reverts to falling
minor thirds, those intervals that had been established, in the very
first phrase of the piece, as a balancing counterpart to the ascent
of the steps. Meanwhile, the lower voices seem to make up for the
preceding sudden drop beyond D by presenting a chromatic
ascent in parallel seventh chords until the bass-note E is regained,
the note from which the fatal slip had occurred. As a result of
these simultaneous operations of attempted recovery, the phrase
ends somewhat appeased yet still tonally unresolved. The thwarted D-minor chord is not heard until far into the next phrase. (See

the open-position chord in the low register in bar 27m that would appear quite unprepared and out of context were it not understood in relation to the preceding phrase.)

bars 20-28

- The third phrases in both sections depict a growing loss of balance and direction. In bars 8-10 (11 in the treble), pervading use of chromaticism endangers the fragile stability of the footsteps. Alto and tenor repeat an ascending semitone step in parallel seventh (bars 8/9: B♭-B/C-C♯), and the three-note ascent, now in the bass, is also entirely chromatic. Thus not only is the diatonic context of the motif completely weakened; what is worse, with all voices ascending, any balancing gesture is suspended and control seems most precarious. Not surprisingly then, the subsequent motions in bars 10/11 paint a rather unstable situation, with many chromatic ascents and descents.

bars 8-11

Meanwhile, as if groping for a new anchor, the bass establishes a new anchoring pitch: C♯, redefined as D♭ in bars 10/11. But hardly has the D♭ been confirmed and strengthened with melodic emphasis under a sustained right-hand chord in the bass line of bars 11-13, than the indirect pedal-note is further lowered to C! Debussy composes this entire first section over two large-scale steps, a chromatic descent of the anchoring pitches from D to C♯/D♭ to C.

bars 1-4,5...6/7, 8...9...10-12, 13,14-15

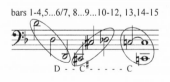

- In the corresponding phrase in the prelude's second section, the middle-D rooting is re-established (bars 26/27), while parallel

94

triads in chromatic descent balance the motif's ascent. But as though the reassuring D-minor chord had been reached treacherously and too soon, the footsteps as well as the tonality are once more completely abandoned. Instead, bars 29-31 sound in an untainted Dorian mode on A♭—a mode diametrically opposed to the earlier Dorian on D![64] The treble recalls (*comme un triste regret* = like a sad regret) the gesture that had marked the moment of greatest panic after the "slip" in the bass. Finally, in a last effort to regain composure, falling minor thirds lead back to D (C♭-A♭, A♭-F, F-D).

- Codetta and coda are opposed in many ways. While the struggle between human hope for survival and nature's force is still unresolved in the former, it is over—but sadly over, it seems—in the latter. The codetta (bars 14-15) deserves special attention for its pitch content: C E F♯ A♭ B♭ constitutes an excerpt from the whole-tone scale on C (or, taking Debussy's accidentals literally, on A♭). This scale is not only as far away as possible from the original tonal context, A♭ being the polar opposite to D. What is more, the excerpt Debussy employs here conspicuously leaves out exactly that pitch which serves as the root of this piece: the D. In the upper voice, the whole-tone context is made possible by raising the motivically essential F (the final note of the footsteps motif that had been prolonged throughout bars 12 and 13) to F♯. In this way, both D and F, the notes that frame the prelude's motif, are explicitly abandoned.

bars 14/15

- The coda, marked slower than the main body of the piece, reassures us that some stability has been regained. The footsteps and the rooting pedal D are heard, albeit in unaccustomed heights, in a register above the continuation of the falling minor thirds—as if somewhat removed from the real effort of walking on earth. The lowest voice, on the other hand, descends to a register below

---

[64] Compare the Dorian mode on D with the same mode on the pitch that is its polar opposite in the circle of fifth, A♭:

$$D \ E \ F \ G \ A \ B \ C \ D \quad \text{and}$$
$$A♭ \ B♭ \ C♭ \ D♭ \ E♭ \ F \ G♭ \ A♭.$$

anything heard in this piece. One cannot help thinking that the middle, where the previous struggle took place, has been given up —and Debussy's *morendo* (dying), while ostensibly referring to tempo and dynamics, might well be read as referring to the dying of pulse and life energy in a metaphoric sense.

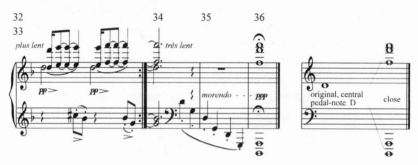

FLOWERS, INSECTS AND BIRDS

Bruyères   (Debussy, *Préludes*, vol. II, no. 5)

English translations of the French noun *bruyère* include the flower *heather*, the *brier wood*, and the *heath* as a type of landscape. Since the word is here used in its plural form, it seems most likely that Debussy had the flowers in mind.

While a French city-dweller will most commonly associate the word heath with the patches of wasteland found around many urban areas in France, the poetic allusion to heather flowers rather implies a longing for undisturbed rural scenes and hints at natural mysticism, fashionable among artists of the time. As Debussy scholars have pointed out, the melodic structure of this prelude is reminiscent of Breton and Celtic folk song. The allusion thus points to a rather humble flower growing in arid ground, in regions with often inclement weather, large clouds and powerful thunderstorms—far removed from the sophisticated society life of cities and stylish resort areas. Through this image speaks a quest for simplicity without sweetness, a quest equally conveyed in the musical language.

The prelude is clad in a very simple, folklike structure, and uses almost pictorially evocative material. The design is ternary on the larger scale as well as, in the middle section, on a small scale:

$A = bars\ 1\text{-}22$		$B = bars\ 23\text{-}37$		$A' = bars\ 38\text{-}51$	
a	1- 5	f	23-28		
b	5- 7	g	29-32	b'	38-44
c	8-14d	f'	33-37	a_{var}	44-51
d	14-18				
e	19-22				

The initial tune, introduced as an unaccompanied melisma, is pentatonic (comprising the pitches E♭ F G B♭ C). It consists of a two-bar subphrase that begins on the keynote, E♭, swings gently downward without touching the lower E♭, and stops inconclusively on C. A one-bar subphrase then complements the melodic gesture, picking up the C and

97

closing on the lower keynote. It is only here, at what amounts to the harmonic close of the pentatonic tune, that other voices enter, extending through the repeat (possibly in the form or an echo) of the complementary second subphrase in bars 4/5.

bars 1-4

These accompanying voices support the cadential closing with various means. The bass presents a traditional formula of V/V - V - I (see B♭-E♭-A♭), the alto contributes a supporting 4-to-3 leading-note and resolution, and the tenor introduces a small contrapuntal line. Thus there are three layers with three points of closure: the pentatonic one, which closes on the downbeat of bar 4, the cadential one, which resolves on the downbeat of bar 5, and the delayed resolution of the contrapuntal line, which does not join the A♭-major chord until the second beat of bar 5.

The subsequent short component *b*, by contrast, is homophonic in texture. Rising waves in the treble supported in chordal structure are set against double octaves in free contrary motion in the bass. While the tonality within these two bars remains uncertain—an original C minor is tainted by G♭s and brightened to C major on the next downbeat—the end (which does not provide closure but instead leads into the next component) is in unequivocal A♭ major, with the same cadential steps in the bass that were already heard in the previous phrase (see bars 7/8).

The third component *c* is determined by a rhythmic motif. Introduced in bar 8 and continued through another five bars, this motif can be read as "twelve sixteenth-notes with a *rubato* at the beginning." The advantage of this somewhat daring interpretation is a greater freedom in the initial beats of each bar—a freedom that enhances the verve of the piece.[65]

bar 8

---

[65]Thus, for instance, the downbeats in bars 8 and 11 could be slightly longer than the eighth-note value suggests, those in bars 9 and 12 fairly accurate, and those in bars 10 and 13 only slight distortions of a regular four-note figure.

Also of interest here is the texture, which Debussy's notation specifies very clearly. There are "entries" of the motif in different voices. After a model in the treble (bar 8), the B♭ in the middle register (bar 9) creates an active contrast to the relaxed (and thus softer) *diminuendo* descent to E♭ in the upper voice. In bar 11, the middle-register *appoggiatura-resolution* G-F completes the motif, while the high-pitched new beginning in the treble should sound in a distinctively different tone color. Finally, the third beat of bar 12 emancipates the tenor whose tied C triggers the motif in the next bar and must therefore be heard slightly above the other voices. Harmonically, this phrase still remains in A♭ major but Debussy emphasizes the plagal rather than the authentic cadence (see both bars 9/10 and, somewhat hybrid, bars 13/14).

In the next short phrase, we seem to be hearing a lark song. Dominated by perfect fourths in both the horizontal progression and the accompanying intervals, this embodiment of pastoral serenity is accompanied once again in plagal steps (see bars 14/15, repeated in 15/16) before its authentic cadence establishes E♭ major as a new tonic. A link in very explicit *ritardando* (see bars 17/18) leads to what sounds like a continuation of the lark's song later in the day, this time presented as an embellishment of a simple tune (see bars 19-22: F E♭ D♭ C B♭, F E♭ G♭ B♭ B♭). This is the first phrase in the piece that remains harmonically suspended.

The middle section, marked *un peu animé* (somewhat lively) and *joyeux* (joyous), appears to rely on previous material, developed freely. Thus bars 23/24 are reminiscent of the rhythmic motif in bar 8; the very prominent contrary motion at the beginning (see bar 23: treble B♭-F, bass F-B♭, bars 23/24: treble descending, middle strand ascending) recalls phrase *b*; and the structure with a model (bars 23/24), its repetition (bars 25/26), and a development of part of the model (see bars 27, 28) recalls the similar design in the first "lark song" (compare with bars 14m-15m, 15m-16m, 16m-17m).

In the central portion of the prelude's middle section, the development is continued in another way. The initial gesture could be described as grand but restrained—grand in its large sweeping rise to the syncopated chord, restrained in that the *crescendo*, felt naturally but also requested by Debussy, is hushed in a *subito p* with the additional warning *doux* (soft). Before the backdrop of the continuing ring of this chord, fragments of the rhythmic motif find new pitch forms (bars 29/30). The entire two-bar unit is then sequenced a fourth higher, before leading into a recapitulation of phrase *f*. Harmonically, the middle section is rooted in

B♭ major (see bars 23/25 and the V/V - V - I bass motion in bars 29-33). Yet while the weak bars in the first occurrence of phrase *f* (bars 24, 26 and 27/28) contain the pitch G representing the major sixth, the corresponding bars in the recapitulation of phrase *f* feature G♭ (see bars 34, 36, 37). The accidental lingers and is only resolved on the final beat of the middle section. This chromatic progression from G♭ to G♮ serves a crucial structural role, acting as an emphasized leading note to the prelude's tonic A♭, which is now reinstated in the large-frame recapitulation (A', from bar 38).

In the final section of the piece, bars 38-44m would be identical to bars 8-14m were it not for the sudden turn to D♭ major at the very end. Bars 44-49 then bring an octave transposition of the initial pentatonic subphrase, followed by rhythmically free reminiscences of the second subphrase, in gradually slower tempo (*en retenant*) and against a new counterpoint with chromatically rising double octaves. The final bars embellish the tonic chord with written-out bass turns around the keynote A♭.

Noctuelles
(Ravel, *Miroirs*, no. 1)

Night moths must be among the creatures that are most neglected in the arts. The entire body of French literature[66] contains only one mention of "noctuelles."[67] Neither conspicuous for beautiful coloring nor apparently useful, these insects are probably perceived above all as an annoyance; killed at worst, impatiently ignored at best. Ravel depicts their unsettling fluttering and wheeling persuasively in multi-layered rhythms and clashing dissonances. One can only speculate whether the abrupt dynamic explosions (see e.g. in bars 23 and 26 where an outbreak from *pp* to *f* is requested in the span of only three eighth-notes) alludes to the fatal collision of a clumsy moth with some object in the room, or with the finally impatient hand of one of its human co-inhabitants.

What Ravel creates in the first piano piece of his cycle *Miroirs* are very intricate rhythmic patterns in frequently changing (or consciously ambiguous) metric organization, and an intriguing play with tonality. All this is wrapped in the conventional structure of a ternary form with coda. More specifically, the structure is reminiscent of the final movements in some Beethoven sonatas (e.g., op. 2, nos. 1 and 3) where the contrasting

---

[66] According to the data base, "Trésor de la langue française" at the University of Chicago library.

[67] See Jean Giraudoux's *Amphitryon*, p. 69.

section contains elements of a development section and the framing sections can be read—in terms of both material and harmonic layout—as exposition and recapitulation. On a small scale, repetitions play a major role in this piece. They influence both the perception of pulse and the size and structure of the musical building blocks. The table on the following page shows the details.

In terms of tonal organization, whole-tones and semitones far outweigh diatonic organization. Instances of the two whole-tone scales appear, e.g., in the left-hand part in bars 1/2 (G♭ A♭ B♭ C D F♭) and at the end of the first section, i.e. in bars 8/9 (from D♭ E♭ F G A [B]). Semitones occur in three guises: quasi-simultaneously as *appoggiaturas*, vertically as bitonal juxtapositions, and horizontally as chromatic lines.

First, there are many bars where clearly tonal triads are tainted on strong beats by *appoggiatura*-like artificial leading-notes, all of them in semitone distance to the subsequent triad note. We find this happening in a melodic setting (as in the right hand's opening figure where the notes of the E♭-minor triad are delayed by A and F respectively; see the example), or in an *arpeggio*-like broken chord (as in bars 6/7, where the E♭-major ninth chord contains the leading-notes F♯, A and, later, D. Such an the accumulation of leading-notes comes close to an effect of bitonality; in bars 6/7, the non-harmonic notes can be heard as a D-major chord against the predominant E♭-major harmony.

bar 1

Second, there are instances where bitonality is even more distinctly realized. Examples include the *arpeggios* in bars 18/19 (F♯^{7} against G major) and in bars 52/54 (G♭ major against F major), the *tremolo* in bar 36 (E♭ minor against F major[68]), and the fifths in bars 51 and 53 (right hand: F♭-C♭, left hand: E♭-B♭). Each of these pairs of tonalities involves primarily if not exclusively semitone clashes.

The table on the following page represents the layout of Ravel's *Noctuelles*. (Note that repetitions and variations are treated as if structurally alike, and are indicated by equations; all bars recurring transposed (down a perfect fifth) appear in *italics*.)

Third, semitones also appear prominently in the form of chromatic lines. They are found on different metric and textural levels. On the smallest scale, in sixteenth-notes, semitones appear as early as in bars 1/2 (see the second half of the bar, right hand). Also in secondary voices but

---

[68]The left-hand chord is certainly intended in *8va*; compare the corresponding *tremolo* in bar 120.

<u>exposition</u>   <u>recapitulation</u>

SECTION I   SECTION I

bars   1   = 2
        ½3   = ½3 [first half of bar = second half]
        4   = 5
        6/7   =   90/91
        8/9   =   92/93

SECTION II   SECTION II

bars   10   = 11   =   94   =   95
        ½12   = ½12 = 13   =   ½96   =   ½96 = 97
        14   = 15   =   98   =   99
        16-18   =   100-102 .
        19/20   =   103/104

SECTION III   SECTION III

bars   21-23   = 24-26   =   105-107 =   108-110
        27   = 28   =   111   =   112
        29/30   =   113/114
        31   = 32   =   115   =   116
        33-34m   = 34m-35   =   117-118m =   118m-119
        36   =   120

                    <u>contrast / development</u>   <u>coda</u>

        SECTION I   SECTION II   SECTION III   121-125
   bars 37   126-131
        38-42   51-54
        42-45
        46-50   ~   55-60
                     61/62   63-89 (development)

more pronounced are the parallel chromatic curves in bars 47-50, 57-60
etc. On a third level, chromaticism invades melodic lines and appears
even in contrary motion; see e.g. bars 21-23 right hand: G-F♯-F, C♮-C♭-B♭
(with D-C♯-C♮, F-F♭-E♭ as a parallel voice in the broken-chord pattern)
against, in the left hand, G♯-A / D♮-D♯, B-C, F♮-F♯-G. Here, an additional
feature is presented by the simultaneous semitone clashes (see bars 21,
24d: G♮/G♯, bars 23, 26d: C/D♭).

Ravel seems to have chosen this conspicuously high degree of satura-
tion with semitones to depict the whizzing, unreal impression that moths
give in their unsteady flight patterns. Owing to the very fast movement of
their tiny wings, they appear almost larger than they are, to reach fuzzily
beyond their actual frame into the border zone around them. The ambivalence of their shape is recreated in the tonal ambivalence perceived as a
result of the myriad semitones.

The time-related elements in this piece contribute another apparently
haphazard dimension. Rhythmically, each beat of bars 1/2 is subdivided
into a pattern of 4 against 3. And while the triple time of the bar is clearly
supported by both the time signature and the left-hand pattern, the right-
hand part seems to consist of two halves. Bar 3 follows with an apparently simpler rhythmic juxtaposition of 6 against 3 in each beat with—on
first inspection—an equal division of the bar into two halves in both
parts. In the process, however, the alleged three-four time is actually
abandoned in favor of six-eight time in the right hand, while the left hand
plays in a metric order that on its own would be fairly odd. In this subtle
way, Ravel's messages within the first three bars are multiple. While
there is the reassuring repetitiveness of bars 1/2 and of the two halves
within bar 3, these multiple metric allegiances, when fully understood,
are quite unsettling.

Similar multi-layered processes continue throughout most of the
piece. Suffice it to mention here the example of bars 33-35. The three
bars in putative six-eight time actually comprise a nine-eight model and
its repetition in the higher octave. While the actual attack rhythm of the
two hands is regular (1:2), the sequencing in the left-hand part divides the
eighteen semiquavers not into three equal groups but creates a pattern of
4 + 4 + 4 + 6!

At times, this rhythmic ambivalence even invades the melody. One example occurs in bars 14/15. The time signature indicates five-eight time, within which the three initial eighths are each subdivided into triplets. In the remaining two beats, the lower part has five notes to each count, but the three-eighth group Ravel has written for the treble actually sounds like a spelled-out *accelerando* of the strongest kind. (Compared to this effect, the *accelerando* in the *arpeggio* of bars 6/7 is gradual and smooth.)

Phrase structure is another area where conscious irregularity is played out. Examples abound; here is one from the third section of the exposition: bars 21-23 and 24-26 each comprise eleven eighths, grouped into 4 + 4 + 3; bars 27-30 consist of nineteen eighths, made up of 5 + 5 + {5+4}. The former sounds like a contraction of an expected twelve-eighth phrase, while the latter is conceived as an extension of a fifteen-eighth unit. The varied sequence of this irregular phrase, launched in bar 31, then expands into the multi-layered bars 33-35 mentioned above.

On a larger scale, the qualities of irregularity and ambivalence of temporal presentation feature prominently in the contrasting section (bars 37-62). The time signature alternates between five-four, three-four and a single indication of four-four. As a mental exercise, one may imagine the melodic part of this section, with the exception of bar 45, as conceived in three-four time, albeit with a very strong *rubato*. (This would mean a *fermata lunga* on the second beat of bars 38, 41, 51, 53 as well as on the third beats of bars 52 and 54). Performers may find it very instructive to play the melody in regular three-four time and thus come to appreciate Ravel's contrivances. Needless to mention, the repeated pedal-note in the left-hand part ticks with utmost regularity in many of the bars thus identified as "odd expansion," and confirms once more Ravel's deliberately ambiguous manipulating of time in simultaneous strands.

As an afterthought to these observations, one wonders to what aspects (of the moths themselves or of the insects as they are perceived by humans) the composer meant to allude when framing a picture with highly ambiguous details—both on the level of spatial (tonal) and temporal organization—in a structure as traditional as the ternary form or modified sonata movement form.

Oiseaux tristes   (Ravel, *Miroirs*, no. 2)

The protagonists of this concert of sorrowful birds are three singers
clearly distinguishable by their calls. Additional choralists join for short
contributions to the composite sound without gaining a discrete identity.
Yet other components in the piece seem designed to serve as a backdrop;
we are tempted to imagine something like "the singing of the forest."

Each of the three principal birds has a rhythm of its own, a fact that
is responsible for the complicated metric notation. This notation includes
simple four-four time (bar 1), four-four time with notated triplets (bar 2),
three-four notation for what is actually six-eight time (bar 3), duple time
in the right hand superimposed over compound time in the left (bars 4, 5),
twelve-eight time for all voices (bar 6), and three-part superimposition
(bar 7), as well as, from bar 8 onwards, a constant alternation of triplet
and duplet understanding no longer reflected in the time signature. For
practical purposes, it may help to re-write all bird calls in triple notation
and look at some of the juxtapositions employed by Ravel (see the
example below).

(1) First bird (as introduced in bars 1/2, re-notated in 12/8 time)

(2) Second bird (as introduced in bars 4/5, re-notated in 9/8 time)

(3) Third bird (as introduced in bars 4/5)

First, second and third birds, re-notated in 12/8

The piece opens with a solitary call of the first bird, consisting of
two components that appear very different but are subtly related in mood.
Each of them is repeated immediately. The initial component comes

105

across as a bird's version of a sigh. It begins with a note repetition in which the connection between the two notes is very close (see the *portato* articulation); it continues in a dynamic gesture that is deeply emotional (an accented note on the strong beat followed by a light note), and the rhythm has a languid quality (owing particularly to the sense of lingering conveyed in the unusual feature of an unaccented syncopation).

The second component of this bird's call begins with a lively chirp but ends, significantly, in a similarly lingering syncopation. It is interesting to note that the duration of the concluding note in both components is almost equal: one-and-a-half quarter values in the "sigh", one-and-a-third quarter values in the "chirp." Moreover, in both cases the concluding note is devoid of any emphasis. This accounts for the particular, mournful character of this call. According to Vuillermoz,[69] Ravel had in mind a *merle* (a European bird referred to in English as blackbird, similar to the American robin).[70]

In the course of the piece, the two components of the first bird's call undergo some variation; more importantly, they recur both as a compound unit and separately. The entire call of the blackbird is heard again in bars 7/8 and, transposed a semitone lower, in bars 21/22. In both instances, the "chirp" is metrically displaced, with the result that the concluding note—by its position at the end of a long slur still specified as dynamically passive—now falls on a strong beat.

The "sigh" on its own is heard almost throughout the entire piece:
- in metric variation in bars 3 and 4/5 (E♭);
  (it helps to hear bar 3 as six-eight time and bars 4m/5 as six-four time)
- in original metric order in bar 10 (D♯=E♭),
- extended to five repetitions, but with much longer silences in between, in bars 26-32 (D♯=E♭).

The "chirp" alone recurs only in the context of the *ad libitum* passage, in what could be described as the second half of the *cadenza* in bar 25. Under the intimation *pressez légèrement* (hurry slightly), a flourish is heard, differing from the original insignificantly in its intervals but quite significantly with regard to the absence of the syncopated extension of the concluding note.

[69]Emile Vuillermoz in: *Maurice Ravel par quelques-uns de ses familiers*, p. 34

[70] Olivier Messiaen, too, adored this bird. Not only did he compose many *cadenzas* for it in his piano music; he even dedicated a flute-and-piano duo, *Le merle noir,* to the virtuoso singer.

The second bird presents itself as a kind of sad cuckoo. It is characterized by a falling major third, in *legato* and with a particularly strong dynamic release, conspicuously marked with an accent and a *diminuendo* hairpin. The actual metric organization of this cuckoo call is in three-four time, as shown in the re-barred representation (2) above.

It is intriguing to observe how this bird call develops away from, and later back towards, its original shape.

- The call undergoes a first rhythmic diminution while still in the same (albeit enharmonically redefined) pitches: bar 6 quotes the cuckoo call in three-eight timing, in a "long-short" pattern with no silence before the repetition.
- Further diminution and metric shifting occur from bar 7 onwards where the falling major third, still in a three-eight frame but now in the middleground of the texture, begins in unaccented position and concludes with a tied note.
- Interspersed in bars 8/9 (see the C♭-A♭) and consistently in bar 10, the cuckoo calls in minor thirds. (This is the interval our folk tunes make us believe is the natural one, although ornithological observation in no way bears that out.)
- In bars 11/12 the call, still in the syncopated three-eight position, is enlarged to the interval of a tritone. The placement inside the texture seems to depict the blending of the cuckoo call into the larger sound picture of the birds' world. It then does not surprise that, after this, the second bird is not heard at all for a while. (One can choose to hear a falling minor third in the bass of bars 17-18d, but the rhythmic structure does not corroborate the connection.)
- Not immediately obvious from the score but very distinctly audible, the call is re-introduced with considerable emphasis in bar 20 (see the upper-voice A followed by an accented F♯).
- In bars 21/22, the falling interval returns to a more prominent position and its original major-third format, in the rhythmic diminution known from bars 7/8.
- Finally in bars 29-31, the "long-short" pattern from bar 6 is heard again, here with a descending sequence instead of the earlier repetition.

(The original three-four format of bars 4/5 never recurs.)

107

The third bird appears as the most pensive and least intense among the singers. Its call is an extended chain of a repeated two-note figure. The interval is a rising major second, and the rhythm is that observed in the second variation of the cuckoo call. This cooing sound is heard throughout most of the piece:

- in bars 4-6, it appears as G♭-A♭, later redefined as F♯-G♯;
- in bars 7-9, its interval is varied to a minor second D-E♭, later E-F;
- in bars 11-12, the rising second C♯-D♯ is heard interspersed with other notes; the notes constituting the call are emphasized in bar 11 by dash-plus-dot notation but less emphasized and more integrated in bar 12;
- in bars 13/14, the call continues with the same pitches but in a varied rhythm that abandons the syncopation (and, in fact, the short-long pattern). Just like the call of the sad cuckoo, the cooing of the third bird thus gradually blends into the surrounding sounds and then disappears for a while;
- in bar 17, a rising minor second (G♮-G♯) gradually emerges as an upper voice from the previously virtuoso texture;
- in bars 18-24, still as a minor third, the original rhythm is re-established;
- in the *ad libitum* of bar 25, the rising seconds A-B♭ and D-E♭ are prominently heard as the leading voice of the right-hand arpeggios; the same pitches actually replicate in the other voices of the broken chords (see, at the beginning of bar 25, D-E♭ in the middle of the chord followed by A-B♭ in the uppermost notes);
- finally in bars 29-31, the original major-second ascent recurs in the second voice, metrically shifted and with a descending sequence instead of the usual repetition.

The only constant figure beside the calls of the three birds is a continuum of supporting perfect-fifth intervals in the bass register. They are:

bars	4/5	5/6	7-9	10-12	17/18	20	21-23	23	24/25	26-28	29-31
	B♭	F♯	E♭/F	C♯	E	G	D/F	B♭	E♭	B/G♯/E	B♭/A♭
	E♭	B	A♭/B♭F♯		B	C	G/B♭	E♭	A♭	E/C♯/A	E♭/D♭

Significantly, the exact center of the piece (bars 15/16 in a total of 32 bars) is marked by a segment in which all three bird calls as well as the supporting perfect-fifth intervals are absent.[71] What we hear instead—as a resounding representation of the bird world at large, as it were—is a fragmentary melodic phrase made up of all-major chords, each of which is tainted in its center by the clash of an added "almost-octave"—a device Ravel uses again in the opening bars of *Alborada del gracioso.*

As the process of tracing the three motivic figures reveals, the three birds and their characteristic calls are intricately interwoven and jointly make up most of this piece. No human presence is suggested, with a sound of its own or even merely as a listener. The austerity and homogeneity of the musical material accounts for the unique atmosphere that we all sense here.

Regard des hauteurs   (Messiaen, *Vingt regards*, VIII)

(Gloire dans les hauteurs... les hauteurs descendent sur la crèche comme un chant d'alouette...)

The dedication of the piece in which "The Heights" contemplate the Infant Jesus is two-fold. In the context of the Nativity scene at Bethlehem, the beginning of Messiaen's subheading, "glory in the heights" seems to refer to the angels' praise and keep us well within the boundaries of traditional Christian imagery: *Gloria in excelsis* or "Glory to God in the Highest." The second part of the subheading, however, causes a shift of meaning when we learn that "the heights descend onto the manger like a lark's song." In his preface, the composer expands by specifying that he is thinking of the nightingale, the blackbird[72], several warblers (which he mentions with full names), chaffinch, goldfinch, "and above all the lark." This enumeration sounds more like ornithology, Messiaen's cherished hobby in later decades of his life, than a contribution to a cycle of scenes at Jesus' manger.

---

[71]This central portion, where all distinct calls seem blended into the larger soundscape, is preceded by a figure that can be heard as a *combination* of all four components. In bars 13m-14, the right hand presents two arpeggios followed by an accented syncopated F♯. The metric value of the F♯ recalls the concluding syncopation of the first bird's "chirp"; the melodic step from one broken chord to the other, a rising third, can be regarded as a combination of the third bird's rising two-note group and the sad cuckoo's characteristic interval, the third; and finally, the arpeggios are supported by perfect fifths, albeit in a register far from the original bass region.

[72] As mentioned before, the "merle" is that bird with the particularly beautiful and highly varied song that the British call blackbird and the Americans, robin. (The American blackbird is a very different birds and a much less skillful singer.)

In the course of the piece, however, the impression that a transcription of natural sounds was intended, subsides. Messiaen marks only three of the piece's components as clearly designated to particular birds. Bar 5 is preceded by the indication "the nightingale," bar 9 presents "the lark"—a clue that is repeated later within the same material, after the rest in bar 28—and bar 60 is verbally announced in the score as "the blackbird and all the [other] birds." The latter indication particularly shows that a faithful recreation of the actual sounds is not the issue here: in nature, "the blackbird and all the other birds" simply do not sing in *unison*.

This brings us to the metaphoric importance of these birds, or birds in general, in Messiaen's music and theology. Both when writing about his aesthetics and in his many interviews, the composer never tired of repeating that his sole aim in creating music was to praise God and His loving presence, which manifests itself threefold in His Divine love (by sending His Son), in our love towards one another (as a reflection of the ideal love), and in the rejoicing of nature (epitomized in bird song).[73]

The Heights' Contemplation contains none of the cyclical themes that pervade the *Vingt regards*, and is not based on modes—neither Messiaen's own nor any other known scalar organization. We do, however, encounter a variety of textures, tonal formations and recurring motifs that convey the impression of having witnessed nature at large expressing its joy over the holy birth. The piece sets out with a twelve-fold statement of what could be described as an elaborate drooping curve. Undulating like a literal sound wave, it increases in volume from *ppp* to *f* through the first six curves and then recedes back to *ppp*. All twelve pitches are used; the effect, however, is far from sounding dodecaphonic. Messiaen creates a juxtaposition of right- and left-hand pitches that appears like a "cheating" arrangement of black over white. (Cheating, because he divides the five black and seven white keys into two groups of six.) Rather than conveying a sense typical for twelve-tone compositions of his Viennese contemporaries, stressing the supremacy of the emancipated individual pitch that is absolutely equal with every other and no longer governed by hierarchical laws, this arrangement communicates a message about wholeness embodied and completeness without clash. The extensive initial bar of

---

[73]See the references to bird song as a symbol of heavenly joie, *symbole de la joie céleste*, in Claude Samuel (1967), p. 167, and in the prefacing remark to V, *The Son Contemplating the Son* where Messiaen speaks of *la joie symbolisée par des chants d'oiseaux*—joy symbolized by bird song.

this piece, then, epitomizes the entire bird kingdom as participating, jointly and jubilantly, in the gleeful praise of God's Incarnation.

The second bar presents a homorhythmic figure that is repeated in bar 3. The tempo is much slower here (*Modéré* against the earlier *Vif*), the rhythm is precise (compared to the extremely fast and blurred oscillation of bar 1), and the grace-notes make it clear that we are listening in on individual birds. Set apart by rests, the nightingale follows with another individualized figure, now in *unison* texture. The section is rounded off by two components that do not seem to form part in the actual bird song: a repeated pitch in receding dynamics, and a sudden outbreak (in *f*) of accented intervals that Messiaen asks to be kept reverberating through the remainder of the bar.

Saying that this initial section of the piece spans eight bars is both correct and misleading, since no degree of metric or structural regularity is proposed here. Nevertheless, the components so far described do recur later in the piece, albeit with two momentous variations. The twelve-fold sound wave introducing the bird world (bar 1) and the two homorhythmic bars that follow it are heard identically in bars 56-58, and the whole-bar rest is retained as well (compare bar 4 with bar 59). After that, what was the nightingale's short call in bars 5/6 appears transformed to the extensive *cadenza* sung, equally in *unison* texture, by "the blackbird and all the birds" in bars 60/61. Messiaen's notation fits the *cadenza* into a mere two bars and thus confirms it as consciously conceived in relationship to the former. The next component in the initial section, the protracted note repetition in bar 7 whose *diminuendo* fades into a quarter rest, is replaced by something apparently very different, though also one bar long. Against a repeated, joyful flourish in the highest register, the left hand rises from the lowest C on the keyboard through the entire circle of fifths, in a dynamic development of *crescendo* and *crescendo molto*. While the relation to the model seems far-fetched here, the six beats heard in bar 62 instead of the four-beat note repetition in bar 7 accelerate (*pressez*), thus matching the model bar in terms of time, and conclude in the original quarter rest, followed by an identical recurrence of bar 8. A rudimentary coda closes the piece in the form of a single chord—very low, very soft, and dry.

The central portion of *The Heights' Contemplation*, framed by these two structurally corresponding outer sections, consists of nothing but an extended bird duet in free counterpoint. Messiaen specifies only the higher voice as that of the lark, leaving us to guess that the second voice

111

may be some kind of warbler. (Not that it matters for anything other than our talking about it.)

Each of the two birds has its own repertoire of highly idiosyncratic calls that it repeats, with or without variation, and groups in ever new ways.

The lark presents five calls and one compound figure that, appearing only once, develops two of them further. Its tonal center is the high B♭; a secondary hinge is E. Five among the six calls—a, b, d, e and e'-d— feature B♭ as a very prominently recurring pitch, while four—b, c, d and e'-d—also stress E. Each individual call is fairly narrowly confined in its range: to a fifth (a), tritone (b, d and e), or even fourth (c). Only the one-time developmental call spans in its two segments a minor sevenths and a diminished ninth respectively. Note repetitions play a leading role in each

THE SONG OF THE LARK

component a

unchanging,
- see bars 9/10,
14/15, 31/32,
44/45, 48/49

component b

changing,
- see bars 11/12,
15/17, 32-37,
45/46, 49-51

component c

virtually
unchanging,
- see bars
12/13, 47

component d

unchanging,
- see bars
18-20, 52-54

component e

unchanging,
- see bars
20/21, 55

component d-e'

free development
of d + e, only once
- see bars 22-25

of the lark's calls, be it directly (as in *a, d* and *e*), ornamented by grace-notes (as in *c*), interspersed with other pitches (as in *b*), or in the form of trills (as in *d* and *e'-d*). The lark's articulation is mostly *staccato*.

The warbler has four calls, two that seem to be the primary repertoire and two others that are interspersed only infrequently. Its vocal behavior does not display any unifying central pitch. However, the two habitual calls are in themselves conceived as infinite variations and regroupings of a few pitches; see in call *x* the groups D-A♭-E♭ and G-D, in call *y* the group E-B-C♯. The intervallic range of this bird is much wider than that of its duet partner, particularly in call *x* where it spans almost two octaves. The warbler expresses itself in an articulation and rhythm that are extremely varied, ranging from thirty-second notes to the dotted quarter note and from *staccato* through different intermediate degrees of resonance to long sounds and slurs spanning large leaps.

THE SONG OF THE WARBLER

Both birds, individually as well as in their contrapuntal interplay, express beautifully the joyousness that Messiaen associates with their song. They thus enrich the cycle dedicated to the *Contemplations of the Infant Jesus* with a musical vignette that shows nature gleeful about the birth of God's Son into this world.

Unlike Ravel's birds, which are heard in an environment apparently devoid of humans, Messiaen's birds relate to us; they can even be seen as bridging the gap between the Creator and His creatures. Their intention, the praise of God, extended daily and without any reservation, defines them as representative speakers for all inhabitants of the Earth. At the same time, the beauty of their song, gladdening all on earth who listen to them, impart to us a heightened sense of what it is to live in God's grace. This twofold reference links them to the role traditionally assigned to angels. (This is a particularly interesting thought since Messiaen intimates, in his piece dedicated to the angels proper, that these might not be entirely agreeable to God's choice of incarnating among humans—rather than among them!)

COMEDIANS AND
OTHER PERFORMERS

Minstrels   (Debussy, *Préludes*, vol. I, no. 12)

As has often been pointed out, Debussy is not referring to troubadours in the title of this piece, but to American black-face comedians whom he saw performing in Paris. This kind of performance originated in America in the early nineteenth century. It was particularly geared towards a working-class audience and reflects racial and social tensions sensed by white workers who found themselves in close contact with black co-workers. A typical American minstrel performance would show a semicircle of four, five or sometimes more white male performers made up with blackened faces and dressed in outrageously oversized or ragged "Negro" costumes. Equipped with an array of instruments that included banjo, fiddle, bone castanets, tambourine and others, the performers would stage a three-part show. One part consisted in a selection of songs interspersed with what passed for black wit and japery. A second segment of the show presented several novelty performances like comic dialogues, incongruous "stump speeches," cross-dressed "wench" performances, etc. The third component, a narrative skit usually set in the South, contained dancing, music and burlesque.

What clearly distinguishes this prelude from any others in typically Debussyan language is a deliberate awkwardness of rhythm and harmonic progression. Both can safely be interpreted as means aimed at representing the vaudeville ambiance in which the caption sets the prelude.

Possibly the most demanding task in this piece for a classically trained pianist is to play irregularly, that is, not on the beat. What Debussy requests for the opening motif: *les "gruppetti" sur le temps* means just that: the "little groups," i.e. the three-note *acciaccaturas*, are to fall *on* the beat, thus shifting the melodic notes they precede into a slightly off-beat position and giving the rhythm of the D-E-F♯ a tottering gait, descriptive of the clumsiness intended by the grotesque comedians. Here are the two prominent melodic snatches. One serves as a kind of character introduction; listeners are led to visualize banjo, cornet and drums:

bars 1-4

The other component seems to evoke the comedian's expression (especially after a minor catastrophe) of an impish kind of reassurance, saying to himself and to the onlookers: "no harm done; let me try once more."

bars 11/12

In-between, one can imagine tap-dancing (from bar 9), perhaps pirouetting (bar 17), an acrobatic stunt (bar 44), juggling (from bar 45) as well as other less unambiguously represented vaudeville acts. Even a "Perils of Pauline" tableau has been suggested for the material after bar 34.[74]

The tonal layout, too, imitates some typical conventions of light entertainment. After eleven bars in very firmly established G major, the subdominant chord on the last beat of bar 12 leads, not to the dominant of the same key, but to that of another: to A, root of the V^7 of D major. The bars thus combine the pretense of a logical modulation, as it appears in the sequence of I-IV and IV-V, with the breaking of this logic by means of an abrupt shift from IV of one key (G major) to V of another (D major). Furthermore, a few bars later the melodic ascent D-E-F♯ that is first heard as a resolution to the preceding, protracted V^7 (see bars 13-16d) is subsequently re-interpreted, with F♯ becoming part of an F♯ major chord. Bar 18 then confirms F♯ major with I-V-I on the first three eighth-

---

[74]I am indebted for this suggestion to Daniel Paul Horn (personal correspondence, January 1995). Pauline is that character in an old series of American silent movies who is always being brought to the brink of disaster. The classic image, often parodied in cartoons, is one of the innocent young woman being tied to railroad tracks by a villain with an on-coming train visible in the distance.

notes. This key, however, is cut off as abruptly as the former ones and G is reinstated with vaudeville nonchalance by a cross-related juxtaposition of F♯ major with the D-major seventh (see bar 18, third and fourth eighth-note). One step further in the process, the repetition (see bar 26) complet-ely omits the resolution into D! Instead, what is heard as the third degree F♯ is enharmonically notated as G♭ (the cornet entering "in the wrong key") and leads into B♭ major and from there onwards to even stranger shores, ending abruptly in an A♭ major (see bar 31).

Another cross-related turnaround (with E♮ pitted against the preced-ing A♭-major chord) brings about a new section, determined this time by parallel motion of augmented chords (see bars 37-44.)[75] More snatches of melodies, harmonic shifts and rigorous confrontations follow (see e.g. bar 49: F♯ major followed in bar 50 by G/C major, then, without transition, in bar 51 defied by A♭ major; another beginning in G/C, followed by A/E major). These seemingly innocent gestures may be read as corresponding to a comic acrobat's endlessly renewed "back to the beginning," after each aborted or failed attempt to get something done.

In bar 58, the minstrels are seen to decide a new game. A tambourine accompaniment begins with full confidence in *f*—but dwindles away without ever being joined by the expected melody. Instead, an old-time Broadway song is recalled, portrayed by the distinctive extended upbeat in diverging chromat-ic voices (see bars 63/64, doubled in the left hand), the har-monic sequence of II^9-V^7-$I^{9\text{-}8\text{-}7\text{-}6}$.

And there the ironic twist happens again: the repetition exag-gerates the chromatic voice-leading by sub-stituting (in bar 73) the earlier II^9 with a $\sharp IV^7$!

bars 63-67

bars 71-75

<hr />

[75]Taking the left-hand into account, what emerges is actually a sequence of alternating whole-tone contexts.

Once more the motto is "back to the beginning" (bars 74/75), but this time the attempt is aborted even earlier. As the clowns get ready to leave the stage, we hear a short recapitulation of snatches from their various motives (bars 78-86). We then literally see them run—undoubtedly to the cheerful laughter of the audience—towards the exit where, just before leaving, they stop short and stomp out in a pretense of dignity as hilarious as their entire number was; see the *serrez* (contract = get faster) and the final *sec et retenu* (dry and held back) that marks the very much accented plagal close.

General Lavine - eccentric   (Debussy, *Préludes*, vol. II, no. 6)

The caption of this prelude makes reference to a performance artist who appeared during the summer of the year 1910 at the Théâtre Marigny in Paris: the American comedian, or clown, Edward Lavine whom the publicity campaign announced as "General Lavine," alluding to the supposition that he had spent his entire life as a soldier. His eccentric performance included impersonations of a wooden puppet, tightrope walking, playing the piano with his toes, fighting a duel with himself, etc. According to a 1945 article in the San Francisco Chronicle, Debussy had been asked to compose incidental music for Lavine's act. Although there seem to be no records that this music was ever performed, one may assume that the composer would have gone to see the comedy act several times before making any decisions. It is thus safe to guess that this prelude was an impression of the American eccentric.

Many of the musical gestures support this scenario. The introduction (bars 1-10) might be heard as a commanding, military-band percussion motif—a "left/right/left" drum roll leading to a cymbal stroke on the strong beat—followed by the awkward steps of an athletically inept soldier. The vivid *f strident* (piercing) marking the percussion motif contrasts effectively with the *p sec* (dry) demanded for the general's somewhat halting *staccato* eighth-notes. The confident, unambiguous C-G of the military call is comically answered by an arch of cross-related triads (E♭ minor, G major, B♭ minor = G♭/B♭ become G♮/B♮, B♮/D♮ become B♭/D♭, etc.) that is comically reminiscent of out-of-tune brass. After a repetition, the discrepancy between the spirit of call and answer widens even more: while the drum-cymbal motif probably remains in confident *p* (Debussy does not further specify the dynamics for the second textural strand), the inept soldier seems to prepare his retreat with more grace (see the D♭-major/B♭-minor triads in bars 5/6 that are not cross-related). But a smooth exit is not to be. A sudden gawky motion (the *ff* in bar 7) jerks his withdrawal and immediately reinstates the cross-related chord progression. A scornful comment in dry *sforzatissimo* on the lowest C of the keyboard concludes the introduction. However, this C is then reinterpreted —during the caesura and pause, as it were—as the dominant of the section to come; it thus expresses at the same time a tension towards the main section of the prelude. (Performers may want to take this into account for their body language during the fermata.)

The main section that follows represents the dance mentioned in the heading that precedes the piece (see the indication *Dans le style et le Mouvement d'un Cake-Walk* = in the style and tempo of a cakewalk). This dance of nineteenth-century black American origin was popularized and disseminated primarily through imitations of its black-face minstrel shows, which fascinated Debussy, as we know from the final piece in book I of his Preludes. More rhythmically moving parody than actual dance, the cakewalk did not prescribe any particular steps. Common elements were a couple's strutting parade, bows backward and forward, salutes to the spectators, high kicks etc. The material upon which Debussy bases his cakewalk is simple and reminiscent of jazz settings. The bass provides cadential steps (in bars 11-18: F, F, F-C-F-C, G-C-F); the off-beat chords add the notes of the most typical jazz harmony, the six-five chord; and the melody keeps close to F major—albeit in a pentatonic excerpt that testifies to Debussy's presence on stage. (Thus what we have here is three-layered: an intentionally comic "dance" of black American origin, parodied by a white American performing clown, in the musical representation of a French composer.)

bars 11-18

Elements of spoof enter at various levels. The heading of the cakewalk section "*spirituel et discret*" bespeaks the original tongue-in-cheek pose of traditional cake-walk dancers who pretend to be all elegance and grace but cannot help bursting out into ostentatious gestures that are anything but spiritual and discreet. The sudden interruption of the smoothly flowing cakewalk by the clumsy soldier's call to duty represents General Lavine's interference with the dance in his comedy act. The disturbance of the relaxed tonal ambiance by a clashing chord (bar 17), an increasing number of altered notes (bars 23/24) and distorted or outright wrong bass notes (see the augmented fourths in bars 25-28 and the comic bitonal effects in bars 39-42) show the composer poking fun at the performer or at the very least participating in his joke. And in the unexpectedly lyrical gesture in bars 31-34, complete with signs of exaggerated emotionality (see the *crescendi* and the sudden, technically impossible hush to *piano* in the midst of a sustained chord), one easily pictures Lavine building himself up to salute the French flag. [76]

The middle section, which commences with the upbeat at the end of bar 45, uses the same two categories of material but reverses their relationship. While the main section of the cakewalk focuses on the dance and the elements of parody inherent in it, and confines the maladroit soldier to an occasional rash disturbance of the elegantly ironic setting, the middle section is dominated by the comic hero of the prelude. Measures 45-47d present a melodramatic variant of the cross-related chord arch from the introduction—now in *legato* instead of dry touch, and *traîné* (sluggish, dawdling) instead of the very rhythm form suggested earlier on. While the tonal context the listener has in mind from the introduction suggests C as a central note, the bass pedal-note (see bars 47-50, 54-57, and 59-62) establishes A♭ as a new root. Not that any of the other voices takes much notice of this fact! The guitar-like strumming in double seconds that re-institutes the cakewalk tempo does not take any definite harmonic stance. Even the accented unison E♭ which, in the middle of bar 48, suggests a V-I motion towards the bass-note, is raised to F two measures later.

The subsequent measures play with new versions of the clumsy protagonist's cross-related triads. At the same time, the melody they create, particularly in bars 51/52, quote the Negro song *The Camptown Races* which, one suspects, may have constituted part of Lavine's routine. The phrase concludes in a distorted cadential pattern, contrasting the bass A♭ with its tritone D♮. As if in comic frustration, the *legato/traîné* version of the soldier's motif opens the otherwise identical repeat (compare bars 58-64 with 46-52) in *ff crescendo* and with a chromatically descending counterpoint launched from *sff!* To complete the irony on the harmonic

[76]For this suggestion I owe thanks to my friend, the British pianist Beryl Chempin.

level, the concluding bars of the middle section (bars 65-69) wiggle their way into the long-expected dominant of A♭ (see the E♭⁹ chord in bar 67, prolonged in melodic augmentation throughout bars 68/69)—but by this time it is too late: A♭ yields to F in the return of the cake-walk. (Bars 70-93 are identical with bars 11-34.)

The coda recalls another familiar element from jazz performances: the shift up a semitone. Thus bars 94/95 and 98/99 are chromatic transpositions of bars 11/12 and 13/14 respectively, while the inserted D-major chord of bar 97 represents once again the "wrong" dominant: the triad on the tritone of the current root G♭. In gradually increasing tempo (*animez*), the most melodramatic version of the soldier's motif—with *crescendo* and chromatically descending counterpoint, is submitted equally to the semitone shift (see bars 101, 102). The concluding coda-within-the-coda, i.e. the final line of the prelude (bars 103-109), hardly surprises us as it provides a harmonic closure worthy of the jazz origins of the piece: a perfect cadence complete with a six-five chord enriched with a seventh (bars 103d and 105d) leading, after a weak-beat drum roll on the tonic, into a dominant-ninth chord (bars 104 and 106) and closing the prelude unambiguously on F.

Hommage à S. Pickwick Esq. P. P. M. P. C.

(Debussy, Préludes, vol. II, no. 9)

This prelude's caption points to one of Debussy's favorite books, Charles Dickens's novel *The Posthumous Papers of the Pickwick Club* of 1836/37. Its principal character, Esquire Samuel Pickwick, whose status as "Perpetual President and Member of the Pickwick Club" is captured in the string of letters following his name and title, is ironically depicted as a fat, unsophisticated, and opinionated clod.

Debussy begins his musical homage to Esquire Pickwick and all he stands for in a stately *grave*, quoting the first line of the British national anthem *God Save Our Gracious King* in the lowest strand of the piano texture. The indications *f sonore* (loud and reverberating) as well as the notation in dashed octaves is reminiscent of the brass instrumentation commonly associated with the anthem. The upper strand, though legato and with some pretense at a melodic line as well as initial harmonic independence, soon merges with the character established by the anthem quotation and two-thirds through the first phrase (see bar 4) gives in to the proposed F major. It is not until the radical diminuendo (from *f* to *p*) in bar 5 that the right-hand part finally takes over—with a syncopated do-ti-do figure in the upper strand that "corrects" the anthem's F-major tonality to D minor!—and a courteous sixteenth-note gesture with beat-2 syncopation in the middle strand.

At this point in the tune, every subject of the British monarchy anticipates the ascending scale in powerful *crescendo* that habitually prepares the second section. Instead, Debussy teases on with four measures that, while containing ascending motion and marked *crescendo molto*, lead quite someplace else. Hemiolas obscure the meter, the whole-tone tetrachord in the bass with its B♮ puts the D-minor tonality as much in doubt as the earlier assumed F-major key, and the irregular exit of the strands, particularly the overhanging treble octave E, give the impression of an eager but somewhat inept musician trying to perform the anthem but getting lost.

bar 9

The jovial but perhaps not quite proper way out of the predicament comes forth with an upbeat of augmented and diminished triads, marked *aimable* (amiable), which contrasts the preceding *f crescendo* with a sudden *p* followed by a further dynamic retreat.

In a thus somewhat subdued voice, but still *expressif,* two partial repeats of the anthem's initial line are heard (compare the bass in bars 10/11 with that in bar 5). The anticipated resolution into a tonic F-major chord, however, remains unaccomplished. With a sudden hush to *pp*, the unlucky anthem player allows the unresolved harmony to fade and concentrates instead on a saucy two-note figure in dotted rhythm.

bars 10-12

Under the driving force of this figure, which Debussy marks as *léger* (light), the music gradually picks up tempo (*peu à peu animé*). One might imagine Esquire Pickwick's speech before the assembled members of his club—according to Dickens a pitifully small group that would have to be addressed with all the more finesse to justify the title of Permanent

President. In this scenario, the busy jingle of many empty words is represented in the very constancy of the little figure (compare the dotted-note line in bars 13/14 with that in bars 15/16 and 17/18), the inconsequential but nevertheless unrelenting deliberations in the long scalar descent of bars 13/14 (complete with *crescendo - diminuendo!*), and the somewhat pathetic pomp of the occasion in the *legato* gestures in bars 15/16 and 17/18.

Pride and grandeur seem restored when, in bars 19/20, a double-note version of the figure rises *crescendo molto*. It culminates in a superbly ironical, overly rich statement of pretentiousness: three triads, fortified beyond the two-hand chord in an accented after-beat supplement, recur after a proud flourish in the simplest of variations! In keeping with the pompousness of the expression, the tempo is appropriately reduced to *retenu.*

As if somewhat ashamed of so much affectation, an attempt to restore the club's agenda begins *pp léger*. Warming to the topic (bars 29/30 are a varied and more exalted repetition of bars 27/28), the various elements merge in a gigantic build-up. A *crescendo* from *pp* in bar 31 to *ff* in bar 40 accompanies an extended, powerful *accelerando* (*animez peu à peu* = increase the tempo little by little, i.e. throughout the ten bars). Scatterings from the anthem (see upper strand bars 31-34, middle strand bars 37-40) are set here against Esquire Pickwick's talkative eagerness. Yet once again, the anthem does not reach any satisfactory close but breaks off abruptly.

As before (compare bars 40-42 with bars 9-11), a conciliatory gesture using a bar from the anthem's first line remains equally unresolved.

After this renewed failure to comply with official ritual, we are in for a real surprise. In a tone color described by the composer as *lointain et léger* (far away and light), we hear what is clearly the imitation of a capricious whistle (see bars 44-46m).

bars 44-45

The tonality in this unison passage gives the impression of D major, the parallel of that often-reached and often-aborted D minor; but the pitches employed are actually those of a pentatony on D: D-E-F♯-A-B.

bars 46-48

A strongly accented trill, soon hushed and concluding in a falling scale that seems to wipe the sound off the keyboard, makes way for the coda in *mouvement retenu* (reduced tempo). The upbeat is taken from the repeatedly unsuccessful attempts to bring the anthem to a close (compare bar 48 with bars 10/11 and 42/43). And while it reaches a solid F-major triad this time performers tuned in to the irony of the piece will certainly play the notes in the lower and middle strands with appropriate triumph and relief—Esquire Pickwick still doesn't get it quite right: the G in the treble, sounding above the augmented dotted-note rhythm with D-C *appoggiatura*, does not find its way into the F-major chord. More pompous bass octaves and a rumbling upbeat are needed. When, at long last, the ambitious Esquire finds himself on an untainted tonic, he smugly emphasizes this in *ff* with dash and strong accent—before realizing that this is a weak third beat, and the chord in six-four inversion. As if fearing to be ridiculed for his unsophisticated way of handling basic rituals, he hastens, in bashful *p*, to correct metric position and inversion.

La sérénade interrompue   (Debussy, *Préludes*, vol. I, no. 9)

This prelude might stand as a good example for what has been called "music as theater." It seems to enact an entire little comedy, with several participants and a number of surprises.

Let us imagine for a moment what a serenade in its original sense was: a lover's song in front of the window of the girl or woman he adored, presented at night time (Italian *la sera* = the evening) when she could be expected to be home and susceptible, and when the environment was quiet. The lover would accompany himself on his lute or guitar or, if he had less talent than money, hire musicians to play for him. Now, many things can happen on such occasions: the loving amateur musician can be nervous, or not so skillful on his instrument or with his voice; the woman may have another admirer who has the bad taste to choose the same night for his approach; parents not in favor of the particular suitor, or neighbors who feel disturbed in their night's sleep, may shout, slam windows, or find other ways of interrupting the sentimental performance; mischievous buddies of the love-sick hero may arrive on the scene with competing music. Each performer will enjoy discovering the "plot" of this comedy, and will, one hopes, convey the fun experienced in the process to his or her audience.

As the tonal language tells us, the story probably takes place in southern Spain. The love-song melody in particular shows strong Moorish influence, while the instrumental sections are predominantly in a scale that is a mix of the Phrygian and the whole-tone scales on F: Phrygian would be **F G♭ A♭ B♭ C D♭ E♭ F**, the whole-tone scale F G A C♭ D♭ E♭ F. (What Debussy has his guitarist play in the "warm-up" section is a descent/ascent on F with the C♭ of the whole-tone scale but the G♭ of the Phrygian—followed by the perfect fifth C♮ in cadencing bars 9/10 and 15-18.)

The rhythmic organization of this mini prelude is also of interest. The opening bars are notated as *hemiolas*—i.e. one should not get the impression, achieved only by artificial stress on the second downbeat, of a triple meter, but perceive a down - - up, down - - up, down - - **stress!** This little emotional outburst, if conveyed with all its inherent quality of surprise, very much sets the stage for the nocturnal plot. In the motif's double stroke with its descent/ascent, listeners will be kept uncertain about whether the time is triple or duple, while the cadential bars clearly state a three-eight. As the phrase is repeated, the two bars of surprising rest are omitted, but made up for at the end by two bars that, characteristically, revert to the *hemiola* grouping.

The first instrumental section has an expressive tenor melody with beat-three accents—prototypical musical gestures pointing to a love song that is most often imagined as sung by a lyrical tenor, with sentimental stresses outside the "orderly" downbeats. It might help to imagine the texture here in three parts: the bass with a slurred group on the downbeat, providing the harmonic framework without specific emotional value; the off-beat guitar chords, which add an old comically dramatic quality, especially since their naturalized notes are at odds with the emphasized

bars 19-24

pitches in the melody that follow; and the lyrical tune focused on the ascents F-G♭-A♭ (bar 19) and C-D♭-E♭ (bar 22). The example shows how it could appear in other than piano instrumentation:

As the nocturnal visitor prepares for the first part of his lyrical declamation, he locks his fingers onto the perfect fifth F/C and, plucking in rapid repetition without double-strokes (and thus without the alternating heavy-light indicated in bars 5-10 etc.), glides this grip up and down in parallel shifts on the finger board.[77]

The first tune (beginning in bar 32) focuses, in the Moorish-influenced style of southern Spain, on a lingering leading note before it finally diverts to the fifth degree, after a *ritardando* that, in the actual setting, would be fairly generous; this is determined in duration by the length of the singer's breath rather than any considerations or structure or sophisticated taste. One can almost see the singers knitted brows and the dramatic thrust of his head at the final, willful *acciaccatura* that leads the music back to the "instrumental" section.

Bars 46-48 contrast in all parameters with what goes before: the tonal root is E, the register much more expansive than that accessible for

---

[77]The typical effect created on a guitar by the combination of plucking right hand and gliding left grip cannot be reproduced on a piano. Debussy's indication to use both pedals and play *staccato* in *pp* or even softer may be an attempt to capture this particular color. It seems unlikely that he intended an ongoing overall blur. Very light and soft *staccatissimo* touch helps as it tends to shorten the vibration of the strings. Where the acoustics of a room are deterrents to clarity, pianists may decide to use flutter pedal through the entire passage.

amateur guitarists, the dynamic indications request f with subsequent increase to a strongly accented sff. This is not part of the sentimental hero's performance; its sounds much more as if a window slammed shut or something was thrown at him! Startled and probably slightly wary of further attacks, he leads from the root E of the interruption back to his own tonal center F (bar 48 middle), and remains there, drastically reducing both volume and speed as if preparing to jump up and run. But as nothing happens, he resumes his playing, beginning once more with the prelude-like ascent/descent (compare bars 50-53 with bars 5-8).

The following part of his lyrical presentation draws, in its first phrase (see bars 54-60) on the first tetrachord of the Moorish, or Arabic, scale (which, on F, reads **F G♭ A B♭** C D♭ E F). The accompaniment here begins, for the first time, a gradual chromatic ascent that will continue until the beginning of the second phrase in bar 63; from there on, the downbeats of every other bar counter with a chromatic descent (bars 63d, 65d, 67d: F♮-F♭-E♭). In the melody, the second phrase begins with a free sequence (compare bars 63/64 with bars 54/55) and expands its second half by means that are again informed by the highly emotional setting: a large-scale *hemiola* (bars 65/66) and increasing prolongations (bars 67/68 and 69-71). In order to appreciate fully the sentimental content, it might help to imagine what a simple rendition of the tune might sound like.

bars 54-72, rhythmically simplified

Two observations are important here. The first regards the strange polytonality of the second half of the phrase that, far from being a statement of a twentieth-century composer about the obsolete nature of functional tonality, sounds rather, in the particular context of this piece, like fun poked at the enamored singer who is so engrossed in his own vocal production that he does two incompatible things: approach a melodic conclusion on the central F while having modulated to D♭ major in the accompaniment (see in the left-hand part the somewhat tainted V^7/V of D♭ in bars 63-64, the V^7 of D♭ in bars 69-72 and 74, and the tonic of D♭ in bars 73 and 75).

The other observation regards the tune itself, which would logically conclude on the root F. As Debussy presents his romantic Spanish hero, the final note is omitted. It enters instead, after an instrumental interlude that acts as a suspense, in the higher octave, with what we are entitled to imagine as the ardor of a fervent lover. (It is important to realize that this *cadenza* represents a vocal line. Thus care must be taken not to exaggerate the speed and create virtuosity at the expense of sonorous intensity.)

Hardly has the rapt man finished expressing himself in a freely declamatory passage that imitates a typical Andalusian vocal arabesque, than he is brutally interrupted again (see the examples below). This time it is rival music, sounding (as Debussy's *lointain* informs us) from far away, but nevertheless upsetting the intimacy of this lover's serenade. Even his final note F, so many times suspended, is redefined as F# in the tonal context of the "other" music. The rival music which, with its D major in a cross-related key and with its square two-four time, stomping beats, and somewhat vulgar pattern that suggest drunken limping, is very much at odds with the atmosphere created in the preceding *cantilena* and makes the guitarist truly furious. *Rageur* (enraged) he intones two bars of his instrumental interlude, choosing *f* for that which had so far always sounded in gentle *pp* (see bars 85/86). When he breaks off (to ascertain whether the other group of musicians can still be heard?) we catch another snatch of the street music before the lover decides that he must keep playing if he wants to retain his lady's attention. Once more he starts with a snippet that Debussy marked *rageur*. This term most probably designates an altogether more aggressive rendition of the music: the motif should sound not only much louder than before, but also considerably faster (see in bar 95 the indication *revenir au movement* = return to the original tempo). Note also that, probably to defend his ground more forcefully, the performer adds treble notes (possibly sung?) to the texture, thus making it somewhat more difficult for pianists to bring out the A♭-G-A♭-G tune in bars 91 and 93.

For a last time we hear a version of the Moorish-inspired chant. Bars 98-104, beginning on a protracted leading note that resolves indirectly into the central F, are related to bars 32-42, and bars 113-124 are reminiscent of what was heard in bars 63-72. The accompaniment in this stanza is rooted first in B♭ (the B♭-minor seventh chord doubles the melody's step from protracted leading-note to resolution—see bars 94-100: chord with E♮, bars 101-104: with F; repeated in bars 105-108/ 109-111). The second half of the phrase appears harmonized with an E♭-major ninth chord, later adapted as an E♭-minor six-five (see bars 121-124) and resolving—this time in accordance with the anticipated melodic close—in F minor. Again, the melody breaks off before the expected final F (which our inner ear adds in bar 125). A development of the guitar motif and a fragment of the opening ascent accompany the serenader's retreat from the scene of his nocturnal devotion (*en s'éloignant*). Is he tired by the time he recalls his *glissando* motif (compare bar 131 with bar 26), and do his fingers no longer have a firm hold, so that he slips to the G♮? We don't know, although the sudden *sfz* in bar 133 with the "corrected" chord seems to point to his frustration. He leaves with a somewhat unprepared and harmonically compromising close in B♭ minor.

Alborada del gracioso   (Ravel, *Miroirs*, no. 4)

The Spanish title of this piece needs some explanation. An *alborada* is the counterpart to a serenade. The latter is derived from the Italian *la sera* (evening) and originally signified a musical greeting, performed in the evening in front of the windows of the person to be honored—a beloved one or a person of rank. The Spanish word for the early morning hours or dawn, *la alborada*, gave the name to an equivalent musical presentation performed at daybreak, also usually out of doors—for instance as the first musical offering to a bride on her wedding morning, to celebrate a traditional festival, or to honor an individual.

While the adjective *gracioso* is used today in the sense of "funny" (with "graceful," the intuitively first translation for English speakers, in the second place), *el gracioso* is more particularly the facetious person in the Spanish comedy (the terms buffoon or jester, while coming close, do not entirely do justice to the meaning of the character). He is someone who, under the mask of wit and frequently professed foolishness, is granted the freedom to jokingly attack and expose ridiculous habits and dubious opinions of any member of the society. That this *gracioso* should perform an *alborada* thus contains irony on several levels.

129

Just as the traditional Italian serenade, of which the typical movement sequence was Allegro (or Moderato) - Minuet - Adagio - Minuet - Allegro, the Spanish "dawn song" also featured a slow and highly expressive central episode framed by more lively sections. It began with a *salute* (greeting) that was typically in moderate three-four time, and ended with a *despedida* (farewell) in swift two-four time. The color Ravel requests for this work differs markedly from the much softer hues prescribed for the other four pieces within *Miroirs*. The performance indications in the initial bar, *sec[,] les arpèges très serrés* (dry, the rolled chords very brisk) point to the instruments we should imagine depicted in the piano score: guitars and castanets, the quintessential representatives of Spanish flair[78]. It is intriguing to observe how Ravel's buffoon "gets things mixed up": the framing sections, notated in six-eight time, oscillate between duple and triple meter with the insertions in nine-eight adding further confusion; and the solemn homage of the solo song in the middle section drips with irony masked as a jester's forgivable clumsiness.

The tonal center of the piece is D. D minor acts as the "home key" in the opening section (as indicated in the key signature and realized particularly in the left-hand part of bars 1-11), while D major reigns from bar 62 onwards into the beginning of the slow *cantilena* and then again in the coda (bars 219-229). These keys, however, are constantly put into question. Ravel's simple but very effective device is what one might want to call an "almost-octave": were we to play, in bars 1-5, all the notes entrusted to the right-hand thumb a semitone lower, the result would be simple, natural D minor!

Another convincing way of showing the jester mockingly pathetic and clumsily out of tune, is the insertion of *appoggiaturas*—either in consecutive order (see e.g. in the second half of the pattern introduced in bar 12, where the treble G of the current C-E♭-G-B♭-D chord is delayed by A and F♯), or simultaneously in several voices (see e.g., under the accent in bar 31/32 etc., the five "leading-notes" [triple F♯ and double B] resolving in parallel perfect intervals into the C-minor chord). The *glissando* runs in bars 44 and 46 feature as their point of departure a double-note that seems like an awkwardly missed G♯; the fact that pianistic technique makes it most likely for these two notes to be played with a squarely

---

[78] As Roger Nichols points out when discussing *Alborada*, "in its treatment of *staccato*, repeated notes and *glissandi,* both single and double—which Ravel could do wonderfully well, probably because of his squarish thumbs—it is really three studies rolled into one." (See R. Nichols, *Ravel*, London: J. M. Dent & Sons Ltd., 1977.)

placed thumb adds to this impression. (See also the similar effect, a "missed F♯ octave", in bars 105-118 and 133-147). Finally, the irony that the double-third *glissando*—quite difficult enough as it is!—appears first in the "wrong" interval of a fourth may be attributed to the same intention of musically depicting clumsiness.

The rhythmic organization, as already briefly mentioned, achieves a similar impression. There are bars where the melodically leading voice suggests triple time; cases in point in the initial section are the left-hand part in bars 1, 3, 5 7, 9-11 and the right-hand part in bars 14, 18, 20. In the same melodic context, the alternating bars (see left hand: bars 2, 4, 6, 8 and right hand: bars 12/13, 16/17) clearly stress the middle beat, thus converting these bars into (compound) duple time. To further complicate the matter, the accompanying chords in some of the first-mentioned triple-time bars may suggest duple time (see right hand: bars 1, 3, 5). The overall effect, especially when regarded in the light of the buffoon performing a musical greeting at dawn, is one of "not getting the time right."

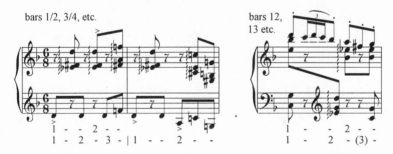

In what follows, the impression is further intensified. After two bars in "duple" time (bars 26/27), two bars in "triple" time (bars 27/28), and an extra three-eight bar (which seems to re-establish the half bar as a basic unit), the next bars are confusingly lengthened. What in the score looks like an extension from six-eight to nine-eight is actually heard as an abridged version of two six-eight bars (i.e. bar 31 is heard as an incomplete rendition of the pattern introduced in bars 14/15). And while the left-hand accent in this bar seemingly keeps track of larger metric units by stressing the fourth eighth-note, this controlling device is abandoned in subsequent bars, so that bars 32-34 are actually perceived as a compound three-four-plus-three-eight time! While fluctuating meters are by no means unusual in Ravel's music, the very extent of these intricate metric confusions here invites a reading as a conscious descriptive intention.

In the second section of the dawn song (bars 43-57), the alternation of conflicting meters seems momentarily suspended in favor of a more floating feeling. Bars 43-51 can be heard as either duple or triple time—a good reason for performers to avoid metric accents as much as possible and thus enhance the contrast created on the levels of material (fast note repetitions and flourishes) and harmony (G♯ as the central note of this section is diametrically opposed to the home key D). The following six bars, in which the color of the contrast (i.e. the note repetitions) is combined with the melodic outline of the main material, necessarily reverts to the metric ambiguity of the main section.

All the more mind-boggling are the surprises—in terms of meter, tempo and color—in the song section of the *alborada*. The homage tune, while ostensibly in structurally corresponding phrases that might be perceived as relating to the lines of the imagined underlying lyrics, is rhythmically so varied that it appears as an *ad libitum* and can be played with corresponding *rubato*. The song itself, however, contains its own two contrasting components. Both take the listener by surprise in that they abandon the *plus lent* (slower) of the passionate unison and reestablish the tempo of the main section. The first internal contrast consists of insertions featuring a single seventh chord (see e.g. in bars 75-79: B-D-F♯-A-C♯) that is rhythmically enlivened by bass octaves in upbeat-downbeat pattern. These patterns are launched in strong support of the purported three-four time (see bars 75-78, 82-85, 89-91, 97-102 etc.) but soon go their own way, establishing a secret five-four time (bars 111-114, 120-122 etc.). The second contrast (see bars 126-129 and 157-160) adds a further, highly expressive and passionate element (bar 126) that, over a sustained left-hand pedal, quickly loses power and impact through three transpositions downwards.

The following page gives an example showing the homage song, stripped of all the interfering internal contrasts, followed by a table outlining the design of the entire piece. As can be seen, *Alborada del gracioso* can structurally be described as a kind of rondo form.

There are, however, two unusual aspects to this rondo. One concerns the refrain that, as the table or a glance at the score shows, becomes consecutively shorter throughout the piece. The second surprise is connected with what is wedged between the rondo's main body and the coda. This insertion contains a medley of fragments from the various sections. Bars 196-199 (both hands) develop component *a* from within the refrain, albeit in a new harmonization including augmented chords. Bars 200-201, 209,

bars 71-74

bars 79-81

bars 85-88

bars 91-96

bars 107-110/
114-119,

con octava

(repeated in bars 137-140/144-150)

The dawn song and its rondo form

refrain	bars 1-21	(a = bars 1-11, b = 12-21)
	bars 22-42	(a' = bars 22-30, b' = 31-42)
first episode	bars 43-57	(c = bars 43-51, c/a = 52-57)
refrain	bars 58-70	
second episode	bars 71-165	(d = bars 71-125, e = 126-129; retransition
		d' = bars 133-156, e'= 157-164; retransition)
refrain	bars 166-173	
first episode	bars 174-190	
refrain	bars 191-195	
(development)	bars 196-218	
coda	bars 219-229	

211, 213-217 recall component b', also from the refrain. The inner voice in bars 202-205, 210, 212 is reminiscent of the final line of the *cantilena* in the second episode. In all regards, then—on the tonal, the metric and the structural levels, the "buffoon" brings considerable confusion into this piece.

Part II

TALES AND POEMS

Sur *Le Tasse en prison* d'Eugène Delacroix[79]

Le poète au cachot, débraillé, maladif,
Roulant un manuscrit sous son pied convulsif,
Mesure d'un regard que la terreur enflamme
L'escalier de vertige où s'abîme son âme.

Les rires enivrants dont s'emplit la prison
Vers l'étrange et l'absurde invitent sa raison;
Le Doute l'environne, et la Peur ridicule,
Hideuse et multiforme, autour de lui circule.

Ce génie enfermé dans un taudis malsain,
Ces grimaces, ces cris, ces spectres dont l'essaim
Tourbillonne, ameuté derrière son oreille,

Ce rêveur que l'horreur de son logis réveille,
Voilà bien ton emblème, Âme aux songes obscurs,
Que le Réel étouffe entre ses quatre murs!

Eugène Delacroix, *Tasso in Prison* (1864).
Bührle Collection, Zurich. Reprinted with permission.

[79]Charles Baudelaire, "Sur le Tasse en prison d'Eugène Delacroix," *Œuvres complètes,*
Claude Pichois, ed. (Paris: Gallimard, Bibliothèque de la Pléiade, 1975), pp.168/169.

On *Tasso in Prison* by Eugène Delacroix

The poet held captive, disheveled, diseased,
A manuscript rolling under a foot unappeased,
Measures with a glance that sheer terror enflames
The dizzying abyss where his soul sees its blames.

Inebriated laughs fill the prison sad,
Inviting his mind towards the absurd and mad;
He's surrounded by Doubt, and encircled too near,
By hideous, ridiculous, multiform Fear.

This genius caged in an unhealthy slum,
These sneers, these screams, these specters whose swarm
Whirls in hordes gathered in his ear's halls,

This dreamer, awakened by the dread of his abode,
Here, then, is your emblem, Soul of dreams without code,
Whom Reality smothers between these four walls!

The Interarts Translation of Narratives

What was it about the Italian poet's imprisonment? At the age of 31, already highly acclaimed for two previous works, the *Discorsi dell'arte poetica* (Discourses on the Art of Poetry) and the pastoral play *Aminta*, Torquato Tasso (1544-1595) completed what would be his masterpiece: his great epic, *Gerusalemme liberata* (Jerusalem Delivered). Its twenty cantos are based on the historic account of the 1099 liberation of Jerusalem from the Moslems by Christian knights. When Tasso shared his manuscript with some friends prior to its intended publication, he met with such harsh and petty criticism that the shock caused him to have a nervous breakdown. The distraught poet was initially placed in mild confinement but escaped. When he was caught again, he was locked up in the lunatics' wing of a hospital, part of the time constrained in chains.

Eugène Delacroix (1798-1863) painted this scene at least three times. After "Tasso in the Madhouse" (1824, 1939), he called his last interpretation of the historic event "Tasso in Prison." Even more than his depiction, this title, which renders as a jail what would nowadays be called a mental institution, encapsulates the situation as it must have impressed itself on the disturbed poet's mind. The painting shows the young nobleman, well-attired with a perfectly groomed beard and no obvious signs of insanity, sitting in the foreground. With his right elbow perched on a gracefully raised knee, his head is resting on his right fist, in a pose that could be perceived as pensive. He appears much more composed than his visitors, of whom one is standing straddle-legged facing Tasso, while others seem to be leaving the cell through a narrow hallway in the background. Their body language and facial expression seem provocative in the one, dismissive and gloating in the other. The room, primitive with a mud floor, naked walls, and hardly any furniture, is eerily dark.

Baudelaire's sonnet, *Sur le Tasse en prison,* is explicitly based on the painting of this compatriot whom he honored with a monograph (*La vie et l'œuvre d'E.Delacroix,* 1928; *E.Delacroix: His Life and Work,* 1947). The poet adopts central features of Delacroix's interpretation but goes far beyond what the artist depicted. There is not literally a manuscript in Delacroix's painting, neither *"sous son pied convulsif"* (literally "under his convulsive foot") nor anywhere else. While Tasso's biography suggests that he was ill at the time of his confinement, the painter's portrayal does not support this. There is also no terror-enflamed glance in the art work; neither are there suggestions of uproarious laughter.

How does this matter? Do we understand the poem better when reading it in light of Delacroix's work? Do we see new things in the painting after reading the poem, not only with regard to details that might otherwise have escaped our attention, but perhaps even more with regard to things significant by their very absence? In other words, could the very interplay of the two representations—by different artistic means and with seemingly different emphasis—broaden our understanding of each?

Take the manuscript. Historically, this was the crucial prop that unleashed Tasso's mental collapse and thus led to what in the eyes of the literary world of the time—Byron and Lamartine wrote extensively about this—constituted the incarceration of the genius by the uncomprehending world. The mention of the manuscript "under his foot" functions in two ways. As a document that is being stepped upon, it refers to the disrespect and contempt the poet's work encountered before its (ultimately very successful) publication. At the same time, Baudelaire's introduction of the manuscript reminds informed readers of the work's title, and thus entails a suggestion of the irony comprised in the fact that Tasso's loss of liberty was caused by his poetic description of the "liberated" Jerusalem.

Many other metaphors in Baudelaire's ekphrastic poem evoke both the story behind the painting and the identification he felt with the older poet, an identification filtered through, and strangely intensified by, the purported primary aim of the sonnet: the verbal representation of Delacroix's painting. Baudelaire apparently attributes various identities to the two men depicted sideways behind Tasso's chair. His prison is filled with the laughter of critics; did he see the men as representatives of the lesser-gifted poet friends whose derision caused Tasso's mind to lose its focus? Baudelaire describes Fear and Doubt as personified, circling around the distressed prisoner; did he take the two men as impersonations of the two states of mind? In this part of his poetic rendition, Baudelaire thus refers to Delacroix's portrayal rather than to the historic context, interpreting the painter's depiction of the two supporting actors as symbolizations of both the external and the internal realities haunting the Italian poet.

Structurally, the two halves of the sonnet reflect two different inter-pretive stances. In the octet, the French 19th-century poet empathizes with his Italian brother of three centuries back, imagining himself in a similar situation. One senses that he can relate only too well to the doubt about the value of one's work, and to the fear (of failure, ridicule, pro-fanity) that may assail a vulnerable bard in all its horrid manifestations (*hideuse et mu1tiforme*). Even more than Delacroix, Baudelaire under-stands that such dual assault may induce madness, "invite his mind towards the bizarre and the absurd."

In the sextet, by contrast, Baudelaire delves even deeper than both the historical data and the painter's representation. It is now the venue rather than the poet that is sick and messy (a *taudis malsain*). The "four walls," whose all-too-concrete, unpoetic reality suffocates the poet, seem no longer merely the boundaries of his cell, but the all-too-square limita-tions of Life itself. The poet is a dreamer, a soul with obscure fantasies. What shocks him is *l'horreur de son logis*, the horror of his lodgings—presumably not merely the physical condition of his hospital room, but rather the spiritual depravity of his larger environment. This "awakes" him, as Baudelaire puts it. Instead of following the common interpretation of a nervous breakdown as a loss of clarity, Baudelaire recognizes Tasso's state of mind as a loss of his dream-world. Where practically-minded members of society assume that one is awakened into lucidity, the fellow poet understands that this confrontation of the genius with the pettiness of the world is an awakening into insanity.

Baudelaire's poem, as I have attempted to show in my brief dis-cussion, belongs to a category of ekphrasis that takes a visual representa-tion (painting, sculpture, etc.) as a point of departure but, rather than describing and recasting the painter's interpretation of a topic, presents a new reading of the same subject matter. Many musical pieces based on poetic stimuli work in just this way, as I will argue.

139

The second part of this study deals with musical miniatures that are based on complex and extensive verbal models. The first group of three pieces share the fact that their captions evoke the entire narrative of the tale from which they are known. This is true for Ondine, whose story is known to audiences world-wide, retold by many authors and in different media; her name alone immediately brings to mind the mermaid's longing for a soul and subsequent disappointment by man. Puck, Shakespeare's mischievous sprite, inevitably trails behind him the entire plot of the *Midsummer Night's Dream*. And while the sentence "The Fairies are Exquisite Dancers" may not be an equally evident allusion for readers in different countries, Debussy evidently thought that *Peter Pan in Kensington Gardens* was enough of a shared heritage for the caption not to warrant explanations. (In the latter case, we are actually dealing with a three-tiered representational derivation. The music is based on an illustration of a particular aspect of the tale; or, "The Fairies are Exquisite Dancers" constitutes a composer's representation of an illustrator's representation of the poet's representation of the fairies in Kensington Gardens)

The second group encompasses three different examples of how a composer may attempt a musical rendering of some atmospheric aspects alluded to in poems. The mode of referentiality is different in each case, spanning from a single line through a title to a collective heading. *Les sons et les parfums tournent dans l'air du soir* quotes a line from within a Baudelaire poem, and the composer's identification of the source underneath the music not only spares us the task of finding out for ourselves, but—more importantly—leaves no doubt that the larger context of the poem should be understood to come into play when interpreting the music. The poetic sources of *La fille au cheveux de lin* and *Feuilles mortes* are left for us to ascertain; but then, neither of them stems from a place hidden in the midst of a larger lyrical text. The first is the title of a poem by Leconte de Lisle, the second quotes the collective heading used by Gabriel Mourey for a section within his volume *Voix éparses*. The analyses will elaborate just how the music captures various aspects represented in the poems.

The third group deals with the three pieces, explicitly called "poems for piano," that Ravel based on poems from Aloysius Bertrand's collection *Gaspard de la nuit*. The musical rendering of that which is poetically represented is specific here, complex and detailed rather than general and atmospheric, and thus complements the two earlier categories.

NYMPHS, FAIRIES, AND SPRITES

Ondine   (Debussy, *Préludes*, vol. II, no. 8)

Ondine's story is one of the most popular recurring themes in fairy tales. With a name *Ondine* deriving from the French word for wave, *onde*, she is the "daughter of the waves". (Undine, another form of the name, stems from the Latin equivalent, *unda*). A close relative of hers is undoubtedly *The Little Mermaid* by Hans Christian Andersen, the Danish poet whose stories Debussy dearly loved. In comparison with the French Ondine, a creature brought up under water who appeared on land as a beautiful and capricious child-woman distinguished from her mortal sisters more in her character than in physique, Andersen's mermaid is literally a creature between two worlds: she has a woman's upper body but a fish tail instead of legs. An important feature that further sets all mermaids apart from humans is the fact that, while they live in undisturbed playful happiness, they are aware that they have no soul. Mermaids can acquire a soul only if they gain the love of a man. The price to be paid, however, is high: the forfeit of the blissful simplicity and innocence of their underwater lives.

In the opera, the Knight Hugo chooses to marry Ondine, the putative daughter of a poor fisherman and his wife. Having discovered that she is a mermaid, i.e. a being without a "soul," he rejects her and turns to Berthalda, a viscount's daughter. The prince of the underwater realm reacts by calling his daughter back to the world from where she came so that she may no longer be exposed to human unfaithfulness. At the same time he vows to take revenge. During Hugo's and Berthalda's wedding, the water spirits appear, destroying the castle and abducting the Knight to the underwater world where full of remorse he sinks to Ondine's feet.

Andersen's fairy tale version precedes a similar story with Ondine's childhood in the underwater realm, her longing to attain a soul, and her infatuation with the world out there. Having rescued a beautiful young prince whose ship is wrecked in a storm, she longs to be able to join him on land and be loved by him. But, as her old grandmother tells her to her dismay, "What is especially delightful here in the sea - your fishtail - they find ugly up there on earth. ... There you must have two clumsy props they call legs to be thought beautiful." Prompted by her longing, the little mermaid asks help from the sea-witch and obtains a drink that will divide her tail. "But it will hurt: it will be like a sharp sword going through you. Everybody who sees you will say you are the loveliest human child they have ever seen! You will keep your gliding motion... every step you take will be like treading on a sharp knife that cuts through you and makes your blood flow."[80]

French literature knows many adaptations of the Ondine tale; among the best-known are those by Frédéric de la Motte-Fouqué and Jean Giraudoux. Two operas, E. T. A. Hoffmann's *Undine* and Albert Lortzing's *Undine*, are based on de la Motte-Fouqué's text. During Debussy's lifetime, de la Motte-Fouqué's *Ondine* was newly published in a beautiful volume adorned with colored plates by Arthur Rackham. Knowing Debussy's admiration for the Edwardian illustrator, whose images inspired his preludes *Les fées sont d'exquises danseuses*, *La dance de Puck* and possibly *Brouillards*, it seems highly likely that one of these plates may have inspired the composer. The plate reproduced on the following page is one of several that could fit here. Captioned "L'enfance d'Ondine" (Ondine's Childhood), it gives a particularly lovely image of the mermaids and of their maritime realm.

Debussy, fascinated as much with fairies, genies and sprites as with diffused light, changing colors and rippling water, has created in *Ondine* a piece that contains almost all the glistening colors of which a piano is capable, evoking gently rolling waves here, sprinkling foam there. The emotional lightness of a world not concerned with "soul" is expressed in diatonic clusters (see e.g. the tonal contents F G A B♭ C♯ F♯ G A B C♯ in the opening waves of bars 1 and 2, and in bars 3/4,5/6).

In terms of harmonic organization, it is interesting to note that those passages that are perceived by most listeners as depictions of the underwater realm contain a prevalence of chords made up of superimposed tritone + perfect fourth. Introduced in bar 4, these chords appear simultaneously in their chordal and linear versions, as melodic waves and as *acciaccatura* sparkle. They recur in bars 6/7and again in the right-hand part of bars 44-53. A variant, combining a perfect fifth with a tritone, characterizes the downbeats of bars 8/9 and the left-hand part of bars 45-49m.

[80] *Hans Christian Andersen's Fairy Tales: A Selection* (Oxford: Oxford University Press 1959), pp. 76-106; quotations from pp. 91 and 94.

Arthur Rackham, *The Infancy of Undine*
Illustration in Frédéric de la Motte-Fouqué, *Undine* (New York:
Doubleday, Page & Co, 1920) Reprinted with permission of
Harlan Hatcher Library, The University of Michigan

The frolicking of the mermaids, as it were, begins in bar 16. After a long section developed with explicit or implied reference to the dominant pedal A (see particularly bars 3-6 and 11-13), bars 14/15 open the window to a new perspective. D, the tonic indicated in the key signature and confirmed in the final bars of the prelude, enters with an arpeggiated triad and superimposed perfect fifths (D-A-E), while the change of perspective is metrically emphasized with a sudden *hemiola* in bar 14. The mermaids' tune, appropriately reminiscent of the Glockenspiel melody in *La Mer*, develops around a repeated inner-voice pedal A, with pitches taken from the Lydian scale on D and characterized by slurred note pairs. The tune's central line (see bars 20-21), enveloped in the small rippling waves of a double-note trill, soon gives way to a more thoughtful

The mermaids' song: introduction, main phrase, transition, contrasting phrase, recap main phrase

frame of "sparkling, splashing water"

passage in chordal texture (bars 22-25). Here, the bass leaves the tonic keynote in the direction of the dominant (A), from where the initial line of the mermaids' song is recapitulated (bars 26/27). Framed by the *scintillant* and *doux* (sparkling and soft) passage of bars 11-13 on the one hand, bars 28/29 on the other hand, this frolicking section seems to present an image of untroubled bliss.

The short unison motif that develops from the "sparkle" brings about the significant change of mood: the playfulness yields to what appears as its opposite: chromatic yearning in *retenu* (slowed down; see bars 30/31).

bars 31/32

One almost inevitably imagines the longing for "soul" depicted in this sad, passionate gesture.

The following, larger section of the prelude is devoted to this longing. Over an augmented triad as a protracted pedal chord (see bars 32-37: E♭-G-B), the yearning chromatic gesture is quoted once in its passionate original version (albeit transposed; see bars 34/35), then with a more resigned ending (see bars 36/37, with *diminuendo* close). The mermaid's tune and the answer from the underwater guardians follows (compare bars 38/39 with bars 16/17 and bars 40/41 with bars 18/19). The yearning recurs in bars 42/43, this time in a tempo requested as *le double plus lent* (twice as slow). While the chordal accompaniment of bars 44-53 evokes the dreamlike atmosphere of the marine world (*rubato* and *un peu au-dessous du mouvement* = somewhat below tempo), the treble recalls and further develops the yearning, now in double minor thirds. The emphasis given to the expression in the earlier indication "twice as slow" is here spelled out in eighth-note values.

Back in tempo regarding both the general motion and the particular figure, the yearning is heard once more in the short section spanning bars 54-61. The inner-voice repeated pedal on A reminds one of the mermaids' tune, but it is here joined by a secondary pedal-note on G, which sounds both in conjunction with the A and as the release of all two-note slurs in the bass. The distinct chromatic outline of the bass figure, enhanced in bars 60/61 by a parallel in the middle strand, speaks once again of the obsession with passionate feelings—feelings that mermaids hope to gain through a loving relationship with a human.

When, in bars 62-64, the listener is reminded of the "sparkling and soft" nature that framed the mermaids' naive frolicking in bars 11-13 and 28/29, the subtle change in the lower register (B♭ rising to a double-octave D♭ instead of the simple pedal-note A before) seems to suggest that on returning to the underwater realm, the framework is by no means quite the same as it was in times of innocence. In the coda (bars 65-74), the tonic pedal D, heard for the first time in the course of the piece, is not presented as the root of an unambiguous harmonic resolution. Instead, the gently gushing and surging arpeggiated chords above it alternate with the two cross-related chords D major and F♯ major before finally settling on the tonic triad: another image of what seems like a very fine but definite fissure. As in most versions of the fairy tale, the mermaid whose love has been accepted by a mortal man but then rejected must return to the underwater realm, never to regain the blissful state.

La danse de Puck   (Debussy, *Préludes*, vol. I, no. 11)

Puck is, of course, the sprite from Shakespeare's *Midsummer Night's Dream*. In this magical fantasy about courtly lovers, an ethereal fairy kingdom ruled by a king and queen, he is the mischievous elf who be-witches them all, before vanishing again swiftly into the depths of the Shakespearean forest.

Debussy is known to have had in his library the edition from the New Temple Shakespeare series, with illustrations by Arthur Rackham.[81] Following is a brief description of the events in Shakespeare's *Midsummer Night's Dream*,[82] with on the facing page Puck as seen by Rackham.

> *There once lived a tiny Fairy King whose name was Oberon. His Queen—Titania—was a beautiful fairy. Fairy King Oberon and Queen Titania often quarrelled because Titania refused to give a little boy, her foster child, to King Oberon for a page. King Oberon finally grew so angry that he determined to punish his Queen. So he sent for Puck. Little Puck was the merriest, maddest elf imaginable. He had the happiest, jolliest face in all Fairyland, and would laugh and laugh while all the time playing pranks and jokes. Everybody loved him. So King Oberon sent for little Puck to be revenged on Titania!*

[81] As mentioned in the previous chapter, Debussy greatly admired this Edwardian illustrator. Representations of characters from various fairy-tales inspired several of his other compositions (see e.g., in the second volume of preludes, the piece *Les fées sont d'exquises danseuses*, after the caption of a Rackham illustration in Barrie's *Peter Pan in Kensington Gardens*, and *Ondine*, after the tale by F. de la Motte-Fouqué, which Rackham also illustrated).

[82] Adapted and excerpted from the tale told by Fay Adams Britton in her book *Shakespearean Fairy Tales* (Chicago: The Reilly & Britton Co., 1907), p. 9-19.

Illustration by Arthur Rackham in William Shakespeare,
A Midsummer Night's Dream (New York: Doubleday, 1929), p.27
Reprinted with permission by Harlan Hatcher Library,
The University of Michigan.

147

"Come hither, Puck," said Oberon to the funny little fellow. "Fetch me a flower which the maids call Love-in-idleness. The juice of this flower squeezed on the eyes of those who sleep will wake them, and when they wake they will love the first thing they see, no matter if it be a cat, a lion, a bear, or a monkey." And Oberon continued to little Puck, "Titania so vexes me that I intend to squeeze the juice of this flower on her eyes as she sleeps, and I will not remove the spell—which I can do with another charm I know—until she gives me the boy for my page." This was great fun for Puck, and he ran off clapping his hands and laughing until his sides ached, thinking how the Queen would act and how angry she would be.

Titania was just retiring for the night. Her couch was a bank of wild thyme, cowslips, and violets, under a canopy of roses. When she was cosily wrapped in her coverlet of snakeskin, a chorus of tiny Fairies fanned her and sang her to sleep, and this being done, they hastened away to perform duties Titania placed upon them. When all had gone, Oberon stole up to the sleeping Queen, squeezed the juice of the flower on her eyelids, and then hurried off into the wood.

As it was about time for Titania to awaken, King Oberon hurried back to her bower, and much to his surprise he saw a clown standing near. After staring at the foolish fellow for a moment, the King quickly waved his wand, and behold! the clown's head was that of a donkey. Immediately Queen Titania awakened, and as her eyes fell upon the strange creature she gave an exclamation of delight. The juice of the flower caused her to believe this monstrous being the most beautiful thing she had ever seen. She wound her arms around the big, big neck of the donkey, and commanded all her Fairy attendants to wait upon him. The foolish donkey finally fell asleep, while poor Titania twined a garland of flowers for his neck. Then, lo and behold! King Oberon appeared, and teased and made so much fun of her that she told him if he would stop he might have the small boy for his page. This, of course, was just what King Oberon wanted, and he was so happy he immediately removed the spell and Fairy Titania was astonished that she should have loved so ugly a beast as the donkey, and asked King Oberon to drive him away. This the King did, but not until he removed the donkey's head and returned the clown his own. King Oberon and his charming Queen were always happy after that and truly loved each other ever after. And Puck—dear, laughing, little Puck! He continued his merry pranks secure in the friendship of everybody.

148

Debussy must have imagined little Puck skipping joyfully as he went about his tasks, perhaps sometimes leaping high from the sheer fun he took in his somewhat mischievous deeds. (He even calls this prelude "Puck's Dance", although Shakespeare does not actually mention the elf's dancing.)

To represent this graceful little sprite, Debussy creates a number of musical gestures that very aptly depict how lovable Puck must have been, and how he obviously enjoyed every moment of his existence. The main motif of the piece is characterized by a chain of dotted-note figures, each slightly "skipping" off the keyboard at the end: the articulation is indicated with two-note slurs and *staccato*-dots, so that the rhythmically short note is even further abridged.

Inserted in this gamboling motion are a shorter and a longer whirl or twist (see the second halves of bars 2 and 3). After a short interruption by King Oberon's motif (see bars 6/7), Debussy has Puck frolicking some more, this time with exuberant leaps (see bars 8-12). A little later (bars 13-16), he can be seen dashing down a slope, with what sounds like an expanding trill *below* B♭ (not, as most trills go, *on* a pitch—but then Puck isn't like most other creatures). Now Debussy advises the performer to hurry *(pressez)*. Is this where Puck surprises the disputing lovers? He certainly seems to be teasing when we hear the *staccato* chords with their chromatically ascending treble line and the jumps through all octaves at the end (bars 18-23). One can almost see him poking fun at the seriousness of the lovers' quarrel when the composer writes signs for exaggerated dramatic expression over "sighs" supported by *tremolo* (bars 24-29).

The subsequent longer section (bars 30-48), is determined by the double second D♭/E♭ in the highest register and a pedal-note E♭ in the bass. At the indication *aérien* (airy), Puck is trying to be quiet—possibly so as to allow the lovers to sleep and get a chance to squeeze the magical juice into their eyes. Or is it Titania resting here? The gentle tune in parallel sixth chords and *doucement soutenu* (softly held back), written in an enharmonic A major / F♯ minor (bars 32/33, 36/37), is interspersed with a slightly more assertive motif in E♭ major (bars 34/35). While the sleepers continue to doze (the right hand and the pedal-note in the bass remain very soft), King Oberon appears once again (bars 41 and 43). Soon afterwards, this part of the story draws to a close (see the *cédez* = give way / slow down in bar 48).

Puck, however, continues to tease (bars 49-52). But what is that? Something really drastic seems to occur, judging by the suddenly exploding *sff*, a very loud, very accented sound, enhanced with preceding *acciaccaturas* (bar 53). Is this the clown with the donkey's head? The subsequent bars might then be depicting the various fairies rushing about their unfamiliar new duties, and Puck in the midst of it all, having great fun. In bars 63-66, Puck is heard skipping in the treble, and the *tremolo* in the lowest part suggests that things are still somewhat dramatic, while in the center of the texture, a melody in C minor might represent—perhaps Titania? King Oberon and Puck—both skipping and teasing—are heard several more times before the sprites, with alternating pentachords from A♭ major, E major and C minor, vanish from our sight into the thicket of the Shakespearean forest.

"Les fées sont d'exquises danseuses"

(Debussy, *Préludes*, vol. II, no. 4)

Debussy has set the epigraph to this prelude in quotation marks, identifying it clearly as a citation. The wording originates from a caption under an illustration by Arthur Rackham in J. M. Barrie's *Peter Pan in Kensington Garden,* which picks up a line from the text that reads "The fairies are exquisite dancers." The composer's daughter, Chou-chou, then seven years old, received the children's book as a Christmas gift from her father's friend, the conductor Robert Godet. Debussy, forever charmed by the world of fairy tales responded with this delightful piano piece. Rackham's graceful illustration is reprinted on the facing page.

In Barrie's *Peter Pan,* the dancing fairies are intrinsically connected with children; in fact he tells us that during the time when children were not allowed in the Gardens, the fairies were completely absent, returning however in great numbers as soon as the children reappeared. It might be interesting to recollect some of the thoughts Barrie expressed in the relevant chapter of his *Peter Pan.* In "Lookout Time" we read the following:

> *"It is frightfully difficult to know much about the fairies, and almost the only thing known for certain is that there are fairies wherever there are children. I have heard of children who declared that they had never seen a fairy. Very likely if they said this in the Kensington Gardens, they were standing looking at a fairy all the*

time. The reason they were cheated was that she pretended to be something else. This is one of their best tricks. They usually pretend to be flowers, because the court sits in the Fairies' Basin, and there are so many flowers there, and all along the Baby Walk, that a flower is the thing least likely to attract attention."

And after describing the fun-loving, purposeless everyday life of the fairies, in which the idea to do things because they are "useful" is completely absent, the poet continues:

"The fairies are exquisite dancers, and that is why one of the first things the baby does is to sign to you to dance to him and then to cry when you do it. They hold their great balls in the open air, in what is called a fairy ring. For weeks afterwards you can see the ring on the grass. It is not there when they begin, but they make it by waltzing round and round. [...] Peter Pan is the fairies' orchestra. He sits in the middle of the ring, and they would never dream of having a smart dance nowadays without him. "[83]

Besides the verbal citation, the music contains its own, often-mentioned quotation: the single-voiced melodic curve in bars 117-120 cites the horn call from the overture of Carl Maria von Weber's opera *Oberon*. Its protagonist, Oberon is, of course, best known from Shakespeare's play *A Midsummer Night's Dream*. While the plot on which Weber's opera is based is somewhat different from that of Shakespeare's play, Oberon is still the Fairy King, and the allusion is very appropriate.

The melodic quotation is not, however, a simple borrowed line. Debussy has incorporated it into the prelude in such a way that the Fairy King's motif takes shape in a gradual development, as if emerging from innocent material. The musical allusion thus appears as the goal towards which the piece was aiming all along, rather than as a sudden revelation:

bars 58-61

bars 67-70

bars 117-120

[83] J. M. Barrie, *Peter Pan in Kensington Gardens*, illustrated by Arthur Rackham (London: Hodder & Stoughton, 1912), p. 52-66

Arthur Rackham, illustration "Fairies are Exquisite Dancers."
In J. M. Barrie, *Peter Pan in Kensington Garden*, plate p. 58.London:
Hodder & Stoughton, 1912. Reprinted with permission by
Harlan Hatcher Library, The University of Michigan.

The prelude begins with broken-chord quintuplets. The overall impression of tonality is of a somewhat concealed Dorian mode on E♭ (a scale with the notes E♭ F G♭ A♭ B♭ C D♭ E♭). This tonal background is colored, particularly in several metrically stressed moments, with chromatic neighbors (see e.g. the very first note of the piece) or significant alterations (see e.g. the G♮ on the third beats of bars 1-4, which converts the harmonic resolution into a tainted but clearly perceptible E♭-major chord!). The perception that E♭ serves indeed as the root of this section is substantiated in bars 5-10. Yet hardly has the listener been reassured than the tonal center is temporarily switched to D♭ (see the Dorian scale on D♭ in bars 11-14). From there it returns via A♭ (bars 15/16) to E♭.

The special features of the initial figure set the stage for the characters we are to imagine. A soft shade, a high register and a very swift motion with quintuplets in the eighth-note in a tempo described as *rapide et léger* (fast and light) provide the basic color; a high degree of repetitiveness (bars 3 and 4 are identical with bar 1) and very restricted tonal material[84] add to the basic shade and give this figure a whizzing, buzzing quality. While many a child may want to imagine fairies in his or her own way—and possibly differently from the picture conjured up by Debussy's music—Rackham's drawing suggests an image of fairies not as flowers (as stipulated by Barrie's words) but as beautiful dragonflies!

This "whizzing wings" motif frames both the first and the last sections of the prelude (see bars 1-4, 18/20-23 and bars 101-104, 106, 108-116, 121). The pictures inside the frame are dominated by trills on octave-displaced B♭s (see bars 5-11d, 17/19 and bars 105/107). Here, a distinct color is achieved through the use of continued fifths intervals underneath the trills, while the *sempre leggierissimo* evokes again the very light flutter of transparent dragonfly wings. The fifths, empty at the outset (bar 5), then supplemented with thirds in the left hand to give an impression of E♭ major, begin shifting in parallel motion as the harmonic anchoring loosens: in bars 11/12 still over a chord, in bars 13/14 varied and without support. After a short halt and a renewed thrust of energy, which leads to interlocking bars of octave-displaced fifths under B♭ trills and "whizzing wings," the initial section ends with scattered utterances interrupted by rests (see bars 21 and 23), a musical image suggesting that the fairies hitherto seen dancing now stop whizzing and settle down one after the other.

---

[84]See that bar 1, beat 1 and bar 2, beat 1 are identical, and bar 2, beat 3 differs from bar 1, beat 3 only in one note.

Between this moment and the resumption of the initial picture in the final section (which never makes it to a similar climax but restrains itself to quoting the color of the image), the spectator watching the fairies' dance is treated to two different scenes. One consists of what might be interpreted as ten separate, short solos and *pas de deux*. The other section is shorter, strongly unified in all aspects of texture, tonal orientation and material, and seems to depict something like a still portrait of the fairy community.

Within the first scene, each of the dance presentations derives from the concept of a four-bar phrase that may then be individually expanded or otherwise changed. Each is individually characterized, but all ten are nevertheless strung together as a delicate chain of events inspired by the same mood and a continuing development of material. (Some of them are shown in the excerpts below).

- The initial four-bar phrase (bars 24-27) retains the Dorian mode on E♭ established at the beginning, but supports it with A♭ as a pedal. The tune is in triple octaves enriched with conso-

bars 24-27

nant chords, the dynamic color is luscious (*mf-p-cresc.*), the attitude *rubato* and the register encompasses five octaves: a statement about as passionate as fairies can get.

- The second phrase, also spanning four bars, prolongs the A♭ pedal and, at its beginning, a hint of the previous chordal texture. The gesture, however, is much more restrained here, almost bashful:

bars 28-31

the tempo is steady (*au mouvement*), with a hesitation at the end (*cédez*), the dynamic level drops suddenly to *pp* from where it recedes even further, the register is low, and the right-hand descent moves in chromatically shifted minor chords.

- The third phrase (bars 32-35) seems to feature a third fairy dancer with yet a different character. Retaining the idea of contrary motion from the preceding phrase (bar 32) and the chromatic outline (particularly in the lowest voice: F♯ G♮ G♯—G F♯ F E), this phrase adds sustained notes in the high register (see the right-hand A, the left-hand A/B and, indirectly, the repeated tied C♯). The ambit is still limited but now plac-

bars 32-35

ed high on the key-board, the movement is somewhat freer (*sans rigeur* = without rigidity in tempo), and the expressive level is raised to a regular *p*.

- The fourth phrase of the dance resentations (bars 36-41) is more complex. The four bars that may be recognized as constituting the essence of this phrase are interrupted by a two-bar echo (see bars 38/39). The texture contains three strands: a repeated A/B pedal retained from the previous phrase (for purely practical reasons played alternately in the right and left hands), a tune in double octaves characterized by a grandiose sweep in dotted rhythm that encompasses four large intervals (a fourth, a fifth and two tritones), and a bass figure in falling fifths (see bar 36 C♯-F♯-B,

bars 36-41

bar 37 A-D). Chromatic steps are absent; instead, there is a chromatic shift from one bar to the other (see the prominent D♯-C♯ in both hands of bar 36 followed by equally prominent D♮-C♮ pairs in bar 37). The two bars after the echo recede in both tempo and textural density.

- The transition to the fifth phrase within this section (bars 42-45) is almost imperceptible on the motivic level: the two upper parts of bar 42 are an enharmonic reading of bar 41, and bars 43 and 44 constitute a pitch development from there. Meanwhile, there is a distinct tonal *caesura* as the bass returns in a tritone step from the previous D to the earlier A♭ pedal.

- Phrase six evolves from phrase five by retaining all pitches (see bar 46). The texture, featuring a gently tumbling treble over a fading chord, is again different from that found in all preceding four-bar phrases. Structurally as well, this phrase establishes a new pattern. Instead of four units there seem to be eight, containing a varied repetition and metrical irregularities. The first half (bars 46-49, beat 1) consists of two three-beat (i.e. whole-bar) units followed by two two-beat units, the last of which brings about an accented (*mf*) harmonic change: E♮/G♮ instead of the earlier E♭/G♭. The distinct *hemiola* effect in the upper voice is countered, and invalidated, as it were, by the downbeat position of the bass pedal. The second half of the phrase continues the *hemiola* pattern (with the pedal A♭ integrated this time) and repeats the E♭/G♭ to E♮/G♮ progression.

bars 46-50

- Phrase seven (bars 52-56) is yet different. It picks up the melodic outline of the previous *hemiola* unit, thus guaranteeing a smooth connection from the previous phrase. At the same time, D♭ is established as a new pedal-note, and a chordally-supported middle-strand tune emerges in bars 53-55 (see B♭-C♭-C♮), while the upper voice develops a simpler figure (bar 53, repeated in bar 54) into a flourish (bar 55). For the structural understanding of this phrase and the following one it is essential to perceive bar 55 as leading into bar 58: both the progressive development in the top voice and the chordally-supported tune with irregular chromatic ascent in all voices endorse this view. Bar 56 is then an extra bar at the end of the seventh phrase (repeating much of what initiated that phrase in bar 51/52), and bar 57 is an introductory bar preceding what is heard as bar 1 of the next phrase.

- The eighth phrase (in its core beginning with bar 58) tags onto the preceding phrase in that it has at the end not one but two extra bars that reiterate the initial bar (compare bars 62/63 with bar 58). Retaining the D♭ pedal and the treble flourish (albeit now in double speed; compare bars 58, 62 and 63 with bar 55), this phrase introduces as its tune the earliest version of what is to become the "Oberon motif."

- The ninth phrase (bars 64-66) serves as a kind of appendix: chord and flourish (again in slower motion; compare bar 64 with bar 60) constitute a continuation from the preceding phrase, while the texture and the *hemiola* organization (bars 65/66 house three two-beat units) are reminiscent of the sixth phrase.

- Finally, the tenth phrase (the core of which spans bars 67-70) varies the "Oberon motif," now in the highest voice over a circling bass line (G-A-B-A♭) complemented by middle-strand arpeggiations. This phrase, once again, is rounded off with two extra bars recalling the phrase beginning, here in a powerful *crescendo*.

The section that follows represents a large-scale contrast in almost every respect. Conceived in ternary form, with bars 73-83 and 89-100 as corresponding outer sections, the twenty-eight bars are united under a continuing trill on the treble A. In contrast to the prelude's preceding section with its clearly defined small phrases, meter and small-scale structure hardly play a role here. Owing to the melodic beginning in duplets (see bar 75), the many syncopations and long tied chords, as well as to the generally reduced tempo (Debussy requests *En retenant* = in holding back / slowing down), the framing sections of the ternary form convey a floating quality. In a mood described by the composer as *doux et rêveur* (soft and dreaming), the fairies are seen dreamily dancing to an allusion of Brahms' famous waltz for piano duet in A♭ major (see bars 79-83 and 96-100). The short middle section (bars 84-88) introduces an element of contrast mainly through accents (see the emphasis in the trill on the downbeats of bars 84 and 86 as well as the obvious *sforzati* in bar 87) and a sudden contraction of tempo at the very end (*serrez*).

After an abridged recapitulation of the "whizzing wings" section in bars 101-116, which ends with the notes of the last five-note chord ringing on in the pedal, the final version of the "Oberon motif" is heard, *più pp*, like a very faint echo. The Fairy King thus enthroned, the prelude concludes in a soft six-bar coda with a single final D♭.

EVENING HARMONY, MORNING DELIGHT, AND DEATH

"Les sons et les parfums tournent dans l'air du soir"

(Debussy, *Préludes*, vol. I, no. 4)

Debussy's fourth prelude in Book I takes as a verbal reference a line from the poem *Harmonie du soir* (Evening Harmony) by Charles Baudelaire. The poem appears in Baudelaire's famous collection of 1857, *Les fleurs du mal* (The Flowers of Evil).

Voici venir les temps ou vibrant sur la tige	1
Chaque fleur s'évapore ainsi qu'un encensoir;	2
Les sons et les parfums tournent dans l'air du soir;	3
Valse mélancholique et langoureux vertige!	4
Chaque fleur s'évapore ainsi qu'un encensoir;	5
Le violon frémit comme un coeur qu'on afflige;	6
Valse mélancholique et langoureux vertige!	7
Le ciel est triste et beau comme un grand reposoir.	8
Le violon frémit comme un coeur qu'on afflige,	9
Un coeur tendre, qui hait le néant vaste et noir!	10
Le ciel est triste et beau comme un grand reposoir.	11
Le soleil s'est noyé dans son sang qui se fige.	12
Un coeur tendre, qui hait le néant vaste et noir,	13
Du passé lumineux recueille tout vestige!	14
Le soleil s'est noyé dans son sang qui se fige...	15
Ton souvenir en moi luit comme un ostensoir!	16

On the next page, I give two translations for this very special poem. One is my own (somewhat inspired by Richard Howard). Since I do not try to rhyme, this version stays closest to Baudelaire's metaphors. The other is by Joseph M. Bernstein, whose translation is of interest in the present context because he has attempted to find an English equivalent for the French rhyme scheme, on which also Debussy's musical realization draws.

(a)   Now come the times when swaying on its stem
Each flower like incense evaporates;
The sounds and perfumes circle in the night—
Languorous waltz and ling'ring, dizzy trance!

Each flower like incense evaporates;
The violin trembles like a heart betrayed;
Languorous waltz and ling'ring, dizzy trance!
The sky is sad and splendid like a shrine.

The violin trembles like a heart betrayed,
A tender heart that hates the vast black void!
The sky is sad and splendid like a shrine;
The sun has drowned in its own clotting blood.

A tender heart that hates the vast black void,
From radiant pasts recalls all its remains.
The sun has drowned in its own clotting blood.
In me your image—like a monstrance—shines.

(b)   The seasons make shake in violent vibration
Flowers that evaporate in a sacred room;
In the air of the night turn in sound and perfume;
- Waltz vertiginous in intoxication!

Flowers that evaporate in a sacred room;
The Violin shivers like a heart in agitation;
- Waltz vertiginous in intoxication!
The sky is sad as a shrine that the flames consume.

The Violin shivers like a heart in agitation,
A heart that hates annihilation like the Tomb!
- The sky is sad as a shrine that the flames consume;
The Sun is drowned in his blood's coagulation.

A heart that hates annihilation like the Tomb
Gathers the Past into an Hallucination;
- The Sun is drowned in his blood's coagulation;
Thy memory haunts me like an aching Womb![85]

[85]The first, more literal translation is mine. The second, rhymed one is by Joseph M. Bernstein, published in *Baudelaire, Rimbaud, Verlaine: Selected Verse and Prose Poems* (Secaucus, N.J.: The Citadel Press, 1947). Reprinted with permission by Carol Publishing Group.

Debussy has taken as his epigraph the third line of the poem, invoking sounds and scents floating in the evening breeze. He may have been intrigued by this poem for a variety of reasons. The poem turns on only two rhyme sounds arranged in the doubled closed-stanza form *abba-baab*. The structure of the poem is unusual because of the abundant use of refrain lines. Beginning with the second stanza, the first and third lines of each stanza repeat the second and fourth lines of the preceding one.[86] The representation of the lines by numbers demonstrates this clearly:

1	5=2	9=6	13=10
2	6	10	14
3	7=4	11=8	15=12
4	8	12	16

Seven topics can be identified within the poem. They are (1) sensual impressions of music (sounds, violins, waltz), (2) scents (flower, perfumes, incense), (3) subtle movements (swaying, gyrating in the evening air, vertiginous, trembling), (4) as well as attributes of a predominantly somber mood (melancholy, languorous, distressed, sad). These sensual impressions are mixed with words reflecting (5) existential aspects (shrine, vast black nothingness, monstrance), as well as with (6) luminous images (sun, luminous past, shining) and dramatic expressions (to drown, clotting blood).

The three outstanding features of the poetic model are thus (a) the limitation to two rhyme sounds, (b) the regular alternation of new material with recall of previous lines, and (c) the seven topic areas. Debussy's musical realization contains correlations with each of them which, while subtle, are nevertheless striking:

(a)   Just as Baudelaire concluded the sixteen lines of his poem using only two rhyme sounds, so Debussy creates this prelude using predominantly two intervals: the perfect fourth and the tritone. These intervals provide the main building blocks both horizon-

[86]Several kinds of French poems, like the *villanelle* and the *lai nouveau*, use lines as refrains. Generally, however, the proportion is different, with fewer repeated lines within much longer poems. The particular line arrangement shown in the table above is derived from a form of Malay origin, called a *pantoum*. Baudelaire's use of it is significant enough to perpetuate the name of the form for students of French poetry. However, it is rare enough to be the one and only example regularly quoted as evidence of the form in Western literature. Thus one may rightly assume that it struck Debussy as quite unusual. In addition, the original *pantoum* (though not Baudelaire's adaptation) closes with the opening line and thus comes full circle.

and vertically. Melodically, the prelude's principal phrase (see bars 1-2) features in its first half an ascending perfect fourth (E-A) followed by a falling tritone (B♭-E); this is complemented in the second half of the phrase by a similar beginning rounded off with a falling perfect fourth (F♯-C♯). The falling fourth is prolonged throughout bars 3, 4, 5 and 7. The melodic fourth also plays a role in bars 13 and 15 as well as, indirectly, in bar 14 (interlocking fourths: A♯-D♯ and C♯-F♯).

Vertically, Debussy constructs (out of the much greater number of possible combinations) four chords made up of a perfect fourth interlocking with a tritone.

If, for easier comparison, we transposed these chords onto C, they would read:

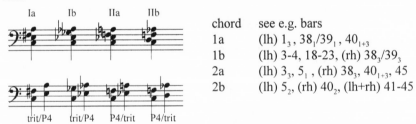

chord	see e.g. bars
1a	(lh) 1_3, $38_1/39_1$, 40_{1+3}
1b	(lh) 3-4, 18-23, (rh) $38_3/39_3$
2a	(lh) 3_3, 5_1, (rh) 38_3, 40_{1+3}, 45
2b	(lh) 5_2, (rh) 40_2, (lh+rh) 41-45

(b) Just as Baudelaire, from the second stanza of his poem onwards, alternates repetition of previously heard lines with new ones, so Debussy creates an evolving structure. Corresponding to the poem's four stanzas, one can recognize in this the prelude four sections followed by a short coda. Each section introduces some new material that, however, is immediately interwoven with earlier components—thus freely imitating the *pantoum* structure. Let us explore this in some detail.

162

- In section I (bars 1-8), Debussy begins by establishing five components: A as the bass pedal, A major as the predominant tonality, the melodic design based on the perfect fourth + tritone intervals, the first of the chords derived from the same two intervals, and the metric design that will remain characteristic for the main theme of this prelude: a five-four bar of, as the dotted bar line shows, three-four and two-four fused, as if in an aborted waltz idea. The introduction of all five components happens virtually at once, within the first bar! After that, the second bar is so obviously derived from the first that it does not need explanation.
Bars 3-5 expand the falling fourth melodic interval, retain the bass pedal, but add new versions of the interlocking-interval chord that, in addition, move in parallel shifts. In bar 5, still supported by the A pedal, the perfect fourth interval C-G is extended into B♭, thus paving the way for the diminished seventh chord in bar 6 that redefines these pitches (D♭-E from chord 2b becomes C♯-E). Bars 7/8 very obviously repeat bars 5/6.
- The second section (bars 9-17) sets out by introducing a new chord and a new texture over a continuing pedal-note A in the bass. The new chord is the augmented triad; the texture features three simple strands, pitting a sustained or repeated three-octave A against chromatically moving three-octave parallels E♯-F♯-G-F♯-E♯ and a three-octave C♯ that is repeated in the left hand and ornamented in the right. During the first four bars of this section that establish these new components, the two characteristic intervals of the prelude are absent. Thereafter, they recur all the more insistently. Bars 13-15 feature shifting superimposed tritones in the middle strand (bar 13: F-B-F, bar 14: E-A♯-E, bar 15: F-B-F) as well as two in the upper part (bar 13: D♯-A-D♯, bar 14: C♯-G-C♯). The melodic progressions in perfect fourths (see bars 13 and 15: D♯-G♯) and the interlocking fourths in bar 14 have already been mentioned. The second section brings something new again: Debussy's favorite trill with octave displacement,[87] here on C♯-D♯. Emerging from the left-hand part in bars 15/16, this idiosyncratic trill figure is then taken over by the right hand,

---

[87]Compare this figure in Debussy's Prelude, *Les sons et les parfums...*, bars 15-24d, with similar ones in his Preludes, *Violes* (bars 33-37) and *Le vent dans la plaine* throughout.

while the left hand comes in by recalling chord 1b (see
F-G♯-B-C♯) arranged in a quasi-melodic pattern. The same
chord is shifted down one semitone in bar 19, up again in bar
20, and down again for the remaining bars. This chromatic
parallel shift is, again, not new in this piece but itself a recollection of the similar chromatic shift back and forth of the
superimposed tritones in bars 13-15, and of the parallel shifts
in bars 3/4.

- Section III (bars 24-30) begins with a "refrain", both on the
level of the musical material, quoting the prelude's initial
phrase in bars 24/25 and 37/38 in the original key, and on the
level of transformation, recalling the chromatic shift downwards (see the semitone transposition in bars 27, 28, 31/32 and
33/34). In addition, there are partial recollections of the principal phrase in the sequenced falling fourths of bars 28/29 (see
in the right hand: G-D, F-C, E-B; the octaves are characteristically filled with alternating perfect fourths and tritones) and in
the extension of bar 39. One of these partial quotations serves
as a link between the old and the new; the G♭-D♭ that, in the
bass of bar 27, opens the section with the A♭-major key
signature, is nothing other than the enharmonically redefined
falling fourth F♯-C♯ from the beginning of the piece.
Only two components are truly new in this section, but they
are conspicuous enough. In bar 30, Debussy uses the established five-four meter to introduce a chromatic version of an
imperfect cadence. Over an E♭ pedal that represents the dominant of the current A♭-major tonality), chromatic lines in triple
parallel octaves (a recalled device) connect a B♭-minor chord
with an E♭^{7} (i.e. ii and V^7 respectively in A♭ major), passing on
beat 4 through a chord that sounds like D major. Immediately
after this new harmonic component, Debussy introduces a new
melodic component: a falling arpeggiated A♭-six-five chord,
rubato, that is later picked up in bars 33 and 37—albeit in
slightly different rhythmic organization.

- Section IV (bars 41-49) is again a blend of recollection and
new elements. We hear "refrain" material in bars 44; also, the
same material is developed in bars 45-47 (right-hand part
only). In addition, bar 49 recalls what in bar 30 was interpreted as the chromatic version of an imperfect cadence, here

shifted one semitone up (compare bar 49 with bar 30). Bars 41-45$_1$ are based on chord 2b, while the three-octave chromatic shift back and forth in bars 46-48 (see in both hands: D♭-C-D♭-C-D♭) is modeled on the same device in bars 9-12. What is new in this section is the texture and melodic treatment in bars 41-44, the accompanying chords in bars 44-47, and the arpeggiated chords in bars 47/48. Finally, the coda (bars 50-53) consists literally of nothing but a fourfold, ornamented A-major chord—old material. Debussy's repeated approach to this chord with all-whole-tone *acciaccaturas* (thus using the raised fourth degree of the A-major scale) is, however, unusual and introduces, together with the little melodic figure in bar 51, two more new elements—thus concluding the prelude, as did Baudelaire's poem, with a line heard only once.

(c)   Just as Baudelaire's imagery in *Harmonie du soir* distinguishes seven realms of sensual or emotive impressions, so Debussy uses seven distinctly different textures in this prelude.

[1]   bass pedal + three-octave tune + doubled chords
     (see e.g. bars 1/2)

[2]   bass pedal + chromatically shifting chords + single-voiced tune (see bars 3-5)

[3]   three-octave pedal note + three-octave, partly ornamented secondary pedal + three-octave chromatic shift back and forth (bars 9-12: three-octave A + three-octave C♯ [partially ornamented] + three-octave E♯-F♯-G-F♯-E♯-F♯-G-F♯)

[4]   trill with octave displacement + chromatically shifted chords (see bars 18-23)

[5]   homophonic *portato* quavers
     (see bars 6, 8, 29, 34-36; even 40)

[6]   single-voiced *arpeggios* (see bars 31, 33, 37)

[7]   two-octave *legato* broken-chord motion in regular sixteenth-notes + four-octave tune (see bars 41-44)

The correlations between the poetic structure and imagery on the one hand and the musical material and coloring on the other hand are thus subtle and complex but, to this musician's mind, exquisitely intriguing and convincing. They paint, as it were, the synaesthetic experience Baudelaire captures so well in a different medium.

La fille aux cheveux de lin (Debussy, *Préludes*, vol. I, no. 8)

The caption of this prelude, which translates as "The Girl with the Flaxen Hair", may have two sources. As a well-documented literary quotation, the phrase is from the title of a poem by Lecomte de Lisle and refers to one of his "four Scottish beauties." At the same time, girls with flaxen hair epitomize naiveté and gentle character in the visual arts. Here is the poem and, on the facing page, an English translation.[88]

La fille aux cheveux de lin

Sur la luzerne en fleur assise
Qui chante dès le frais matin?
C'est la fille aux cheveux de lin,
La belle aux lèvres de cerise.
 L'amour, au clair soleil d'été,
 Avec l'alouette a chanté.

Ta bouche a des couleurs divines,
Ma chère, et tente le baiser!
Sur l'herbe en fleur veux-tu causer,
Fille aux cils longs, aux boucles fines?
 L'amour, au clair soleil d'été,
 Avec l'alouette a chanté.

Ne dis pas non, fille cruelle!
Ne dis pas oui! J'entendrai mieux
Le long regard de tes grands yeux
Et ta lèvre rose, ô ma belle!
 L'amour, au clair soleil d'été,
 Avec l'alouette a chanté.

Adieu les daims, adieu les lièvres
Et les rouges perdrix! Je veux
Baiser le lin de tes cheveux,
Presser la pourpre de tes lèvres!
 L'amour, au clair soleil d'été,
 Avec l'alouette a chanté.[89]

[88]To my knowledge, no published translation of this poem exists. My own rendition tries to stay close to the French metaphors, but unfortunately changes the rhyme scheme.

[89]Leconte de Lisle: *Poèmes Antiques* (Paris: Alphonse Lemerre, 1874; Société d'édition "Les belles lettres" 1977), p.296/7. Leconte de Lisle's title is reminiscent of Robert Burn's poem of 1794, "Lassie wi' the lintwhite locks." The translation is mine; unfortunately, it changes the rhyme scheme.

The Girl with the Flaxen Hair

Sitting amidst the alfalfa in flower,
Who sings from the cool morning hour?
It is the girl with the flaxen hair,
The beauty with cherry lips so fair.
    Love, in the summer sun so bright,
    Sang with the lark for sheer delight.

Your mouth has colors so divine,
it tempts a kiss, o, were it mine!
Come chat with me in the flow'ring grass,
Girl with the long lashes, the silken tress.
    Love, in the summer sun so bright,
    Sang with the lark for sheer delight.

Do not say no, o cruel girl!
Do not say yes! Far better still
To read your large eye's longing gaze,
your rosy lips, which I so praise!
    Love, in the summer sun so bright,
    Sang with the lark for sheer delight.

Farewell to deer, farewell to hare,
And to red partridges! I shall dare
a kiss of your crimson lips to steal,
your flaxen locks to caress and feel!
    Love, in the summer sun so bright,
    Sang with the lark for sheer delight.

The composer has captured the overall impression of naiveté[90] in a piece that is fairly simple in texture and, particularly with regard to its harmonic language, considerably more traditional than other Debussy compositions of this time. While the melody seems drawn partly from the pentatonic scale E♭ G♭ A♭ B♭ D♭ (see the treble in bars 1/2, 4-7m, 8/9, 23-30 and the double-note ascent in bar 35), the underlying accompaniment features distinct plagal and authentic cadences. The rhythmic design, too, is simple; it is characterized by repeated short-short-long

---

[90]Debussy communicates the character of the girl in an easily accessible way through allusion to another of his preludes. The piece about the gentle, unassuming maiden shares two significant features with the prelude dedicated to the simple, unassuming flower, the heather. Compare the opening melodic gestures (*La fille au cheveux de lin,* bars 1-3; *Bruyères,* bars 1-4) and the idiosyncratic subdominant pedals (*La fille au cheveux de lin,* bars 28-31; *Bruyères,* bars 44/45).

patterns, framed by longer notes that are often tied into a silent downbeat or, as the initial note of the piece, sound indeterminate with regard to their metric position and thus somewhat floating.

Phrase structure and setting in this prelude admirably depict the gentle nature and the innocence of the girl Debussy must have had in mind. The first phrase is launched from an unaccompanied, lingering dotted quarter and continues in gentle waves up and down through a four-note excerpt from the pentatonic scale. A chordal accompaniment appears in bars 2/3 with the plagal steps IV-I in G♭ major. The main clause of the phrase literally concludes with a "feminine", i.e. weak-beat ending in the middle of bar 3, after which the chord is passively prolonged into the next bar. (The descending, long-short-short-long tetrachord of this melodic ending will from here onwards be referred to as *x*.)

bars 1-4

Two eighth-notes serve as a link to the shorter second subphrase. Here, the listener at first perceives the dominant that had previously been omitted (D♭ major, see bars 5d and 6d), but is then surprised by a sudden modulation and perfect cadence in E♭ major (bar 6). As in the first half of the phrase, metric stress is carefully avoided and the conclusion occurs on a weak beat that is only passively prolonged into the following downbeat. The texture in this subphrase is in chordal homophony and thus differs strongly from the lighter first part of the phrase.

The second phrase, prepared by a bridge in bar 8, begins with a variation of the first subphrase. The originally unaccompanied part is now supported by alternating G♭⁷ and A♭⁷ chords (see bars 8/9). In the conclusion, the C♭ major subdominant chord competes with D♭/A♭, notes that represent the dominant of G♭ major, as if plagal and authentic cadence struggled with one another for control.

bars 2-4

The prolongation of the concluding note of this subphrase (see bar 10/11) is this time filled with free imitations of component *x*. The complementing subphrase, even shorter here than before, is launched after an upbeat and centers in a pentatonically derived chord and melody (see bar 12: G♭ A♭ C♭ D♭ E♭). At the same time, however, the inherent dominant-seven effect of the chord in the tenor range strives for resolution and launches an authentic cadence in G♭ major. The by now familiar passive prolongation and avoidance of a strong final downbeat are provided by a syncopation of the G♭s in both the upper voice and the bass—thus earlier than in preceding phrases. The melodic conclusion in bar 13 is once more the segment *x*.

After another link, the second section of this piece begins with new material. This can be read as a progression in twofold double fourths (beginning E♭/A♭-F/B♭ in the right hand, G♭/C♭-A♭/D♭ in the left) where the upper voice is rhythmically varied.

After yet another link, several variations of component *x* appear, harmonized as a diatonic modulation via the subdominant (bar 16: C♭) and the dominant-seven (bars 17/18: D♭, preceded by a V⁷/V) but concluding with a sudden twist towards E♭ major. This key is again reached in a hybrid plagal + authentic cadence, i.e. through a chord that comprises notes from both the B♭ major and the A♭ major chords and thus points back to the cadential close in bars 9/10. (It should be mentioned that, while it is *theoretically* possible to explain this hybrid chord as an eleventh-chord over the dominant root—i.e. as a further extension of the dominant-ninth chord, such an interpretation fails to give account of what is *practically* being experienced in this harmonic turn.)

bars 18-19

Melodic ascents, stemming from the pentatonic scale B♭ C E♭ F G (a transposition of the scale used in bar 12) lead to a repetition of the hybrid cadence in the two following bars. The section concludes with varied recurrences of component *x* (see bars 21/22 and bar 23-23m). An authentic cadence resolving into an added-sixth tonic in distinct *cédez* prepares the return of the primary material.

The third section is a free recapitulation. The melodic material of bars 1/2 appears in a new variation, in a homophonic setting completely derived from the original pentatonic scale[91]. The section ends in what amounts to some kind of a deceptive cadence: the downbeat of bar 28 is not the anticipated G♭ major but instead C♭ major (the subdominant, a suspending pedal point). The original melody is repeated and finally concludes, with augmented values in component *x*, on the tonic G♭ major. The coda recalls material from the middle section (bars 33/34 are a development of bar 14) before the prelude ends in pure, high-registered G♭-major chords.

As the short analysis has shown, the simplicity of the setting is matched by the structural layout, which keeps very close to traditional ternary form. What emerge as distinctive features in this prelude are

[1] the phrase-concluding component *x*;
[2] the duality of plagal and authentic cadences emphasized through the repeated use of the hybrid chord; and
[3] the striking fact that this piece, apparently so functional, actually has two tonal centers. This deserves more attention.

One tonal center is, very obviously, the G♭ confirmed in the cadential closes. This G♭ establishes the connection with the preceding prelude that is built over a pedal-note F♯. The secondary tonal center is E♭. An E♭ appears as

[1] the root of the first pentatonic scale (bars 1/2);
[2] the goal of the first modulation (bars 6/7);
[3] the root of the melody in bars 8/9 and
[4] in bar 12;
[5] the goal of the threefold hybrid cadence (bars 18-21);
[6] the melodic trigger for the climax of the piece (bars 21/22 and 23d);
[7] the melodic root of the pentatonic scale in the recap (bars 24-31);
[8] the goal of both bass and treble in the coda's development component (bar 35).

Finally, there is a most intriguing musical equivalent to the particular structure in Lecomte de Lisle's poem. As the text reprinted above shows, the poem consists of four stanzas, each of which ends with a refrain. The

---

[91] See bars 24-27 (except for bar 25, beat 3 and bar 27, beat 2, which contain C♭).

connection between Debussy's phrase-concluding component x, the gently descending tetrachord, and the refrain feature in the poem seems almost too obvious to be mentioned.

What is particular in the poem, however, is not the refrain itself, which is a common enough phenomenon, but the fact that its content is detached from the deliberations in the stanzas in both speech attitude and time. Whereas the action-carrying lines of the poem appear in either narrative present tense (stanza 1) or direct speech (stanzas 2-4), i.e. very much in the here and now, the refrain contains a statement about love in the summer sun in general and, quite surprisingly, is in the past tense. Whether the poet is here musing, imagining himself in the young man's role or, more likely, presenting to his audience as a still inconclusive development something that happened earlier and the outcome of which he knows, remains intentionally open. The refrain thus causes a repeated, slightly surprising shift of perspective at the end of each stanza.

This shift of perspective has found its way into Debussy's musical rendering of the poem. Four times in the course of the prelude the listener is surprised by a harmonic turn that, while gentle in itself, seems to give the events depicted a new twist.

[1] There are harmonic twists into an unexpected key. In bars 6/7, the cadential resolution into E♭ major quite unexpectedly brightens up the preceding G♭-major phrase. The very similar perfect cadence in E♭ major in bars 18/19 has the same effect: bar 17 with its A♭^{7} and D♭^{7} chords gave the impression of wanting to return to G♭ major, so that the E♭-major conclusion creates something of a revelation.

[2] There are hybrid cadences in which the tonic is preceded by a superimposition of its subdominant and dominant chords, as happens in bars 9/10 and 18/19.

[3] There are cross-related progressions. In bars 21/22, two syncopated chords cause a slight startle. The C♭ major chord that subsequently resolves into E♭ minor is cross-related with the preceding E♭-major six-five chord (the pitches G and C clash with the brusquely occurring G♭ and C♭), and the A♭-major chord in bar 22m sets its C♮ against the C♭s in both the preceding and the following chords. (The same process is then repeated in bar 23.)

[4] Finally, there is a deceptive cadence. The phrase in bars 24-27, and particularly its conclusive cadence with $A\flat^7$-D major, clearly seem to prepare the return to G♭ major. Instead of this expected tonic of the piece, however, Debussy writes a C♭-major chord—astounding even when regarded in the context of other deceptive cadences. It is a major eye-opener for the understanding of this piece that not one of these startling twists seems in the least geared to question tonality, or to shock and awake the listener from all too pleasant expectations. What they create is a musical shift of perspective.

The four musical shifts of perspective, corresponding with the four occurrences of the refrain in the poem, should be regarded as major eye-openers for the understanding of this piece. The hybrid cadences can now be read as musical metaphors for conclusions that allow more than one interpretation, and the dual tonal center seems to stand, in this context, for the dual frame of reference that underlies this and any other budding love stories: the obvious, unquestioned, enchanted involvement here and now (as presented in the stanzas), and the knowing, slightly wistful look backward at past elation (as apparent in the refrain).

Feuilles mortes (Debussy, *Préludes*, vol. II, no. 2)

Given Debussy's well-documented affection for the work of the Edwardian illustrator Arthur Rackham, it has been suggested that the title of this prelude, *Dead Leaves*, may recall the caption of one of Rackham's drawings for J. M. Barrie's *Peter Pan in Kensington Garden*. The illustration in question shows three young girls caught in a flurry of wind and dry leaves, and is accompanied by the lines: "There is almost nothing that has such a keen sense of fun as a fallen leaf." The guess was that the French translation for "fallen leaf" might have read "feuille morte" and thus prompted the title of the musical work. Yet considering the utterly sad, desolate character of the piece, which Debussy describes in his heading as *Lent et mélancholique* (slow and melancholy), the happy spirit of the illustration seems a highly unlikely source. At the time of writing this prelude the composer was at the height of his career but had just discovered that he had cancer, and one imagines that the "dead leaves" struck him as particularly appropriate to express his mood because of their image of decay.

A much more likely source for the wording of this prelude's title can be found in a collection of poetry by Debussy's friend of many years, Gabriel Mourey. Debussy met the poet, playwright and critic, with whom he planned several operas, in the early 1880s at the newly opened cabaret *Chat Noir* where he accompanied singers and met many different literary personalities for whom this locale had become a favorite gathering place.

Looking at Mourey's collection of poems, entitled *Voix éparses* (Scattered Voices), one cannot help thinking that the influence between the composer and the poet was mutual: *Voix éparses* is itself composed rather like a piece of music.

- It consists of an opening poem, three sections very much reminiscent of the three movements of a symphony, and a closing poem. The opening and closing poems are named in tribute to the greatest artists of the Italian Golden Age, *Michel-Ange* and *Dante Alighieri* respectively.
- The first section following *Michel-Ange*, significantly called *Adagios*, comprises the largest number of poems (forty-five in all) and is the most complex of the three, particularly with regard to moods expressed and metaphors employed.
- The central portion, entitled *Feuilles mortes*—just as its counterpart, the central movement of a cyclical work of music—represents the shortest section with only ten poems, but the melancholy mood of these poems gives them much extra weight.
- The nineteen poems of the third section are compiled under the heading *Croquis rêvés* (Dreamed Sketches). This portion of Mourey's collection is significantly more lighthearted than the two preceding ones and thus confirms the analogy with the musical work by presenting a similar mood to that expected in the final movement of a sonata or symphony.

Debussy's title does not make reference to any one particular poem but to the entire middle section of Mourey's poetic cycle. Here are two of the ten poems included in the section *Feuilles mortes*. They capture a mood that seems very similar to that expressed in Debussy's prelude:[92]

---

[92]Gabriel Mourey, *Voix éparses* (Paris: Librairie des Bibliophiles, 1883). The English translations are mine. (I wish to thank Professor Guy Mermier from the Department of Romance Literatures, University of Michigan, for his critical reading and several very helpful suggestions.)

I

Les bonheurs envolés, les ivresses fiévreuses,
Les rêves disparus, les choses du passé,
Tout ce que le destin a naguère effacé,
Tout cela se retrouve en vous, forêts charmeuses!

Dans la sonorité des horizons lointains,
Dans le bruit solennel de vos grandes ramures,
On sent gémir sans cesse, avec tous leurs murmures,
Les espoir, les soupirs et les sanglots humains.

Moi, j'ai senti ton charme ineffable et sublime,
J'ai saisi dans tes voix les voix de l'Infini.
Et dans mon rêve immense, ô forêt, j'ai béni
Les grands enchantements de la main qui t'anime!

VII

La forêt gémissait sous le vent de l'automne
Mélancolique et froid: les arbres défeuillés
Tremblaient sinistrement sur leurs vieux troncs souillés
En un lugubre écho de plainte monotone.

Et la nuit descendait sous le ciel sans lueurs,
Rapide, enveloppant comme d'un noir suaire
Les horizons éteints; dans le bois solitaire
S'agitaient vaguement d'indécises pâleurs...

Des ombres qui fuyaient, tendrement enlacées...
Les âmes de tous ceux qui s'aimèrent jadis
S'envolant vers l'azur des lointains paradis
Après l'expiation des ivresses passé.

Turning to the music, we find that the utterly sad character of Debussy's prelude is achieved by means of various harmonic devices, multiple layers of often tonally independent texture, a prevalence of motions that (often palindromically) fall back to where they came from, and a generally very soft dynamic level with *p marqué* (enhanced *piano*) and two very short *mf* outbreaks as its most expressive moments.

In a key signature of C♯ minor (confirmed both in the initial bass notes and at the end of the piece), the prelude begins on an F♯-major ninth chord that falls, as if with a noticeable sigh, a whole-tone downwards to an E^9 chord. This initial "sigh" is very powerful in setting the mood for this musical expression of desolation.

I

The bliss of lost days, their feverish trance,
The disappeared dreams, events of our past,
All that which fate has recently erased,
Is recouped in you, o magic forests!

In the resonant sounds of horizons at far,
In the solemn rustle of your foliage so vast,
One ceaselessly hears the murmurs and moans
Of human hopes and sighs and sobs.

I have felt your charm, ineffable and sublime,
I have caught in your voices those of Eternity.
And in my great dream, o forest, I have blessed
The magical spells of the hand that makes you live.

VII

Under the melancholy and chilly autumn wind
The forest groaned and moaned: the trees, stripped of leaves,
Full of foreboding trembled on their stained old trunks
As with a gruesome echo of monotone lament.

And the night fell under a lightless sky,
Swiftly, enveloping as with a black shroud
The extinguished horizons; in the lonely wood
Wavering pallors vaguely hastened by...

And shadows went fleeing, tenderly embraced...
The souls of those who loved each other long ago
Flying towards the azur of a distant paradise,
Past ecstasy and madness atoned for and effaced.

As a result of this harmonically ambiguous beginning, the notes of the lowest textural layer, the keynote and fifth of the presumed home key C♯ that join after the downbeat of bar 2, are heard as dissonances. The tonal incongruence is continued in bar 3 where the F♯-major ninth chord is reinstated in the upper layers while the bass ascends a whole tone to D♯-A♯; C♯ appears in double octave in the melodic line. But while the pitch is conceived as a relaxation in the horizontal context, it is actually perceived, due to the harmonic environment, as highly suspenseful.

Both the eight-part chords and the bass harmonies are then suspended during the two remaining bars of the first phrase, and attention is thus directed entirely to the melody in unison octaves that was so far almost concealed behind the many-layered harmonic processes. Despite this apparent simplification of texture, however, the sense of tonal certainty remains elusive. Written-out chromatic slides create the impression of horizontal clusters (see bars 4/5: A♯-G-G♯-A and C♯-D-D♯-E-C), while the two most essential melodic pitches so far, F♯ and C♯, are abandoned in favor of F♮ and C♮. The melodic A-minor chord that concludes the unison line reveals itself only with hindsight as a preparation for the pedal-note of the following phrase. While it is, strictly speaking, the resolution of the E⁹ in bar 2, it can hardly be heard as such and thus does not create the impression of tonal closure.

Rhythm and metric order in this phrase support the image of vagueness. The initial three-beat chord in very slow tempo comes to the listener as a suspended sound that does not reveal any sense of pulse or metric placing. The phrase then centers on two very regular bars with clear downbeat feeling before falling into a syncopation. From here, the unaccompanied melody, while rhythmically unambiguous, nevertheless creates an effect of metric floating owing to two devices: the abridged bar 5 (see the change from the earlier three-four time to two-four for this bar) and the concomitant shift of the "chromatic slide" figure from a weak to a strong beat.

The second phrase reworks some of the features into a new pattern. Tonal grounding is provided by a four-bar pedal-octave A followed by a five-bar pedal on G. The first pedal is active in both space and time: rhythmically non-repetitive, it moves up and down through three octaves.

176

The second pedal is locked into one place, both on the keyboard and in the bar where it invariably strikes the second beat. However, closer inspection reveals that there is much correspondence behind the apparent contrast. The two segments of the phrase are actually identical in duration since, owing to the change in time signature in bar 12, the five bars of the second half (bars 10-14) add up to the same total of twelve beats as do the four bars of the phrase's first half (bars 6-9). Consequently, the apparent rhythmic evenness of the pedal-note in the second half of the phrase is all but monotonous. For the listener tuned in to the previous three-four time, it results in a *hemiola* (read bars 10-14 as 1 **2** 3 1 **2** 3|1 **2** 1 **2** 1 **2**).

Vertically, the phrase is characterized by chords that encompass diatonic clusters—reminiscent of, but not immediately related to, the chromatic clusters in the initial phrase. These diatonic clusters have three sources: some are inverted and contracted ninth chords (see, in bars 6/7, the B-major ninth chord and its interspersed chromatic neighbor on B♭); others are conceived as inverted triads with added fourths (see in bars 8/9); or, finally, they result from the invasion of various upper-strand chords by the pedal-note (see bars 10-14 where the G, in addition to its prominent position in the bass, also appears in every chord of the upper strands).

This subtle play with the inter-relatedness of all components conveys a strong sense of resignation. It is hardly surprising, then, that the melodic contours of the first phrase, too, find their correspondence in the second phrase. The falling consecutive fourths from bars 2/3, one of the distinctive horizontal features of the opening bars, recur in bars 8/9 as sequences of a chord-pair of falling fourths. The harmonic mirror effect created in bars 1-3d by the shift back and forth (F♯⁹-E⁹-F♯⁹) is taken up at both the beginning and the end of the second phrase (see bars 6/7: B⁹-B♭⁹-B⁹, and bars 12-14: F/A-G/B-F/A).[93] Even the melodic line of bar 10 and its repeat in bar 11 can be traced back to a model—one whole tone higher and slightly different in rhythm—in bar 2 (compare bar 10: D- - -B-C with bar 2: E- -C♯-D-[B]).

The third phrase (see bars 15-18) is a shortened, lightened and varied version of the first. While the phrase recalls the melodic line and tonal progression of the initial bars, it is shortened in that it is deprived of the

[93]The lowest note of the left-hand chord in bar 14 in fact reads D and not, as expected in the palindrome and realized in the right-hand chord, G. What harmonic or melodic meaning this D might have remains utterly unclear both within these bars and in view of the transition to the following. This might be a misprint.

suspended first chord, and lightened insofar as it comes without the octave doubling in both melody and chords, and without the seventh within the two ninth chords. Variations concern register and details in the accompanying broken chords. The ambit in the two trunk bars is narrowed from both sides: the treble appears an octave lower than before and the lowest bass notes (C♯ and D♯) an octave higher. The after-beat *portati* that were originally part of the bass are now taken over by a third layer, a kind of overhang from the end of the previous phrase (compare bar 15, third staff, with bars 12-14, first staff.) The fact that they are written underneath the melodic part as in bars 2/3, rather than above as in bars 12-14, shows Debussy's concept of a fusion of the two components.

A small detail at the end of the phrase takes care of the transition to the prelude's second section. To appreciate this, it is necessary to glance back at the initial phrase. In bars 4/5, the sequence of the chromatic-slide figure adjusts the final interval: the F-C♯ from bar 4 does not appear literally transposed to C-G♯ in bar 5, but is instead narrowed to C-A and thus prepares the coming pedal-note A. This adjustment is not retained in bar 18. The seemingly inconspicuous G♯ turns out to be highly significant: it prompts a pedal-note G♯ that, extending over a total of sixteen bars (see bars 19-30, 37-40), covers the largest portion of the prelude; it also reinstates the augmented chord that originally concluded the figure (see bar 4: A-F-C♯ and bar 18: E-C-G♯). This, in turn, lays the ground for the whole-tone organization of the following bars.

In bars 19-24 (excluding the last sixteenth-note in the treble), the two upper strands are built on the whole-tone scale C-D-E-F♯-G♯-A♯. The scale informs both the vertical organization of chords (bars 21-24) and the horizontal progression of the melodic line. The third strand is taken up by an *ostinato* derived from the "chromatic slide" figure that, apart from its chromatic passing-note, fits into the same tonal frame. The absence of tonal tension, the slightly increased tempo, the reassuring repetitiveness of the *ostinato* and particularly the rising line of the melody with its emphatic *crescendos* and dotted-note rhythm, all contribute to an effect of hope in this phrase.

The second phrase in this section (see bars 25-30), while again reworking many of the elements established in the previous phrase, constitutes a stark contrast in terms of mood. Its *ostinato*, now in the higher register, consists of

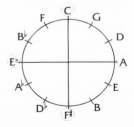

four major triads. In the circle of fifths, these mark the four poles: A and D♯ major, F♯ and C major.[94] This horizontal pattern of harmonic vagueness is matched vertically where the downbeats unite representatives of the chromatic steps G, G♯, A and A♯: G is the metrically emphasized melodic note (see downbeats except for bar 27), and G major the implied tonality of the melodic line in bars 25-28; G♯ is enhanced as the pedal-note (both in the lower notes of the third-strand chords and in the few low bass notes); A major is the metrically emphasized chord of the *ostinato*, and finally, a diminished triad on A♯ rings through the repeated chords in the third staff.

Within the third phrase of this section, the *toccata* component in bars 31-33 and 33-35 recalls the palindromic patterns from the first section (see also its simpler melodic equivalent in bars 37-39d, and the symmetric A♯/E-G×/D♯-A♯/E in the middle-strand chords of the same bars). At the same time, the connection to the preceding phrase is maintained on the level of harmonic organization: While bars 29/30 conclude with a repetition of a two-chord excerpt from the original four polarized chords (i.e. only the enharmonically notated D♯ and C-major chords), the third phrase begins with repeated statements of the other two chords, F♯ and A major (as well as D major, which, however, is related to the pivotal A).

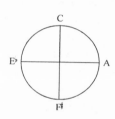

bars 25-28	29/30	31-35
A, D♯, F♯, C	D♯, C	A, F♯

The end of this phrase sees the return of two features that contribute to the retransitional cadential effect in bar 40. The pedal-note G♯, tonal center of the entire second section, is converted into a dominant bass and as such leads to the now clearly established tonic C♯ (see the bass progression V-I in bars 40-41). At the same time, the dominant-ninth chord is reminiscent of the prelude's first section where it constituted the initial and most prominent chord. As an E♯-major ninth chord, first heard in bar 38 and melodically enhanced in bar 40, it has its own cadential tendency that would demand resolution into A♯. Before the backdrop of this harmonic expectation, the actually occurring F♯ major in bar 41 is heard as a deceptive cadence (VI of A♯ minor). The emotional effect of these superimposed cadences, combining the impression of completion with that of deception, is awesome in its subtle beauty.

[94] The triads on D♯ and C are enharmonically concealed; see D♯-G-A♯ instead of D♯-F×-A♯, and B♯-E-G instead of C-E-G.

The short third section of the prelude "Dead leaves" is recapitulation and coda in one. The initial phrase of the piece recurs, now securely rooted in a pedal on the tonic C♯, with melodic enhancement in triple octaves and slight, though harmonically inconsequential changes in the right-hand chords. After a short extension (see bar 46), harmonic dissonance returns with cross-related chords (see bar 47: F♯/F♮ and A♮/A♭ in D major/f minor) and a harmonic sidestep to B♭ (bar 48/49). The tonal ambiguity is retained in that the chords in these bars support B♭ major while the descending melodic line emphasizes the pitches A♭ and G♭ before resolving into F. The three final bars of the piece, however, "correct" this impression. A five-octave C♯, endorsed in the low register by the fifth G♯, clearly marks the return to the tonic. The melodic gesture, now in augmentation (compare the octave descent in bars 48/49 with that in bars 50-52 where the note values are exactly twice as long) is enharmonically redefined so that A♭ G♭ F become G♯ F♯ E♯. In this form, the melodic gesture thus presents a segment from the C♯-major scale and, with its resolution into a C♯-major chord, confirms the tonality—after all. One is tempted to read this metaphorically: The final reconciliation of the "prevalent surface motion" and its "progression in time" with the "preconceived and ever-present basic key" points to a—desired or achieved?—similar reconciliation in life.

APPARITIONS AND VISITATIONS

Ondine   (Ravel, *Gaspard de la nuit*, no. 1)

The first poem Ravel selected for his composition *Gaspard de la nuit*, named after Aloysius Bertrand's collection of prose poems, is from the Third Book in Bertrand, a section that is entitled *La nuit et ses prestiges* (The Night and its Distinctions). As shown in the chapter discussing Debussy's *Ondine*, the water-spirit in its fairy-tale version is not literally related to the night. In the Bertrand poem, however, the allusions point very much to the realm of the not-clearly lit, the dream-like, the surreal. Moreover, it was the story of the mermaid—cool and shimmering, attractive but without deep feelings—that had made Hoffmann famous above all. In the narrative version of Frédéric de la Motte-Fouquet's romance of two women—one a mortal, the other the immortal daughter of the waves—in love with the same man, as well as in the famous fairy-tale version, Hans Christian Andersen's *The Little Mermaid,* the story captivated wide audiences. Various adaptations for the stage included E. T. A. Hoffmann's and Albert Lortzing's operas *Undine*, Antonin Dvořák's opera *Rusalka* and Jean Giraudoux' acclaimed play *Ondine*. The tale as it was perceived by romantic audiences is of the paradise in the depths of the waters, left with high hopes in search of a man's love that alone can give a mermaid her soul. Mortality thus gained seems a small price to pay for that unfathomable asset called "soul," but when human incomprehension and rejection cause the return to the waters without a return to blissful innocence and joy, one is inclined to weep in empathy with the betrayed creature from that strange, beautiful world.[95]

Bertrand in his poem clearly focuses differently. (For Bertrand's poem *Ondine* and a fairly literal translation, see the following two facing

---

[95]For a synopsis giving the plot of the opera *Ondine* and a brief account of Andersen's fairy-tale version, *The Little Mermaid,* see above under Debussy's *Prélude Ondine* (pages 123-126).

The three Bertrand poems Ravel selected for his composition are quoted here from Aloysius Bertrand, *Gaspard de la nuit* (Paris: Payot, 1925). The English translations are mine.

"Ecoute! - Ecoute! - C'est moi, c'est Ondine qui frôle de ces gouttes d'eau les losanges sonores de ta fenêtre illuminée par les mornes rayons de la lune; et voici, en robe de moire, la dame châtelaine qui contemple à son balcon la belle nuit étoilée et le beau lac endormi.

"Chaque flot est un ondin qui nage dans le courant, chaque courant est un sentier qui serpente vers mon palais, et mon palais est bâti fluide au fond du lac, dans le triangle du feu, de la terre et de l'air.

"Ecoute! - Ecoute! - mon père bat l'eau coassante d'une branche d'aulne verte, et mes soeurs caressent de leurs bras d'écume les fraîches îles d'herbes, de nénuphars et de glaïeuls, ou se moquent du saule caduc et barbu qui pêche à la ligne."

*

Sa chanson murmurée, elle me supplia de recevoir son anneau à mon doigt, pour être l'époux d'une Ondine, et de visiter avec elle son palais, pour être le roi des lacs.

Et comme je lui répondais que j'aimais une mortelle, boudeuse et dépitée, elle pleura quelques larmes, poussa un éclat de rire, et s'évanouit en giboulées qui ruisselèrent blanches le long de mes vitraux bleus.

pages.) His accent is not at all on those qualities that, in the various fairy tale versions as well as in the operatic and theatrical realizations, appear in the foreground. Indeed his poem does not present the story from Ondine's perspective but from the man's point of view. His Ondine is "murmuring a song" and begging to be married. When learning, in answer to her plea, that the man is in love with a mortal woman, she overcomes her dejection very quickly and returns to—or remains in?— her playful state. Thus not pity but smiling indulgence with the child-like creature is what Bertrand's poem evokes, and what Ravel chose for his piano work.

The poem is in five stanzas. The initial three deal with Ondine; the remaining two, separated by an asterisk, with the man whom she hopes to marry. The bipartite structure thus corresponds very directly to the two main characters. That this twosome is, however, a hope primarily embraced by Ondine is mirrored in the fact that her three stanzas contain several further instances of pairs, while his stanzas don't; see the two-fold "Listen! Listen" in the first and third stanzas, the juxtaposition of Ondine with the "lady of the manor" in the first stanza, the "each..., each..." in the second stanza, and the mention of father / sisters in the third stanza.

"Listen! - Listen! - It's me, it's Ondine who brushes with these drops of water the resonant diamonds of your window lit by the gloomy moonlight; and there in her silken robe is the lady of the manor contemplating from her balcony the lovely star-bright night and the beautiful, sleeping lake.

"Each ripple is a 'child of the waves' swimming with the current, each current is a path winding towards my palace, and my palace is built fluid, at the bottom of the lake, in the triangle of fire, earth and air.

"Listen! - Listen! - My father beats the croaking water with a branch of green alder, and my sisters caress with their arms of foam the cool islands of herbs, water lilies and gladioli, or make fun of the sickly, bearded willow that is fishing with rod and line."

*

Having murmured her song, she begged me to accept her ring on my finger, so that I would be the husband of an Ondine, and to visit her palace with her, so that I would be king of the lakes.

And when I replied that I loved a mortal woman, she wept a few tears, sulking and peevish, then broke into laughter, and vanished in showers of rain that drizzled white across my blue window pane.

Focusing on the content of Ondine's words, one finds that she characterizes herself by way of contrast and metaphor. In the first stanza, she distinguishes her own immediacy, naiveté, enthusiasm and playfulness from the noble attire (silken robe), noble demeanor (contemplate) and noble place (balcony of a manor) of the rival. She also associates herself with gloomy moonlight—and thus with mystery, unpredictability, emotioality, while the lady is presented with the much more rational and conventional perceptions of the "lovely star-bright night and the beautiful sleeping lake." In the second stanza, she asks to read each ripple as an *"ondin,"* [96] each current as a path, thus interpreting the entire lake as a manifestation of the water spirits.

How complete and perfect her realm should be imagined is expressed through the use of the four elements and the perfect geometrical symbol: her palace of water is located in the "triangle of fire, earth and air." In the third stanza, metaphoric and non-metaphoric images merge into a real fantasy. The father strikes the water (which, as we have learned before, actually constitutes his children, the *"ondins"*); the sisters' arms—of foam, of course, since each sister is a ripple—caress the islands, and in doing so foster flowers and plants. Their anthropomorphizing mockery of

[96]French *onde* = wave, *ondin* = child of the waves, *ondine* = female child of the waves.

the pitiful weeping willow at the lake shore as well as the father's use of an alder branch depicts the water spirits as integrated in a larger natural environment.

In terms of structure, Ondine's three stanzas form an entity distinguished by both symmetry and progression. The very conspicuous repeated "Listen! Listen!" at the beginning of the fist and third stanzas creates the impression of an A B A form. At the same time, a strong sense of continuity is achieved. The contemplation of the "sleeping lake" at the end of the first stanza leads to a further description of that lake in stanza II, and the mention of Ondine's home at the close of the second stanza prompts more details about her family in stanza III.

The speech attitude in the remaining two stanzas is distinctly different from that in the first three: immediacy gives way to narrative, logic ("Having..., she...") and reasoning ("so that..."; "and since..."). The fourth stanza gives an account of what Ondine hoped with regard to the man, and why; the reasons as perceived by the man—"so that I would be the husband of an Ondine," and "so that I would be king of the lakes"— sound very different indeed from those familiar from the fairy tale! The fifth stanza briefs us about the man's reply and Ondine's reaction—that of a child who sulks for a moment and forgets immediately as she continues to play.

In terms of the images and metaphors employed, the final stanza creates a bridge back to the first stanza: the "mortal woman" is, of course, the "lady of the manor"; Ondine is once again volatile and playful, splashing water around; and the rain on the window panes recalls the initial setting in stanza I.

The fact that the first three stanzas are presented in quotation marks seems to suggest that we are dealing with direct vs. indirect speech. However, a closer look at stanzas IV and V reveals that they, too, are in the first person singular. The two speech patterns are thus rather to be read as the man's voice as narrator beginning with a verbatim quotation of what he heard (or: thought he heard) the water spirit say.

Going even one step further and considering the setting that, according to both his own and Ondine's stipulated account, provides the backdrop for the encounter, one wonders even more who—and whether anybody at all—is actually speaking. The two-fold mention of the window pane makes it clear that Ondine is "out there" and the man "in here." Furthermore, at the end of the poem Ondine seems to vanish into the rain drops streaming down the window, the same rain drops that first brought her into the picture. Is she, then, not just an hallucination of a man about to be married (to a mortal woman, of course), a fantasy inspired by the play of rain drops, in which the narrator pits the playful, child-like creature against the noble, well-dressed and poised woman who will be his wife? The "reasons" why he should marry her—"so that I would be the husband of an Ondine," and "so that I would be king of the lakes"—seem to confirm this interpretation: they focus entirely on what he would be; no mention of Ondine's longing for a soul, and her need for his love to obtain it.

While the fairy tale can usefully be read as a metaphor of a girl's initiation into adulthood with, especially in the more explicit versions, the very problematic image of the fish tail split into two legs that are needed to love a man, and the interpretation of the painful loss of virginity as a precondition for attaining a soul, the message of Aloysius Bertrand's poem is quite different. This is clearly a man's fantasy, in which a luring water spirit sings a "murmured song," evoking options the waking mind rejects. The dream of being king in a realm of perfection, beauty and irresponsible playfulness is but a delightful backdrop for the more serious and responsible obligations in real life, and the mate thus rejected is not hurt but remains in her element.

The epigram that precedes Bertrand's poem sheds further light both on this interpretation of the poem and on the music it inspired. Taken from Charles Brugnot's *Les deux Génies*, the excerpt reads:

> .... *Je croyais entendre*
> *Une vague harmonie enchanter mon sommeil,*
> *Et près de moi s'épandre un murmure pareil*
> *Aux chants entrecoupés d'une voix triste et tendre.*

> (.................... I thought I heard
> A vague harmony that enchanted my sleep,
> And near me a scattering murmur similar to
> Songs interspersed with a sad and tender voice.)

Vagueness, sleep and what is thought to be heard point to the illusory quality of the story; the enchantment perceived suggests wish fulfillment, and "murmur" and "song" refer directly to the way Bertrand's male narrator describes Ondine's utterances.

Ravel's musical rendition of the poem integrates all significant aspects shown in the poem. The "vague harmony" is embodied in the characteristic chord combination of the piece (not shown in the example): the

Maurice Ravel: *Gaspard de la Nuit* - The "song" in *Ondine*

Line 1
establishes the trunk of theme 1,
and complements it with the first
three components: a, b and c.

Line 2
re-groups two of the components (c, b, b var)
to create the more natural and folk-song like
component d, the main complement of the song.

Line 3
is a free development of theme 1; the complementing component is new (e) and appears
as a phrase-group (e, e, e extended).

Line 4
presents a contrasting character. Its initial impulse stems
from theme 1 (see the variant of a); at the same time, it
creates continuity by picking up the triplets from line 3.

Line 5
establishes the trunk of theme 2, which it
complements with a substantial segment of d,
the complement of theme 1 from line 2.

Line 6
repeats and reinforces line 5 but
distorts what came from theme 1.

Line 7
recalls theme 1, with a free rendering of
of component a and a new complement, g:
the first to reach into the bass register.

Line 8
is a transposition (up a major sixth)
and a reinforcement (in partial octave
doubling) of line 7.

Line 9
recalls the trunk of theme 2, complemented
with an abridged version of of component d.

Line 10
reinforces the trunk of theme 2, and complements it
with the bass-register component h introduced in line 7
in theme 1 context - here extended much beyond the
scope of a song line.

Line 11
is a free development of theme 2; the
complement derives from d and appears in
the structure of a phrase group (d, d, d extended).

Line 12
recalls the contrasting character from line 4
which is here heard also in continuity of line 11
(compare line 12, second bar with line 11 last bar).

Line 13
is a final reminiscence of theme 1
with its two main complements:
a free version of component a,
followed by the complete d.

bitonal juxtaposition of a six-five chord with a melodic development in another key. It is intriguing to ponder the fact that the six-five chord invariably mixes the two tonal genders: it is either a major chord with a minor sixth or a minor chord with a major sixth.[97]

Most notably, Ravel's work is definitely a *song*. The texture allows clearly to distinguish two components: vertically, a tune supported by an accompaniment in varying patterns; horizontally, the different lines of a clearly phrased song. In three instances, a line is preceded by one or two introductory bars, and the whole song is rounded off by what would in a vocal piece be an instrumental coda.

The example, given on pages 188-189, shows the thirteen lines of the song. Both the music-analytical letters within the example and the verbal remarks at the margin give a short account of the thematic material and its structural organization. (In addition, the indentation pattern aims to reflect the overall structure: Ondine's lines are flush left, the man's lines are strongly indented, while "the other woman's" two short contributions are set to begin half-way between those of the principal characters.)

Relating the music to the poetic text, one can make the following eight observations:

[1] Just as there are two main characters and "the other woman" in the fairy tale, so Ravel invented two themes and, in addition, a melodic line that, for the time being, will just be referred to as "contrasting character."

[2] Both themes consist of a "core" (or "trunk") and a number of complements. The characteristic features of the "trunks" seem to relate the themes to the protagonists of the tale: on the one hand there is the somewhat languishing, wave-like, repeated outline of the theme-1 trunk (see bars 3/4) that might stand for Ondine; on the other hand there is the less accommodating (owing to the whole-tone tetrachord descent), more narrative character of the theme-2 trunk that one would connect with the man, the first-person narrator of the poem.

---

[97]Here are the details:

bars 3/4, 15/16: C♯-major six-five chord with lowered sixth, against melody in G♯ minor;
bars 9/10: G♯-minor six-five chord with major sixth, against melody in A♯ minor;
bars 33-38: G♯-major six-five chord with lowered sixth, against melody in D♯ Phrygian;
bars 45/46: D♯-major six-five chord with lowered sixth, against melody in A♯ minor;
bars 83/84: G♯-minor six-five chord with raised sixth, against melody in D♯ minor, with additional alternation D♯/D♮ and juxtaposition of B♮/B♯ within the G♯ chord;
bars 92-94: C♯-major six-five chord with lowered sixth in both hands, no melody.

[3] The intriguing fact that for Bertrand, Ondine may be a product of a man's fantasy rather than a real creature encountering him on some level of reality, is mirrored in two musical details:

- First, the two themes exchange their most significant complements. This is most noticeable in the case of what, in my
example on the following pages, I have labeled component d,
the "slow-waltz," folk-song like subphrase that is

established	in line 2	as a complement to theme 1,
taken up	in lines 5/6	as a complement to theme 2,
recalled	in lines 9,11	as a complement to theme 2,
and again	in line 13	as a complement to theme 1.

The same holds true for the bass-register component g which, at the beginning of the second half of the song, is

| introduced | in lines 7/8 | as a complement to theme 1 |
| and taken up | in line 10 | as a complement to theme 2. |

- Second, the two themes also share accompaniment patterns.
The principal accompaniment pattern of the piece, in which a
repeated triad alternates with a single note—the sixth over the
triad's root—creates the impression of shimmering. This quality has often been associated with the water Ondine calls her
home. In light of the poem, however, the shimmering quality
could equally well be descriptive of the fantasized girl herself,
depicting attributes the man's longing would have her represent. Rhythmically, the pattern is both irregular and safely
predictable: the unusual grouping of 3+3+2 repeats very
reliably on each beat of the bar—a woman delightfully volatile
but well under control. The "shimmering" pattern

accompanies	lines 1/2,	i.e. theme 1,
is gradually altered,		
then given up in	line 3,	i.e. the theme-1 developmt,
reinstated in	lines 5/6	i.e. theme 2,
		(varied and infiltrated by another pattern).
It continues through	lines 7/8	i.e. the return of theme 1, (albeit increasingly pene- trated by other material),
recurs with the end of	line 11,	i.e. the theme-2 developmt,
and once more in	line 13,	i.e. with the theme-1 trunk.

[4] The only complement that does not connect with theme 2 is component *a*. In its original form, it is launched from a weak beat after the longer version of the theme-1 trunk (see Ravel's metrically irregular slurring in bars 5, 47 and 52, as over the metrically regular slurs in bars 10/11, 16/17 and, surprisingly, 85). This component—the first complement associated with Ondine—can be recognized in the initial gesture of the "contrasting character" and thus links the musical representative of "the other woman" to the female protagonist.

[5] A symmetrical counterpart can be found in the recurrence of the melodic material (see line 12 or bars 75-82). Here what is last heard in connection with theme 2 makes its way into the "contrasting character"; the concluding bar of line 11 is inserted in line 12 between component *a* and its sequence. By means of this musical reference, Ravel seems to show the link of "the other woman" to the male protagonist... when all is said and done, so to speak.

[6] In terms of accompaniment pattern, the two lines dedicated to the contrasting character use similar material. The opening gesture derived from component *a* is set apart from the remainder of the phrase; it is heard against a G♯-major scale (bar 23), a C-major scale as white-key *glissando* (see bar 75), a black-key *glissando* (bar 77) and an arpeggiated B^7 wave (bar 27). Component *g*—the one that is unique to this character—is first accompanied by a figure reminiscent of Ondine's "shimmering" pattern. Closer inspection, however, reveals significant differences: the pattern in bars 24-26 and 28 is both much more regular (consisting of a four-chord figure and its inversion) and more "grounded" (see the pedal-note D♯ in bars 24-26 and the $E♯^9$ chord throughout bar 28) than the water spirit's floating figure, just as the prospective wife is distinguished from the fantasy mate. In line 12, component *g* is enveloped by a pattern that surrounds the melodic note D♯ (bars 78/79) with a repeated 6-against-4 figure featuring A♯-C♯-E♯-D♯ in the lower part, E♯-A♯-D♯-A♯-F♯ in the upper part. Subsequently this envelope, rather than abiding by harmonic or otherwise independent rules, follows the melodic line in perfect parallel shift—a musical metaphor that seems to epitomize the lady's "adaptability" in contrast to Ondine's capriciousness.

190

[7] An accompaniment figure shared by parts of the contrasting character and theme 2 is the ninth-chord in a large two-fold wave. First heard in bars 29/30 (A^9/B^9), the chord recurs in bars 39-42 ($F\sharp^9$), bar 82 ($D\sharp^9$) and, slightly varied, in bar 91 ($C^{9\flat}$). It is both intriguing and revealing to notice that these bars, which musically link the male narrator to "the other woman," are harmonically entirely conservative: no hint of the bitonality that pervades all that is under Ondine's spell.

[8] Finally, Ravel's choice of key signatures deserves a mention. He employs two diametrically contrasting signatures—seven sharps vs. no sharps—as well as, towards the very end of the piece, an "other" signature (five sharps). The piece opens with seven sharps and thus links this key signature to Ondine. The first half of the song (more precisely: line 1-6 as well as most of line 7) remains in this tonal realm. All sharps are canceled at exactly that moment when component g reaches into the bass register—as if to suggest that everything is allowed to appear from Ondine's perspective until the moment when she actually reaches for the man. Thereafter, the transposed theme 1 (line 8) and theme 2 (lines 9 and 10) appear without accidentals. The seven sharps are reintroduced on occasion of the developmental processes spawned from theme 2, but given up again immediately thereafter. Thus line 12 (the other woman) begins in a notation without accidentals (the man's tonal realm, as one may be tempted to interpret) but then turns to a tonal organization of its own, with five sharps (see from bar 77). The final line of the song begins under the tonal influence of the third party with five sharps and then returns to the man's no-accidental key signature. The coda, however, concludes by re-empowering Ondine: after an unaccompanied phrase without accidentals (perhaps a last, already almost disembodied longing for the mate that was not to be?), the final three bars return to the seven sharps and the original C$\sharp$-major triad with added minor sixth, thus placing the mermaid back in her element.

Le Gibet (Ravel, *Gaspard de la nuit*, no. 2)

This poem's relentless directness is reminiscent of François Villon and Arthur Rimbaud, poets known for their fascination with the lowest and even criminal elements of society. Rimbaud treats a basically similar topic in his *Le Bal des pendus* (The Ball of the Hanged Men), and both he and Villon heroicize outlaws at the margins of society. (Jean Genet later followed the same track.) Nineteenth-century France was well acquainted with blood-and-murder ballads. Encouraged by Victor Hugo, the chansonnier Maurice Rollinat performed such ballads in the salons of Parisian nobility, and Hugo himself evokes eerie pictures. Debussy had plans to compose an opera based on Edgar Allan Poe's "The Fall of the House of Usher."

The poet's choice of epigram is intriguing. Bertrand quotes Faust with the words *Que vois-je remuer autour de ce Gibet?* (What do I see moving around this gibbet?) The attention, then, centers neither on the ghastly vision of a human life ended by strangling, nor on any delving into the personality of the criminal, the motives for his deed, or the reception of his death by fellow human beings. What struck Faust and inspired Bertrand is the movement around the gallows, which may be an intrusion of non-related agents or the reflection of an inner movement related to the subject of the hanging. The poem confirms this direction of thought. Below is the text, with my translation on the page facing it.

Ah! ce que j'entends, serait-ce la bise nocturne qui glapit, ou le pendu qui pousse un soupir sur la fourche patibulaire?

Serait-ce quelque grillon qui chante tapi dans la mousse et le lierre stérile dont par pitié se chausse le bois?

Serait-ce quelche mouche en chasse sonnant du cor autour de ces oreilles sourdes à la fanfare des hallali?

Serait-ce quelque escarbot qui cueille en son vol inégal un cheveu sanglant à son crâne chauve?

Ou bien serait-ce quelque araignée qui brode une demi-aune de mousseline pour cravate à ce col étranglé?

C'est la cloche qui tinte aux murs d'une ville sous l'horizon, et la carcasse d'un pendu que rougit le soleil couchant.

Bertrand draws our attention to two facets of a transitional space. On the one hand, there is the very moment between life and death. The question that pervades all six stanzas of his poem asks after the origin and nature of a sound. The two framing verses clearly stake out this ground. In the beginning, the lyrical "I" is wondering whether the sound may be the sigh of the hanged man; there may still be life. But the end speaks unequivocally of a carcass, a corpse. Even the choice of articles traces the same development. "The sigh of *the* hanged man" (*le pendu*), with its use of the direct "the" still implying individuality, gives way to "the corpse of a hanged man" (*un pendu*), the indirect form insinuating that personality and distinctiveness cease at the moment of death. The entire poem can thus be read as an unfolding of that moment between almost-no-life and definite death. The elements evoked to set this effigy off in the framing verses paint an image of suggestive power with a gothic undertone. The screeching nocturnal breeze invites us to imagine the punished body not vertically still but swinging; the setting sun imbues the corpse with red, summoning the memory of bodies burned on the stakes but also painting a larger-than-life picture of the human shape.

On the other hand, Bertrand elicits, in the four central stanzas, the interaction between the living and the not-quite-dead. Significantly, the creatures proposed as possible sources of the puzzling sound are not animals whom a man could look in the eye, but insects—representatives of transition. Cricket, fly, beetle, spider are all related to the hanged man in ways that evolve from the innocuous to the downright morose.

Ah! might what I hear be the nocturnal breeze that screeches, or the hanged man who sighs on the fork of the gallows?

Might it be some cricket that sings, crouched in the moss and the infertile ivy with which out of pity the forest shoes itself?

Might it be some hunting fly, sounding its horn around those ears that are deaf to the fanfares of the hallali?*

Might it be some beetle that in its uneven flight plucks a bloody hair off his bald skull?

Or might it be some spider that crochets half a yard of muslin as a neck scarf for this strangled neck?

It is the clock that chimes on the walls of a city below the horizon, and the corpse of a hanged man whom the setting sun reddens.

* The proper English translation for "hallali," which is "mort," risks being misunderstood by contemporary readers, who place it in the context of romance-language words for death. "Mort" or "hallali" refers very specifically to a fanfare played over the death of a prey at the end of a hunt.

- The cricket keeps a certain distance. Neither its place in the moss underneath the gibbet nor its singing associates in any way with the dying or dead body. Only its chosen habitat, the infertile ivy, alludes to the bleakness of the site, while Bertrand's suggestion of pity as nature's motive to grow moss and ivy introduces a trace of compassion. The hint of this emotion alerts the reader to the successive loss of empathy through the following stanzas.
- The fly transgresses the boundaries of personal space, buzzing into the ears of the man who can no longer defend himself. The ears, however, are already deaf to the hunting call or any other activity. While the hanged man and his impending death form part of this scene, the reference does not contain elements of gross disrespect or horror.
- The beetle plucks a blood-soaked hair from the hanged man's skull. This image epitomizes the complete loss of dignity, the intrusiveness of the world upon one for whom physical punishment is not yet cruel enough; there is also clearly an element of exploitation.
- Finally, the spider crochets a necktie for the strangled man, mocking him beyond any decency.

The identification of the sound serves Bertrand as a device for holding this poem together. Through a series of ostensible attempts to ascertain the source of the sound, several layers are being connected. On the layer of poetic language, the fivefold *serait-ce* that in the sixth verse leads finally to an assertive *c'est* invokes a syntactic parallelism, which induces a sense of unity between the objective scene (depicted in the first and last stanzas) and the alternative potential subplots traced in the four central verses.[98]

Looking closer, one is struck by the fact that, on any level of credibility, this chain of sonic imagery is not realistic. There is no bell the sound of which could be mistaken for the sigh of a man, the screeching of the wind, the chirping of a cricket, the buzzing of a fly, or the humming of a beetle; and spiders produce no sound at all.

---

[98] I owe thanks to my friend Fred Bookstein, Distinguished Research Scientist at the University of Michigan, for drawing my attention to an eerily related American prose composition, Ambrose Bierce's short story "An Occurrence at Owl Creek Bridge" (reprinted e.g. in *The Amis Story Anthology*, Kingsley Amis, ed. [London: Hutchinson,1992]).

In fact, overriding the alleged musing over the source of the sound is a string of images for which the insects serve as allegorical impersonations. Sophus Bugge, in his study of folk-tale motifs, makes a strong case for the constant intermingling, particularly in medieval sources, of the gibbet with Christ's Cross.[99] According to Bugge, the gothic expression "galga Xristaus" denoted Christ's Cross, and Nordic *galga* as well as Anglo-Saxon *gealga* led to the modern words for gallows (see, e.g., German *Galgen*). Similarly, the Latin word from which these translations of the Christian Cross stem was *patibulum*—the direct etymological ancestor of one of the French terms for the gibbet, *patibulaire*. While the early Roman meaning of *patibulum* was the cross-beam laid across the criminal's neck, a beam to which his arms were tied (in a practice of crucifixion), ever since the early middle ages *patibulum* denotes the structure that we understand today as a gibbet: a cantilevered beam from which an offender is hanged by a rope around the neck.

While Bertrand chooses the common term for gallows, *gibet*, for the title of his poem, he substitutes the more formal *patibulaire* at the end of the first verse. The preposition *sur* in the same stanza equally invites us to pause; a hanged man is literally not "on" the fork of the wood (as a crucified man might be), but far below it. There is, then, an intentional mixing of metaphors that ties the image of the anonymous hanged man to that of the crucified Christ.

In light of this *double entendre*, the four sub-plots also carry additional meaning in a subtext, alluding to the entire spectrum of reactions to the Crucified, from pity through derision, exploitative violation and cruel mockery. All this is accompanied by the death bell, not yet identified but all the while heard tolling at the walls of a far-away city, *une ville sous l'horizon*, a place so distanced that its inhabitants (i.e., unrelated people in general) need not feel involved, much less responsible.

On all these levels of interpretation, the sound of the bell is thus the only thing that is real. Its tolling constitutes the link among the different aspects embedded in the poem. It marks the transition of a human from life to death, and from embeddedness in an empathetic nature to a state in which nature violates and ridicules the human. By extension, it also points to the paradigmatic image behind all tales of hanging, the crucified Jesus, who is surrounded, at the moment of transition from one realm to the other, by little pity but much defilement and derision.

[99] Sophus Bugge, *Studien über die Entstehung der nordischen Götter- und Heldensagen* (Munich: Christian Kaiser, 1889); particularly the chapter "Odin am Galgen," pp. 317 f.

Ravel captures many of these nuances in his deceptively easy piece.[100] As in the poem, the tolling of the bell is the unifying feature. The bell never pauses and never changes its pitch (which is B♭ throughout, though for a short span of five bars enharmonically notated as A♯). Its rhythm, however, makes it clear that all is not in order here.

Three aspects seem important: the metric position, the way the basic rhythmic pattern structures the four-four time, and the interruptions or distortions this pattern undergoes in the course of the piece. The piece begins with the bell rhythm alone, which enters in syncopated position after the second beat of the bar. In the absence of any clue as to what the intended meter is and where its units (the bars) begin and end, this bell rhythm establishes itself as a temporal reality of its own.

This reality—secondary or primary, one wonders—will persist throughout the piece, parallel to the temporal organization of the thematic elements with which it shares its extension of 8 eighth-note values. It is the metric structuring of the 8 eighths in the bell pattern that is accountable for the sense that the tolling of the death knell happens in a reality different from that in the thematic components. While these (cf. bars 3-5, 6/7) endorse an unambiguous four-four time, the bell's rhythm contains three constituents, in a repeatedly irregular pattern of 3/8-3/8-2/8. One cannot help being reminded, in this pitting of 4/4 time against a tripartite formation, of the spiritual significance associated with these numbers. In this piece, which deals with the moment between this world and the beyond, Ravel persistently pits 3 (for the divine and Trinitarian) against 4 (for the earthly-human). And while this "Trinitarian" rhythm is broken several times, not once does it change enough to coincide with the metric order of the "other realm."

The interruptions the bell rhythm undergoes as the piece unfolds present an interesting process. One can observe a gradual "deterioration" by which the spans featuring the originally established regular pattern become shorter, while the moments of distortion interspersed with the reassuring regularity become more and more invasive. The occurrences of the

[100]Ravel dedicated this piece to an old friend, the critic Jean Marnold, adding with amiable malice that this was the only one among the three that he might be able to play.

regular pattern decrease from thirteen (in bars 1-14) through eleven (bars 17-28) to two (bars 30-32) and down to several single appearances (bars 33/34, 42/43) and one metrically shifted pattern (bars 36/37, appearing an eighth-note early and in addition overrun at the end by a new beginning):

It is not until the very end of the piece that the original rhythm is firmly reinstated. Bars 47-52 close with five statements of the complete pattern, of which, however, the final one is significantly deprived of its concluding note. In view of the fact that the bell that is tolling here is the death-knell, this elision can be read, as I have argued, as a metaphor for the moment of passing away. In view of Ravel's dynamics indications (*ppp diminuendo*), the incomplete rhythmic pattern may also be heard as a fading out: henceforth the listener is excluded from a reality that continues—an indirect sign of respect offered one who has been ridiculed, despised, and put to death.

In this light, the distortions of the bell's basic rhythm are significant. While the procedure of hanging a man does not normally provide much of a threshold between life and death, both Bertrand and Ravel draw our attention to this very moment. Bertrand's device, as shown in some detail above, is to leave open until the very last verse whether or not the man is already dead; only the identification of the puzzling sound as the chiming of the death-knell launches the sentence that states the *fait accompli* by alluding to a corpse. If Bertrand's continued questioning of a mysterious sound leads merely in retrospect to the insight that the bell must have been tolling ever since the man was hanged, Ravel takes this as a given. He presents us the bell rhythm as the first and last thing we hear, yet he manages to avoid prematurely concluding the psychological process of transition.

Recall that the four central verses of Bertrand's poem present a gradual development of the attitude in which nature, represented by the four insects, deals with the transition from life to death. From the cricket chirping without taking much notice of the dying man, to the spider whose web is seen to be intended as a contemptuous scarf for the strangled throat, the creatures of transitory space relate in ever more intrusive ways to the hanged man. Ravel's music traces a similar development: he sets the various melodic elements and their specific harmonic contexts against the perpetual B♭ of the death-knell.

A first melodic element *(a)* is heard in bars 3-5. Its melodic line contains no semitone, no minor sixth or any other "emotional" interval. The vertical setting is equally objective, featuring parallel motion of superimposed perfect fifths, the uppermost of which is doubled in the higher octave). The central superimposition E♭ B♭ F, repeated three times on downbeats, can usefully be read as B♭ with a fifth above and a fifth below, thus strengthening rather than challenging the bell's pitch. Moreover, the structure of this motif—a one-bar segment, its literal repetition, and a simpler single stroke—is related in its tripartite design with the similar structure of the bell's basic rhythm.

bars 3-5

The objective nature of this motif appears in direct correspondence with the character expressed in Bertrand's framing verses, in which the presence of the hanged man is acknowledged without giving rise to any response or interaction.

The second motif *(b)* appears in bars 6/7. While its vertical organization in double octaves is neutral as before, its tonal reference is ambiguous. Heard alone, this motif would be perceived as relating to D♭ minor. In the combination with the bell's B♭ pitch, however, it is unclear whether this constitutes a change of tonal center or a B♭ minor context with diminished ished fifth. The horizontal organization with the semitone F♭-E♭, the dotted C♮ that is melodically heard as a leading note to the root D♭, and the lingering *appoggiatura* at the end creates an impression of heightened emotional involvement, temporarily appeased again by the shortened recurrence of motif *a* in bars 8/9.

Motif *b* recurs in bars 10/11 with doubling by the (upper!) third, thus enhancing the impression of a secondary tonality rooted in D♭. Ravel heightens the sense of emotional tension expressed in the descending semitone by duplicating it in the upper third with the aid of a G♮.

As motif *a* recurs in bars 12-14, it is much changed, as if infected by the challenging attitude of the previous component. Transposed in such a way that its root chord bears no tonal relation to the bell's B♭, it is now modified in vertical structure as well. The neutral perfect fifths of the original motif are replaced with triads expanded by minor thirds added below their roots. Horizontally, the chords follow one another in constant cross-relationship. The combination of these two devices defies tonal centering in every respect. As though that was not enough, Ravel intensifies the second-bar repetition of the motif with a triplet introducing the chromatic downward shift of the augmented chord.

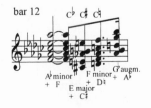

bars 1/2

bars 12-14

One element counteracts the dramatic slide here. In the third strand of the texture, thus far silent, Ravel now introduces a pedal in double octaves. This pedal rings on B♭, reinforcing thus the bell's central pitch, and in a rhythm that seems like a varied augmentation of the basic bell pattern.

The final melodic gesture of the varied motif *a* in bar 14 begins a transition confirmed in the contrasting setting of the next two bars. The meter changes to three-four time, bringing with it the first distortion of the bell rhythm. The tonal organization, featuring simultaneous perfect-fifth (in the lowest strand) and perfect-fourth parallels (in the middle strand) over E♭ and B♭, progresses to a phrase over E♭ as a new pedal. The fact that the pedal recalls the rhythm heard in bars 12-14 in faithful transposition enhances the sense that the centrality of B♭ has now been abandoned. The two upper strands in bars 17-19 also present a direct transposition of the varied motif *a* from bars 12-14, including the transition gesture at the end. As a logical consequence, the pedal is transposed one more time down the circle of fifths. Only now, over an unrhythmicized pedal-note on A♭, does Ravel introduce the new material that his harmonic progressions have already made the listener anticipate.

The texture has now expanded to four strands. Two strings of chords in regular eighth-notes converge in contrary motion, deriving their pitches from the A♭-minor seventh chord with sixth and diminished fifth. Supported by the protracted A♭ octave in the bass, they surround a metrically misplaced bell rhythm. Soon after the bell has regained its regular pattern, the chords settle in reluctant parallels: see, in the right hand of bars 21/22, the threefold chromatic descent in double thirds and its complement in the left hand that evades parallelism for every other third. The "disturbance" is exacerbated in the sequence of the three-bar phrase (bars 23-25). Here, the bass has left the harmonic tie to the circle of fifths and moved chromatically (or.emotionally) down a semitone. The bell, beginning with the same metric distortion as before, is surrounded by contrary-motion chords that neither relate to the pedal-note nor derive from any one tonal context. Finally, the "reluctant" parallels have split, developing even more gestures that seem to epitomize the musical equivalent of an unwillingness to empathize. In the left-hand part, the double-notes meet only momentarily in octaves, and the descending three-note chords in the right-hand part are framed by harsh major sevenths.

These six bars constitute the third of the emotionally loaded musical steps the composer takes in the course of relating motivic material to the central bell or, in the image drawn by Bertrand, of relating the creatures of transitional space to the hanged man. While the affective quality of motif *b* simply introduces another presence beside that symbolized by the death-knell, the first transformations undergone by the two thematic elements move into realms (tonal as well as spiritual ones) that seem ever less sympathetic—just as Bertrand portrayed his cricket as "just another presence," whereas his fly is already somewhat disrespectful. The tonal movement away from the central B♭ can be heard as a musical correspondence to Bertrand's consecutively visualized movements away from sympathy and awe centered on the punished man, towards the more and more macabre action of the insects approaching his body.

The fourth step and climax of this development is the passage from bar 26 to bar 34 (see example on the next page). Horizontally, this section comprises a long melodic theme with extensions at both sides. The core of the theme unfolds in bars 28-30. It features a repeated descending semitone F-E in the first subphrase (see bars 28 and 29) and a traditional melodic closing formula constituting most of the second subphrase. The melodically leading part in the two bars preceding this phrase can be identified, in hindsight, as an anticipation of the phrase's final gesture (cf. bars 26 and 27 with bar 30 with regard to both melody and harmony.) The second phrase, triggered by an octave displacement of the closing gesture, unexpectedly clad in transformed harmonic attire (see bar 31), plays further with the descending step and ends in the same closing formula, transposed upward by a perfect fourth. The harmonic underpinning continues with dominant-ninth chords. The reiteration of the chord in the prolongation matches that in the anticipation (cf. bar 31 with bars 33, 34) and thus creates a symmetry that makes this climactic phrase stand out even more

In terms of tonality as well, this passage reaches the height of disjunction. The theme, taken alone as a horizontally designed entity, is conceived in D minor; but pedal notes flanking its phrases—C♯ in bars 26/27 and E♭ in bars 33/34—are placed a semitone above and below that central pitch. Moreover, the vertically defined elements themselves are full of deception. The chord in bars 26/27, clearly a dominant-ninth chord (C♯-E♯-B-D) that suggests resolution into F♯ or one of its usual substitutes, lingers unresolved (half-heartedly challenged by a weak-beat seventh-chord on A, see bar 29), then suddenly moves on to another dominant

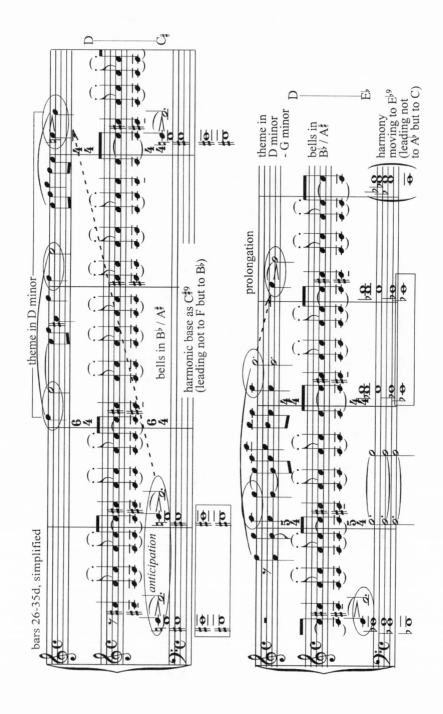

bars 26-35d, simplified

theme in D minor

anticipation

bells in B♭ / A♯

harmonic base as C♯♭9
(leading not to F but to B♭)

D

C♯

prolongation

theme in
D minor
- G minor

bells in
B♭ / A♯

harmony
moving to E♭♭9
(leading not
to A♭ but to C)

D

E♭

function, the seventh-chord three semitones lower (B♭-D-A♭). This chord, transposed, turns into another dominant-ninth chord (E♭-G-B♭-D♭-F♭), again to resolve into a seventh-chord three semitones lower (C-E♭-G♭-B♭). These repeated deceptive progressions must be considered sarcastic, as is the strikingly unsupportive character of the harmonic movements surrounding the theme. One is reminded of the inappropriate neck scarf offered to the hanged man by Bertrand's spider.

Bertrand stuns the readers of his poem when, at the height of horror over the degraded man, we are ingeniously reassured about the original of the sound that gave rise to all his speculations. It's nothing but the traditional death-knell, he lets us know, and whatever the insects might do can no longer touch this corpse. But Ravel proceeds differently. His music began with the death-knell associated with a gibbet—no possibility of surprise there. How, then, can Ravel extricate himself and his listeners from the emotional turmoil into which he has led them?

Once the multifarious clashes of realities have passed, epitomized in the D-minor theme and its harmonic surroundings, Ravel takes pains to "undo" what has happened, step by step. In bars 35-37, extended to the downbeat of bar 40, he presents a variation of motif *a* similar to the one that triggered much of the disjunction. Now, however, the parallel chords are much more closely related, both among one another and to the bass pedal. A long extension gives us time to restore ourselves and prepares the return of the bass to the central note B♭ (see bar 40 onwards). The contrary-motion figure recurs as well (see bars 40/41). Its pitches are taken from a single chord based on the pedal (as was also the case in bars 20-22, before the major distortions began to happen), and this time they also agree with the bell's B♭.

Next in this process of undoing, motif *b* is heard once more. Its pitch line stems from the variation presented in bars 10/11, but its texture in simple double octaves points even further back to the original of this motif. After a partial recurrence of the contrary-motion figure, Ravel undoes even the melodic strain exerted by the F♭-centered melody of the motif-*b* variation. A string of decreasing intervals over B♭ reduce the tension from that of the tritone F♭-B♭ to the much softer one experienced in the original motif *b*, D♭-B♭ (cf. bars 44m-48). One step further back, the original motif *a* with its superimposed fifths centered in B♭, recurs, and the regressive process concludes with the return to the unaccompanied bell.

Scarbo (Ravel, *Gaspard de la nuit*, no. 3)

Il regarda sous le lit, dans la cheminée, dans le bahut; - personne.
Il ne put comprendre par où il s'était introduit, par où il s'était évadé.

Oh! que de fois je l'ai entendu et vu, Scarbo, lorsqu'à minuit la lune brille dans le ciel comme un écu d'argent sur une bannière d'azur semée d'abeilles d'or!
Que de fois j'ai entendu bourdonner son rire dans l'ombre de mon alcôve, et grincer son ongle sur la soie des courtines de mon lit!
Que de fois je l'ai vu descendre du plancher, pirouetter sur un pied et rouler par la chambre comme le fuseau tombé de la quenouille d'une sorcière!
Le croyais-je alors évanoui? le nain grandissait entre la lune et moi comme le clocher d'une cathédrale gothique, un grelot d'or en branle à son bonnet pointu.
Mais bientôt son corps bleuissait, diaphane comme la cire d'une bougie, son visage blémissait comme la cire d'un lumignon, - et soudain il s'éteignait.

Who is this Scarbo to whom Bertrand has dedicated two poems in his collection *Gaspard de la nuit*? Although clearly an apparition, he is addressed in a manner that suggests he is real and we might all know him. Is there no need to introduce him? Is he, as we are led to believe since he is referred to by his proper name, a close acquaintance? Early on we guess that he must be a creature who, in the light of a silvery moon under a star-studded sky, intrudes into people's bedrooms. But not until the fourth of five stanzas do we learn that he is a dwarf—only to be confused immediately by being told that he is seen growing tall "like the belfry of a Gothic cathedral."[101]

When the pianist Vlado Perlemuter studied the *Gaspard de la nuit* under Ravel's guidance, the composer is reported to have admitted that he had planned the piece as a caricature of romanticism; but—and there his voice allegedly died down to a whisper—he feared he may himself have been caught in the spell. In fact, the passionate ascending-seventh interval (bar 32 etc.) under which Ravel wrote the words "quelle horreur" (what horror) is closer to genuine romantic emotion than to its caricature.

---

[101] While "Scarbo" as a proper name for a nocturnal ghost does not seem to have a history in French folklore or literature, Bertrand, surprisingly, uses it twice. One of the Scarbo poems forms part of book III (*La nuits et ses prestiges*) of *Gaspard de la nuit*; that is the section from where Ravel took the text for *Ondine*. The poem appears here in the context of two others with a similar general topic, *Le Fou* (The Madman) and *Le Nain* (The Dwarf). The other Scarbo poem, the one Ravel chose, is number 12 of the *Pièces détachées* that form the coda of the *Gaspard* collection, following, as in the music, *Le Gibet*.

He looked under the bed, up the chimney, in the chest; nobody.
He could not understand from where he had entered,
or where he had escaped.

O! how many times have I heard and seen him, Scarbo, when at midnight the moon shines in the sky like a silver crown on a blue banner emblazoned with golden bees.

How many times have I heard his laughter resound in the shadow of my alcove, heard his claw scrape on the silk of my bed curtains!

How many times have I seen him come down from the floor, pirouette on one foot and roll around the room like the fallen spindle of a sorceress's distaff.

Did I then believe him vanished? The dwarf grew tall between the moon and me like the belfry of a Gothic cathedral, a golden bell swinging on its pointed cap.

But soon his body turned blue, diaphanous like the wax of a candle, his face grew pale like the wax of a candle stub—and suddenly he expired.

The epigram preceding the poem corroborates this idea. The lines are from the French translation of the collection *Nachtstücke* by that most romantic poet, E. T. A. Hoffmann.

Using a number of intriguing devices in this poem, Bertrand creates the impression of creepy immediacy and at the same time a sense of the perennial exposure of our lives to forces from the realm of "Scarbo." In the first three, structurally parallel stanzas, the accent is on the triple "how many times." The sleeper, speaking in the first person, seems eager to assure us that an intruder seen and heard again and again must have some reality—if merely a subjective one. His specification about the time that usually brings Scarbo to his bed chamber, however, is a giveaway; while midnight is undoubtedly the hour of preference for phantoms and specters, the suggestion that "the moon resembles a silver crown" and the star-studded sky a "blue banner emblazoned with golden bees" tells us that visionary fantasy by no means begins with the entrance of the ghost, but is in the eyes of the beholder well before the event occurs. One thus begins wondering, at this early point in the poem, what causes what: does the arrival of Scarbo cause strange sounds and sights that haunt an innocent victim, or rather, does the narrator's obvious susceptibility to fantastic visions bring Scarbo into existence? There is, then, a peculiar mutual causation between the lyrical "I" and the phantom, a relationship that challenges the picture of an active visitor intruding upon a passive sleeper.

While the first stanza seems to set the stage for the fact that this ghost is "heard and seen," the second and third verses ostensibly undertake to detail each of the two sensual experiences separately, focusing explicitly on "How many times have I heard" in the one and "How many times have I seen" in the other. On closer inspection, however, stanza 2 does not only concern itself with the sounds of Scarbo's resounding laughter and the grating noise his finger nails or claws create on the bed curtains; nor does stanza 3 exclusively report visual impressions, as its opening line seems to suggest. The specter's reverberating laughter emanates from the shadow of the sleeper's alcove and the scraping noise from the silken bed curtain, prompting us to visualize the intruder, eerily close to the narrator's body. Similarly, the image of Scarbo whirling around the room on a single foot inevitably evokes accompanying sounds, and one cannot picture him rolling around "like the fallen spindle of a sorceress' distaff" without hearing the clattering noises that would accompany such mayhem. On this level there is, then, a mutual causation of sounds and images that defies the apparent semantic distinction and separation into two stanzas dedicated to things either heard or seen.

The two final stanzas change perspective—in both meanings of the word. Semantically, the initial sentence of stanza 4 completes the series of statements in which a lyrical "I" is the subject perceiving (if not conceiving) the apparition. After *je l'ai entendu et vu...* (stanza 1), *je l'ai entendu...* (stanza 2), and *je l'ai vu...* (stanza 3), there is, as a conclusion, a single question, *le croyais-je ...?*, portraying the narrator asking himself what he makes of all this and thus stressing the interpretive aspect. From there on, the language changes. The grammatical subjects are henceforth the dwarf, his body, and his face respectively. Consequently, the verbs no longer refer to perceptions, whether sensual and real or mentally induced as a result of an overstimulated imagination. Instead, the two earlier verbs denoting sensation and interpretation (I heard, I saw) are now matched with three verbs describing transformations. These transformations are not presented as "seeming as if" but as ostensibly real; the dwarf grew taller, his body turned blue, his face turned pale. Finally, accompanying this change of rhetorical perspective we find a change of perspective in characterizing the ghost. No longer determined by what he does, Scarbo is now portrayed as someone to whom strange things are happening. No longer noisy and vivacious, he suddenly seems frozen into a spot where he metamorphizes into something gaunt and diaphanous.

In spite of the conspicuous triple comparative "*comme*" that follows the verbs of transformation in these two stanzas (*grandissait... comme le clocher d'une cathédrale, bleuissait... comme la cire d'une bougie, blémissait comme la cire d'un lumignon*), the three visually diverse and psychologically significant images are not conjured up as a direct match to the three verbs but overlap them. They are cunningly chosen to refer to all the mixed feelings an apparition might cause in the involuntary host. There is a sense of awe, embodied in the image of the majestically high spire of a Gothic cathedral; there is a nervous urge to ridicule, captured in the sudden twist that reinterprets the belfry and its bell as the pointed, jingling cap of a buffoon; and there is an anxious need to be reassured of one's ultimate safety, epitomized by the candle that, a single line later, has turned into a mere candle stub, assuring the disturbed sleeper that sooner rather than later this apparition will expire.

Behind the ambiguity of attribution captured in the question "what causes what?," the ambiguity of visual and auditory impressions, the change of perspective in talking about the ghost, the change of behavior in the ghost himself, and the psychologically significant metaphors, there is an interesting numerical play in this poem. One part of it is presented as a cross-arrangement of THREES and TWOS:

- THREE stanzas framed in the clauses of "how many times have I (perceived him)!" are followed by TWO stanzas with ostensibly unmediated descriptions of the transformations the specter undergoes.

- The THREE initial stanzas contain TWO verbs denoting the narrator's sensual impressions of the nocturnal visitor (to hear and to see), as well as a TWOfold interplay between the TWO protagonists (the ghost generating the perceptions and the perceptions generating the ghost) and the TWO sense impressions (sounds heard that imply visual images, and scenes observed that evoke the accompanying noises).

- The TWO final stanzas are framed by a question and an assertion that indicate the ghost's dissolving into thin air ("Did I believe him vanished? .... and suddenly he expired.") Within this dualistic frame are contained THREE layers of THREE observations, covering Scarbo's physique (the dwarf, his body, his face), his metamorphoses (becoming tall, blue, pale), and the metaphors attached to him (belfry, buffoon, candle).

207

However, this apparent increase in verbal intensity and imagery in the last two stanzas is a matter of metaphoric interpretation, while the phantom's actions are much more uniform than they were in the stanzas explicitly dedicated to that which was heard and seen. Only two (related) processes are evoked here: metamorphosis and extinction. As a result, the total of Scarbo's actions as described in this poem equals SEVEN—another momentous number.

He
- laughs,   - twirls,   - transmutes, and
- scratches,   - rolls around - disintegrates.
- plunges,   the room,

The number SEVEN will be read, for want of any more specific clues, in its usual symbolic sense, epitomizing the seven traditional sins, along with the temptations to commit these sins, or the seven demons that Jesus exorcises. While there is hardly a religious theme here, the musical analysis will show that Ravel was eager to portray the nocturnal phantom luring the sleeper away from a sober perspective into excitement and frenzy.

To sum up, Bertrand's poem can be read in several different ways: as a Gothic tale about a midnight ghost, as a hidden psychological interpretation of the phenomenon of phantom experiences, and as a witty play with TWO VS. THREE, TWO in THREE, dual (= ambivalent) vs. triple (= perfect or complete, giving all aspects), and with SEVEN as a special interpretive twist on the moral nature of what Scarbo signifies in the life of his host.

Ravel's piano piece, too, can be approached in several significantly different ways, revealing parallels to what is expressed in the poem.

On the level that might be considered the most straightforward by most musicians, viz. the level of structure, *Scarbo* represents a not so unusual case of sonata movement form. One recognizes the exposition in bars 1-188, the development section in bars 189-393, the recapitulation in bars 394-541, and a second development plus coda in bars 542-626. As is common in sonata movements, there are clearly two tonal centers, D$\sharp$ and B—though the question of which is primary and which is secondary will have to be answered in a way that transcends normal concerns of sonata form. Beyond this traditional structural scheme, however, there are two overlapping realities expressed in SEVENS; one of them regards the design when seen under aspects other than those of the manifestation of an extant form, the other concerns the thematic material.

The SEVEN thematic units in this piece constitute three motifs and four themes. They differ in extension from one bar (= three eighth-notes for motif *a*) to sixty-nine bars (for theme 4). The cunning way in which they are interlinked is worth investigating in more detail (see below). Suffice it here to observe that the SEVEN is composed of TWOS and THREES —AND this goes way beyond simple, additive composition.

- The TWO-fold division regards   2 in 7:
  motifs vs. themes, while   motifs and themes

- THREE counts the groups formed on   3 in 7:
  the basis of thematic interrelation-   groups of themati-
  ship These comprise,   cally related
  first, motif *a*, motif *b*, and theme 1,   material
  second, motif c and themes 2 and 3,
  and third, the extensive and thematically independent theme 4.

On the larger scale, this grouping of the thematic material is responsible for the SEVEN-part form that is perceived beneath the sonata movement. These audibly discerned portions—as against the sections that traditional analytical tools would have us report—are of very different length and complexity.

I	bars	1-31	exposition 1	with motifs *a*, *b*, *c*
II	bars	32-119	exposition 2	with themes 1, 2, 3
III	bars	120-188	exposition 3	with theme 4
IV	bars	189-393	development 1	with themes 1, 2, 3, 4
V	bars	394-446/476-541	recapitulation	with motifs *a*, *b*, *c* and themes 2, 4
VI	bars	447-475	insert	with foreign material
VII	bars	542-626	recapitulation 2	with motifs *a*, *b* and themes 4, 1, 2

This brings us to the small-scale analysis, and to the messages conveyed on that level. The initial section of Ravel's piece *Scarbo* introduces, and subsequently plays with, three motifs. Motif *a* consists of three eighth-notes in diminishing *pp legato*, delineating the perfect fifth G♯-D♯ preceded by its leading-note F*. Motif *b* comprises a protracted chord topped by a melodically falling perfect fourth. For reasons that will soon become apparent, this chord (C*-E-G♯-B) can usefully be read in terms of classical harmony as a VII^7 with diminished third of D♯. Functionally,

209

these two motifs support the tonal center D♯ by way of its subdominant (motif a = G♯D♯ = IV) and dominant (motif-b chord = VII^7). D♯ itself appears as motif c, an extensive, fifty-six-fold note repetition marked *très fondu* (very much blended or blurred). Ravel's second indication for the sound of this note repetition, *en trémolo*, carries a double meaning. Understood as an expression within established musical terminology, it refers the pianist to a style of execution better known to string players. (A *tremolo* in piano repertoire characteristically involves at least two different pitches that alternate in fast shakes.) As a literal translation of a word of Italian origin, the term means "trembling" and thus sets the emotional stage for midnight phantoms and other supernatural apparitions—real or imagined, involuntary or sought out. The three motifs are rounded off by a further element, easily overlooked in the score but never in a good performance. This is the rest that follows, extending the conglomerate of motifs to a total of SEVEN bars! With its *fermata*, magnified by Ravel's instruction *très long*, this silence adds considerably to the eeriness that pervades the piece from its very beginning.

bars 1-7

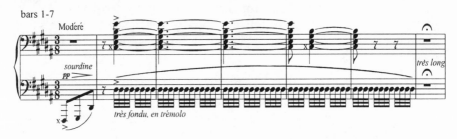

This is not, however, all there is to the initial material. Above and beyond the visually presented SEVEN bars of three beats each with their three motifs, there is an auditory reality that presents quite a different angle. Owing to the omission of the downbeat in the second bar and the two syncopated chordal attacks in the right hand (on the second beats of bars 2 and 5 respectively), no listener will, or should, have an idea what metric order is designated here. What is actually being perceived by listeners is a BI-partite event of strange proportions. The first component is a unison motif comprising four beats (three attacks and a rest) in decreasing volume; the second is a "trembling" chord of practically unfathomable duration. Within this second component, the nine beats of the first chordal attack are heard as one long shudder that, while exceeding intuitive comprehension, is basically measurable. The five notated beats of the second chord, by contrast, vanish into silence and extend for what must seem like an indefinite time—for however long a performer can keep up the tension.

This brings us to the psychological message contained in the first phrase of the piece. Ravel seems to give us a sneak preview of what the story is all about. There is an initial stirring, murmur, or commotion that indicates, to the imagination of the fantasy-inclined sleeper anyway, the presence of a ghost. After a short, startled silence (one imagines the sleeper nervously listening into the dark), there is a long shudder, accompanied by a sigh ... "growing ever longer and paler" ... and finally dissipating.

Subsequently, the entire, multi-layered seven-bar combination expands into a tripartite structure of its own. After a complete repetition (with the right-hand part an octave lower; see bars 8-14), the third component on this larger scale is a development of motifs a and b. Growth occurs on many levels here. A two-fold motif a,[102] reinforced half-way through by two pitches representing the chord of motif b, rises through six consecutive octaves. The first statement of this extended motif a retains the original rhythm, the next two squeeze four attacks into the space of three, and the remaining three statements assume rhythmic values twice those of the original. In addition to this ascent (through the ranges of the keyboard) and intensification (in a three-step process of ever denser material), Ravel prescribes *crescendo accelerando*. The climax of this multiple increase presents a *tremolo* in which a chordal version of motif a (the pitches are simultaneous but also inverted) alternates with the chord from motif b, building a powerful dynamic curve of *pp-ff-(pp)* followed by two additional bars of silence.

To sum up, this first section contains THREE segments (a phrase, its repetition, and its development/intensification). The seminal phrase can be perceived in TWO ways: as TWO subsequent auditory "events" (of 4 beats and 19+ beats respectively) or as THREE textual components (motifs a, b and c). The seminal phrase contains the events of the poem in a nutshell; the entire section with its three-fold exploration of the ghost's initial stirring speaks of the "How many times!" that Scarbo has been

---

[102]Note that Ravel has adjusted the lowest pitches to the reality of the keyboard, writing A♮-A♯-D♯ instead of F×-G♯-D♯, apparently trusting that our ears find it hard to discern those extremely low frequencies and will hear what is intended rather than what is actually played. Performers playing on pianos with extended keyboards can, of course, substitute the "correct" notes here.

heard and seen. It also reasserts, with its protracted (SEVEN-bar!) chordal *tremolo*, the creepiness of the experience.

The second section of the piece is much more extensive and introduces three themes rather than three motifs. However, behind this tripartite material there looms, once again, a dualistic aspect. On the one hand, there are two occurrences of the first theme framing the section; on the other hand, the second and third themes are related to one another in several ways, thus offering a united front of contrast.

Theme 1 is, in terms of its thematic material, a metamorphosis of two of the motifs introduced in the initial section; in terms of its tonal organization, it is significantly bi-layered, i.e. ambiguous, contradictory. The double-octave line in the right-hand part of bars 32/33 presents an extended variant of motif *a* (F×-G♯-D♯ transposed to D♯-E-....-B).

bars 32-44

(melody still D♯ - - -)

accomp. D♯ - - - - - - - - - - - - - - - C♯ -
(already)

Once this connection has been established, bars 34 and 35 easily fall into place as two further variants. After a bar of melodic rest, the descending perfect-fourth interval in the treble of bars 37-44 with its two syncopated attacks clearly recalls the same melodic step in motif *b*. Keeping the subdominant function of motif *a* in mind, the melodic part of bars 32/33 would thus refer to B as a central pitch. Both the middle-voice A♯ and the left-hand *arpeggio*, however, suggest D♯ major as the still reigning tonal focus. Yet hardly have the listeners adjusted their ears to respect the vertical over the horizontal message and convince themselves that D♯ is more "real" than B here—an adjustment that comes easy in bars 34/35 with its repeated melodic D♯—than the accompaniment changes to C♯ major. This new bitonality continues through bars 37-40. In the poem, the initial ambiguity whether Scarbo, referred to as being "heard and seen as," is a product of the narrator's visionary fantasy or an actual intruder, gives way to the unmediated descriptive statements of what Scarbo actually is. Similarly in the music, the extended tonal ambiguity that might be read as an emotional outbreak of a soul torn between two realities recedes. As the "sigh" dies off, the *arpeggio* is triply reduced: in dynamics (from *mf-ff-mf* gradually diminishing to *pp*), in rhythmic intensity (from three triplets to three duplets per bar), and in range (from a broken chord spanning over more than three octaves to a simple "trembling" fifth; see the four stages in bars 35/36, 37-40, 41-44, 45-50). The anticipated but omitted next stage in this reduction would be the note repetition of motif *c*—the reality of trembling excitement has won over the skepticism that labels the whole scene as nothing but a hallucination.

Instead of the expected note repetition, theme 2 is launched in bar 51. In several respects, this theme can be recognized as a development of certain aspects from the initial section, while continuing to embody the play with the numbers 2, 3 and 7, with THREE layers expressing various aspects of DUALism in SEVEN-bar phrases. The lowest strand is taken up entirely by a repeated pedal on B, the second tonal center of the piece, briefly suggested but not realized in theme 1. The second layer contains a three-note group and its transposition. The group relates negatively to motif *a* in that its whole-tone/diminished fifth outline conspicuously subverts the semitone/P5 structure of motif *a*. Erected over the current tonal center B, the chord B-F-G is heard in bars 51-55, its transposition (transformation?) G♯-D-E appears in bars 51 and 56 (right hand), and the concluding bar of the phrase, bar 57, combines the two versions. The uppermost, melodic layer of the theme plays structurally with the number TWO. A one-bar rest followed by a one-bar segment, and a two-bar rest followed by a two-bar segment, are wrapped up by the dualistic bar 57. Tonally as well, the entire theme 2 is dualistic. While the pedal-note creates a strong orientation towards B, the melodically prominent pitch is D♯, supported by the G♯ that prominently concludes the second segment of the phrase. The fact that the melodic line is marked *staccato* and the central pitch D♯ is thrust from a note repetition is strongly reminiscent of the repeated D♯ in motif *c*.

In its overall structure, theme 2 is an extended ternary form. Note that each segment is SEVEN bars long.

bars 51-57	main phrase
bars 58-64	main phrase repeated
bars 65-71	contrasting phrase
bars 72-78	main phrase recurs, varied
bars 79-85	extension 1 (still on pedal-note B)
bars 86-91	extension 2 (now on pedal-note G♯)

Theme 2 is rounded off with a dynamically dissipating *arpeggio*, consisting of a G♯-minor triad with its leading-notes F𝕩, A♯ and C𝕩. The chord subsequently resolves into a D♯-major chord, thus re-establishing the tonal center of the initial section, that of the hallucinatory realm.[103]

Theme 3 is launched from the second beat of bar 93. It begins very innocently with an extremely regular phrase structure: a first phrase of 2 + 2 bars followed by its varied repetition, accompanied in repetitive rhythmic patterns. The tonal center holding the melody and the underlying intervals together is D♯. This and the prominence of note-repetitions link this theme to theme 2 and, further back, to motif *c*. Two facets, however, make this seemingly harmless embodiment of the nocturnal guest's boisterous behavior somewhat more disconcerting. Tonally, the distinct orientation towards D♯ minor in the melodic part struggles with a persistent major third F𝕩 in the accompaniment; dynamically, the open-ended extension increases powerfully towards *ff* and then suddenly breaks off with an almost threatening gesture.

Finally in this section, the recurrence of theme 1 (see bars 109ff) is at the same time different from and significantly in tune with the original version in bars 32ff; it is different with regard to surface features while in tune with regard to the underlying message of ambiguity that characterizes this theme. The accompaniment starts out as a D♯-major ninth-chord and it does not shift to C♯ as before but stays on the central note. Instead, the melody performs the shift (see bar 112), reasserting the essential ambiguity and skepticism (Is this really happening? Or is this just an imagined scene?). However, D♯ as the tonal center is unequivocally confirmed in the last bars of the section (see bars 115-119), thus establishing what is to be the reigning interpretation of reality.

To sum up, section II can be read as filling in details to a plot outline given in the seminal first phrase of the piece. The bitonally conceived theme 1, which seems to challenge the validity of that which the central pitch D♯ stands for, is thematically derived from motifs *a* and *b* of section I, whose tonal function would remain unclear without the D♯ added by motif *c*. In that sense, motifs *a* and *b* and the theme derived from them

---

[103]More on the play with TWOS and THREES:

- The contrasting phrase begins with *hemiolas*, the prototypical metric device asking the question "TWO or THREE?"

- The first TWO of the THREE bars of silence at the end of this phrase (cf. bars 70-72) constitute the "vanishing" perspective of the preceding phrase, reminiscent of the two bars of silence concluding the initial section (bars 30/31); the third one-bar rest corresponds with bars 51 and 58 (where, however, the accompaniment did not pause).

may be said to stand for the perceptive angle, the emotions experienced by the narrator, while motif *c* in this scenario represents that which is being perceived (and taken for real and frightening), i.e. Scarbo and his alleged antics.

If we accept this reading, closer observation shows the narrator's experience musically characterized by intense emotional involvement. This can be ascertained both horizontally (prepared in the *legato* articulation of motif *a* and the falling fourth of motif *b*, and fully realized in the dramatic ascending major-seventh in theme 1) and vertically (expressed in the full chords in motif *b* and particularly the sweeping accompaniment of theme 1). By contrast, when Scarbo appears directly and not mediated through the perceiver's reactions, he sounds very different. Themes 2 and 3 feature a light touch set against a sparse accompaniment. Motif *c* informs not only the melodically predominant pitch D♯ (as shown in the example below) but also the instances of "shaking" (see particularly the trill-like accompaniment that begins in bars 51-64 and turns into a doubly fast *tremolo* in bars 65-67, and the shakes in bars 103-107 that wrap up the two Scarbo themes), confirming once again that D♯ designates the realm in which Scarbo's appearance is taken at face value.

theme 2, bars 51-57 (repeated in bars 58-64)

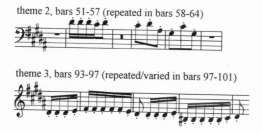

theme 3, bars 93-97 (repeated/varied in bars 97-101)

Last but not least, the more rhythmically distinct repeated D♯s in themes 2 and 3 and their musical characterizations in the different contexts shed light on the verbs Bertrand's narrator uses to describe the actions of his nocturnal visitor in the first three stanzas of the poem. All the sounds Scarbo is heard to make—laughing, scraping, pirouetting or rattling like a fallen spindle—are presented as derived from the repeated-note *tremolo*, and thus interpreted as auditory manifestations of the trembling triggered by the unidentified nocturnal sound.

Beneath the seemingly balanced duality of textual reality, which pits two thematic units (the recurring theme 1, epitomizing the narrator's emotional reaction) against two others (themes 2 and 3, enacting Scarbo's mischievousness), the auditory reality is clearly tilted. Interestingly, it is the theme that plays with the ominous figure SEVEN that dominates the section. The forty-four bars of its extended ternary structure, consisting of the above-mentioned six SEVEN-bar phrases and the concluding two-bar cadential sweep, make up exactly half of the 88-bar-long section II.

In the poem, the shift of perspective from the perceiving narrator towards Scarbo as the second protagonist occurs after the first sentence of the fourth stanza when the grammatical subject changes from the previous "I" to the "he" that determines the remainder of the text. In the music, the analogous shift, prepared somewhat with the spatially dominating theme 2 within the still ambiguous thematic and tonal contexts, is completed in the third section of the exposition. In Bertrand's version, the refocusing of the attention on Scarbo himself (rather than on the way the narrator hears or sees him) completely alters our impression of him. No longer raucous and vivacious, laughing, jumping and whirling, he suddenly reveals himself as subject to a bizarre metamorphosis, appearing in turn awesome, ridiculous and ultimately even reassuringly weak. Correspondingly in Ravel's music, the third section consists of nothing but theme 4, which fills its sixty-nine bars entirely with ever new metamorphoses of a small basic unit.

The theme's original phrase is heard in bars 120-131. The auditory impression it creates is in stark contrast to that of the preceding material. The texture is in a chordal five-to-six-part setting, and bass pedal-notes, a conspicuous feature of section II, are absent. The "trembling," now vertically expanded to a three-octave *tremolo*, appears "inside" the material rather than alongside it or, as in themes 2 and 3, in transformations that can be heard as laughter, rattling or otherwise roguish, intentional behavior. The twelve bars of the phrase can usefully be read as a three-bar skeleton, fleshed out with nine bars of trembling insert, an interpretation corroborated by the subsequent transmutations. [104]

What happens to this skeleton as well as to its "trembling flesh" in the course of this section seems like an uncanny musical depiction of the metamorphoses Scarbo suffers in the two final stanzas of the poem.

---

[104]The multi-voiced chords of the skeleton continue the number play with TWOS and THREES. The THREE pairs of chords (as shown in the example) are actually only TWO: the opening pair is taken up after the "trembling" insert and only then answered by a different closing pair. The five consistent parts of these chords move in chromatic steps in TWO directions (a sequential ascent in the upper voice against a continued descents in the four lower parts). Moreover, the lowest note, splitting into TWO (an apt pictorial image!), undertakes a THIRD motion by leaping a tritone downwards.

Stretched out in time beyond anything previously heard in this piece (just as Bertrand depicts the ghost as visually stretched to the dimensions of a Gothic belfry), the musical image of the phantom is progressively reduced with regard to both the color of its frame and the space inside it; while "growing longer," it turns "paler" and more and more diaphanous. Ravel achieves the impression of an oddly protracted shape by having the seminal phrase undergo five transmutations. At first glance, the modifications seem insignificant enough to create the sensation of more and more of the same, a sensation heightened by the fact that each of the transmutations is heard twice. In the process, however, the multi-voiced frame is gradually drained of color and substance.

One means Ravel employs to depict the reduction of substance is the shrinking of that which fleshes out the ghost's appearance. The three-octave *tremolo*, originally stretching over nine bars and thus giving the phrase the substantial length of twelve bars (see phrase 1 in the example on the next page), is progressively diminished to seven (phrase 1 repeat), five and a half (phrase 2), three (phrase 2 repeat), and two bars (phrases 3 and 4). At the same time, the stability of the frame, established in the seminal phrase by the reiteration of the opening chord-pair after the *tremolo*, is given up from the first transmutation onwards, where we first hear a sequence of three descending chord-pairs, in which the slipping sequence conveys a sense of lost control.

While the opening pair of the first transmutation (see bars 141/142) constitutes a literal transposition of that launching the original phrase, the repetition of this pair (bars 149/150) deviates slightly, simplifying the upper two voices so as to include one tied note. In the two pairs that wrap up the first transmutation (see bars 148/149), the number of "paralyzed" voices is extended to four and the active movement thus reduced to the two upper parts with their chromatic steps in contrary motion. The splitting of the lowest part is retained, but it occurs now no longer in the form of a high-tension tritone leap but in the much tamer perfect fifth. While the number of parts is actually increased in the closing portion of the first transmutation, the harmonic complexity is diminished.[105] The fact that in the repetition, the final pair is extended to a three-chord group in which the third chord appears as a very soft after-beat, adds to the impression of

---

[105]The pairs do not close, as in the original phrase, with six-pitch chords involving the superimposition of minor and major thirds (see bars 130/131: C♯+C×/B+B♯) but instead with seven- and eight-part version of the much more relaxed F♯-major seventh-chord and B-major six-five-chord respectively (see bars 148/149).

increasing passivity. Finally, even the pitch on which the trembling takes place in these two phrases contributes to the sizable loss of vitality. In the first phrase, the *tremolo*-note E establishes an additional cross-relationship with the E♯ in the skeleton chord, while this same note in the first transmutation merges with the E that is part of the framing chords there.

theme 4
bars 120-131, 132-141

phrase 1 with repeat — (9 bars *tremolo* on E)

(repeat: 7 bars *tremolo* on E)   (repeat: [-])

bars 141-149, 149-154

phrase 2 with repeat — (5½ bars *tremolo* on E)

(repeat: 3 bars *tremolo* on E)

bars 155-162, 162-166 — (introduction: 3 bars *tremolo* on A♭)

phrase 3 with repeat — (2 bars *tremolo* on A♭)

(repeat: 2 bars *tremolo* on A♭)

bars 167-172, 173-177

phrase 4 with repeat — (3 bars *tremolo* on B♭, continuing as accompaniment)

(repeat: 2 bars *tremolo* on B♭, continuing as accompaniment)

bars 178-183, 184-188

phrase 5 with repeat   = varied sequence of phrase 4, a perfect fourth higher, *tremolo* on E♭

In the subsequent transmutations of the phrase, the framing pairs consecutively lose the independence of contrary motion (from bar 158 onwards), and the color in the chords, whose original five-to-six-part richness is reduced further and further until no more than a simple double octave plus sixth is left (from bar 167 onwards), pales. The trembling is no longer merely happening inside the frame, but becomes all-pervasive, accompanying the waning transmutations (without repose from bar 167 onwards) and even invading the frame (see the short shake in the closing pairs from bar 172 onwards).

Yet, while the phantom disintegrates musically and one expects its immediate demise, pedal notes reappear, their pitches B♭ and E♭—enharmonic reinterpretations of A♯ and D♯—tie the listener firmly back into the realm of the hallucinatory. The story isn't over!

Let me sum up the results of the interpretive analysis so far. On the level of traditional structural analysis, this section completes the tripartite exposition of the sonata movement. Meanwhile, the relationship of the composer's musical representation to Bertrand's poetic representation of the Scarbo story is all but plain. As was shown above, the initial phrase of the piece—and, based on it, the short first section as a whole—present something like a psychological account of what lies behind the ghost tale. Literally in a nutshell, i.e. in a mere SEVEN bars, we witness a short, unconnected (and thus presumably inexplicable) commotion, followed by extensive trembling that, accompanied by a sigh, gradually dies down and ceases—to give way to a long silence. In a similar way, a disturbing sound of unknown origin, heard at midnight in a bedroom filled with the light of the full moon, may incite a susceptible insomniac's imagination. The mind may react by creating frightening visions, the body by emitting a sigh and trembling violently. Although the shivering will eventually cease, it may need a long moment of absolute silence before one feels truly reassured.[106] The second section with its three themes juxtaposes the narrator's horror (remember Ravel's note "*quelle horreur!*" under the ascending major seventh of theme 1 in the Perlemuter score) with Scarbo's

[106]This section is audibly set apart from the two following ones by means of a tempo indication whose full impact does not become evident until much later, when Ravel explains the proportion. At the transition to the recapitulation, the composer specifies that one eighth-note in the bars following bar 394 equals three eighth-notes, or a full 3/8 measure, in the preceding bars. Since no acceleration was explicitly demanded since the *au Mouvement (Vif)* in bar 32, we must assume that the proportion of that *Vif* to the preceding *Modéré* is equally that of 1:3—a striking change in character from a more poised, observant attitude to a fully involved, highly emotional one.

allegedly rambunctious behavior. The ambiguity as expressed in the coexistence of both tonal centers, reminds us that it is still unclear—as it remains in the three initial stanzas of the poem—who it is we are being told about: the ghost as though he existed, or the sleeper, scared up by a noise and now "seeing and hearing" a ghost. In the latter part of the second section, this ambiguity is suspended. In the third section as in the two final stanzas of the poem, the narrator's perspective is only implicit, and the phantom, now the sole focus of attention, is shown in the form of theme 4 with its multiple transmutations: elongated and gradually losing life and color, fading to more and more extensive shudders. But just before it threatens to dissolve completely, the narrator's fascination with the eerie realm takes over once again, and the tonal center D♯ is reestablished.

If the second and third sections can thus be read as analog to the viewpoints expressed in the initial three and the remaining two stanzas of the poem respectively, or as the mind's reaction, in the form of a narrative enactment, to the triggering event suggested in the first section, the following, long fourth section of the music undertakes to show both the repetitiveness of the experience for the mesmerized narrator ("how many times ...!") and his considerable confusion. In the course of altogether 205 bars, the previously introduced musical metaphors recur in myriad combinations of snippets and transmutations, tumbling over one another, melting in various ways, and painting the image of a victim both terrified and charmed by the nocturnal apparition.

The section comprises SEVEN segments—a number that strikes one by now as hardly surprising. The first, laid out with a phrase, its repetition and a subsequent development, recalls the "objective" opening section of the piece. The second segment is devoted to Scarbo's mischievousness, playing with and expanding on "his" theme 2 in the form of only slightly irregular six-times-seven bars. After a chain of the ghost's three themes in the third segment, all of them in slightly distorted format, the fourth segment returns to Scarbo's boisterousness, playing with its other symbol, theme 3, in a three-fold pattern. Hereafter, the perspective changes. The fifth segment seems to focus again on the narrator's perception, casting his interpretation—in the form of theme-1 variants—on the three Scarbo themes. This applies particularly to theme 3, which (as a consequence, one is tempted to say) undergoes ever stranger distortions and liquidations in the subsequent sixth segment. Having recalled, at the climactic beginning of segment 7, the horrifying images of the metamorphosing phantom (with a theme-4 fragment launched from $f\!f$ and subsequently plunging through four octaves), the development section ends by reinstating the aspect of subjective perception with a grandly sweeping version of theme 1.[107]

With the first installment of the recapitulation, we return to the moderate tempo and the more sober perspective of the first section, juxtaposed without pause with a reminiscence of Scarbo's friskiness in theme 2 (from bar 429 onwards). Of the three motifs constituting the initial seven-bar phrase, the first comes with a distorted octave parallel, a device recalled from bar 15 that is, literally, an adaptation to the confines of the piano keyboard, but might simultaneously serve to render the commotion that triggers the entire story told in this piece all the more harrowing. After a repetition of the phrase, the development consists this time in an augmentation and mystification involving all parameters. Motif a, softer than ever before, is stretched to one-and-a-half times is former size; motif b, lower than ever before, is also elongated (from a 9/8+3/8-sigh to a 12/8+6/8-one). Motif c, also an octave lower than before and protracted

[107]Here is a short account of what happens in each of these seven segments:

[1] bars 189-213   syncopated chord rhythmically reminiscent of motif b paired with a progression of chords rhythmically reminiscent of the transmutations of th 4, over pedal notes D♯ and B (= the two tonal centers of the piece); repeat; development of the combination, loss of tonal mooring, dying down.

[2] bars 213-254   th 2 on V (7 bars);
varied repetition, elision of bar 1 made up by extension (7 bars);
extension with cadential close as in section II (7 bars);
th 2 on V/V, with repetition, make-up for elided bars later (6 + 8 bars);
extension with cadential close see section II (7 bars).

[3] bars 255-275   th 3 + repeat (melody on D♯, pedal G♯); extension: distorted intervals;
th 2 trunk, launched from distorted metric position, with repetition;
th 4, initial chord-pair of the final transmuted phrase.

[4] bars 276-312   th 3 with repetition (melody on D, pedal B), extension + th-4 fragment;
sequence 1 (melody on B, pedal G♯); sequence 2 (melody on F, pedal on A♯ [= G♯]).

[5] bars 313-323   th 1 var. (intervals from motif a) + half th 3 (chromatic distortion)
th 1 var. (hemiolic suspension) + first chord-pair of th 4;
th 1 var. (intervals from motif a) + half th 2 (metrically distorted);
th 1 var. (hemiolic suspension) + half th 3 (now in diatonic shape);
first half of th 1 (interval structure form motif a) + second half of th 3;
second half of th 1, + repetition of second half of th 3.

[6] bars 344-364   th 3, distorted across several octaves, over D pedal with neighbor notes; extension with rhythmic distortions and metric irregularities.

[7] bars 365-393   th 4 var. (in $f\!f$), repetition, and liquidation (initial fragment plunging through several octaves); rhythmically augmented th 1.

along with motif *b*, subsequently plunges yet another octave, where its "trembling" slows down to four bars of an eerily slow shudder. But instead of fading away and thus giving the anxious sleeper reason to assure himself that all is well, the shuddering D♯ repetition spawns a crooked little figure, effectively (though not indicated as such in the score) in triplets to the preceding slow note repetition. This figure is repeated four times in the piano's lowest register before it starts ascending octave by octave. As it reaches the middle register, it reorganizes its pitches to form a smoother curve (bar 428) and in this shape undergoes a drastic change of speed.

From here onwards, the dimension of tempo plays a major role. It thus seems meaningful to take a moment and look back on what Ravel's treatment of tempo and pulse is in this piece. Throughout the initial 393 bars of "Scarbo," i.e. for the length of the entire exposition and development section of the sonata movement, the composer gives only four indications regarding temporal organization. The initial signification *Modéré* is inflected by the *en accélérant* of bars 17-22, which leads to *vif* in bar 23, confirmed by *au Mouvement (Vif)* in bar 32. This lively tempo is not explicitly modified until the climax of the development section, and here, the marking *Un peu retenu* adds weightiness rather than reducing intensity. It is only at the opening of the recapitulation that one gets a sense of what specific proportion of pulse between the section-I *modéré* and the *vif* Ravel had in mind. His instruction, at the transition to the recapitulation of section I in bar 393/394, determines that one eighth-note of what follows is to equal one dotted quarter-note in the preceding tempo—or, each of the three eighth-notes in motif *a* takes the duration of what was heard, for most of the piece, as an entire bar. Looking back, this specification determines retrospectively that the beginning of theme 1 in bar 32 sounds three times as fast as the notes in motif *a* in bar 1 from which it derives! At the end of the development section, on the other hand, the pulse of these same three theme-1 notes in bars 385-387 is the same at that in motif *a* of bar 394. These proportional tempo changes seem drastic, and one might feel like approaching them with some doubt were it not for the remainder of the "recapitulation," where further indications seem to corroborate the seriousness of Ravel's instructions. These give the interpreter reason to suspect that what is being "recapitulated" is only the material (or part of it), while the new play with temporal dimensions gives the remaining sections of the piece an expressive slant not based on anything heard before.

This becomes strikingly evident on occasion of the return of theme 2, launched with the equivalent to the original seven-bar phrase in bars 429-435. Ravel's change of time signature at this point causes, at one and the same time, a radical increase in turbulence and a slowing down of the thematic material to one third of the tempo in which it was heard in the exposition.[108]

No sooner has this puzzlingly distorted Scarbo theme been presented (with 7 + 4 + 7 bars only, instead of the six-phrase format of section II), than Ravel turns to entirely unexpected material and, with it, to a new play with the dimensions of temporality. In the right-hand part, a major second is shifted by chromatic increments, in a variety of combinations of the two basic shapes shown in the diagram.

see bars 447-466

shape 1   shape 2

For twenty bars, the pitch outline of these figures remains the same with only minute modifications.[109] The dynamic level, however, develops from *ppp* (in bar 447) to *f* (in bar 467), the tempo changes (see Ravel's indications *En accélérant* in bar 451ff and *Toujours en accélérant* in bar 459ff), and even the visual representation takes this intensification into account in a rhythmic/metric reinterpretation (see bar 458/459 where eighth-notes turn into sixteenth-notes while the meter reverses from the recent three-four time to the original three-eight). The result, as the composer makes clear, should be a return to *vif* at bar 463. This means

---

[108]The manifold indications here are somewhat confusing at first sight. As a quarter-note in the new three-four time equals an eighth-note in the preceding three-eight meter, there is no actual change in the duration of the bar or the pulse of the beat. This, however, means that theme 2 is still in the tempo of section I (*modéré*, as of bar 394), and not in the *vif* that first informed it in bars 51ff.

With regard to the emotional undertones, it may help to try and get a sense of the strange change from "trembling" through "eerily slow shudder" to "turbulence" by simply coun ting attacks per measure at a consistent speed. This would reveal the following variations of temporal density:

bars	410-416	417-420	421-427	428	429
number of attacks	12	6	9	8	24

[109]There are THREE irregularities in this pattern: TWO momentary intervallic splits at the apex of the figure (bars 454, 456), TWO intervallic displacements of the major second at the same point (bars 460, 462), and TWO skips at the end of the ascent (bars 465, 466).

that the section based on the chromatically shifting whole step ends in a tempo three times as fast as that in which it sets out, thus recapitulating in entirely foreign material the drastic change of vibration that, in the initial section of the piece, distinguishes the reasonable reaction to an unidentified noise from the exalted state of hallucinatory enactment.

While this re-immersion into the world of the fantastic takes place on one level, the accompanying broken triads counter this powerful acceleration by adjusting their density so as to keep an approximately equal level.[110] This inverse development results in what could be referred to as a split reality: a paradox that mirrors the one encountered earlier, where increased "turbulence" accompanied what appeared almost like frozen motion in the ghost's theme 2. Here, ascending pitches, increasing dynamics and run-away acceleration in the pulsing of the right-hand figure are counteracted by factually frozen density in the accompaniment.

This parameter (which links sections V and VI) adds yet another aspect to the musical representation of the *Scarbo* poem. At the same time as the first installment of the recapitulation suggests a new look at the psychological trigger of the apparition (embodied in the seminal phrase with its three motifs) and at one of the phantom's images as they are "heard and seen" (in the short recollection of theme 2), there is a strong suggestion that the distortions happen in the narrator's mind rather than in the reality of his bed chamber. Immensely growing agitation makes the ghost's previously rambunctious behavior appear in grotesque slow motion. But no sooner has the excitement reached a peak, than the mind, ostensibly dealing with neutral material that is entirely unrelated to phantom experiences, soars to further heights and runs out of control.

It is in this state, after a sudden, drastic hush (from *f* back to *ppp* in bars 467/471 to 476), that the final section invites the listeners to experience once again the phantom's weird metamorphoses. In the musical material, what follows is the strangely extended second installment of the recapitulation. However, what is being recalled—in excerpts and with significant modifications—is not only the third section of the exposition

---

[110]Here is an account of what happens on the level of left-hand pulsation:

bars	(446)	447-452	453-458	459-466	
number of attacks	24	19/18	9/8	2	(one or both of them as arpeggiated chords; thus 4-6 notes)

Note that the six notes comprising the two arpeggiated triads in bars 460-462, were they broken regularly (which is not, of course, the idea), would roughly equal the tempo of the eighteen attacks in the three times slower bars 447-450.

but part of the development section as well![111] On the level of interpretive signification, what is being so lavishly called back to memory in this second installment of the recapitulation are the phantom's metamorphosis and overwhelming ubiquitousness.

Meanwhile, the impending return to a reality where Scarbo is allotted his proper place as a creation of the imagination is corroborated on the tonal level. As one will recall, the entire piece oscillates between two tonal centers, D♯ and B, of which D♯ was so far clearly predominant. It is introduced as the note characterizing the ghost-induced trembling in section I, and as the melodic root pitch for Scarbo's raucous behavior, depicted in themes 2 and 3 in section II. The narrator's emotional response to the intruding specter, musically embodied in theme 1, is equally launched from D♯, but it soon expresses its ambiguity in vertical bitonality. Theme 2 itself, the first musical depiction of a frolicking phantom, is pitted against a pervasive pedal B in the bass. Doubts from the skeptical mind, heard when D♯ is occasionally contested by B, thus exist but are soon overrun by the narrator's undiminished fascination with his vision.

[111]The bare structural facts are as follows:

bars 476-541 — recapitulate theme 4, in a layout vaguely following that of section III. The initial phrases show a change of texture, a very erratic phrase structure, and a strongly modified tonal coloring; bars 510-541, however, are a close recollection of bars 158-188, transposed to the key of the fifth.

bars 542-552 — recapitulate the beginning of the development section; cf. bars 189-199. The motif-*b* chord and theme-4 fragment are linked by a bar that recalls motif *a*, i.e. that which our interpretive reading identified as the original trigger noise (see e.g. bar 543, lowest part right hand). The first eight bars are in the key of the fifth, the remainder is not transposed.

bars 562-571 — recapitulate the climax of the development section; cf. bars 365-370. An unequivocal reminiscence, it even retains the tempo inflection, substituting the *Un peu retenu* in bar 365 by an *Un peu moins vif* for the analogous passage launched in bar 562. The newly introduced use of a varied motif *a* in replacement for the simpler "trembling" continues and is even heard in prominent double octaves here (see bars 563-565, 568-570, as well as in the extension of bars 573-576).

bars 579-582 and 616-(621?) — recapitulate the end of the development section. Compare the version of theme 1 with strongly overstretched syncopation and (as a consequence) omitted fourth bar, heard in bars 385-393, with the structurally similar one in bars 579-582. The other aspect of this part of the development, the gothic amplification, is split off as a separate entity here, returning motif *a* to its original, slow tempo in bars 615-621 and thus finally bringing the nocturnal experience full circle.

What, then, does this second tonal center B, that never establishes itself melodically in the course of the depiction of the Scarbo story, stand for? As the continuously sensed and secretly apprehended alternate truth that only manifests itself at the very end, it recommends itself strongly as the musical signifier for the realization that Bertrand has his narrator express twice—once as a question and finally as a statement: that this is but an apparition, born from a visual and auditory delusion, and will dissipate any moment. ("Did I then believe him vanished?" the lyrical "I" asks at the poem's midpoint, only to confirm later "and suddenly he expired."

The seventh perspective of the poem, then, embodied in the seventh representational section of the music, is much more than what the surface features bring to our attention. It starts out, in bars 476-509, with a bass figuration that, in addition to its familiar trembling, contains a downbeat leading-note (E♯-F♯-F♯) that is strongly reminiscent of the leading-note in motif *a*, i.e. the thematic component interpreted above as the factual commotion that gave rise to the perception of a ghost—and thus something like a musical reminder that all this is just happening in the mind's eye. At the beginning of the piece, this leading-note supports G♯ and, indirectly through this pitch, the tonal center D♯. Here, however, it leads to F♯, the dominant of the other tonal center, B, or the preparation for the other reality, the voluntary dissolution of the phantom. Just as in the poem, the astute question "Did I then believe him vanished?" does not succeed in chasing the specter away, so also in the music are we hardly surprised to find the E♯-F♯-F♯ bass figure shift (in bar 512) to D-E♭-E♭, thus reinstating E♭ (=D♯) and its fascinated acceptance of the ghost as virtual. But, once questioned, this re-immersion into the world of the attractively horrifying (musically realized in the fairly literal transposition of bars 158-199 in bars 510-552) cannot be held up for long. The untransposed bass note A (bars 550, 555) serves as a point of departure for a descent in what we have come to recognize as the "Scriabin scale" or as Messiaen's mode 2: a linear alternation of semitones and wholetones. In this case, the resulting octatonic scale descends in a powerful eight-bar *crescendo* to a *fff* B (see bars 555-562: A-G♯-F♯-F-E♭-D-C-B)!

With this B, one is tempted to interpret, Scarbo's disappearance is imminent. From here onwards, Ravel concludes his musical ghost tale with a fairly traditional sequence in the bass,

bars	562-571	572-578	579-582	583-590	591-613	614-626
bass notes	B	E	C♯	G♯	F♯	B

thus strongly confirming the second tonal center B and reassuring the captivated but frightened sleeper.

In conclusion, in his piano poem *Scarbo* Ravel uses two organizational devices—one structural, the other numerical—with which he explores separately each aspect expressed in Bertrand's text, as well as a single, all-pervasive musical metaphor. The musical metaphor is that of trembling. Components explicitly marked *tremolo* obviously fall into this category, but so do conspicuous note repetitions and effective shakes, be they across octaves or other intervals. This trembling is in itself an element of ambiguity. Throughout the piece one cannot help wondering whether it is the ghost who is shaking, or whether the suggestion of spookiness gives us the sleeper's perspective of the nightly visitation. The numerical play explores the meaning of the dual or ambiguous as alternatively part of, and opposed to, the supposedly more balanced and complete "triple" aspect of reality. Beyond both, the figure SEVEN (striking whenever it appears in the context of a text system like the musical one that bases its countables—rhythmic values, meters and bars in a phrase—primarily on multiples of 2 and 3), pervades the piece with myriad connotations of teasing and tempting, reminding us that the nocturnal apparition is not an unavoidable hazard of life but something that we allow to possess us as we give in to its luring powers.

As for the organization of the material, Ravel sets out and ends with perspectives that seem closest to an objective assessment of the kind of reality that might explain the apparition of a midnight specter, while playing, in the middle section of his work, with the many ambiguous interactions of perceiver and perceived. Having opened his piece in section I with a musical version of a level-headed suggestion of what might cause this and similar hallucinations (or, to use a language that seems strangely inappropriate in discussing a musical work, the neurological chain that might translate into an entire mental ghost tale), he proceeds to give voice to the narrator's emotional and sensory responses in section II, and to a depiction of the metamorphoses we are told the ghost undergoes in section III. (In this regard, sections II and III can be said to correspond with stanzas 1-3 and 4-5 of the poem respectively.) The composer then turns to Bertrand's rhetorical assertion of "How many times," painting a vivid musical image of the phantom's frequent, scattered and unpredictable appearances. In sections V and VI, the narrator's psychological overreaction takes the foreground. The result of this frenzy is two-fold. In the state of utter excitement, the ghost appears as if frozen in slow motion but not, for that matter, less confusing. As a result, the confused mind ostensibly turns away from all images related to the phantom, towards neutral material; but even this distraction does not have appeasing effects, and the mind's excitement continues to increase uncontrollably. In this state, the other aspect of the phantom's metamorphoses are recalled—those that, in the poem, precede Scarbo's timely extinction—this time in the light of a growing assurance that there is indeed a sane and safe reality beyond the story produced by an anxious mind. As the music moves confidently towards the second tonal center B, the nocturnal spell is broken.

Part III

SPIRITUAL CONCEPTS AND DIVINE ATTRIBUTES

James M. Whistler, *Nocturne in Blue and Gold: Old Battersea Bridge*
Tate Gallery, London. Reprinted with permission.

The Meditative Transfiguration of Imagery

Under a stagnant sky,
Gloom out of gloom uncoiling into gloom,
The River, jaded and forlorn,
Welters and wanders wearily — wretchedly — on;
Yet in and out among the ribs
Of the old skeleton bridge, as in the piles
Of some dead lake-built city, full of skulls,
Worm-worn, rat-riddled, mouldy with memories,
Lingers to babble to a broken tune
(Once, O the unvoiced music of my heart!)
So melancholy a soliloquy
It sounds as it might tell
The secret of the unending grief-in-grain,
The terror of Time and Change and Death,
That wastes this floating, transitory world.
What of the incantation
That forced the huddled shapes on yonder shore
To take and wear the night
Like a material majesty?
That touched the shafts of wavering fire
About this miserable welter and wash —
(River, O River of Journeys, River of Dreams!)
Into long shining signals from the panes
Of an enchanted pleasure-house,
Where life and life might live life lost in life
For ever and evermore?
O Death! O Change! O Time!
Without you, O the insufferable eyes
Of these poor Might-Have-Beens,
These fatuous, ineffectual Yesterdays!

William Ernest Henley (1849-1903), "To James McNeill Whistler"[112]

[112]*The Works of W. E. Henley*, London: D. Nutt, 1908, vol. I, "Rhymes and Rhythms,"
XIII, p. 216/7.

A poem about a painting can be even more evocative than Charles Baudelaire's interpretation of Delacroix's *Tasso in Prison* (discussed on pp. 137-140) Works with religious content in particular are likely to cause viewers—including poets—to transcend that which is actually shown. The same holds true for images that suggest melancholy moods, and verbal intimations like "forlorn" or "in vain." Rather than merely absorbing the details of the particular visual representation or the means employed by the artist to achieve specific effects, our mind's eye conjures up the much larger context connected with the image, a context created by our culture and inflected by our personal creed and attitude.

Similarly, the poetic imagination may take the visual representation as an inspiration to delve deeply into the realm of concepts and to meditate on eternal questions regarding God's design for the world and Man's place and purpose in it. By doing so, the poet assumes perhaps less than in other cases that readers are acquainted with the particular work of art. Instead, the poetic rendering is based on the premise that both the author and the readers share with the painter a doctrinal or archetypal framework that the artist's work activates without any need for explicitness. What results might be best described as a communication between the poet and the audience about a philosophy familiar to all, triggered by a work of visual art.

In this constellation, one may want to argue that James Whistler's rendition of Old Battersea Bridge acts as a vignette rather than as a text that conveys a particular message. Neither the structure and colors of the painting, nor the actual situation it depicts and the metaphors the painter chose are instrumental in determining the poet's focus. Instead, what speaks to the painter's audience and what informs the poet's reception are the archetypal aspects, evoked in the metaphoric value of bridges in general, reflected in myriad layers of interpretation in lyrical and pictorial media, and now brought back to memory and submitted to renewed reflection by the particular visual rendering.

W. E. Henley's "To James McNeill Whistler" provides a good example for such a relationship between a poem and a work of visual art. While there is no doubt about the art work Henley refers to, and little reason to quarrel over which of Whistler's works inspired the poem, the case could be made that one of these two references is strangely arbitrary. The particular nocturnal bridge W. E. Henley had in mind can only be determined in reference to the poem's title; the poetic text itself does not in any way betray any detail of the visual composition.

In a similar way, a piece of music may refer to a vignette—extant visually or merely alluded to verbally—in a manner that sees details "into" the stimulus rather than deriving them "out" of it. Again, the condition for this reaction is that the object depicted exists in the viewer's —and the composer's—imagination prior to and independently of the particular visual or verbal allusion.

The third part of this study examines pieces from Messiaen's cycle *Twenty Contemplations of the Infant Jesus*. The collective title clearly suggests a series of visual images—especially in the French form, where *regard* suggests not only the eyes that are laid upon the Child, but by extension the people who are looking upon the Infant Jesus, and thus a series of scenes around the manger. In this respect, the music renders visual representations suggested by verbal titles alone. But as in the case of W. E. Henley and Whistler's *Old Battersea Bridge*, a particular artist's vision of each scene remains largely irrelevant to meditative representation in another artistic means, and is not even suggested here.

Instead, the composer's subheading remarks draw us into the realm of his often mystical symbols, associations, and allusions. These verbal utterings, deliberately fragmentary in both style and imagery, do not seem devised to expound either the religious image evoked in the title or the music that "interprets" the image. Rather, the sentences, by virtue of their very incompleteness and often startling symbolism, draw us away both from the all-too-familiar topic that is to be depicted and from the compositional result as an end in itself. Messiaen sets out to guide us—by way of his musical representation of aspects about which our logical language can only stutter—to a deeper understanding of the religious concepts and truths themselves.

GOD'S LOVE

Regard du Père   (Messiaen, *Vingt regards*, I)

*(Et Dieu dit: "Celui-ci est mon Fils bien-aimé en qui j'ai pris toutes mes com-
plaisances"...)*

The initial piece of the cycle is called *The Father's Contemplation.*
The apparently simple and straightforward wording of this title is interesting when compared to other titles that refer to persons looking upon the
manger. These include *The Virgin's Contemplation* (not *the Mother's*),
*The Prophets, the Shepherds, and the Magi Contemplating the Infant
Jesus*, and *The Angels' Contemplation*. In this context, a semantic equivalent that one might have expected are *The Lord's Contemplation*. The
wording chosen by Messiaen stresses the personhood of God the Father,
and thus points in a direction that is further corroborated in the prefacing
subtitle. There, Messiaen quotes from Matthew 3:17, Mark 1:11 or Luke
3:22, "And God says: 'This is my beloved Son in whom I am well
pleased'..." The message here is clearly that of love, a message supported
even in the composer's indication of the desired mood of the piece, which
he describes with the words "mysterious, with love."

In terms of thematic content, the piece is uniquely uniform.

- All nineteen bars are based on a chordally supported melody
  designated as *Thème de Dieu* (Theme of God). The initial subphrase of this theme is laid out as a simple, supremely calm line
  of a three-eighth up-beat in repeated A♯ followed by a strong-beat
  (and accented) C♯ and concluded by the return to A♯. The vertical
  support of this melody consist of triads and four-note chords.
  (More on the harmonic layout later.)

- No contrasting material is
  introduced anywhere. The
  Thème de Dieu develops,
  after a repetition of its initial subphrase, through two

Theme of God

free transformations of the same unit into a longer climaxing subphrase (see bars 5m-7m). The first stanza is rounded off by a very

235

short two-chord element. An inserted three-fold repetition of the treble-octave C♯ constitutes a textural change and alerts the listener to the structural *caesura* at this point. The second stanza is designed correspondingly; bars 9-14m are identical with bars 1-6m; the climaxing portion of the phrase (bars 14m-15m) and the rounding-off component present new melodic and chordal details, but the transitional three-fold treble-octave C♯ recurs as before. A three-bar coda completes the piece, in all its elements still derived from the *Thème de Dieu*.

-   The implied, though not explicitly indicated, meter is four-four, and no change whatsoever occurs in the course of the piece. This is worth noticing in a composer who for the most part has abandoned regular and especially repetitive metric organization.
-   The rhythmic organization features a pulse of continuous sixteenth-note triplets. These are created by means of a repetition of each chord, in the first octave in four-note version and then in the second octave with only the doubled melody note. This pulse is not interrupted once in the entire course of the piece. Most surprisingly and in stark contrast to common traditions, it even continues throughout the final bar, i.e. after the concluding melodic note.

In terms of tonal organization, two aspects play an important role; one concerns "key" and the other mode. The word "key" comes in quotation marks here because we are not dealing with the term in the sense usually implied in Western music. However, Messiaen's choice of the key signature for F♯ major is significant, despite—or perhaps even in light of—the fact that the pitches that actually occur then require a wealth of additional accidentals. This key signature gives us several important clues.

To begin with, it confirms the tonal center established in the initial subphrase of the *Thème de Dieu*—where the first as well as the two last chords represent inversions of the F♯-major chord. Since all occurrences in this piece of the F♯-major triad or the F♯-A♯-C♯-D♯ four-note chord appear in inversion (see particularly the first and last chords), the key signature provides a kind of symbolic reassurance that we are not dealing with a tonal context centered in A♯. This, in turn, is crucial for the interpretation of the final chord. In the context of F♯ major, this is an F♯-major chord with added sixth, albeit in inversion. As is expounded in considerable detail in the introduction to Messiaen's tonal language given in

Appendix II, the F♯-major scale as well as this particular chord represent the most symmetrical—and thus, symbolically speaking, the most perfect —pitch content and vertical organization thinkable. (Refer back to the visual representation on the keyboard.) For the two most prominent occurrences of the F♯-major chord with added sixth in this piece see the climax of the second stanza, bar 14m, and the final chord.

Last but not least, the fact that the characteristic chord is indeed a chord with added sixth turns out to be consequential in the context of the eighth piece in the cycle, *The Cross's Contemplation*, which features as a prominently recurring element an A♭-minor chord with added sixth. The spiritual relationship between these two chords—and thus between aspects alluded to in the two pieces—will be explored in more detail in the context of the later piece; it is critical to the understanding of the tonal symbols within this cycle.

While the key signature thus serves as a spiritual pointer and rooting principle, the actual pitch content is based entirely on Messiaen's favorite mode 2.[113] This mode, one recalls, allows for only three transpositions (counting, with the composer, the version from C as transposition 1) before the original set of notes reappears. Here is a visual aid to imagine the three versions as they appear on the keyboard.

If we concentrate on the characteristic pattern of this mode (i.e. the unit made up of a semitone followed by a whole tone), it becomes clear that each transposition can be read from four different starting points:

- transposition 1 from C, E♭, F♯ and A,
- transposition 2 from C♯, E, G and B♭, and
- transposition 3 from D, F, G♯ and B
  respectively.

In the course of *The Father's Contemplation*, Messiaen employs the three transpositions of mode 2 in such a way that they clearly create the illusion of representing the functional areas of tonic, dominant and sub-

[113]There are, actually, two chords that do not abide by the rules of the mode. One of them is clearly the result of a misprint: on the middle beat of bar 14 we find a chord that, following the natural sign earlier in the bar, seems to contain F♮ instead of the F♯ expected in the mode. Fortunately in this case we can be sure, since the entire *Thème de Dieu* recurs twice in the course of the cycle, and both times (compare V bar. 56 and XX bar 187), Messiaen has added the accidentals for the F♯ in the chord.

The other chord not in accordance with the modal design of the piece remains a mystery. The penultimate chord (see bar 18, beat 4) does not derive from any of the three transpositions of mode 2. Since it recurs with the same pitches in pieces V and XX, there is no simple way of knowing what Messiaen may have had in mind.

MODE 2 -
an alternation of semitones and wholetones
that exists in only three transpositions

mode 2^1
on C, though not necessarily centered there

mode 2^2
transposition to the second semitone

mode 2^3
transposition to the third semitone

dominant with reference to F♯; one may imagine reading transposition 1 from F♯, transposition 2 from C♯, and transposition 3 from B, or

tonic	= mode 2^1:	F♯ G A A♯ B♯ C♯ D♯ E
dominant	= mode 2^2:	C♯ D E E♯ G G♯ A♯ B
subdominant	= mode 2^3:	B C D D♯ F F♯ G♯ A

This play with the functional-harmonic representation of the three versions of the mode subtly enhances the impression of tonality in the piece—an impression otherwise not truly supported by the modal pitch content. Let us sum up the evidence laid out above:

- the multiple verbal references to God's love;
- the extraordinary regularity of meter and pulse, phrase structure and texture;
- the extremely slow tempo (with a metronome indication that refers to a triplet-sixteenth!) resulting in an impression of superhuman serenity and composure;
- the divine perfection epitomized
  on the one hand in the choice of the key signature and its most significant chord,

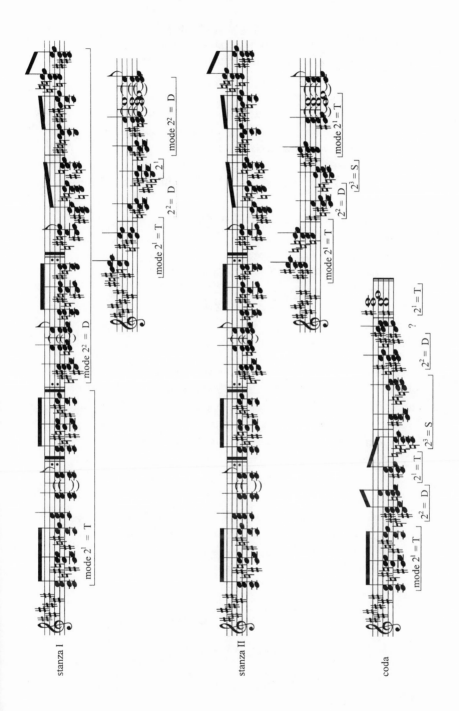

- on the other hand in the singular combination of modal organization and tonal-functional design;
- the "omnipresence" of the material that spans the five central octaves of the keyboard and remains undisturbed by any contrasting element.

In conclusion, all musical features adopt the hermeneutic implications connected with the *Thème de Dieu*. One would, then, interpret the *Thème de Dieu* as the thematic symbol of GOD'S LOVE.

This conclusion in turn sheds light on the spiritual significance of the other phenomena characterized so far. We can thus propose the following first group of symbols:

attribute	*symbol*	*musical category*	*appearance*
GOD'S LOVE	Thème de Dieu	thematic phrase	horizontal
	F♯ major +sixth	chord	vertical
	F♯ major	tonal context	overall
	mode 2	pitch content	overall
	A♯	predominant pitch	at the beginning and at the end of the *Theme of God*; at the outset and the close of the piece

The example on the preceding page represents the complete melodic and tonal argument of the piece in excerpt, i.e. without the further octave doublings and their mini-rhythm. That a theme epitomizing GOD'S LOVE should be the first and main musical "thought" in Messiaen's cycle is not at all surprising when seen in light of the composer's own assertions. One of many similar statements was:

> "I am, above all, a Catholic composer. All my works, whether religious or not, are documents of faith glorifying the mystery of Christ. Through my poor stammerings about *Divine Love* I have tried to find a music signifying a new epoch, a loving and chanting music."[114]
> (Italics added)

---

[114]This by now famous saying of Messiaen's is quoted here from Claude Rostand, *French Music Today* (New York: Merlin Press, 1950), p. 46.

Regard du Fils sur le Fils   Messiaen, *Vingt regards*, V)

(Mystère, rais de lumière dans la nuit - réfraction de la joie, les oiseaux du silence - la personne du Verbe dans une nature humaine - mariage des natures humaine et divine en Jésus Christ...)

What is immediately striking about this piece is the fact that *The Son Contemplating the Son* is a variation of *The Father's Contemplation*. It literally quotes the entire thematic argument of the opening piece, which appears here as the lowest of three strands within a texture that could be described as three homophonically singing choruses. The middle and upper strands each contain chord progressions that are tonally related neither among themselves nor with the *Theme of God*.

Who, then, is looking upon or contemplating whom here? In his "Author's Note," Messiaen declares that thisias "obviously the Son-as-Word looking upon the Son-as-Infant-Jesus." The music, however, seems to define the two sons along different lines: the Divine Son—fated to suffer on the Cross in order to save humanity—looks down upon Mary's son, the son of Man, the WORD INCARNATE. As I will show in some detail below, this reading is corroborated by the musical symbols employed.

As shown above, the first piece of the cycle, *The Father's Contemplation*, is laid out in two stanzas, differing only towards their ends and followed by a coda built from the same material. The tonal material in the homophonic theme is derived entirely from the three transpositions of mode 2, and the meter firmly rooted in regular bars of eight-eight time (albeit without an explicitly stated time signature). The thematically relevant eighth-notes of the *Theme of God*, requested in *The Father's Contemplation* in the almost unfathomably slow tempo of 20, appear here, in *The Son Contemplating the Son*, as quarter-notes. The difference, however, is deceptive; the tempo indication ($\flat$ = 76) requires an even slower pace than in the first piece, in that the thematic notes are now spaced at 19 to the minute.[115] The register of the *Theme-of-God* quotation is not that of either of the lower octaves heard on the melodic beats in the first piece, but centers around middle C. The color suggested by the composer is a "luminous" *piano*, the mood is described demanded as "solemn."

The two higher strands are composed as a rich text of symbols epitomimizing the simultaneously different and identical natures of Jesus.

[115]One wonders, of course, whether this distinction matters—quite apart from the question of who would be there to tell. The important message here is probably that the pace of the *Thème de Dieu*, despite the apparent change of note values, is exactly the same in both pieces.

241

Strand 1 contains only three-note chords, strand 2 exclusively four-note chords. The notes of strand 1 are taken (as the composer informs us in the score) from the third transposition of mode 6, while those in the second strand all represent the fourth transposition of mode 4. Furthermore, rhythm, chord structure and pitch outline also appear entirely unrelated.

Whereas in the score, the two strands are visually segregated in different staves, they actually share the same register; both are notated with *octava alta* indication throughout and center in the third octave above middle C. Messiaen answers the question of prevalence by marking strand 1 as *pp*, in slight distinction from strand 2, which is requested *ppp* and *doux et mystérieux*. This distinction invites us to begin an analysis of the duple higher layer with strand 1.

The chord progression in strand 1 is repeated twice (see the new beginnings on the middle beat of bar 7 and on the downbeat of bar 14). The third statement of the phrase is followed by one more recurrence of the first group of three chords before it is abandoned until the end of the first stanza of *The Father's Contemplation* (bars 22-33). Each phrase of the strand-1 progression thus spans 13 quarter-notes (or, as most analysts prefer to describe it for better comparison, 26 eighth-notes). The layout of the phrase, interestingly, mirrors that of *The Father's Contemplation*! Where the representation of GOD'S LOVE is designed in two similar stanzas followed by a coda, the phrase representing the *Son* consists of two subphrases (repeated with regard to the pitches but different in rhythm, and thus in a different way largely similar) followed by a tail.

Each subphrase encompasses two groups of three chords, in themselves distinctly individualized and graded through the use of different interval colors and, concomitantly, different degrees of tension. The first group of three chords is designed in a curve of ascent and descent. Flanking an inverted major triad (D♭-G♭-B♭, enharmonically written) are two chords in which a perfect fifth is laid over a perfect fourth, and thus keeps a very low tension profile. The second group of three chords swoops steeply upwards and embodies much more tension than the first. It begins with a perfect fifth laid over a tritone, proceeds through a sequence of this chord on the next higher semitone, and climaxes in a chord whose framing interval is a diminished octave. After both groups have been repeated in different rhythmic shapes, the complementing five-chord tail combines two chords from the second group with two new chords. The first, heard as a dominant-seventh chord without fifth, is the most relaxed, while the fourth chord (and its transposition upwards in the fifth chord) contains a diminished octave laid over a tritone, thus expressing the highest degree of tension so far.

The rhythmic organization of the phrase is itself an important symbol. Suffice it for now to say that it coincides with the grouping suggested by the interval structure of the chords. The four three-chord groups constitute palindromes—rhythmic units that read the same backwards as forwards—while the tail shows a vectorial development of time values.[116]

The table on the following page shows the chord progression in strand 1 of *The Son Contemplating the Son*. The different chords are represented by letter names (with a' denoting the inversion of a). The rhythmic spacing is visualized with blocks of proportionate sizes; as the analysis progresses, these blocks will prove more useful representations than the actual rhythms. The patterns created by Messiaen in the rhythmic design of the chords are indicated by arrows; thus double-headed arrows designate rhythmic palindromes, while a single-headed arrow denotes a straight rhythmic development in one direction. The interval analysis aims to show in an overview the different degrees of tonal tension in each chord. This is crucial particularly for performers. More than the simple pitch outline (with which, however, it thankfully coincides), the degree of tension in the chords determines the development of dynamics within the phrase. Finally, the sketch of the keyboard concretizes the tonal background (for those of us who tend to forget which of Messiaen's modes is which).

---

[116]Robert Sherlaw-Johnson, in his excellent book on Messiaen (London: J.M.Dent & Sons, 1975), proves that the origin of this rhythmic phrase is a combination of the three Hindu rhythms *râgavardhana, candrakalâ,* and *lakskmîça.* He finds the phrase in many of Messiaen's works, from *Chants de Terre et de ciel* (1938) onwards. While there can be no doubt about the composer's interest in, and familiarity with, Hindu and Carnatic (southern Indian) rhythms, the interpretive value of this knowledge remains unclear. Messiaen has expressed fascination mainly with one of the phenomena encountered in the Hindu context, their metrically uninhibited nature, the fact that they are engendered as growth from a smallest unit rather than as patterns that have to fit within larger, preconceived measures.

Larry Peterson, who touched on this subject when interviewing the composer in the spring of 1971, confirms this ambiguity by cautioning: "He [Messiaen] demonstrated and explained them [the Indian rhythms]. Yet even though he uses the rhythms, he does *not* use them for their symbolic meanings. He *knew* the meanings but ignored them, he said. Also, he certainly did not expect his audience to know anything about them. So trying to interpolate Indian meanings to the *deçî-tâlas* Messiaen employs is not a fruitful task if you are trying to get to Messiaen's meaning." (Larry Peterson, private correspondence, 20 September 1994.)

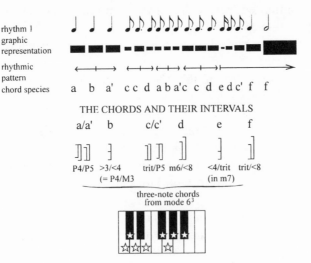

Strand 2, as has already been mentioned, is both independent from and subtly related to strand 1. Like its neighbor, it is based on a phrase of seventeen chords; this phrase, however, takes much longer to unfold, ending with the third eighth-note in bar 10. (While the phrase in strand 1 spans 26 eighth-notes, the one in strand 2 is 39 eighth-notes long.) Like the phrase in strand 1, the one in strand 2 is repeated; not twice, however, but only once. As in strand 1, the repetition is followed by an aborted new beginning; in strand 2, however, this truncated version comprises only two chords (see bars 20/21). Like the phrase in strand 1, the one in strand 2 also mirrors the layout of *The Father's Contemplation* with two subphrases, repeated with regard to the pitches but different in rhythm, followed by a "tail"; the inner structure of the repeated subphrase, however, is different.

Considering the interval structure of the four-note chords, one discerns a group of six chords repeated in identical intervals but different rhythms. Spotting transpositions is sometimes difficult owing to the composer's choice of a notation that retains the designation of the pitches rather than the nature of the intervals, and thus entails frequent enharmonic redefinitions; but careful inspection reveals that there are several simple patterns. Within the six-chord group, the second chord is a transposition of the first, the fourth a transposition of the third, and the sixth an inverted transposition of the fifth. Focusing on the superimposed intervals of these chords (their "color,") one finds that the first (and

244

second) consist of two interlocking perfect fifths; semitone, tritone, and augmented octave as additional intervals provide a high degree of tension. The third (and fourth) are built from interlocking minor and major sixths, a pattern entailing tritone and diminished octave but no semitone and thus more easygoing. The fifth (and sixth) chords feature a tritone interlocking with a major sixth, resulting in a relatively relaxed combination without semitones, again contained in a diminished octave. The five-chord tail, drawing on three new chords integrating the initial chord of the phrase, begins from a point of lowest tension: its framing interval is, for once, *not* a distorted octave, and the entire chord can be heard as a minor triad with added sixth.

Strand 2

THE CHORDS AND THEIR INTERVALS

The phrase structure in strands 1 and 2 is thus both related and dissimilar. In strand 1, the six repeated chords are organized as 3 + 3, while in strand 2, their pattern is 2 + 2 + 2; the five-chord tail that follows, too, is differently ordered. The relationship among the phrases with regard to rhythmic organization is even more intriguing: the pattern in strand 2 is derived from that in strand 1 by a process of augmentation by 150%, i.e. by increasing each time value by one half. The proportional relationship creates utterly complex constellations before it almost miraculously causes the repetition of the longer phrase to conclude simultaneously with the third statement of the phrase on the first level.

rhythm 1
graphic
representation

rhythm 2
graphic
representation

What are we to make of all that has been found so far? Let us consider the different parameters separately.

- The two modes used for the two strands, modes 6 and mode 4, relate to the two aspects of Jesus—to the SUFFERING ON THE CROSS overshadowing the INCARNATION OF THE WORD. Significantly, the same combination of modes 6 and 4 recurs in piece VII of the cycle, *The Cross's Contemplation*, musically emphasizing that in this situation the dual nature of the Christ is put to its hardest test.

- The fact that strand 1 consists exclusively of three-note chords, while strand 2 contains four-note chords throughout, confirms this interpretation. The Trinitarian 3 is an established symbol for the divine, while 4 stands for the material, perishable world of Aristotle's four elements (fire, water, air and earth). The three-note chords thus represent the divine nature of the Son, "shining down upon" the four-note chords that stand for the mortal aspect of the son. The essentially related structure yet apparently different shape of the phrases may be read as a symbolic rendering of the essentially identical yet apparently dissimilar appearance of the *Son of God* and the *Son of Man*.

- The use of rhythmic palindromes is connected, throughout Messiaen's work, with the concept of THE ETERNAL. The particular rhythmic sequence heard here combines four palindromes with a tail in vectorially increasing rhythmic values. The composer seems to employ this rhythm to symbolize the alliance of timeless, eternal qualities with temporally-determined, i.e. earthly concerns. This category of rhythmic organization (which recurs several times in the cycle, always attached to the same symbolic meaning) will be referred to as THE MANIFESTATION OF THE ETERNAL IN TIME.

- The fact that both strands are based on this same rhythmic pattern, that they are thus only seemingly different (and will remain unrelated for any listener, even after several consecutive exposures)

246

but intrinsically identical—proportionate to the degree that they "meet in the end"—corroborates the interpretation of the two strands as two aspects of the Christ. The divine and the human natures of Jesus, His mission to shoulder our sins and die for us on the Cross, and the hope He incorporates as a manifestation of the WORD INCARNATE, appear musically recreated as two differently sized perspectives of the same truth—perspectives that literally converge in the end. (In the subheading remarks to this piece, Messiaen speaks of "the Word in human nature—marriage of the human and divine natures in Jesus Christ.")

The superimposition of the two strands over *The Father's Contemplation* in the third strand occurs three times in this piece (see bars 1-21, 34-53m, 66m-73). A small, easily-overlooked detail distinguishes the three combinations at the point of their respective inceptions. The first stanza of *The Father's Contemplation* begins with GOD'S LOVE entering in the middle of bar 2. This means that for the time of three extremely slow quarter-notes, the Son alone is heard, exposed in His two natures. The complete initial three-chord palindrome in the first strand (the eternal aspect) is heard against the two initial chords in the second strand (and, with them, the rhythmic proportion, or the "other aspect"). At the beginning of the second stanza, only the initial chords of both strands—not yet rhythmically divided—precede the entry of GOD'S LOVE. And as a spiritually logical consequence, the coda is launched in all strands simultaneously. This adds a further dimension to the hermeneutic reading of the different parameters:

- The fact that *The Son Contemplating the Son* quotes *The Father's Contemplation* in its entirety should be read as Messiaen's musical embodiment of the Christian conviction that GOD'S LOVE, in its encompassing and original scope, supports the difficult duality of the Divine Son and the Child of Bethlehem. This support may seem as though withheld at a first glance; but a second exposure reveals that the blessing is present before the two aspects even begin to split. Finally, hindsight—the view from the coda—reassures us of the perfect coincidence of the Father's love with the Son's fate.

How, then, do the phrases representing the Son relate musically to the layer symbolizing the Father? Interestingly, Messiaen has structured his material in such a way that not a single subphrasing in the entire piece concurs! The musical excerpt below shows the juxtaposition of the leading part of the dual representation of the Son (strand 1, the SUFFERING

247

ON THE CROSS) and the beginning of *The Father's Contemplation*—not last
in the aim of stressing the supreme independence of one *Gestalt* from the
other at any given moment, particularly in terms of metric organization
and dynamic development. (Bar lines in the strand-1 phrase have been
omitted here to facilitate the recognition of rhythmic units and, particularly, the detection of the palindromes.)

This is, however, still not all there is to this piece. As was briefly
mentioned before, the dual layers representing the Son are suspended
during several bars at the end of each stanza of the *Theme of God* as well
as the very end of the coda. In its stead, the right-hand part embarks on
the most joyous play of pianistic bird-song imitations.

While in the lowest strand, *The Father's Contemplation* swells to
forte sonority—a dynamic level it has not ever reached before, neither in
the course of this piece nor in the initial *The Father's Contemplation*—
the stately half-note chords are contrasted and complemented in the treble
register by gleeful bird rhetoric. Among the multifarious chirping and
trilling, much of which is similar in the two stanzas, two calls stand out.
The first, noticeable for its short articulations, appears in bars 23, 27, 55
and 59. The second, concluding both shorter exchanges and the sections
themselves, is heard in bars 27, 30, 33, 59 and 64-65. (Moreover, the
pitches of this second call, characteristic in their superimposed fourths
A-D-G with semitone neighbors E♭ and A♭, creep into several other
chirps; see e.g. bars 29m, 31 [twice], and 60.) The bird responsible for
this call is also the only one who will persist, an octave higher, in the
coda.

The musical representatives of both the SUFFERING ON THE CROSS and
the INCARNATION OF THE WORD are thus absent for extended periods during

(The sketch on the following page gives an overview of the entire layout
of Messiaen's *The Son Contemplating the Son*.)

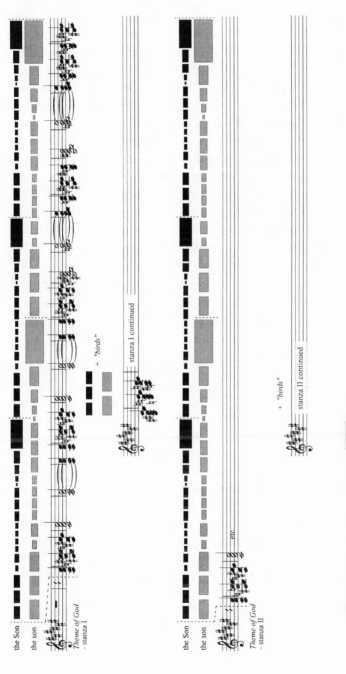

the piece dedicated to just this relationship. What we hear instead is GOD'S LOVE in, as it were, two of its many versions. As Messiaen never tired of assuring his interviewers, bird song is for him the manifestation of God's love in nature—just as he sees the "ideal love" as expressed in the Tristan myth as the manifestation of God's love among humans.

Exactly when the change from one texture to the other occurs in each of the three instances is highly significant. In the first stanza, the merger of Jesus' two natures, i.e. the coinciding conclusion of the second repetition of the strand-1 phrase and of the first repetition of the strand-2 phrase, is followed by the portion of both phrases that was heard "apparently without the support of GOD'S LOVE at the beginning of the stanza (compare bars 20m-21 with bars 1-2m). In the second stanza, by contrast, where no exposed split of natures was heard to begin with, the bird-song imitation follows directly after the concurring conclusion of the phrases (see bar 53m). Finally in the coda, the process is yet different. The two strands dedicated to the Son break off, abruptly and without any inner logic within their respective phrases, immediately before the attack of the final chord of *The Father's Contemplation*. (I like to read this as a musical symbol for the belief that Jesus' mission is, in a sense, ongoing; but I might be taking this too far.) This F♯-major chord with added sixth—the "chord of love," as one will recall—diverges from the established pattern of protracted middle-register chords and ascends with four accented sixteenth values, in a *crescendo* through four octaves.

The bird-song cadenzas, then, add a crucial dimension to the theological message of this piece. The "merger" of the two proportionate rhythmic sequences, i.e. the completion of the process in which Jesus' dual nature again falls together, leads to a powerfully reinforced manifestation of divine Love. The spiritual interpretation is further corroborated and widened by the composer's own words. Messiaen's prefacing remarks speak of the "refraction of joy" and mention "the birds of silence." Beginning with the latter wording, we are reminded that birds can only be heard in silence, and may thus stand for the representation in sound of that which is characterized by an absence of human noise. The former expression points to a different aspect. As in many of his other compositions, Messiaen's translates the joy he experiences (as do most of us) in the presence of lively bird song into a musical symbol. Bird song, then, stands both for our silent awe and for the "refraction of joy" in which nature exuberantly celebrates God's love as manifested in the Incarnation of His Son.

Première communion de la Vierge   (Messiaen, *Vingt regards*, XI)

(Après l'Annonciation, Marie adore Jésus en elle... mon Dieu, mon fils, mon Magnificat! - mon amour sans bruit de paroles...)

The eleventh piece marks the beginning of the second half in this cycle of twenty. The accompanying wording ("After the annunciation, Mary worships Jesus within her... my God, my son, my Magnificat!—my love without the sound of words ...") assigns the piece to Mary. She is pictured in the moment when, having learned in the Annunciation that she is carrying the divine Child, she adores that which is growing in her, saying her "Magnificat."[117] Meanwhile, the musical language establishes its own connections, above all through themes, modal organization, and rhythmic patterns. This connection points to GOD'S LOVE as that which supports throughout, to the human aspect (in referring both to the *Son of Man* and to the Star and the Cross, symbols of Jesus' earthly life span), and to the ecstatic happiness over the birth of this child. Let us look at each of these components separately and then seek to understand their combined message.

The piece is overwhelmingly based on the *Theme of God*. Interestingly, the phrase structure underlying this theme in the cycle's initial piece, *The Father's Contemplation*, can be recognized twice within the *First Communion of the Virgin*. We are thus dealing not only with two stanzas of a song (as in I and V), but actually with two related songs, each of which shows the entire original design. Here is a first overview:

I *The Father's Contempl.*		XI *First Communion,* I		XI *First Communion,* II	
First stanza		*First stanza*		*First stanza*	
phrase I	bars 1-2	phrase I	bars 1-2	phrase I	bars 21-22
repetition	bars 2-3	repetition	bars 3-4	repetition	bars 22-24
develop.1	bars 3-9	develop.1	bars 5-8	develop.1	bars 25-28

[117] In his *Note de l'auteur*, Messiaen evokes a painting showing the Virgin on her knees, withdrawn into herself in the night, a radiant halo overhanging her womb. "Her eyes closed, she dwells in adoration for the fruit hidden within her." While, as any anthology of "Maria del parto" or "Marie enceinte" reveals, there are hundreds of paintings depicting the Virgin at this moment and in this state of mind, the very unusual halo around the womb seems like a giveaway that might help us identify which particular work of art the composer had in mind. However, neither my own search nor my persistent questions to several art historians brought any fruit, and unfortunately Messiaen's widow, Yvonne Loriod, could not help either.

Second stanza		Second stanza		Second stanza	
phrase I	bars 9-10	phrase I	bars 9-10	phrase I	bars 29-30
repetition	bars 10-11	repetition	bars 11-12	repetition	bars 31-32
develop.2	bars 11-17	develop.2	bars 13-16	develop.	bars 33-36
Coda	bars 17-19	Codetta	bars 16,20	Codetta	bars 37-42
		Contrast 1	bars 17-19	Contrast 2	bars 43-72
				Coda	bars 73-80

The *Theme of God* is presented in the key of B♭ major and the corresponding, second transposition of mode 2 (which, read from this key note, contains the pitches B♭ B C♯ D E F G A♭). Within the original phrase, we hear the three characteristic chords followed by the melodic climax; the relaxation that concludes the phrase in *The Father's Contemplation* is omitted here. Also, the rhythmic shape has changed somewhat, in that the climax is not just two beats long, but occurs in a variety of uneven durations (thirteen or fifteen half-beats in bars 2 and 4, five in bar 6, eight in bar 8, eleven in bars 10 and 12). The melodic outline, by contrast, does not change in the development; neither do other transpositions of mode 2 occur. What structures the phrases in the way outlined above are the events in the accompanying right-hand part.

The four components that can be distinguished here stem from different tonal sources and carry with them the symbolic meaning attached to these sources. The two-bar phrase and its repetition (see bars 1-4 and 9-12) are accompanied by two figures. The first, which will be referred to as component *a*, coils in very soft, very swift motions in the highest register. Its tonal background is the second transposition of mode 4. Throughout the cycle, this mode stands for one of Christ's aspects, that of the WORD INCARNATE.[118] The musical symbol is thus ideally placed to mark the moment when Mary becomes aware of the manifestation of God's grace growing in her womb. The complementing component *b* is more than five times slower than *a*, placed closer to the central register and, with the indication *p tendre,* also closer to the color of the *Theme of God.* Its firm rooting in the third B♭/D relates it further to the underlying theme. With a

---

[118] For the pitches of Messiaen's modes in all their transpositions, please refer to the table in Appendix II. The symbolic meaning of mode 4 as representing the WORD INCARNATE was discussed in greater depth in connection with piece V, *The Son Contemplating the Son.* The composer also uses this mode in the same sense in XIII, *Christmas,* and in X, *The Spirit of Joy Contemplating the Infant Jesus* (see the two chapters in part I of this book). Mode 4 further plays a role in VI, *Through Him All Was Made* and in VII, *The Cross's Contemplation.*

pitch content that is derived from the second transposition of mode 2, this component thus clearly reinforces the symbolism of GOD'S LOVE.

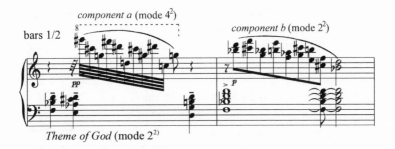

Theme of God (mode 2^2)

In the developmental part of the stanza, two new components are added. Component *c*, heard in bars 6/7, is reminiscent of component *a* in that it is launched in the same, high register from where it winds its way down. The pitches represent an excerpt from the second transposition of mode 7. This mode is both tonally and spiritually related to mode 4. Tonally, mode 7 constitutes and extension of mode 4 by one note in each half-octave:

mode 4^2: C C♯ D D♯   F♯ G G♯ A
mode 7^2: C C♯ D D♯ E   F♯ G G♯ A A♯

Spiritually, mode 7 is the tonal character determining the *Theme of the Star and the Cross*. This theme—by virtue of its double-duty name as well as through its usage in II, *The Star's Contemplation* and in VII, *The Cross's Contemplation*—marks the two end points of Jesus' life on earth. The comet announcing the birth of the divine Child, and the Cross representing the fulfillment of His mission among humans, are tonally conceived as an emanation of the INCARNATION OF THE WORD. Both the promise and hope at the beginning of this life and the grief at its end are thus emotionally anticipated in this moment when Mary first understands, and enters into communion with Jesus.

The fourth component is not necessarily modally determined, although one could read it as an excerpt of mode 7^3. More significant seems the designation as bird song (see Messiaen's indication, *oiseau*, in bar 7). The juxtaposition of the *Theme of God* with bird song harkens back to the developmental phrases in the fifth piece of the *Vingt regards*, thus reinforcing the connection of this piece not only with the initial *The Father's Contemplation,* but also with the first variation of the two stanzas as heard in *The Son Contemplating the Son*. Here as there, the introduction of bird song stands for the participation of nature in the blissful event.

While component *a* remains without any modifications (cf. bar 1 with bars 3, 5 and 9), component *b* never recurs in the same form. In fact, so much is this symbolic reassurance of GOD'S LOVE expanded that it overruns everything else: component *a*, which we would have expected in bar 11, component *c* and the bird call, which might have featured in the development of the second stanza (bars 13-16), but also the *Theme of God* itself, which is not literally present in these bars (although, strangely enough, we hear them as the expected developmental phrase). And as if this was not enough, Messiaen uses two further details to enhance the message that GOD'S LOVE is stronger than any other aspects. One is captured in the dynamic intensity of this second development, which leads up to *f* before it concludes in the original soft shades. The other can be recognized in the way the composer uses the mode here. From the beginning of the second stanza, the third B♭/D in its function as a reinforcement of the key note and B♭-major chord of the *Theme of God* is given more and more room (see bars 9/10, 11/12). In the two bars that open the development, another major chord, G major, assumes importance. Finally in bars 15/16, we hear nothing but major triads (in second inversion). In fact, B♭ major, D♭ major, E major and G major constitute all the major triads that can be built from mode 4^2. These chords thus corroborate even in their multi-faceted appearance the priority of the mode epitomizing GOD'S LOVE.

As if to disturb this untainted optimism, Messiaen concludes this section in the second half of bar 16 with a *ppp* plunge to the lowest key of the keyboard, in pitches that still stem from mode 2^2 and are thus subtly linked to the preceding two stanzas. The gesture of the sudden plunge, metaphoric for the awe experienced in view of the momentousness of the Incarnation, occurs in a similar way in the other piece dedicated to the Virgin. In *The Virgin's Contemplation*, the first half of the piece concludes with an unmediated three-note cluster over the same lowest A of the keyboard, carrying the same spiritual connotations of Mary's overwhelming awe. The connection is confirmed in the *au movement* of bar 20 that picks up the B♭-major chord after the short contrast and closes with the full A/B♭/B♮ cluster heard in bar 62 of piece IV.

This musical "bracket," as it were—comprising part of bar 16 and the confirming or correcting bar 20—constitutes the first codetta in this piece. It encloses three bars that, by virtue of their consistent E♭ pedal, fit convincingly into the B♭-major context. However, this first contrast actually represents a quotation from another work of Messiaen's on the topic of Christ's birth, *La nativité du seigneur*. The first movement of that organ composition of 1935 is entitled *La Vierge et l'Enfant* (The Virgin and the Child). Its opening theme appears here almost literally, albeit transposed a fifth lower. Messiaen acknowledges the connection with the explicit remark *Rappel de "la Vierge et l'Enfant"* (Reminiscence of "the Virgin and the Child").

La nativité du seigneur,
"La Vierge et l'Enfant,"
bar 1

Vingt regards sur l'Enfant-Jésus
XI: "Première communion de la Vierge,"
bars 17-19

Both the quoted melody with its supporting chords and the large curve of four-note chords in the accompanying right-hand part derive from mode 2³. They thus remain closely related to the general message of this piece, which is the manifestation of God's all-encompassing love, present in this moment of Mary's first communion. Messiaen scholar Aloyse Michaely, in the context of her discussion of *Nativité*, speaks of this melodic gesture as "the Incarnation theme."[119] This reading further corroborates the symbolic value of the other components, especially of mode 4 as a symbol for the WORD INCARNATE.

The second half of this piece, and with it the second recurrence of the complete *Theme of God* in the version established in *The Father's Contemplation,* while retaining many of the characteristics just heard before, introduces a whole new set of symbols and cross references.

As in the first half of the piece, the *Theme of God* is rooted in B♭, and the developmental phrases do not present transpositions of the mode but rather developments in the rhythmic patterns and in the accompanying components. As in the first half of the piece, the second stanza differs from the first from the very beginning with regard to the accompanying events in the treble and with regard to rhythm.

In contrast to the first half of the piece, the second half presents the three characteristic chords of the *Theme of God* in a rhythmic pattern that

---

[119]A. Michaely, *op. cit.*, page 284.

was introduced in the piece preceding the *First Communion*. Piece X, *The Spirit of Joy Contemplating the Infant Jesus*, features in its very prominent central section a "hunting song" whose conspicuous feature is the repeated long-short-long rhythm leading up to a climx that, with its long halt, interrupts the melodic flow.

XI, *First Communion of the Virgin*, bars 1/2: *Theme of God*

X, *The Spirit of Joy Contemplating* bars 60/61: hunting song

XI, bars 21/22: Mary's exuberant Magnificat, the *Theme of God* in the rhythm of the hunting song

The connotations are manifold here. In the context of the verbal clues provided in piece X, the hunting song stands for the exuberant joy of both the "blissful God" and the Spirit of Joy. At the same time, as was elaborated in detail in the chapter dealing with that piece, the hunting song is related to Messiaen's *Theme of Love*. This theme, on the other hand, stands symbolically for the LOVE OF GOD that mirrors GOD's LOVE. And that is exactly what Messiaen has set out to express here, as his remark in the score, *Magnificat - enthusiasme haletant* (Magnificat; breathless enthusiasm) indicates. If the first half of the piece, kept in very slow tempo, depicts the more contemplative aspect of the scene—Mary's state of blissful withdrawal into herself with closed eyes—then the second half portrays her exhilation and "breathless" joy, related in kind to that of the Spirit of Joy.

The developmental phrases (bars 25-28 and 33-36) expand and significantly alter the rhythmic pattern of the hunting song, reinforcing the sense of elation in a wide variety of unpredictable rhythms and ecstatic *rubato* flourishes, all the while remaining securely rooted in mode 2^2. The second codetta is launched in bars 37/38 with an enhanced version of the hunting-song transformation of the *Theme of God*. Bars 39-42 follow with a powerful *crescendo*, which develops through three mode-2 bars and is completed in a twelve-tone flourish. In the three modal bars, a middle-register B♭-major chord (i.e. the opening triad of the *Theme-of-God* phrase) serves as a recurring upbeat to ever higher inversions of a five-note chord, reached in increasingly spread-out tempo. In the concluding flourish, the process is repeated with regard to the ascending motion (which comes here as a broken chord in increasingly smaller intervals) but inverted with regard to speed (see the *pressez* that breaks off in an abrupt *caesura*).

The following, second contrast is much longer than the first, encompassing three segments from bar 43 to bar 72. All segments are based on elements of the B♭ chord that, in this piece, stands for the tonality of GOD'S LOVE. Each of them plays, in increasing intensity, with the paradox of simultaneously occurring reiteration and change.

- In the first segment (bars 43-46), the rhythm does not undergo any changes. There are seven versions of a six-note chord that, preceded by an *acciaccatura*, is topped by the B♭/D of the central tonality. After four identical attacks, the right-hand part changes only slightly by moving back and forth between octaves, while the left hand juxtaposes new, unrelated chords. No dynamic development whatsoever happens in the prescribed *ff*.

- Bars 47-51 present a chain of five chord pairs, strung together by a recurring pitch and a pattern of rhythmic progression. In each pair (which can be regarded as a development of the preceding coupling of *acciaccatura*-plus-chord), the second attack features a D in the treble, thus retaining the melodically leading note from the *Theme-of-God* B♭/D that rang through the preceding segment. Besides the reiterated pitch and the persistent use of chord pairs, the outstanding feature is one of progressive growth: a gradual rhythmic expansion of the first chord, involving only prime numbers. Counted in sixteenths, the five bars establish the following sequence:

$$2 + 4, \quad 3 + 4, \quad 5 + 4, \quad 7 + 4, \quad 11 + 4$$

The five-bar segment is rounded off with a five-chord bar that is reminiscent of a very similar bar in the Creation piece *Through Him All Was Made* (cf. VI, bars 23/24 etc.). In the context of the growth in prime numbers, which was also first heard in the Creation piece (cf. VI, bars 62, 64, 66, 68), this quotation gains particular importance, and connects the growing of the Child in Mary's womb to God's Creation of the world at large.

- In the third segment of this contrast, repetition and growth are taken yet one step further, in what amounts to a combination of all devices heard just before. Regarding pitch, the original unit is now a doubled chord pair—a chord with *acciaccatura* (as in bar 43) coupled with its repetition. This unit occurs four times (see the four identical versions of the chord in bar 43). Still with regard to pitch only, the following four bars are triggered from two of the "Creation" chords and move through three more unrelated chords. In bar 61, the pitches of bar 53 are reinstalled and form yet another pattern, featuring an expansive broken-chord *acciaccatura*-group complemented by repeated notes in the low bass. Messiaen marked this repeated F as "heart beats of the Infant." Above it, the pitches change only slightly.

As for "growth," the entire segment is held together by a *diminuendo* from *ff* to *ppp*, and by two aspects of slowing down. One regards the *acciaccatura*-groups, which Messiaen specifically requests to be taken ever slower. The other expresses itself in a deepening of the growth experienced in the second segment. Here, both parts of the pair expand in equal increments. Counted in sixteenths, this is the sequence:

1+3, 2+4, 3+5, 4+6, 5+7, 6+8, 7+9, 8+10, 9+11, 10+12, 11+13

The segment, and with it the entire contrasting section, is wrapped up after a rest with a chord that prolongs the heartbeat F in its lowest voice and thus underscores the sense of dominant within the reigning B♭-major tonality.

The coda consists of two segments. Both pick up elements from the very beginning of the *First Communion of the Virgin*. Bars 73-74 recall component *a* and its symbolism of the WORD INCARNATE over an ascending bass of F and C. Bars 75-80 quote once more the initial phrase of the *Theme of God*, accompanied with component *b*, the reinforcement of GOD'S LOVE, which is here designated as an expression of an "inner kiss" or "inner embrace."

All elements of the coda undergo a process of fading out of existence. In component *a,* the continuous motion is interrupted by a sudden suspension of the initial note, after which the remainder is fragmented and disappears. In component *b*, a nineteen-beat version in bar 76 is reduced to a more excerpt in bar 78 and nothing but its final dyad B♭/D in bar 80. Even the *Theme-of-God* phrase recedes with disjointed utterings in bars 79/80.

The larger symbolism in this piece is manifold. Its various, sometimes contrasting elements reflect the elements of Messiaen's subheading lines. With all due caution, one could recognize a focus on the idea of

Jesus as Son of Man in the first half, and on the notion of Jesus as Son of God in the second. The central message underlying the Annunciation, that God's Son is growing in Mary's womb, is present throughout the piece with the *Theme of God.*

Mary's first reaction is musically depicted as a contemplative mood: the tempo is very slow, the *Theme-of-God* phrase very quiet, and the accompanying thoughts center in the concept of the INCARNATION OF THE WORD (component *a* with its mode 4^2) and the key events of the prospective child's life on earth, its birth and death as symbolized in the Star of Bethlehem and the Cross of Golgotha (see component *c* with its mode 7^2). Embedded in this reflective mood is a short expression of nature's rejoicing in the form of bird calls. The contrast complementing this first mood is equally intimate, centering entirely on the tender relationship of mother and child.

Mary's second reaction is her powerful Magnificat. This shifts the focus from her child to God's Child, as it were. The musical expression Messiaen chooses is the hunting-song rhythm from piece X, *The Spirit of Joy Contemplating the Infant Jesus.* Instead of the tender happiness of the expecting mother, we now hear the exuberance of the blissful God. Wild runs inside each stanza and a powerful outburst in the codetta pave the way for the contrast. It concentrates again on God's role and plan: "growth," the symbol for human TRANSFORMATION, is coupled with a reminder that "through Him all was made."

The conspicuous fragmentation of elements in the coda can be read as a musical depiction of the process of renouncing utterance. This ties in with the last sentence in Messiaen's subheading, "my love without the sound of words," a rephrasing of the *sine strepitu verborum* from the *Imitatio* (III. 43, 3) which Thérèse de Lisieux, the little saint whom Messiaen so revered, quoted in her autobiography when she wrote, "He ... teaches without the sound of words. Never did I hear Him speak, and yet I sense that He is within me." After Mary has expressed her motherly love and devotion, and God His elation and bliss, Jesus teaches us that no words are needed.

Regard de l'Eglise d'amour   (Messiaen , *Vingt regards*, XX)

(La grâce nous fait aimer Dieu comme Dieu s'aime; après les gerbes de nuit, les spirales d'angoisse, voici les cloches, la gloire et le baiser d'amour...toute la passion de nos bras autour de l'Invisible...)

This is another piece built powerfully on the concept of GOD'S LOVE, both musically and theologically. It ends with a complete restatement of the entire tonal argument of *The Father's Contemplation*, in the original F♯-major context and concomitant mode 2, and thus brings the cycle of *Twenty Contemplations on the Infant Jesus* full circle.

Messiaen's title and subheading point us in the direction of his thinking. The Church is very explicitly "the Church of Love." Rather than an institution that guards and perpetuates agreed-upon doctrines, the Church the composer has in mind is the manifestation of God's love in the form of a community and brotherhood, the mystical body of Christ (Messiaen: *"l'église qui est le corps du Christ"*) or, by extension, the mystical body of "the Word." It is thus, in a first sense, a process by which the gift of the Incarnation of the Word is handed on from brother to brother-in-spirit, from Christian to fellow Christian, as in a lateral mirroring of that which was given from above. In the context of our ability to love God as we should, Messiaen speaks frequently about grace —usually in the sense of the grace that makes us all God's adopted children.

According to Messiaen, "The grace makes us love God as God loves Himself." The composer's wording is remarkable here, and evokes a second degree of mirroring. God loves Himself, and His Church fulfills its destined task best if its love equals that which God feels for Himself. This statement contains a most intriguing dual reflection on the familiar quest to love one's neighbor as one loves oneself. But while the instigation to true brotherly love takes human self-love as a point of comparison, thus demanding a degree of love that is by definition available to everyone, the quest to love God as God loves Himself requires that humans strive to imitate God's ability to love, which is boundless and supreme. This is a goal that, were it not for God's grace, would remain forever out of reach. (Even aided by grace, however, one imagines such human attempts to match divine Love to fall pitifully short of their model.)

The opening section of the piece depicts this two-fold mirroring process, along with parameters symbolizing the dimensions of love within the Church. The six-bar section contains two components with two transformations each. Component *a*, introduced in bar 1, features in the right-hand part a swift, steeply curved figure in perfect bilateral symmetry. The rhythm is even, and the process of mirroring thus concentrates on pitches (along with dynamics). The left-hand counterpart, while equally mirror-symmetrical in the horizontal dimension, presents at the same time a somewhat distorted vertical reflection of the right-hand figure. Both the perfect-fourth intervals in the treble and the connecting steps appear slightly "too small" in the lower part. Component *b*, first heard in bar 2, is scored in simple *unison*. The bilateral symmetry is one of rhythmic values here, not of pitch. The two components in their original forms combine, then, the spiritual aspects of passing on to one's brothers the gift of the Incarnation (horizontal symmetry), attempting to imitate God's love of Himself (vertical symmetry), and many-sided action, guided by the same spirit but different in each situation (rhythmic palindrome with free pitch allocation).

The transformations of component *a* in bars 3 and 5 constitute an internal extension: the climactic moment in bar 1 is surpassed in bar 3 where, at the center of the figure, an additional development heightens and deepens the effect. The step is repeated, with further intensification, in bar 5. As a counterpart to this internal extension, component *b* undergoes external extension. The three-note palindrome of bar 2 is expanded in bar 4 by two further eighth-notes at both flanks, and by a sixteenth-note suspension plus another eighth in bar 6. As in the original, the bilateral mirror is perfect with regard to rhythm but corresponds only gesturally with regard to pitch. The transformative processes carry their own powerful symbolism. The internal extensions undergone by component *a* portray a heightening and deepening of the love that is the topic of this piece, while the external expansions of component *b* seem to point at the spreading of this love, in all directions an in different forms.

The entire opening section recurs later in the piece (bars 85-92), with important modifications. One way of perceiving it is to say that the order of the two components is reversed, and that each spawns three instead of only two transformations. Another way of looking at it reveals the original opening section (compare bars 1-6 with bars 86-91) as extended in two directions, horizontally (with an additional bar at each wing) and vertically (in that component *b* now adopts the two-part contrary-motion of component *a*). The second view allows for particularly interesting nuances of interpretation. Component *b*, heard in its original, simple *unison* in the "additional" bar 85, reopens in a new format in bar 87 where it presents its three-note palindrome in vertically imperfect mirror symmetry.[120] The two palindromic extensions familiar from bars 4 and 6 appear here, in bars 89, with no further change other than the significant fortification by contrary motion, which is thickened even more in bar 91. The extension, then, is one that regards the vertical dimension; the task of spreading the message of divine love is tied in once more with the model to be followed, God's love for Himself. Similarly with other means, *component a* also deemphasizes the dimension of horizontal mirroring. The "additional" bar 92 forgoes bilateral symmetry altogether, taking up only what was the second half of the model bar. Expanding its vertically mirrored, contracting motion into a large sweep in *crescendo molto* and *rallentando*, the two hands meet climactically on a single, central pitch: E.

In the context of the *Vingt regards*, the pitch E has a very solid symbolic significance. In piece III, *The Exchange*, the unchanging E in the midst of asymmetric growth process represents God's unchanging presence. This connotation is taken up in the third section of *The Spirit of Joy Contemplating the Infant Jesus,* where E is again a reliable anchor in a depiction of exponential growth. The introduction of this pitch with its spiritual significance in *The Exchange* is particularly intriguing because of a shared image in the subheadings of that piece and *The Church of Love Contemplating the Infant Jesus.* In both cases, Messiaen speaks of "showers of sparks" and "spirals" (see III: *Descente en gerbe, montée en spirale* [Descent in a shower of sparks, ascent in a spiral] with XX: *après les gerbes de nuit, les spirales d'angoisse* [after the showers of sparks in the night, the spirals of anguish]). Just as in the piece speaking of the

---

[120]It would have been easy indeed for Messiaen to write this figure in a form that was as perfectly symmetrical vertically as it is horizontally. Since he has decided not to limit himself by the use of any of his modes, no tonal logic kept him from inverting the intervals of the treble in the bass. Taking the trouble of writing out what the perfect mirror image would have been (left hand: D♮-D-F♯/B-F-G♯/C♮), we even discover that, owing to Messiaen's choice of the pitches from which the two voices are launched, the climax would have fallen on the doubling of the perfect fourth in the right hand! On this improbable level of comparison with the assumed "ideal," the left-hand part thus presents indeed a distorted mirror image—as helplessly distorted as man's love in striving to equal God's love.

Exchange of Natures, God becoming Man and Man becoming God, so also in this context does the word *gerbe* designate both the tail of a comet (the Star of Bethlehem) and the gift of God's love, handed down to us in Jesus' Incarnation. The spiral as a symbol both for spiritual purification and for continuing growth denoted Man's imitation of Christ's love of God in piece III, just as it represents Man's attempts to mirror God's love of Himself in piece XX. The explicit, strongly emphasized pitch E at the end of bar 92 can then be taken as a signifier for the unwavering presence of God's grace in the midst of our imperfect attempts to learn boundless love.

In this spiritual framework, it feels especially reassuring that GOD'S LOVE, in its musical representation by the *Theme of God*, is explicitly present. As a single phrase, it is interspersed in all structurally significant moments of the piece that glorifies the Church of Love.

- In bars 7/8, following the metaphoric delineation of spatiality both internal and external, the *Theme-of-God* phrase is heard in mode 2^3. The tonal rooting in B major is strongly emphasized here; of the thirteen eighth-notes allotted this phrase, twelve manifest the B-major chord, with only one eighth-note left for the theme's second and third chords. During the final three-eighths, the B-major chord is joined by a bass attack whose pitches, A/B♭/D♯/E, bring with them significant allusions. A is the lowest key on the keyboard; A/B♭ stands for the chromatic cluster over the lowest pitch that, by the time listeners reach the final piece of the cycle, they have heard on several occasions. The earliest instance of this lowest-possible chromatic cluster occurs in the piece dedicated to *The Virgin's Contemplation* which, as we shall see, is quoted two more times in *The Church of Love Contemplating the Infant Jesus*. In bar 62 of piece IV, the bass cluster A/B♭/B♮/C can be interpreted as Mary's sudden awe when she grasps the full importance of the Incarnation, and the shock that accompanies her insight. In bars 16 and 20 of piece XI, *First Communion of the Virgin*, two clusters over the lowest key A frame the quotation from *The Virgin and the Infant*, the opening movement of Messiaen's *La nativité du seigneur*, thus establishing a very similar context. The role of the cluster over A as an expression of awe in front of the divine will is confirmed in XIII, *Christmas*, and particularly in XII, *The Almighty Word*.

The chord A/B♭/D♯/E in the present context, that of the "Church of Love," may be read to serve two symbolic purposes, in that it combines the significance of the cluster over the lowest A with that of the distinctive pitch E, here also enhanced by a chromatic neighbor note.

- In bars 17/18, the phrase sounds in D♭ major with pitches from mode 2^2. The beginning is rhythmically analogous, but ornamentation at the end is extended and lacks the bass attack. These two phrases assume the role of two beginnings not followed by further development.

- The third beginning, in mode 2^3 and F major, carries the manifestation of GOD'S LOVE somewhat further (see bars 27/28 and 29/30, and compare with I, bars 2/3).

- In bars 105-107, only the melody (presented in the rhythm that, unchanged throughout all these beginnings, is by now familiar) recalls the *Theme of God*. The accompaniment consists of a four-beat *ostinato* in curved shape that strikes us as strongly reminiscent of the similar *ostinato* heard in bars 42-44 and 49-51 of piece IV, *The Virgin's Contemplation*. The development at the end of the phrase, however, leads to other material.

- Finally, launched in bar 161, the *Theme of God* is heard in the original mode (2^1), the original key of GOD'S LOVE (F♯ major, underscored by an explicit six-sharps key signature), and in the complete form of two stanzas and coda.

Compare I,	with XX,
The Father's Contemplation,	*The Church of Love Contemplating*
stanza I bars 1- 9d	bars 161-173d
stanza II bars 9-16d	bars 177-189d
coda bars 17-19	bars 193-199 (extended to 220)

The bass cluster is retained in the four opening phrases of each of the two stanzas, and the low A also prominently concludes the piece—and with it the cycle, leaving the listener with something akin to a musical admonition to be mindful of the awesome aspect of the Incarnation.

Meanwhile, the development in each stanza is rounded off with an insert that constitutes, after the bass attack and the chordal *ostinato*, the third quotation from piece IV, *The Virgin's Contemplation.* The treble part, here complemented with a new left-hand

264

counterpart, was first heard as an accompaniment to Mary's heart-rending lament.

Compare IV,	with XX,
The Virgin's Contemplation,	*The Church of Love Contemplating*
bars 35/36, 95/96	bar 173, 189
bars 37-39, 97-99	bars 174-176, 190-192

Returning to the beginning of *The Church of Love Contemplating the Infant Jesus*, we find a third large section, after the section of palindromic expansions and the *Theme of God*. In fast tempo (*vif*) and in powerfully growing intensity (from *pp* to *ff*), the left hand presents a motif that starts out as a horizontal cluster (C/C♯/D/E♭/E/F). The line then undergoes asymmetric growth, in such a way that the three higher semitones rise by one chromatic increment in each of the three following bars, while the three lower semitones fall step by step. In a transposition of this four-bar segment, the process is repeated a perfect fourth higher (cf. bars 13-16 with bars 9-12). After an interjected *Theme-of-God* phrase, we hear a first variation of the two phrases, placed a semitone higher and enriched with an inner-voice chromatic descent that later adjusts freely to the changing surroundings in the asymmetric growth (cf. left hand, bars 19-26 with bars 9-16). Much later, after the recapitulation of the opening section, a second variation sounds three semitones higher than the original, keeps the inner voice, but breaks the octaves (cf. left hand, bars 93-100). Finally, bars 101-104 repeat the pitches of bars 19-22 with broken octaves, thus adding another half variation that is perceived as an extension and intensification of the preceding one.

The treble counters this expansion with a twelve-tone row (see the first two sextuplets in bar 9) whose immediate repetition is delayed until the bass is finished. In subsequent bars, the pitches of the row are somewhat rearranged without, however, following any of the rules of transmutation defined by Schoenberg and his followers. Most significantly, the octave allocation of each pitch remains unchanged, and each row begins unfalteringly on E. What is more, the four versions of the row established in the original bars 9-12 recur unchanged in each of the six transformations.

The symbolism of this section harkens back to the first piece within the *Vingt regards* that uses asymmetric growth. In III, *The Exchange*, the process of gradual distortion is attached to the idea of the human-divine commerce: God becomes human so that humans may become God-like. The immutable pitch E stands there for the reliable, never-changing presence of God. (For an in-depth discussion of the symbolism, see the chapter dealing with *L'échange*.) The combination of asymmetric growth and a stable pitch E recurs several times in prominent places within the cycle. Piece VI, *Through Him All Was Made*, contains three passages that employ the combination of the two devices. The irregularly growing left-hand figure in VI, bars 50-58 contains an untouched major-seventh leap from F to E as a fixed anchor; the leading voice in the three-part stretto of VI bars 130-141 as well as its continuation in the bass of bars 142-153 features, in the midst of a gradually widening warp, four unchanging notes that lead invariably to E; and finally, the contrapuntally used version in the treble of bars 142-154 ends with three constant pitches, concluding once more with E. And in piece X, *The Spirit of Joy Contemplating the Infant Jesus*, the section employing wildly contorting asymmetric growth is even more firmly rooted in the pitch E, heard in *unison* at the end of every single unit. In *The Church of Love Contemplating the Infant Jesus*, both the contention regarding the necessity of gradual transformation and the promise of God's unwavering presence are thus renewed one more time.

At this stage, it may help to visualize the layout of the entire piece in table format.

exposition

recapitulation

bars
  1-6   palindromes
  7-8   *Theme of God*
  9-16   asymmetric growth
  17-18 *Theme of God*
  19-26 asymmetric growth
  27-30 *Theme of God*

bars
  85-92   palindromes (expanded)

  93-104 asymmetric growth (enlivened)
  105-111 *Theme of God* (expanded)

contrast 1

contrast 2

bars
31-54   *Theme of Love*
55-84

bars
112-160   bell rondo

conclusion

bars
161-196   *Theme of God*
196-220   external extension (coda)

The first contrast, then, begins in bar 31. As Messiaen's marking in the score makes clear, what we hear is a variant of the *Theme of Love*. This theme was first heard in bar 170 of piece VI, *Through Him All Was Made*. In the original version, it consists of three different chords in four attacks (the fourth chord constitutes an inversion of the third); the pitch content does not stem from any of the modes; it shares with the *Theme of God* the melodic beginning on A♯ in the top voice over A♯ in the lowest voice, and the conclusion on the F♯-major chord with added sixth. These shared features, together with the allusion to the concept of bilaterality in the pitch content (for more details, see the chapter on piece VI), invite an interpretation of the *Theme of Love* as a symbol for the human LOVE OF GOD, as well as the love of one another. In the piece currently under consideration, *The Church of Love Contemplating the Infant Jesus*, the *Theme of Love* appears in a transformation that is reminiscent of the hunting song in *The Spirit of Joy Contemplating the Infant Jesus* (see X, bars 60/61, etc.). As was shown in the discussion of *First Communion of the Virgin*, there is a strong inner connection between the hunting song and GOD'S LOVE: Mary sings her Magnificat with the chords of the *Theme of God* in the rhythm of the hunting song (see XI, bars 21/22). Here, the connection is further expanded. Not only GOD'S LOVE towards His Son and all of us is filled with ecstatic bliss, and represented as such in Mary's song; even the LOVE OF GOD as manifested among his believers in the community of the Church is characterized, or so Messiaen convinces us, by this element of elated happiness, as the combination of *Theme-of-Love* melody with hunting-song rhythm demonstrates. And to spin the connective web even further, the melodic notes in the first bar together with the inverted seventh chord (and its arpeggiated extension) in the second bar stem from mode 2, the mode of GOD'S LOVE. The composer's hope for the Church, then, is that divine love, love of one another, and spirited joy work together.

The two-bar phrase of the *Theme of Love* is heard in four transpositions (bars 31-38), followed by four statements of an intensified version, in which the thematic phrase (in *ff*, a little slower than before, and "with a feeling of intense joy") is juxtaposed with its diminution in the higher register (bars 39-46) and an even more powerful development (bars 47-54, *mf-fff*). Then, the entire process is repeated. Each phrase is transposed to a different semitone, and several extensions create further intensification (see bars 55-84).

267

In light of this mighty manifestation of *Love and Bliss*, the specifics of the recapitulation assume an enhanced signification. The fact that the palindromic opening section is here directly combined with the "growth" section emphasizes the task faced by the Church of Love: to cover ever more ground (see the horizontal expansions described above in detail), to develop ever more depth of insight and ever new ways of mirroring God's example (see the vertical expansions and completions of the imperfect reflection process), and to become ever richer and more alive (see the asymmetric-growth section with its leading left-hand part enlivened by broken octaves). The *Theme-of-God* phrase, rather than being interspersed as it was at the beginning of the piece, follows the two expanding sections and develops its own expansion (see bars 107m-111).

The second contrast is determined both by its musical quotations from within the *Vingt regards* and by its almost unrelenting pedal-note C♮, a pitch that is prepared in the *Theme-of-God* variant heard at the end of the recapitulation, with its reiterated C♯ in the bass. Messiaen wraps the section with a refrain of three bars taken from the second piece of the cycle. In bars 3-5 of *The Star's Contemplation*, we hear three chord pairs, specified as *comme des cloches* and *accords de carillon* (like bells, carillon chords). These chords were originally based on C but appear here a semitone higher. The transposition centers the refrain in the pitch around which revolves the Virgin's tune from piece IV, *The Virgin's Contemplation* often quoted elsewhere in *The Church of Love Contemplating the Infant Jesus*.

The refrain (see bars 112-114/115-117, bars 129-131/132-134, bars 140-142) frames two episodes that are both closely related and ostensibly different. The first, in bars 118-128, consists of a pattern of downbeat C$^\#$s followed by *acciaccatura*-decorated chords developed from Messiaen's *Theme of Chords*; moreover, there is a slight reminiscence of bars 40/ 41 of *The Virgin's Contemplation*. The second episode, in bars 135-139, spreads these pairs out equally by giving each *acciaccatura* full value (compare bar 135, right hand and part of left hand, with bars 118/119, middle beats). Meanwhile, the regular "bell" of the downbeat C♯ is transformed here into a rhythm of composed *ritardando*. For the listener of the final piece in the cycle, this rhythm recalls bars 74-82 of XVI, *of The Prophets, the Shepherds and the Magi Contemplating the Infant Jesus,* thus establishing an inner link to the first devotees of Jesus, the first "Church of Love," if one wills. "Here are the bells, the glory and the kiss of love... all the passion of our arms around the Invisible...": this is how Messiaen describes it in the subheading.

In summary, *The Church of Love Contemplating the Infant Jesus* is motivated by three concepts: love, joy, and growth. Love is predominantly evoked as GOD'S LOVE (in the *Theme of God*), but also as the LOVE OF GOD (in the *Theme of Love*) and as the tender love of the mother (in the numerous quotations from IV, *The Virgin's Contemplation*). Elation and celebration are present in extended sections of bell chiming and the rhythm of the hunting song. Finally, there are myriad musical representations of growth and development. Internal as well as external symmetric extension of material on the one hand, vertical expansion in register and horizontal expansion in rhythmic values on the other hand can be read as representing the growth of faith in both depth and breadth, passionate dedication and profound understanding.

THE CHILD

Le baiser de l'Enfant-Jésus

Messiaen, *Vingt regards*, XV

(A chaque communion, l'Enfant-Jésus dort avec nous près de la porte; puis il l'ouvre sur le jardin et se précipite à toute lumière pour nous embrasser...)

At face value, this is the most directly programmatic piece in the cycle. Messiaen picks up expressions from his subheading remarks and allocates them to particular sections. Thus the first phrase, "At each communion, the Jesus-Child sleeps with us close to the door," appears in the score as *Le sommeil* (the sleep), the title for the large first section. The second phrase, "then He opens the door into the garden," is represented in a section marked *Le jardin* (the garden). The subsequent image, which has the Jesus-Child "rush, in full light," is musically portrayed in a fast, passionate section marked *Les bras tendus vers l'amour* (arms extended towards love), preceded by a shorter section with carillon chords. The subheading's concluding words, "... to embrace us," informs the final section of the piece, which the composer introduced with *Le baiser* (the kiss) above the staves and *avec amour* (with love) as a modifier to the dynamic indication *ff*.

Before we explore in detail what lies beneath this seemingly very simple pairing of phrases with musical sections, the verbal images used in the subheading as well as a further, visual image found in the "Author's Note" deserve more comment. The word communion, etymologically related to "union" and phonetically also suggestive of "communication," is often represented in the metaphor of opening a door, to allow union and communication to happen. Thus through the act of communion, Jesus opens us to the act of communicating with the Divinity. The image of Jesus sleeping close to us, close to the door, bears connotations of the mother-child image: someone to guard our sleep, keep us warm, and protect us. When He rushes out into the garden (i.e. into the world), Messiaen describes Him as "in full light": we are reminded of the Star of Bethlehem announcing the beginning of the journey into this world in a bright light. (The appearance at just this juncture of the carillon chords, reminiscent of piece II, *The Star's Contemplation*, corroborates this

271

reading.) At the same time, this expression contains a curious surprise effect. A French speaker hearing *Il se précipite à toute* ... will automatically complete the familiar expression with *vitesse* (speed)—He rushes at full speed. Noticing almost belatedly Messiaen's idea of Jesus' rushing "at full light" thus places special emphasis on this image.

Like the *First Communion of the Virgin*, this piece was influenced by a visual image. In his "Author's Note," Messiaen tells us that when writing this piece he was inspired by an etching "which represents the infant Jesus leaving his mother's arms in order to kiss the Little Sister Theresa." And he adds, "All this is a symbol of the communion, of the divine love." Almost as though he wanted to counter possible reservations against the unusually strict programmatic determination and the perhaps over-sweet images (and sounds), the composer further admonishes us that "one needs to love to be able to love this subject and this music whose desire it is to be tender like the very heart of heaven—and there is nothing else." The Little Sister Theresa is, of course, the saint Thérèse de Lisieux. The life of this Carmelite nun, who entered the order at age 15 and died of tuberculosis before she was 25, had the greatest influence on French Catholics intent on finding a renewal of true, simple spirituality. Her autobiography of 1889, *Histoire d'une âme* (History of a Soul or, in the translation of Ronald Knox, *The Autobiography of Thérèse de Lisieux*) speaks eloquently of her particular devotion, her struggles to overcome willfulness, pride and doubts, and of her "little way" of self-perfection. Messiaen regarded her as one of his most cherished models, as his acknowledgments at the beginning of the "Author's Note" reveal. The most outstanding aspects of her spirituality, no doubt present in this piece, are the fact that she was not ashamed of being nothing outstanding, and her intimacy with Jesus, facilitated by her very unimportance.

Through her writing as well as that of a saint whom both she and Messiaen treasured, St. John of the Cross, we gain a wider understanding of the composer's wording. When Thérèse de Lisieux, in the first pages of her autobiography, speaks of "the world of the souls, which is the garden of Jesus," she adds depth to the image of the Jesus-Child sleeping close to a door that he subsequently opens "to the garden." In another context she describes, with an almost childlike joy, an exquisite miniature barge found in a bowl in her room. The barge, she tells us, held the Jesus-Child sleeping under a sail on which was written "I sleep, but my heart wakes," a wording that has no doubt inspired both the image of the sleeping Jesus in this piece and the explicit title Messiaen chose for piece XIX.

On the other hand, the composer's admonition that one needs to know (mystical) love in order to be able to love this music is most probably inspired by a similar warning with which St. John of the Cross prefaces his *Canto Espiritual*. The Spanish mystic cautions that these songs, composed in the love of mystical insight, cannot be fully interpreted; for mystical wisdom as alluded to in these stanzas will only be understood through love. No analysis is needed in order to create the effect and affect of love in the soul.

Taking to heart this reiterated caution, this analysis will be prudently sparse, giving only the essentials of the main theme, the general outline, and focusing then on the use of symbols. The main theme is derived from the *Theme of God.*

Messiaen marks it as *Thème de Dieu en berceuse* (*Theme of God* in the form of a lullaby), probably alluding to the image of the sleeping Child rather than to any specific lullaby rhythm.

(Le sommeil)

Thème de Dieu en berceuse

The significant difference to the form in which the *Theme of God* was introduced in *The Father's Contemplation* is that this version is conceived with a strong sense of tonality, referring clearly to F♯ as not only its central note but its tonic. After the familiar three-chord beginning, in the pitches of I and V and in the register of the *The Son Contemplating the Son* (cf. XV, bar 1 with V, bars 2/3), the downbeat of bar 2 presents an unequivocal dominant-seventh chord (inverted and over a tonic pedal). This chord resolves, after a sequence of the three chords, on the downbeat of bar 3 into the "chord of love," the F♯-major chord with added sixth. This simple message of the rootedness in GOD's LOVE, all the more striking for its very simplicity, pervades the entire piece, for the thematic phrase is not only frequently repeated, but is itself built on a half-phrase (bars 1-3m) and its varied and extended repetition (bars 3m-5).

The following outline utilizes Messiaen's own descriptive wording, complemented by the implied but not explicitly marked "in full light." (*Theme of God* refers to the version established in the initial piece of the cycle, *The Father's Contemplation*, while the derived version that is particular to this piece will be abbreviated as "*ToG-lullaby.*")

"The sleep"

bars 1-5	*ToG-lullaby*		bars 6-10	*ToG-lullaby*, repetition
bars 11-15	transformation 1		bars 16-20	transformation 1 repeated
bars 21-25	*ToG-lullaby*, original			
bars 26-32	transformation 2		bars 33-39	transformation 2, repeated
bars 40-46	*ToG-lullaby*, var. 1		bars 47-62	*ToG-lullaby*, var. 2
			(bars 53-60	internal extension)

"The garden"

bars 63-65d, 65-67d, 67-69d, 69-71d *Theme of God*, different variations
bars 71-72 *Theme of God* in stretto development

("In full light")

bars 73-78 *Theme of chords* alternating with carillon chords

"Arms extended towards love"

bars 79-84 two-note slurs in predominantly chromatic motion; developed in bars 85-89, newly developed in bars 90-94

"The kiss"

bars 95-102 melody in triads, over ascending *arpeggios*; developed in bars 103-118

"The shadow of a kiss"

bars 119-123	*ToG-lullaby* (new rhythm)	bars 123-136	*ToG-lullaby*, rep./varied (bars 127-134 internal extension)

Finally, *The Kiss of the Jesus-Child* contains an abundance of symbols epitomizing GOD'S LOVE. F♯ major, the tonality of GOD'S LOVE, is present in the key signature with six sharps throughout the "sleep" and "garden" sections as well as in the sections entitled "kiss" and "shadow of a kiss." An F♯ bass pedal reverberates through sixty-two of the 136 bars of this piece (see bars 2-25, 41-52, 119-136).[121]

Every half-phrase within the main theme leads to the F♯-major chord with added sixth, the "chord of love" shared by Messiaen's symbols for GOD'S LOVE and the LOVE OF GOD. Both the "sleep" section and the entire piece end, in bars 60/61 and 135/136 respectively, with identical cadences toward the "chord of love." And what is more, the internal extension in bars 127-134 consists of nothing but this chord, thus making for an overwhelming impression.

---

[121]This pedal is even indirectly supported in another twenty-six bars featuring the "dominant" pedal C♯; see bars 54-60, 73-76, 79-89, 108-111.

Mode 2 as the modal representation of GOD'S LOVE is also prominently represented. The *Theme of God* in its lullaby version uses all three transpositions of mode 2. The internal extension in the second variation is restricted to mode 2^2 over a C♯ pedal, thus enacting the "dominant" both tonally and modally (see the use of mode 2^2 as dominant in I); this is followed in "The garden" with the original *Theme-of-God* phrase using, as the "tonic," mode 2^1 exclusively The "shadow of a kiss"—musically rather a "shadow of the sleep" since it is based on the lullaby version of the *Theme of God* and not at all related to the material in the "kiss" section—uses modes 2^1 and 2^2 in alternating bars.

Besides the prevailing symbolism of GOD'S LOVE, a reminder of another aspect of this loving Child's fate appears. Significantly, this is the section with the strongest eruptions of dynamics and tempo within the piece, speaking to the high emotive content evoked here.[122] In "arms extended towards love"—the only section marking not reflected in the subheading remarks—Messiaen emphasizes what we know as the sigh motif: a slurred note-pair with a strong accent at the beginning (note, in bar 87, the composer's reminder *marquez beaucoup les accents*) and, frequently, chromatic progression to the second note. The fact that Messiaen begins in bar 79 with four-part sighs of which all but the treble move exclusively in semitones is strongly reminiscent of similar four-part sighs in piece VII, *The Cross's Contemplation*, where they stand for the sorrowful mourning over the crucifixion. The "extended arms," then, gain a double meaning. As a result of His loving willingness to rush out and embrace us, Messiaen tells us, this Child's extended arms will later be nailed to the beam of the Cross of Golgotha.

Je dors, mais mon cœur veille   Messiaen, *Vingt regards,* XIX

(Ce n'est pas d'un ange l'archet qui sourit - c'est Jésus dormant qui nous aime dans son Dimanche et nous donne l'oubli...)

If *The Kiss of the Jesus-Child* told us about several mystics' perception of the sleeping Child, and *The Virgin's Contemplation* gives Messiaen's image of the mother cradling her child, this piece presents the

---

[122]See in bars 81-85 *p, crescendo, crescendo molto // pp subito*;
   in bars 85-90, beginning "somewhat slower and with very intense expression,"
   pp, crescendo (gradually pick up the tempo),
   sempre crescendo (push forward),
   rallentando, rallentando molto, ff;
   in bars 90-95 *ff*, somewhat slower, *rallentando,* very much slower, even slower.

sleeping Child in the most direct intimacy. The title, *I Sleep But My Heart Wakes*, taken from the most beautiful poem of mystical love, the Song of Songs, is phrased in the first person (without so much as telling us who is saying "I" here).

The subheading begins with a sentence ("It is not an angel's bow that smiles") in which Messiaen paraphrases Saint Francis of Assisi.[123] Having asked God to give him a foretaste of the immeasurable splendor and the blissful joy of eternal life, Francis sees an angel of magnificent brilliance, holding a violin in his left and a bow in his right hand. Saint Francis is still transfixed by the lustrous apparition when the angel strikes the bow once across the strings. Instantaneously, Francis hears a melody of such beauty, that his soul is filled with sweetness and he loses all sense of physical sensation. As he will later tell his followers, he fears that his soul might flee his body from such unbearable bliss, were the angel to complete his bowing. But, as Messiaen assures us, the unbearable sweetness perceived here is not that of the angel's bow. "It is the sleeping Jesus who loves us in his Sunday and gives us oblivion."

Messiaen speaks about this piece as "a love poem, a dialog of mystical love." Love is the central and only issue here, bliss so sweet that it makes our souls want to leave our bodies. Oblivion follows, as a respite from all that worries us whenever we distance ourselves from that generously offered love.

This love, GOD'S LOVE, appears in multiple symbolic layers. F♯ major is not only indicated in the key signature but actually appears, in the opening section of the piece (A, bars 1-8) as well as in the varied reprise of this section towards the end (A', bars 69-78), in completely untainted

---

[123] See *The Little Flowers of Saint Francis of Assisi* (New York: Heritage Press, 1965), p. 173. Originally published as *Vita e fioretti di San Francesco d'Assisi* (Venice: Nicolaus Girardengus, 1480).

chords. Listeners are thus bathed, as it were, in pure love—for what in the extremely slow tempo of this piece lasts for more than three minutes![124]

The sections following the opening section and preceding its reprise (see B, bars 9-23 and B', bars 53-68), are prominently built on and around the F♯-major chord with added sixth. This "chord of love" opens the sections (see bars 9 and 53 downbeat), closes its phrases (see bars 14, 22/23, 59 and 67), and serves as a conclusion particle (see the final beats in bars 17, 18, 62 and 63 as well as the downbeats in bars 20 and 65). In the middle section of the piece (see C, bars 24-52), the "chord of love" seems conspicuously absent at first. But once it recurs, it soon gains absolute prominence. (It is heard in bar 45 for two eighths, in bar 47 for two quarter-notes, and in bars 50-53 for altogether two half-notes.)

The remaining symbols in this piece highlight various aspects of love —both the love God extends (and Jesus, too) and the love we feel for God (our reaction to the bliss given us). As a symbol of GOD'S LOVE, Messiaen's mode 2 reigns almost supreme in the B sections. In fact, the only notes that violate the pitch content of mode 2^1, sound like inserts from another realms: the high-registered chord pairs in bars 12, 16, 57 and 71). The *Theme of Love,* standing for human LOVE OF GOD, informs section C, where it is heard nine times (bars 24-27, 32-35, 40-49). Finally, the characteristic melodic interval of the *Theme of Love*, the descending fourth, stands out as the single most important gesture in the entire piece.[125]

Messiaen thus musically defines Jesus' love for us not only as identical with GOD'S LOVE, but even as the purest manifestation of that love (see the passages in pure F♯ major), as well as a further source for the human potential of love.

---

[124]In the opening section, bars 1-8 contain 83 sixteenth-notes; in the reprise, bars 69-78 even count 119 sixteenth-notes; in the coda, bars 84-87 add a stretch of another 30 six-teenth-notes. This adds up to 232 sixteenth-notes. In a tempo designated as 72 sixteenths to a minute, the result amounts to 3 ¼ minutes of pure F♯ major.

[125] Here is an overview over the appearances of this interval:
In the A sections and coda, the falling fourth appears nine times in the bass,
   namely in bars 2, 4, 7, 70, 72, 77, 80, 84, and 87.
In the B sections, it is heard six times in the form of its complementary interval,
   the falling fifth, namely in bars 10, 14, 22, 55, 59, and 67.
In the middle section, it dominates as a twelvefold melodic gesture;
   see bars 25, 27, 33, 35, 41, 43, 45, 47, 48, 49, 51, and 52.

Regard de la Vierge   (Messiaen, *Vingt regards*, IV)

(Innocence et tendresse... la femme de la Pureté, la femme du Magnificat, la Vierge regarde son Enfant...)

At face value, this piece appears as an instrumental version of a cradle song. In his "Author's Note," Messiaen writes that his aim was to express "purity" in music; that this required a certain effort—and above all a great degree of naiveté and childlike tenderness.[126] This aim is also reflected in the subheading remarks which translate as "Innocence and tenderness... the woman of purity, the woman of the Magnificat, the Virgin looks at her Child..."

The musical realization of innocence and tenderness can be observed in several parameters. Among them, particularly the structural layout and the motivic material express simplicity, and the tonal organization contains numerous components that, in the larger context of the cycle *Vingt regards*, serve as symbols for unconditional love.

Structurally, the piece is determined on all levels, from the overall layout to the composition of a two-bar cell, by processes of varied repetition. Here are the details.

[1] *Within the entire piece,*
   a general overview of the design reveals two corresponding halves: bars 1-62 correspond with bars 63-102. Or, in greater detail,

bars 1-15	correspond	with bars 63-75
bars 16-24	correspond	with bars 76-86
bars 25-34	correspond	with bars 87-94
bars 35-39 + 59	correspond	with bars 95-102

[2] *Within each half of the piece,*
   there are further correspondences; these reveal a layout in four quadrants:

bars 1-15	correspond	with bars 25-34
bars 63-75	correspond	with bars 87-94

Were one to depict this observation in letters, the design would appear as

$$A \quad B, \quad A' \quad C; \qquad A_{var.} \ B, \ A'_{var.} \ C.$$

---

[126] *"J'ai voulu exprimer la* pureté *en musique: il y a fallu une certaine force—et surtout beaucoup de naïveté, de tendresse puérile"* (enhancement by Messiaen).

[3] *Within each of the recurring A sections,*
all phrases are identical except for their endings. Even
honoring these distinctions, the rate of recurrence is high:

bars 1- 5	bars 11-15
= bars 6-10	= bars 30-34
= bars 25-29	
bars 63-67	bars 73-75
= bars 68-72	= bars 92-94
= bars 87-91	

[4] *Within each phrase* of the A sections,
subphrases are identical except for their very endings:

bars 1/2	= 3/4,	bars 6/7	= 8/9
bars 63/64	= 65/66	bars 67/68	= 69/70

[5] *Within each of these subphrases,*
pitch motions recur twice. The two halves of the subphrase
are distinguished only by a slightly varied rhythm:

short-short-*long-long* turns into *long-long*-short-*long*.

This unusual rhythm can usefully be heard as an irregular
cradling motion. Only the final, expanded component of
each phrase uses exclusively the shorter values. (See e.g.
bar 5: the four initial sixteenth-notes are repeated and
then rounded off by an expansion which presents a new
rhythm, new pitches, and even a dynamic surprise.)

The entire section is designed in what appears superficially as a
homophonic texture. Closer inspection reveals several layers within this
texture. The highest, innermost and lowest pitches in the initial unit (not
counting the expansion in bar 5) comprise a three-octave, repeated pedal-
note A♯. As a second layer, we hear a four-note descent, a modest but
very touching little chant to which the composer himself draws our
attention in a footnote.[127] On a third layer—the uppermost part of the left
hand—there is a G♯ that splits, in its step downwards, into two notes, the
chromatic neighbors G and F♯. Finally, the fourth level (the one above the
left-hand pedal A♯), presents a whole-tone step downwards: D♯-C♯.

---

[127]*Faites sortir le chant à la main droite: sol, fa, mi, ré.* (Bring out the chant in the right
hand). Note that the Frenchman Messiaen uses fixed-do solmization. His syllables designate nothing other than our letter names G F E D or, more accurately, actually: G F♯ E♯ D♯.

In terms of tonal organization, the pitches in this basic unit (and its fifty-five repetitions) are powerfully reminiscent of some of Messiaen's musical attributes of GOD'S LOVE. In the first piece of the cycle, *The Father's Contemplation*, A♯ is also the melodically predominant pitch. There, the note appears as both the central pitch that launches the theme and, owing to Messiaen's preference for the first inversion of the F♯-major chord, as the predominant bass note. The fourth piece of the cycle, *The Virgin's Contemplation*, thus corroborates the interpretation of the pitch A♯ as the "note of love."

Furthermore, as the example above shows, the basic unit of piece IV can be read harmonically as an embellishment of A♯-C♯-D♯-F♯, the inverted F♯-major chord with added sixth that emphasizes GOD'S LOVE in the piece *The Father's Contemplation*.

Just as the expansion within each phrase (bars 5, 10 etc.) brings a sudden deviation from the pitches established in the basic unit, the special dynamic marking also stands out from the even *pp* of the section. The moment where the right-hand perfect fourth is transposed a third up (to C♯/G♯) and the left-hand pedal-note A♯ a third down (to F♯) is prepared by a *crescendo* and marked as emphasized (see the dashes); yet despite all these enhancements, Messiaen imagines it extremely soft (see the *ppp*)! The conclusion of each little phrase thus contains a musical expression of particular tenderness that complements the basic mood of "innocence" and "purity" in section A.

While the structural process of repetition and variation—a process which can be observed on every level, from the smallest to the largest perspective—is most obvious in section A and its recurrences, a similar relationship of varied reprise exists between section B and its reprise. Let us first observe and then interpret.

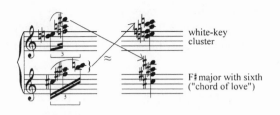

white-key
cluster

F# major with sixth
("chord of love")

[6]   In the first phrase of section B, not only is bar 17 a repetition of bar 16, but both consist in themselves of four-fold repetitions of a small triplet unit.

In bar 18, however, a further repetition suddenly sounds an octave lower, much faster, slightly reshuffled, and expanded with a plunge down to the very low register of the keyboard.

In the second half of the piece, the corresponding bars 76-79 are built on a triplet unit with identical rhythm but a retrograde of the pitch order. Again there is an extra repetition in the lower octave, which here appears as a complete retrograde of the model bar (compare bar 78 with bar 18), while the expansion follows the direction of its model but uses new pitches—a varied reprise.

[7]   The second phrase of section B (see bars 20-22) consists of a one-bar unit whose two sequences are subjected to a process of asymmetric contraction. The perfect fifth interval on the downbeat and the bass-register attack with its *appoggiatura* move chromatically upwards from one bar to the next, while the double-notes in the higher register sink chromatically downwards.

In the corresponding bars 80-82, the process occurs in retrograde (or, to express the same fact in different terms, bars 20, 21, 22 recur as bars 82, 81, 80). In terms of dynamic rendering, these bars are the first to demand a considerable increase in loudness: from *pp* through *p* to *mf.*

[8]   The transition connecting the initial B section to the first recurrence of the A section is short (see bars 23/24). It is built on one chord which is transposed at increasingly larger intervals.[128]

---

[128] The downbeat chord in bar 23, consisting of tritone + perfect fourth, is moved down in consecutively larger steps: a major second, a major third / diminished fourth, a perfect fourth, and from there in octave displacements through a large-scale curve. (Note that the pitches in bar 24 are enharmonic reinterpretations of those in the last chord of bar 23.)

The corresponding transition in the second half of the piece is longer. Bar 83 is a retrograde equivalent of bar 23, while bars 84-86, still based on the same chord, constitute an expanded counterpart to bar 24.

The tempo of this section is faster than that of the first section (*plus vif* = more lively, in a proportion of approximately 3:2 to the preceding section). The irregular cradling rhythm gives way to a more regular motion here which, however, undergoes a gradual release from phrase to phrase: the triplet sixteenth-notes in the first phrase turn into a motion of duplet sixteenth in the second phrase and slow down to eighth notes in the transition, a process further enhanced by the prescribed *rallentando*.

In terms of tonal organization, the triplet unit from which this section is launched is conspicuously built over an inversion of the F♯-major chord. If one adds the prominent highest pitch D♯, one may even discern a version of the "chord of love": the F♯-major chord with added sixth, heard here in second inversion and open position. The two transitional bars (see bars 23/24) also blend with the main tonal hue of the piece by featuring A♯ (in bar 23 as B♭) as their most prominent treble pitch.

These observations clearly invite us to pause a moment and consider the spiritual message of those phrases that are dominated by either the pitch A♯ or the F♯-major chord with added sixth (or both). To give an idea of the sensual importance of the single pitch, one is tempted to count. In the course of the piece, A♯ is heard 122 times as a treble-register pedal-note, 300 times altogether if one includes the occurrences of the pitch in all three octaves. This unusually high number of reiterations of the same pitch contributes powerfully to the effect of innocence and naiveté. Combining only those instances where A♯ sounds in clearly audible, exposed register with moments determined by the F♯ chord with added sixth, one finds that these two symbols of LOVE jointly determine 79 of the 102 bars, or more than three quarters of the piece! Messiaen thus clearly declares the Virgin as the epitome of all-embracing LOVE.

Asymmetric growth, on the other hand, throughout Messiaen's work stands for TRANSFORMATION. The "heart" of section B thus alludes to Mary's knowledge that this child is more than just another human.

While section A is extremely unified in all regards, and section B contains three components with, as we saw, two slightly distinct messages, the degree of diversity is greatest in section C and its recurrence. Indeed, the reprise departs from the model in such a way that it is tempting to seek a specific explanation for the structural layout. Here are the facts:

[9] The initial phrase (bars 35-39) consists of a melodic unit arranged around the pitch C♯. Since this unit is used motivically throughout the remainder of the piece, it will be referred to as component *x*. Sounding in the lower voice of bars 35-37, it is accompanied by a repeated, sparkling figure in the treble, and marked *mf* for the right-hand figure and *f* for the melodically leading left hand. On the final note of component *x*, this accompaniment figure gives way to an octave *tremolo* in *staccato* which Messiaen marks as "percussive, like a xylophone." In a powerful *crescendo*, the *tremolo* explodes into a rhythmically leveled, shortened and enhanced repetition of component *x* before the phrase breaks off in two fast *ff unison* attacks. With its pervasive accents, the explosive *crescendo* in the middle, and the *ff* at the end that breaks off after two thirds of a triplet, this phrase expresses a sudden intensity that comes as a shock after the extended depiction of soothing motherly love. (The corresponding phrase in the reprise is identical; see bars 95-99.)

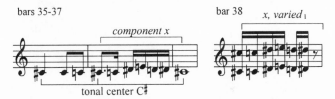

bars 35-37   component x   bar 38   x, varied₁

tonal center C♯

The spiritual message expressed in this component, whose intensity is surprising in proximity to Mary's gentle, loving smile, becomes clear in the larger context of Messiaen's works. The component has a closely related precursor in the two-piano cycle *Visions de l'Amen,* composed one year prior to the *Vingt regards.* Occurring in the third piece, entitled *Amen de l'agonie de Jésus,* the precursor is marked "heart-rending lament"! Messiaen thus uses component *x* as a lament over Christ's agony, which Mary anticipates already when cradling her new-born infant.

[10] The second phrase in section C (see bars 40-46) consists of three segments that, with the exception of a common pitch, are clearly different from one another. However, they all contain

elements of repetition within themselves, thus continuing the main developmental procedure in this piece. The first segment (bars 40 and 41) repeats a gesture with entirely changed pitches over an identical, accented octave C♯. In the second segment (bars 42-44), the melodically leading upper voice of a left-hand chord progression unfolds as a little tune under a chordal *ostinato* in the right hand. The third segment (bars 45-46), in four-part unison, is derived from component *x*. Bar 46 presents an identical recurrence of bar 45, and in addition, each bar consists of a six-note figure that is reiterated except for the elision of its initial note. This variant of

the "heart-rending lament" is strongly reminiscent of the final segment of the *Theme of the Star and the Cross* in *Vingt regards* III; moreover, Messiaen scholar Aloyse Michaely points to a resemblance with the *Theme of the Cross* in Messiaen's orchestral work *Les offrandes oubliées*. These two cross-references invite an interpretation of component *x*—as well as of the pitch shared by all three segments of this phrase—an allusion to the fate of the child Mary is cradling here.

At the corresponding moment in the second half of the piece, after bar 99, this entire second phrase does not recur. In search of some compensation we discover that instead, the phrase recurs immediately after it is first stated, i.e. in bars 47-55. Here, the *unison* figure reminiscent of several allusions to the Cross is even expanded (compare bar 52/53 with bar 45).

[11] The final components of the two C sections have one segment in common (compare bars 100/101 with bars 59/60). The distinctive feature is the intensifying process undergone by the contrary-motion unit in bar 59. Dynamically powerful (*ff*) and rhythmically very intense at its inception, the collapse of descending right hand and ascending left hand creates further tension which erupts into *sff* in the following bar.

At the conclusion of the first half of the piece, this collapse is framed by two derivatives of component *x* (see right hand, bar 58 and left hand, bar 61). The former is accompanied by two-note sighs in the left hand, the latter by a hectic figure that

looks like a flash of lightning and feels like a flash of pain. At
the conclusion of the second half of the piece, i.e. in the final
bar, only component *x* recurs. But it does so as an extremely
hectic, abrupt flash, faster than ever before (in thirty-second-
notes in *plus vif*) and in very extreme registers, in a *unison* at
the distance of six octaves. The *staccato* demanded for the
final attack creates an additional shock. This version thus
incorporates the pain with the Cross. One remembers that the
Christmas narrative Messiaen quotes most often, that in Luke
2, continues with the visit to the temple and the prophesy of
Simeon that, in verse 35, reads, 'and you yourself a sword will
pierce, so that the thoughts of many hearts may be revealed'.)

The predominant pitches in this section are C♯ (or D♭) and D♯ (or E♭).
In the context of A♯, the tonal center of sections A and B, these two
pitches strike us necessarily as reminiscent of the inverted F♯ major chord
with added sixth heard in the initial unit of the second section, the "chord
of love." While D♯ (as E♭) only plays a role in the initial bars 35-38 where
it serves as a repeated treble accent, C♯ is ubiquitous. It is the central tone
of component *x* and thus reigns supreme in bars 35-38, 45/46 etc.; it is
also the repeated octave in bars 40/41, and finally, as D♭, provides the
treble note from which the chordal tune in bars 42-44 is launched and to
which it returns.

Returning at last to section A, we are now equipped to take a closer
look at the variation in the second half of the piece. What Messiaen has
composed here is a superimposition of material from two sections. The
cradling motive characteristic of section A sounds in its many rhythmic
shapes, exactly as before in bars 1-15. As a newly added treble melody,
we hear a plaintive tune which now discloses its identity as a new
rhythmic version of component *x*. In this register, tempo, and color, the
chromatic tone collection underlying component *x* sounds, for the first
time in the piece, extremely sorrowful.

The composer's admonitions to play really softly and gently are
worth noting as they express spiritual rather than mere dynamic qualities.
While the cradling parts are marked *pp* and *tendre*, the treble melody is
designated *p* and enhanced with many accents and dashes, but at the same
time requested as *très tendre*! The tempo in this section, significantly, is
also indicated as slightly slower than that suggested for the A sections in
the first half of the piece.

In conclusion: In his piece *The Virgin's Contemplation*, Messiaen depicts many facets of what is encompassed in the relationship between this loving mother and her child. The innocence and purity of the Virgin, as well as her great tenderness, are expressed in section A, together with the overwhelming love (see the overwhelming occurrence of the "note of love," A♯). The same love frames, in section B, a knowledge of her son's transformative role. Section C, while tonally still partaking in the general theme of love, introduces a premonition of the Cross, and anticipation of pain, with its new melodic component. Once introduced, this premonition remains present throughout the return to the innocence of the cradle song.

Probably the most extreme and disturbing musical gesture in this piece happens at the conclusion of the first half, where a high-registered, clashing chord (see bar 62) is followed by a four-note chromatic cluster using the lowest keys available on our piano keyboards. Messiaen employs the bass cluster consisting of the three or four lowest notes as a musical symbol of *awe*. This *awe*—at once the proper attitude of man towards God and an expression of the distance that humans on their own are unable to bridge—is thus introduced here as a complement to its spiritual opposite: Love.

INCARNATION AND SUFFERING

Regard de l'étoile

(Messiaen, *Vingt regards*, II)

(Choc de la grâce . . . l'étoile luit naïvement, surmontée d'une croix)

The Star's *Contemplation* or *The Star Looking Upon the Infant Jesus* contains a wealth of coded messages. In this relatively short piece, everything seems to point beyond the music—its structure, its play with various homophonic textures and tonal contexts, its rhythmic, metric and tempo contrasts, and its use of visual symbolism.

The two parts of Messiaen's subheading assist in developing a first association to the different components: The line translates as "Shock of grace... the star shines naively, surmounted by a cross." The star, assuming a personality, is shocked at how the incarnation manifests the presence of grace—a shock that may have overtones of the dismay that the incarnation finds its destiny at the Cross. The two contrasting elements, the "shock" and the "naive star shine," create a tension that is mirrored in the contrasting blocks of the composition: the five-bar *Modéré* with its abrupt dynamics, and the *unison* chant in *Modéré, un peu lent* (moderate, somewhat slower) identified by Messiaen as *Thème de l'étoile et de la croix* (Theme of the Star and of the Cross).

As Aloyse Michaely has pointed out,[129] the representation of the Cross above the manger can be found in several paintings of the nativity; see e.g. Roger van der Weyden's "Adoration of the Magi" of 1460 where we find a cross (with corpse!) hanging from the central beam of the stable, above Mary with the child, and Albrecht Dürer's "The Birth of Christ" of 1502/3, which shows a large cross among the rafters with, immediately beside it, the star of Bethlehem. And to add an example from twentieth-century literature: in T. S. Eliot's poem "The Journey of the Magi," verse 24 reads "And three trees on the low sky," an allusion to the three crosses of Golgotha.

---

[129]Aloyse Michaely, "Verbum Caro: Die Darstellung des Mysteriums der Inkarnation in Olivier Messiaens Vingt Regards sur l'Enfant-Jésus," in *Hamburger Jahrbuch für Musikwissenschaft*, vol. 6 (Hamburg: 1984), p. 252.

The *Modéré* is heard three times in identical repetition (bars 1-5, 18-22, 35-39). It consists of three strongly diverse elements, which express contrast along with linear developments. The contrast is accomplished
- with regard to dynamics:
  the first component (bar 1) is marked *f* and leads to and accent,
  the second component (bar 2) is a smooth *ppp* without any enhancement,
  the third component (bars 3-5) demands *ff* with accents on every attack;
- with regard to discontinuity vs. continuity of motion:
  the first component comes to a sudden accented halt,
  the second component evolves in absolutely even motion,
  the third component contrasts this once more with what sounds like syncopations;
- with regard to pitch outline:
  the first component embodies a single upward thrust,
  the second component combines gradual contraction of the lines of the two hands with gradual shrinking of the double-note intervals in each hand (from major ninth / augmented octave on the first beat to augmented fifth/perfect fifth toward the end of the bar),
  component 3 is dominated by the triple repetition of the treble C, after Messiaen's indication *comme des cloches* (like bells).

The linear development is realized
- with regard to rhythm:
  the flourish in bar 1 is in thirty-second-notes, followed by sixteenth-notes in the regular motion of bar 2, and rounded off in the third component by the triple repetition heard rhythmically as two eighth-notes plus a two-eighths suspension—a process of gradual calming down;
- with regard to duration:
  the three components can be counted as 5/16, 12/16, 24/16 —a gradual expansion;
- with regard to vertical density:
  the first component consists of double-notes leading up to a triad, the second alternates four-note superpositions with two-note ones, and the third component (owing to its overlapping sounds) continues this trend with a succession of a five-note

chord (bar 3), a six-note chord (bar 4), and a twelve-note chord (bar 5)—a gradual increase.

The tonal organization of the three components seems to epitomize three different versions of "completeness".

- The six double-notes constituting the flourish in bar 1 establish a tonal link to the preceding piece in that they replicate, in hurried contraction, the three transpositions of mode 2; the accented target chord explicitly leaves this tonal context: the augmented triad is incompatible with mode 2.[130]
- The contracting motion in bar 2 employs all twelve semitones, in no discernible order but fairly equal spread.
- The three "bell" chords in bars 3-5 with their increasing number of pitches develop from a four-pitch chord (emphasizing tritones and avoiding any semitone neighbors) through a six-pitch chord to a comprehensive twelve-tone chord without any repeated pitch.

Taken together, all these symbols seem to relate to what the composer calls the "shock of grace": the combination of contrastand linearity as well as the multifaceted comprehensiveness of aspects far surpasses human grasp and concept.

Before turning to details of the other component, the *unison* chant, here is an overview of the structural layout of the piece.

bars		bars	
1-5	"shock of grace" with three components	6-17	*Theme of the Star and the Cross* with three lines
18-22	"shock of grace" identical repetition	23-34	*Theme of the Star and the Cross* tune identical, texture varied
35-39	"shock of grace" identical repetition		
		[40-41m	final half line of the *theme* followed by short coda]

While the title dedicates this piece to the Star of Bethlehem, the designation of the theme refers to the inner relationship between the symbol of Christ's birth and that of Christ's death. Messiaen has represented

[130]In the flourish, the initial four-note group with D♭-E-G-C stems from mode 2¹, the next four-note group with F-G♯-B-E represents mode 2², and the last four-note group with A-B♯-D♯-G♯ stands for mode 2³. Pianists characteristically memorize these three chords as "four-note major chords with a chromatically raised keynote"—a C-major chord over D♭, an E-major chord over F, and an A♭-major chord over A—typical formations for this mode.

his insight in this close relationship between beginning and end, heavenly greeting of the Son of God and utter human cruelty and contempt for the son of Man, in two symbolic ways.

The first is a visual symbol. If one were to try and adjust the shapes commonly associated with the Star of Bethlehem and the Cross of Golgotha, one  would end up with the Cross tilted to the side. In this perspective, the Cross is reminiscent of Jesus' struggle on earth, his CARRYING OF the Cross rather than his DYING ON it! It seems very possible that this was the aspect Messiaen wanted to stress when he conceived the first four-note turn of each line of the *Thème de l'étoile et de la croix* as a visual symbol depicting both the Star and the (tilted) Cross.[131]

The example on the next page shows the theme in the form of a chant, which undoubtedly informs its texture. As can be seen in the excerpt, the *Theme of the Star and the Cross* consists of three lines. Each of them begins with the four-note depiction of the symbol (in the third line, the beams are simply seen in reverse order), and each ends on the pitch A♭. Each line consists of two clearly distinguishable halves, ending in a half-note. The texture in which the theme is first presented is a *unison* at a distance of four octaves, enriched only for the final half-line: here, the continuation of the chant comes in four-part *unison*, while a newly introduced second voice is doubled four octaves apart. If one took the liberty to fold this spaced vision of the Star and the Cross into its center, obliterating the note-doubling in favor of the assumed line from which Messiaen's voices keep an equal distance (as shown in the excerpt), one recognizes that this theme is extraordinarily centered. Finally,

---

[131] Given the fact that in music, both the performance and perception in time and the notation on paper are horizontal processes only enriched and textured by vertical ones, the choice for the reclined version of the symbol of the Cross is, of course, also a practical one. And yet: while most musical representations of the Christian symbol for suffering trace the four corners of the Cross in a suggestive rather than in a pictorially "true" way—one thinks of Bach's anagram B-A-C-H (B♭-A-C-B) in the *Art of the Fugue* and of many fugue subjects (e.g. the main subject from the fugue in C♯ minor, *Well-tempered Clavier*, volume I)—Messiaen's so much more visually evocative choice of pitches "as they are on the keyboard" seems to invite envisioning the carried tool of martyrdom.

in terms of tonal organization the *Thème de l'étoile et de la croix* is built from the third transposition of Messiaen's mode 7—a mode that, within the *Vingt regards*, is exclusively used for this theme![131a]

Thème de l'étoile et de la croix

The question has often been asked: why did Messiaen design seven modes, no more and no less. An obvious answer points to his known fascination with number mysticism, and the biblical importance of the number 7. The question becomes all the more meaningful when one discovers that several of his modes are actually closely interrelated—one being a mere slight variant of another. This is most obvious in the case of the rarely used mode 5, which is almost identical with mode 4. In the context of the *Vingt regards*, it seems utterly significant that mode 7, exclusively restricted to the thematic representation of the Star and the Cross, can be read as a combination of modes 4^4 and 6^3—two modes that, as *The Son Contemplating the Son* has shown, are related to the different aspects of Jesus in just these transpositions.

mode 7^3 : A♭ A B♭ B D♭D E♭ E F G
mode 4^4 : A♭ A B♭ B D E♭ E F
mode 6^3 : A♭ B♭ C D♭D E F♯G

To appreciate the second musical device Messiaen chooses to depict the essential relationship of the Star and the Cross one needs to turn to the seventh piece in the cycle, called *Regard de la Croix* (*The Cross's Contemplation* or *The Cross Looking Upon the Infant Jesus*) and discover that the composer has not only employed the *Thème de l'étoile et de la*

[131a]Halbreich, in his excellent and admirably comprehensive study of Messiaen's music (Harry Halbreich *Olivier Messiaen*, Paris: Fayard / Foundation SACEM, 1980), seems to err when he declares this theme to be based on the third transposition of mode 4 (p. 221).

croix here—in doubled note values—but that the entire piece VII actually figures as a third "stanza" complementing the layout of piece II. In order to elaborate this point graphically, the table given above (on p. 289) can be specified further as follows:

II:	bars 1-5 "shock of grace" with three components	**II:**	bars 6-17 *Theme of the Star and the Cross*; lines: bars 6-9, 10-13, 14-17
II:	bars 18-22 "shock of grace" identical repetition	**II:**	bars 23-34 *Theme of the Star and the Cross*, var. 1 lines: bars 23-26, 27-30, 31-34
II:	bars 35-39 "shock of grace" identical repetition	**VII:**	bars 1-29 *Theme of the Star and the Cross*, var. 2 lines: bars 1-8, 9-19, 20-29

In this highly symbolic and yet dauntingly commanding way, Messiaen seems to share his conviction that the Cross was indeed the "necessary completion" for that which began with the Star.

Regard de la Croix   (Messiaen, *Vingt regards*, VII)

(La Croix lui dit: tu seras prêtre dans mes bras...)

The theme that determines *The Cross Contemplating the Infant Jesus* is familiar to listeners by the time they come to this seventh piece of Messiaen's cycle. Explicitly designated by the composer as *Thème de l'étoile et de la Croix* (*Theme of the Star and the Cross*), it was introduced in the second piece, *The Star's Contemplation*. There, it formed the major segment of a stanza consisting of a musical as well as theological contrast—the "shock of grace" constituted in the Incarnation of the Son of God, pitted against the "chant" defining the frame for this Incarnation: the prophetic annunciation of the birth of the Son and His Crucifixion as a completion of His destiny. As was shown in some detail above, the tripartite layout of the earlier piece remains incomplete, as the third evocation of the "shock of grace" is not followed once more by the theme but instead breaks off with only a short coda.

This seventh piece provides exactly that missing complement for the third stanza begun in "Regard de l'étoile." Messiaen thus creates the powerful suggestion that, in order to be complete (and in the Christian sense, this necessarily means: to be shown in "comprehensive" threefold representation), the aspect represented in the Star of Bethlehem must be complemented by that of the Cross of Golgotha.

In the sense that the entire piece VII presents the complement of that which was left unfinished in piece II, the musical layout does not require to recall the "shock of grace" that marked the birth of the Son of God. Beyond this structural logic, it seems also theologically significant that all elements that musically embody the notion of the "shock of grace" are repressed in the piece foreshadowing His death on the Cross.

As before, the chant format of the theme is realized in unison. What appears, in *The Star's Contemplation*, as a simple unison at a distance of four octaves, is heard as a fourfold unison over the same keyboard range here. The phrase structure with three lines, each of which comprises two clearly distinguishable segments, is preserved:

line 1 of the chant appears in   bars 1-3/5-7,
line 2   in   bars 9-12/14-18, and
line 3   in   bars 20-22/24-29.

On another level, the relationship between the complement (the aspect of the Cross) and that which it consummates (the Incarnation at Bethlehem as announced by the star) mirrors the structure of the chant itself. One will recall that in *The Star's Contemplation*, Messiaen composes two basically analogous lines and begins the third line still in the same character, but then changes three aspects of the musical setting in the middle of line 3:

[1]   He enriches the final half-line by scoring the chant in four-part unison;

[2]   he adds a secondary voice that is doubled four octaves apart, thus considerably increasing the intensity; and

[3]   he articulates each note in *non legato*, as if to give particular stress to this second half of the third aspect.

Intriguingly, this approach recurs on two further levels and thus appears itself in threefold (= "perfect") realization. In the design that unites *The Star's Contemplation* with *The Cross's Contemplation*, this change of aspect is reproduced in augmentation. The large-scale equivalent to the second half of the chant's third line, the second half of the third stanza, is set apart not only in that it appears as a piece of its own, but also in terms of its musical realization. The three distinguishing aspects correspond with those listed above:

[1]   Messiaen enhances the chant's texture to four-part unison;

[2]   he heightens the intensity by thickening the setting with additional, eight-part middle-ground chords (discussed below) and by choosing a different intensity (*mf* with *crescendo* to *f* and occasionally even *ff*); and

[3]   he increases the stress placed on each single note of the theme, both by choosing a much slower tempo for the chant's basic rhythmic value[132] and by setting the middleground chords not *against* the pitches of the theme but after each note, in an entirely different tone color.

The third instance of this change of aspects occurs when the last half-line of *The Cross Contemplating the Infant Jesus* is once again drastically set apart from what precedes it. Here, however—and that may be theologically crucial—the relationship is inverted. In bar 24, the pace of the "chant" loses all of its heaviness:

[1]   The extremely slow quarter-notes are suddenly given up in favor of sixteenth-notes (i.e., in this tempo, moderately paced notes);

[2]   the eight-part chords that filled the gap between the two ranges of the chant are abandoned; and

[3]   the subphrase is extended with multiple repetition that generates a single *crescendo molto*, thus tying the group of notes together all the more rather than stressing individual attacks. (A further modification is as unexpected as it is revealing. As soon as the powerful *crescendo molto* has reached the level of *ff*, it is enhanced by the recurrence of *non legato* articulation.)

In the context of Christian symbolism, any significant occurrence of THREE will necessarily be read not only as manifesting perfection and comprehensiveness, but also more specifically in light of the Trinity. In this sense, it is not far-fetched to perceive the chant-theme as representing the threefold image of that which is the same in substance but different in appearance. This encourages us to try and match the analytical details given above with a corresponding interpretive reading.

---

[132]The melodic quarter-notes in *The Cross's Contemplation* are drawn out to practically four times the duration of the melodic eighth-notes in *The Star's Contemplation*; compare *Vingt regards* VII, in which the tempo indication requires 1/8 = 40 and the chant thus moves at 20 notes per minute, with *Vingt regards* II, where the tempo of the relevant section is specified as 1/8 = 76 and the chant moves predominantly in eighth-notes.

The cycle of *Twenty Contemplations of the Infant Jesus"* in general, and *The Star's Contemplation* in particular, center on the moment of the Savior's birth—i.e. on the moment when the complementing second aspect of his nature, His suffering in order to take upon Himself the sin of the world, is still in the future. This future will be the completion of the higher design, marked by the words "It is fulfilled" on the Cross. Correspondingly, the musical component that represents this future under the aspect of the Star of Bethlehem appears significantly enhanced and intensified. The intensification appears first as an integral part of the design (as the last half-line of the chant in no. II), then as a momentous reality all of its own (when the omitted final half-stanza of piece II manifests as piece VII), and finally as a pulling together and return to simplicity—both in tempo and in articulation (as the last half-line in piece VII).

As a separate piece in the cycle, *The Cross's Contemplation* thus both *is* the consummation and *contains* within it once again the full design that is to be fulfilled. At the same time yet from a different angle, Messiaen depicts the "perspective of the Cross" through the way in which he accompanies the first two-and-a-half lines of the theme, namely as a view *during* the time when this aspect is being realized. Towards the end of the third enactment of the consummation, he seems to offer a view backwards that is informed by the full understanding of the Crucifixion.

The textural middle-ground that accompanies the theme through most of this piece is twofold, divided once again by the way the event is perceied from within and from without. Both portions consist of eight-part chords, both encompass pedal-notes, and both derive from sigh motifs.[133] The way in which these elements are realized, however, differs both in musical detail and in theological message.

- The chords that accompany the ongoing chant (see e.g. bars 1/2) are simply structured both in their horizontal and in their vertical designs. Vertically, the left-hand chords double the right-hand chords an octave lower, so that the effective texture comprises only four different parts. Horizontally, the uppermost part constitutes a sequence of separate, three-note sigh motifs. The lowest part in each four-note strand doubles these "sighs" at the unusual

---

[133]Sigh motifs, well-known from Bach's music, are those three-note motifs in which an upbeat precedes an *appoggiatura*-resolution pair. (They may also occur without the upbeat, especially when in chain setting.) Typically, the accented *appoggiatura* follows the upbeat in the form of a note repetition, and the resolution is reached in the step of a major or minor second. The most characteristic case is that in which the resolution constitutes a chromatic descent.

intervallic distance of the major seventh, thus enhancing the pining quality. The line described by the entire sequence of sigh motifs is a chromatic descent and ascent through three beats each. The remaining two voices in the four-part chordal texture, constituting the unchanging interval F-A♭, act as pedal-notes. (To compare these details, see the example on the next two facing pages.) The dynamic level is determined as *pp* at the beginning of the piece, and while it later rises somewhat, it always remains way below the intensity of the chant.

- The middle-ground events that follow the attack of the long note at the end of each of the chant's half-lines (see e.g. bars 3/4) are more complex. The eight-part chords, while still based on *appoggiatura*-resolution, are no longer in octave transposition of one another; nor do they contain any static inner voices. Instead, the now very expressive four-part chords in the right hand take their pitches from Messiaen's mode 6, while those in the left hand stem from mode 4. The juxtaposition of these two modes remains intact throughout the piece, although the actual pitches change. The sighing occurs no longer in regularly phrased succession, but first in much increased density (see the triple *appoggiatura*-resolution pair in bar 3), later after dramatic interruptions and much wider chord settings (see bar 4). The pedal-notes, extracted from the "sighs" and enriched to five-part chords of their own, appear now in reinforced position on the two strong beats of the last bar (see bar 4). These A♭-minor chords with added sixth remain the same throughout the entire piece.

bars 3/4

mode 6⁴ — A B C♯ D E♭ F G A♭

mode 4⁶ — B♭ B C D♭ E F G♭ G

The interpretation of these musical symbols is multi-faceted. The pedal-note chord on A♭, anticipated already "within," i.e. during the accompaniment of the subphrase, but only fully realized "outside," suggests two tonal ties. On the one hand, its root A♭ links it to the central note of the theme itself, the pitch A♭ with which each of the chant's three lines concludes. On the other hand, the nature of the chord is strongly reminiscent of the other significant chord with added sixth in Messiaen's cycle, the one in F♯ major that, from the first piece onwards, has a constant semiotic value as one of the musical symbols of GOD'S LOVE; as an obvious variant of the "chord of love", it shows Messiaen's interpretation of the Crucifixion as an ultimate confirmation of God's love.

Sigh motifs traditionally denote human lamenting over the sinfulness of the world, as well as, by extension, over the fate this sinfulness made necessary for Christ the Son of Man. Furthermore, extensive use of chromaticism has the rhetorical value of pitting Man, his small and faltering steps, against God's magnificence.

The juxtaposition of modes 6 and 4 in the right-hand and left-hand chords of the texture goes back to piece V, *The Son Contemplating the Son*, where it was shown to denote two aspects of Jesus—His SUFFERING ON THE CROSS and His birth as the WORD INCARNATE. The recurrence of the same juxtaposition seems intuitively comprehensible in a piece dedicated to the looming shadow of the Cross over the manger. While the sighing and lamenting inside the phrases is thus realized as the immediate, immersed way in which the completion of Christ's destiny on the Cross can be perceived, Messiaen presents another, more reflected reaction literally from outside the (sub-)phrases, after the completion with the advent of the final melodic note. Jesus' divine and human natures, His mission as a manifestation of the Word Incarnate, and His reconciliatory appearance as a child born to Mary, appear as a consistent and thus somehow necessary juxtaposition. They are supported by a chord that brings with it reassurance of GOD'S LOVE, albeit in the slightly tainted form of the chord with added sixth built from mode 7 on A♭. This is the mode whose exclusive symbolic function in the cycle is to link the Star with the Cross, while the original chord with added sixth epitomizes pure Love.[134]

[134]In retrospect, the same chord can also be detected in the earlier context of the *Theme of the Star and of the Cross* as well. In bars 3-5 of *The Star's Contemplation*, immediately preceding the onset of the chant, we hear three instances of resonant downbeat chords followed on the second sixteenth of each bar by three further chords. These after-beat chords are built over a descending bass line that progresses chromatically from B♭ through A to G♯. The chord built over this G♯ fulfills two tonal functions. On the one hand, its pitches complement those of the downbeat chord to a full twelve-tone assortment; this provides an aspect of completion not achieved or thematized in any of the preceding bars. On the other hand, the chord's pitches G♯-C♯-D♯-E♯-B appear, particularly with hindsight, as an enharmonic variation (A♭-[D♭]-E♭-F-C♭) of the A♭-minor chord with sixth.

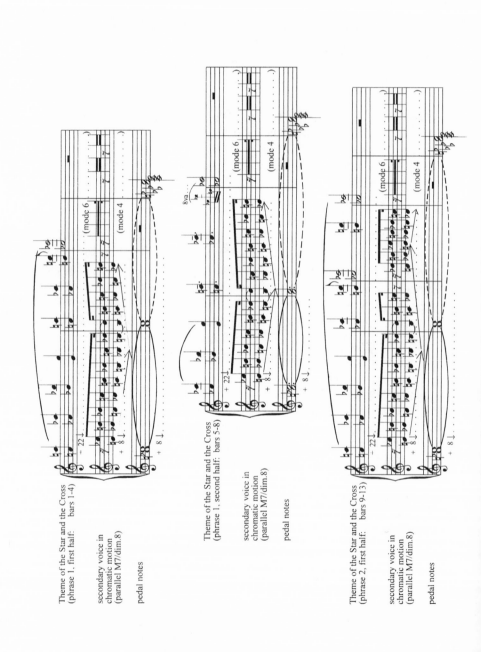

Theme of the Star and the Cross
(phrase 1, first half: bars 1-4)

secondary voice in
chromatic motion
(parallel M7/dim.8)

pedal notes

Theme of the Star and the Cross
(phrase 1, second half: bars 5-8)

secondary voice in
chromatic motion
(parallel M7/dim.8)

pedal notes

Theme of the Star and the Cross
(phrase 2, first half: bars 9-13)

secondary voice in
chromatic motion
(parallel M7/dim.8)

pedal notes

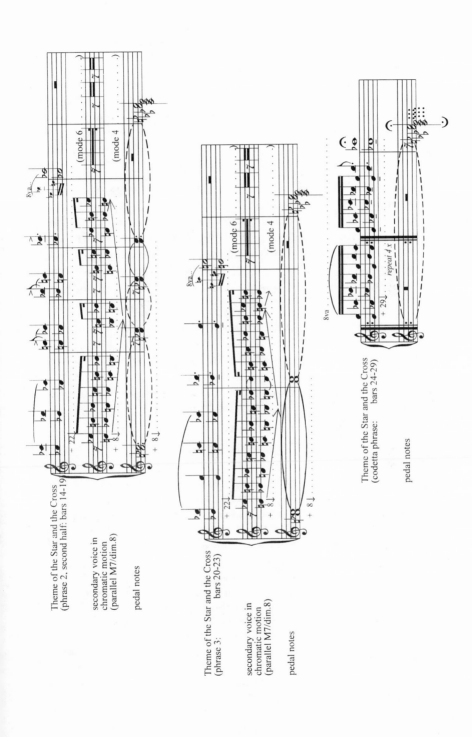

Theme of the Star and the Cross
(phrase 2, second half: bars 14-19)

secondary voice in
chromatic motion
(parallel M7/dim.8)

pedal notes

Theme of the Star and the Cross
(phrase 3:   bars 20-23)

secondary voice in
chromatic motion
(parallel M7/dim.8)

pedal notes

Theme of the Star and the Cross
(codetta phrase: bars 24-29)

pedal notes

Towards the end of the piece, the "consummation" within this perspective of the Cross (see bars 24-29) uses musical devices that are equally expressive of theological interpretation. The protracted *legato* articulation that precedes the expected *non legato* of this subphrase speaks of a tying together of larger contexts, and the soaring *crescendo molto* achieved in the course of the repetitions sounds triumphant. The crucifixion is thus not merely reason for lamenting and sighing, but ultimately an act of triumph. "The Cross says: you will be priest in my arms....," this is what Messiaen associates in his subheading. On the Cross Jesus is a priest; the bloody death of Christ is the priestly sacrifice redemptive of the world.[135]

The piece concludes with a renewed combination of the foremost aspects. The downbeat of the final bar with its four-octave A♭ completes the link between the Star and the Cross; throughout the remaining thirteen pieces of the cycle, this particular pitch will never recur as a melodically dominant or harmonically determining note. On the sixteenth-note after the downbeat, the A♭-minor chord with added sixth reasserts one last time the presence of GOD'S LOVE, albeit in the inflection characteristic for this situation.[136] As a third element in the final bar, two chords in *p* represent once more the two modes that stand for the two aspects of the Son, modes 6 and 4.[137] Interestingly, they are not directly juxtaposed here (which would have been just as easy to write and play) but slightly set off beside one another. What is more, the chord embodying mode 6, i.e. the aspect of the SUFFERING ON THE CROSS, is notated as a pre-beat *acciaccatura*. This gives much greater weight to the left-hand chord and thus to the aspect of the Child as the WORD INCARNATE—which is indeed the one we are still primarily concerned with in the *Contemplations of the Infant Jesus*.

[135] The idea goes back to the Letter to the Hebrews. This particular devotion emerged and was popular during the first three or four decades of the 20th century and led to the iconography to which Messiaen alludes here. Interestingly, the church authorities discouraged portraying Jesus as a Christian/ Catholic priest on the Cross.

[136] In this context, one is reminded of the correspondence between piece VII of the *Vingt regards* and piece VII of the *Nativité* whose title is "Jesus accepts the suffering." In another instance of correspondence within the larger oeuvre of Olivier Messiaen, the third movement of *Visions de l'Amen* with the title "Amen of Jesus' agony" is characterized by constant chromatic sighing (Messiaen's "*gémissement chromatique perpétuel*") and by a minor chord with added sixth.

[137] For readers who wish to verify this, it is important to know that the after-phrase chords throughout the piece stem from the fourth transposition of mode 6 (right hand) and the sixth transposition of mode 4 (left hand), while the two final chords are taken from the third transposition of mode 6 and the second transposition of mode 4 respectively.

Regard des prophètes, des bergers et des Mages
(Messiaen, *Vingt regards*, XVI)

(Tam-tams et hautbois, concert énorme et nasillard...)

Among the twenty pieces in Olivier Messiaen's *Vingt regards sur l'Enfant-Jésus*, two are musically related through a very potent structural device. Both XVI and XVIII have palindromically conceived framing sections. While the frames of XVI are somewhat simpler than those of XVIII, the latter clearly develop the former, using the same basic pitches in the same chordal arrangement undergoing the same rhythmic development.

Significantly, the two pieces are the only ones in the cycle that feature an explicit framing section. What is more, the musical framing device is here not an identically recurring section or recapitulation, but a palindrome: a retracing of steps, an image of perfect, symmetric, and inevitable closure. As if in conscious contradiction to this stringent sense of closure, *The Prophets, the Shepherds and the Magi Contemplating the Infant Jesus* ends with a coda that, after the conclusion of the retrograde, picks up the two main musical gestures heard inside the frame. (*The Awesome Unction Contemplating the Infant Jesus*, by contrast, does not add anything to the image of perfect containment, as will be discussed in the next chapter.) Neither the position of these pieces within the cycle nor any other purely musical reason seems to account satisfactorily for this strikingly close relationship. One might therefore search for an extra-musical stimulus.

In an attempt to account for the connection Messiaen must have intended, let us look more closely at the musical material that makes up these framing sections. The chord A/D♯/G♯ in the lowest register, on which the framing sections of both pieces build, bears its own connotations. This A, the lowest key on the modern keyboard, is used throughout Messiaen's cycle as a symbol of awe. It occurs repeatedly as the base of a chromatic cluster (A/A♯/B or, as in bar 62 of *The Virgin's Contemplation*, A/B♭/B♮/C). Significantly, the cluster also functions as a device that links two images that appear at first irreconcilably different: XII, the abstract *Almighty Word*, and XIII, *Christmas,* a straightforward rondo with a re-frain suggestive of Christmas bells.

The interval arrangement of the chord built over this awe-symbolizing lowest A, a perfect fourth over a tritone, has two forerunners. In II, *The Star's Contemplation*, the chord constitutes the building block of a coda that is strangely outside the otherwise tightly strophic structure of the piece, unconnected to its main body in every sense, and distinctly unrelated to any of its tempi (as if "outside of time"). This coda material later turns into the cell that generates the second theme in IX, *Time's Contemplation*, where it stands for "eternity." (For more details, please refer to the chapters dealing with these pieces, pp. 287-292 and 360-367.)

Let us now take a closer look at the rhythmic layout, dynamic development, and texture in which this chord A/D#/G# appears in XVI. In both framing sections, the chord undergoes incremental rhythmic transformations. The opening section presents a gradual tightening of the repeated attacks, in a diminution process leading from a whole-note down to sixteenth-notes. Correspondingly, the mirroring section towards the end of the piece allows the same chord to grow longer and longer, more and more weighty from one attack to the next, featuring an augmentation from repeated sixteenth-notes up to a whole note. The almost viscerally convincing depiction with decreasing time spans in the opening section and increasingly large values in the closing section imparts a very straightforward statement, and one can hear these developments as an actual marking of time. This is especially obvious for the opening section: as history approaches the moment when the Promised One will come, time grows shorter and shorter. After the event, which counts rhythmically as something like "day zero" (an understanding reflected in our Western calendar), time takes a new beginning. With it, a newly informed and confirmed prophesy starts its own expansion process.

Furthermore, not only the rhythmic but also the dynamic developments in these framing sections recur in retrograde. The increasing urgency of the rhythmic diminution, clad in a process of lessening tension (*sfff—p*), is reversed into an incremental augmentation of values presented in triumphant *crescendo (p—ff)*. The fact that the marking of time towards the long-announced central event is realized in decreasing intensity, reaching its goal in a whisper, gives much to ponder. We might have expected—and so did most of the pious Jews, as the Bible tells us very vividly—that when God took on human flesh, it would be with fanfares and triumph: the birth of a king. Instead, this incarnation takes place in a small village, to a poor family, in a place where animals are housed. Messiaen's music invites us to approach the birth at Bethlehem from this angle as well, to prepare ourselves, in our listening attitude, to something ostensibly humble, whose greatness is not on the visible level. The theme of smallness to greatness resounds through the stories of Jesus' birth. His public ministry, and his message to the world, is meant to grow both wider and louder, as the framing section at the and of the piece epitomizes so persuasively.

Against both halves of this perfect palindrome, the *ostinato* in the treble remains completely unchanged (as indicated by repeated curves in the example below). Moreover, of the four chords in each bar, the third repeats the first, and they are arranged in such a way as to form a continuous wavy line of ups and downs. The pitches are taken from the fourth transposition of mode 5. Messiaen does not otherwise employ this mode within the *Vingt regards*. However, it is certainly no coincidence that mode 5, along with mode 7, can be read as a derivative of mode 4, one of the very important modes in this cycle.[138] Mode 5^4 in particular is an excerpt from mode 4^4, the most prominent transposition of that mode, and gleans from it the signifying power of the WORD INCARNATE.[139]

bars 1-21

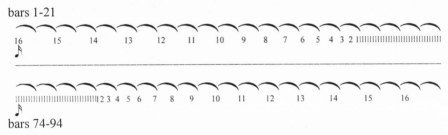

bars 74-94

The simultaneity of the rhythmic acceleration in the lower register and the *ostinato* in the treble posits a most revealing thought: the marking of time toward the event of the Incarnation, on one level so clearly depicted as a development with a clear goal, at the same time forms part of an ongoing, ever-repeated, ever-identical process: God's continued communication with His prophets throughout all ages, His unchanging invitation to trust His guidance and rely on His assistance.

[138]Where mode 7 is conceived with more closely packed chromatic ingredients and thus potentially more emotionally intense, mode 5 presents itself as a more transparent version of mode 4 and thus lends itself well to the prophetic dimension. Compare the fourth transpositions of all three modes:

mode 5^4:	D♯ E		G♯|A A♯			D
mode 4^4:	D♯ E F		G♯|A A♯ B			D
mode 7^4:	D♯ E F F♯		G♯|A B♭ B C			D

[139]In V, *The Son Contemplating the Son*, Messiaen employs mode 4^4 as the modal symbol for the WORD INCARNATE, realized in the middle strand of the three-tiered texture. It is contemplated by that aspect of the Son which is characterized, in the upper strand, by the SUFFERING ON THE CROSS, whose symbol, there and elsewhere in the cycle, is mode 6.

To sum up what we have discovered with regard to the framing sections: the contextual connotations given the central note A in the remainder of Messiaen's cycle carry into these pieces an element of awe. Similarly, the vertical interval structure of superimposed perfect fourth and tritone imports its own symbolic baggage and thus comes to us with a connotation of "outside of time" and eternity. The developmental features within the framing sections speak a distinct language: there is the marking of time towards the event and the broadening of the perspective afterwards, the hush before the incomprehensible humility of this birth, and the increase of confidence as the ministry develops. Both are accompanied by an unchanging *ostinato*, God's continuing revelation and communication with those who hear Him (before and after the historic event of the Incarnation). Finally, the mirrored structure is broken as the closing section is extended with a coda. It is as though that which is divinely fulfilled in the moment of the birth at Bethlehem still needs to trail a span of "life within time" behind it before its completion at Golgotha.

As we turn to the central section that the above-discussed features frame, we need to recall what agents other than prophets Messiaen had in mind, and what place these onlookers take in the spectrum depicted in the *Vingt regards*.

Interestingly, the titling of the two pieces that share the conspicuous framing sections places them at opposite ends of the spectrum of entities contemplating the Infant Jesus. In his "Author's Note," Messiaen tells us that he imagined the *regards* to represent looks of creatures on a scale from real (*The Virgin's Contemplation*) through metaphorical (*The Spirit of Joy Contemplating the Infant Jesus, The Church of Love Contemplating the Infant Jesus*) to immaterial and symbolic (*Time's Contemplation, Silence's Contemplation*, etc.).

In XVI, the agents are people: generic representatives as real as they are picturesque. The vignette picturing prophets, shepherds, and Magi at the manger, points not so much to contemporary Christmas imagery (which usually does not feature the prophets) as to medieval liturgical dramas. Particularly in the *Carmina Burana* play from the 13th century, the three groups appear united in the stable of Bethlehem.[140] The wording in the subheading is restricted to an evocation of sounds heard (tam-tams,

---

[140]See Karl Young: *The Drama of the Medieval Church*, I-II (Oxford: Clarendon Press 1962), vol. 2, p. 172-196 for the (Latin) text; also p. 125-171 on the procession of prophets, according to Young a fairly widespread Christmas practice in the Middle Ages, on which the *Carmina Burana* play draws.

oboes), and Messiaen apparently saw no need for further elaboration in the preface.

Indeed, there is no need; the musical symbolism is very transparent. The middle section begins (in bars 22-29) with a single-voiced figuration that could hardly be more evocative. Even without the composer's instruction (*"hautbois"* [oboe], he specifies, and *un peu criard* [somewhat shrill]), one cannot imagine that anybody would have missed the allusion to the instruments with which shepherds were traditionally often depicted, the chalumeau (literally a forerunner of today's bass clarinet) or the recorder. And as with shepherds who play to pass the time, what we hear sounds like an excerpt of something that might go on much longer: manifold repetitions of the same three-note figure, sometimes embellished with an initial grace-note and concluding—at the end of a breath, one is tempted to guess—with an equally simple, often slightly embellished closing particle.

The recurring pitches of this shepherds' signal, C B A D♯ C♯, are subsequently employed to form various improvisatory figures; see the five pitches in the treble peak line of bars 30/31, in generous octave displacement in the *arpeggio* of bar 33, and, abridged, in the four-part unison of bar 35.

Now that prophets and shepherds have presented themselves, one expects a musical rendering of the Magi. Sure enough, the following section (bars 36-59) consists of three segments and presents three melodic ideas in a variety of textures with, mostly, three strands: an apt image of the three wise men from distant lands who, united at Bethlehem to worship the poor-born child and acknowledge it as the new king of kings, do so each in his own way, yet in perfect harmony.

The first melodic component *(x)* consists of four accented fourths, in a pitch curve that is reminiscent of that heard in the *ostinato* (compare C♮-C♯-C♮-A with the wavy outline of the treble in bars 1-21). The second component *(y)*, much more virtuoso and rhythmically alive, stresses the pitches F♯-G♯-A-G♯-F♯. In its basic design, it is metrically congruent with component *x*, but irregular extensions and elisions soon create a vivid contrapuntal interplay (see bars 38-42d). After a *caesura* marked by *ff*

chords that stress the augmented octaves F♮/F♯ and C♯/D, the second segment shows components x and y joined by a third figure *(z)*. Interestingly,
the new material does not make its entry with the beginning of polyphonic three-part texture. Instead, bar 44 turns first from the previous x/y
juxtaposition to a setting where component x in the upper voice is contrapuntally superimposed over a stretto imitation of y in the middle and
lower voices. In bar 45/46, component x rests, while the two lower voices
continue their stretto with the new component z. The following bars
repeat the same process with considerable internal extension (cf. bars
47-51 with bars 44-46).

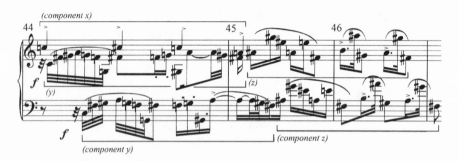

The third segment of this section, once again set apart from the previous one by contrasting bars in f with strongly emphasized F♮/F♯ and C♯/D
clashes, plays freely with the pitches of x (see the upper voice in bars 55/
56 but also the diminution in the upper and lowest voices of bar 57) and
concludes again with a closing attack distinguished by augmented and
diminished octaves (see here particularly the triplet parallel in bar 58).

When the shepherds's chalumeau figuration returns in bar 60, it does
so not only with parallel thirds in its first three-note particle, but over an
"energetic" bass (according to Messiaen) that quotes the leader of the
Magi. Not surprisingly then, the final bars before the mirror image of the
frame begins combine the pitches of this component x (C♮ C♯ C♮ A) with
the pitch representation of the shepherds (C B A D♯ C♯).

The shepherds, beyond their pictorial value so familiar to us from
Christmas art, stand for the common people—people whose humble
circumstances Jesus has come to share from the moment of His birth in a
stable; they also represent the local, i.e. Jewish element. The Magi, by
contrast, epitomize the class of distinguished persons from different
ethnic backgrounds and different parts of the world, and thus the global
aspect, both in terms of "all humanity" and in terms of "all social and

intellectual classes." Messiaen's musical rendering recreates this complementarity by conceiving the two groups with material that could hardly be
more contrasted: simplicity of melodic, rhythmic and textural design for
the shepherds, complexity in all parameters for the Magi. The mirrored
recurrence of the prophets' preparation for the coming of Christ then
functions as a musical symbol for the new prophetic power that emanates
from this moment onwards. After the birth, seen somewhat like a stillpoint, the announcement made in past history through the voices of the
poets now finds its own voice. As the rhythmic and dynamic growth process in which Messiaen has laid out this second part of the framing section
makes clear, the message is not just for the Jewish people, but for all of
humankind. Correspondingly, it is being spread, in terms of both an ever
broader and wider scope, and an ever more triumphant voice. However,
as Messiaen seems determined to remind us: under the aspect of this very
concrete birth in the stable there is first of all a life to live for the Son of
Man, a life among shepherds and kings. Reassuringly, the coda concludes
with a unison of the leading component representing the Magi, in triumphant *fff* and an equally triumphant expansive gesture from the center to
'the corners of the universe.'

Regard de l'Onction terrible   Messiaen, *Vingt regards*, XVIII

(Le Verbe assume une certaine nature humaine; choix de la chair de Jésus par la
Majesté épouvantable...)

When playing, listening to, or analyzing the score of the five final
pieces of Messiaen's *Vingt regards sur l'Enfant-Jésus* in the order in
which they occur, one becomes acutely aware of the close resemblance
between the framing sections of this piece with the XVIth. And one
wonders why the composer might have chosen such a powerful linking
device, given the almost complete lack of obvious connection between
the two titles, both with regard to imagery and in terms of the degree of
abstraction suggested.

As was mentioned above, the protagonists in XVI—prophets, shepherds and Magi—are real, tangible people. They include the characters
historically chosen by God's revelation (the prophets), the ones addressed
by the angels' announcement (the shepherds), and the ones informed by
their dreams and guided by the Star (the Magi). Together, these generic
representatives cover the entire spectrum of humanity, past and present at
the event of the birth, humble and noble. As we find them united around

the manger, they are as real as they are picturesque. By contrast, one could hardly find anything more insubstantial and symbolic (see Messiaen's *créatures immatérielles et symboliques*) contemplating the infant Jesus than the "Awesome Unction" of XVIII.

It is these two pieces, however, that Messiaen offers us as counterparts through the use of the strongly related framing device. Their musical ties thus link a particularly pictorial piece to the one possibly most mystically inspired. Beyond the titles of the two pieces, the additional remarks contained in the composer's subheading and preface as well as the information gleaned from the musical layout must be consulted in oder to understand in which respects and on what levels Messiaen might have seen an intrinsic relationship between the "prophets, shepherds and Magi" on the one hand, and the "Awesome Unction" on the other.

The "Awesome Unction" of XVIII posits Jesus as the Anointed One. In it, similarly to what was observed in *The Cross's Contemplation*, a future yet ontologically pre-determined aspect of Jesus glances upon the child in the manger. The wording elicits three possible sources. The adjective "awesome" reflects the understanding that God's decision to send His Son into a life of suffering that will end at the Cross is both gruesome and awe-inspiring. The unction, which consecrates the anointed person and endows him with divine powers, was seen by many medieval theologians in the context of the Incarnation itself, which could be regarded as an anointment, in the sense that the Word anoints the human nature of Jesusre with divinity.[141] The expression further reminds us of two events from Jesus' life time. Understood literally, the word points to the biblical scene in which Mary Magdalen washes and anoints Jesus' feet. Since Jesus interprets this act as done in anticipation of his funeral, the sinner's deed is given a prophetic meaning. Finally, in its figurative sense the "unction" can also be read as referring to Jesus' baptism by John the Baptist, during which the Spirit descends upon Him and brings about the manifestation of an ontologically determined destiny. This baptism also acts as the beginning of Jesus' ministry, and in this sense too can be compared with the anointment for office habitual for kings and priests. Messiaen's subheading refers somewhat cryptically to the interpretation of Jesus as the Anointed One: "The Word takes on a certain human nature; choice of the flesh of Jesus by the dreadful Majesty..."

---

[141] On this meaning see also Psalm 45, 8: "You love justice and hate wrongdoing; therefore God, your God, has anointed you with the oil of gladness above your fellow kings." See also the original meaning of the word *Christos*, which is "the Anointed One."

Let us begin by looking at the framing sections, and comparing them with those in XVI, *The Prophets, the Shepherds and the Magi Contemplating the Infant Jesus*. The initial section of XVI features gradually accelerating repetitions of a bass chord, a process that is then reversed in the closing part of the frame. As was shown above, this ever faster, ever softer rush towards the zero point depicts one essential aspect of the prophets—their preparation for the long-prophesied birth of the Savior—while the ever more triumphant broadening towards the end of that piece speaks of the spreading of the new prophesy. In XVII, The *Awesome Unction Contemplating the Infant Jesus*, these two processes happen simultaneously. The same bass chord initiates the same rhythmic acceleration in the initial section, but the reverse process of gradually increasing values is now superimposed in the treble. Moreover, the juxtaposition is intensified by a vertical contraction. The chords are here not simply repeated as in XVI but move, by chromatic increments with each attack, towards the center. The result adds a further dimension to the overlay: chromatically ascending chords in the left hand are pitted against chromatically descending ones in the right hand in such a way that the two lines finally meet on the same inner pitch, the central $E\flat$, which is reached in the thumbs of both the right and the left hands. (See bars 1-19 in the graphic illustration below. The figures denote the rhythmic values of each chord in sixteenth-notes, from $1 = \eighthnote$ to $16 = \whitenote$).

As in XVI, the final section of this piece also presents a retrograde mirror, thus concluding the *Awesome Unction* with an expansion process that sets out in central proximity and spreads into the extreme registers of the keyboard (see bars 180-198).

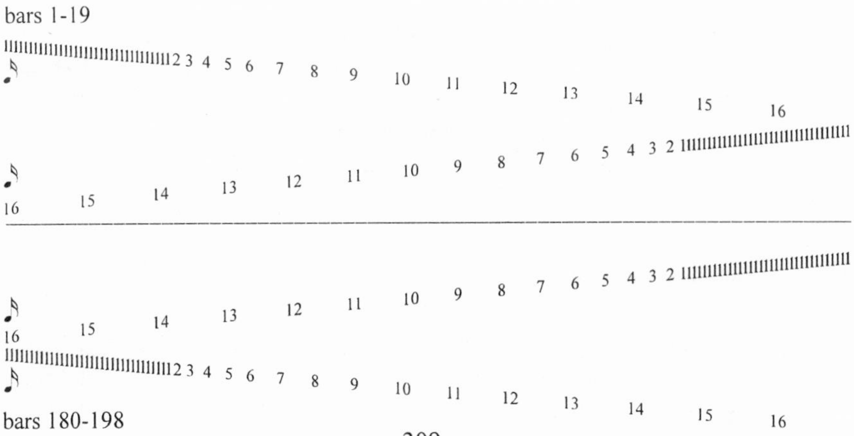

bars 1-19

bars 180-198

In light of the crucial connection of this frame with that of XVI, both the common musical material and the particular process observed in this piece must carry some of the same interpretive implications—in other words, it can be expected to contain an aspect of prophesy. The word "unction" provides a clue here. In its adjective form, "anointed" leads to another Biblical figure, John the Baptist, who has been anointed for his task of pointing people to Jesus in His very lifetime. At the same time, the baptism of Christ by John in many ways functions as the tangible part of Jesus' unction.[142] What Messiaen may thus be depicting in his impressive texture of juxtaposed accelerating ascent and decelerating descent is John the Baptist's famous prophesy according to which

"He [Jesus] must increase, but I must decrease." (John 3:30)

Following such lines of thought, Messiaen may thus have been prompted to use the same musical device in the two pieces, and thus create a connection between two ostensibly unrelated visions, by the wish to emphasize that both comprise the element of prophecy. Earlier prophets are imagined among the shepherds and Magi at the manger, witnessing and confirming in a somewhat quaint picture the birth of the Child who is to be the world's savior. John the Baptist, by contrast, is the contemporary prophet. He bears witness to destiny and mission of the man who lives among men, marked but not yet recognized. The first relation, then, is between a past prophecy fulfilled in the birth at Bethlehem, and a prophecy born in the moment of Jesus' baptism and pointing into the future.

Yet there is more. While the parameters used in the framing section of XVI focus on the temporal aspect (marking the ever-shorter time span left before the stillpoint of the birth at Bethlehem, and the ever-broader mission after the crucial event), the more complex processes in XVIII seem to depict a forceful collapse and equally powerful re-expansion. Rather than indicating pious worship and obedient service in ministry, as evoked in the vignette around the manger, the *Awesome Unction* suggests suffering and battles both internal and external.

In his "Author's Note," Messiaen mentions the inspiration derived from a piece of art. "An old tapestry," he writes, "represents the Word of God in battle under the features of Christ on horseback: One sees only His two hands on the handle of the sword that He waves in the middle of

---

[142]Furthermore, baptism typologically relates to the death of Christ (see Paul's letter to the Romans, chapter 6). Finally, the term baptism is also used metaphorically for the crucifixion in at least two places in the New Testament, Mark 10: 38-39, and Luke 12: 50.

flashes of lightning. That image has influenced me." At first reading, this description seems utterly puzzling. To take it literally: if all we see is a sword handle with two hands holding it, how do we know that Christ is on horseback? The fact that Messiaen does not give us any clue as to the country or time of origin, or even its present location does not make the identification any easier. However, a systematic study of the foremost Christian tapestries brought a result that Messiaen's widow, Yvonne Loriod, was later able to confirm. The tapestry to which the composer refers is part of the medieval cycle of tapestries known today as the "Apocalypse of Angers." More precisely, catalogued as no. 69, it is one of the surviving seventy-eight panels that are estimated to have been created in the years leading up to 1380 and, despite a fate of changing locations over the centuries, are miraculously conserved almost intact, carefully restored and since 1954 exhibited in the gallery of the castle of Angers in France.[143]

The story told in the sequence of panels follows very closely the Revelation received by St. John while in exile on the Greek island of Patmos. The narrative speaks of great dangers to the Church—internal dangers for the faith, hope, and charity of Christians as well as external dangers through persecutions. As we read in various chapters, the apocalypse presents itself as a prophecy, and its writer repeatedly acknowledges his role as that of a prophet.[144] The Biblical book itself is highly allegorical, and thus lends itself well to visual retelling.

Panel no. 69, entitled *Le Christ à cheval poursuit les bêtes* (Christ on horseback chases the beasts), shows Jesus mounted on a horse, His two arms raised in such a way that His face is hidden and all attention is drawn to the sword that He holds with both hands—hence Messiaen's enigmatic observation "one sees only His two hands on the handle of the sword... ." The beasts He is pursuing are intermingled with soldiers who, while clearly in retreat, have not quite given up fighting back. (See the reproduction of the panel on the following page.)

---

[143]For a fascinating account of all that led to the exhibition as it has been shown in the Castle of Angers since 1954, and for more details on the panels themselves, see Pierre-Marie Auzas et al., *L'apocalypse d'Anger. Chef-d'oeuvre de la tapisserie médiévale* (Paris: Editions Vilo, 1985). The panel mentioned by Messiaen is reprinted in black and white on page 178, and page 179 shows a color excerpt.

[144]See, e.g., Rev. I:3, X:11, XXII:7, 10, 18, 19. John distinctly identifies himself as a prophet in I:1 and I:19, recognizing that his specific mission is to reveal certain divine secrets regarding the present and future of the faithful and of the Church of Christ.

Messiaen visited Angers several times. No doubt he saw all the panels available to visitors, but he probably also studied the documentation that identifies the Biblical verses on which each panel is based. The panel we are considering here comes with a quote from Rev. XIX: 11-14, which reads as follows: "Then I saw the heavens open, and a white horse appeared; its rider was called Faithful and True, the one who judges and fights justly. His eyes were like a fiery flame, he had several diadems on his head and a name written that no-one knows but Himself. He was clad in a cloak soaked in blood, and calls Himself the Word of God. The heavenly armies followed him, mounted on white horses and wearing clean white linen."[145]

Le Christ à cheval poursuit les bêtes (Christ on horseback chases the beasts);
Panel no. 69 from the tapestry *L'apocalypse d'Anger.*
Reprinted from the catalogue of the Galerie d'Anger, France.

[145]"Je vis alors le ciel ouvert et il parut un cheval blanc; celui qui le montait s'appelait le Fidèle et le Véritable qui juge et qui combat justement. Ses yeux étaient comme une flamme de feu; il avait plusieurs diadèmes sur la tête et un nom écrit que nul connaît que lui. Il était vêtu d'une robe teinte de sang et il s'appelle le Verbe de Dieu. Les armées qui sont dans le ciel le suivaient sur des chevaux blancs, vêtus d'un lin blanc et pur."

Both the particulars of the visual image and the additional text thus contribute crucially to the full understanding of Messiaen's piece. On the one hand, the connection between Jesus' chasing of the beasts in times to come and His *Awesome Unction* expands the interpretive scope of Messiaen's titling beyond the meaning given the term in the Incarnation and in the baptism, to embrace tasks and struggles beyond Golgotha. On the other hand, the text from the apocalypse alerts us to the silent presence of yet another prophet in Messiaen's cycle. This is crucial, since it extends the notion of the event at Bethlehem as far into the future as it was presaged in the past. Where the prophets whom we found worshipping around the manger in XVI reach into Jesus' lifetime from times long past, and where John the Baptist, the contemporary prophet, bears witness to the universal importance of this man in front of him whom he recognizes as the Son of God, John the Apostle reaches from Jesus' lifetime into times far away.

This understanding sheds new light on the interpretation of the material and design of Messiaen's *The Awesome Unction Contemplating the Infant Jesus*. The framing sections, in their derivation from those of XVI identified as symbolic representations of prophets or prophesies, now take on a meaning that links them to John the Baptist and John the Apostle respectively. Both sections have a dynamic development that points forward, to the future. In the opening section, the accelerating ascent meets the decelerating descent in a way that may be read as symbolic for the moment of Jesus' baptism: for John the Baptist, the moment of his contact with Jesus represented the fulfillment of his life's mission; for Jesus, the moment marks the beginning of His three-year ministry. Correspondingly, the accelerating ascent and the decelerating descent in the closing section begin in close proximity and depart from there in different directions, just as John the Apostle's prophetic task begins after his contact with Jesus during the years as His disciple.

The *Awesome Unction*, then, while generally the "choice of the flesh of Jesus" and thus the fact of the Incarnation, refers here specifically to that which is awaiting Him after his baptism in the Jordan river, immediately before and in infinity after Golgotha.

This brings us to the extensive central section that these framing passages embrace. The immediately adjacent bars 20-22 and 178-179 function as transitions. The two components of which these transitions are made up seem closely linked to the framing sections in gesture and structure respectively. The *glissandi*, which are neither alike nor exact retrogrades of one another, duplicate and thus reinforce the forward-pointing *crescendo* in the framing sections, and the broken chords in contrary motion are laid out as mirror images of one another. What is more, these chords take the above-mentioned meeting of the two chordal strands one step further. In *arpeggios* that Messiaen requests to be played *arraché*, (literally, snatched), the chords cross over one another and in this interwoven position descend or (in preparation for the closing section) ascend jointly! The messengers are thus shown in close intimacy and mutual support with the Messiah.

The long innermost section (bars 23-177) is structured as a "solemn" rondo. The cycle contains only one other case of a rondo, to be found in XIII, *Christmas*, where the main expression is prescribed as "joyous." In this aspect, too, as in the case of the related framing sections, Messiaen thus explores the use of the same device for very different ends.

For a first overview, here is the layout of this rondo (R = refrain, E = episode, R^m = refrain with mirrored elements, R_4 = refrain transposed to the fourth semitone):

bars 1	20	23	38	53	68	83	98	113	128	143	158	178	180
frame	transi-	R	R^m		R_4		R_8		R	R^m		transi-	frame
(open)	tion			E1		E2		$E1_8$			$E2_8$	tion	(close)

The refrain and the two interlocking episodes are derived from a few cells of shared material. The first particle is a vertical stacking of five notes based on a perfect fifth. and its octave doublings. Paired in the refrain with its transposition by a tritone (see, e.g., in bars 23, 26, 27, 30, 30/31 as well as in the convex curve of bars 35/36), this symbol launches each of the refrain's phrases. The first and second subphrases are rounded off by a zigzagged flourish that shoots up into the highest registers of the piano before falling more gingerly, marked *"comme la foudre"* (like a flash of lightning, bars 24, 28 etc.), followed by broken chords in *staccato, martelé*. The third and fourth subphrases conclude, respectively, with an ascending *toccata* pattern and a descending figuration over repeated broken chords.

As the overview above shows in one glance, the recurrences of the refrain are organized in a supremely regular manner, and its transformations follow objective laws. At the beginning and at the end of the rondo section, the refrain is followed immediately by a version that contains significant mirror effects (cf. the two tritone ascents in bars 45/46 and 150/151 with the descents in bars 30/31 and 135/136, and the concave curves in bars 50/51 and 155/156 with the convex ones in bars 35/36 and

140/141). In between, two other instances of the refrain, separated by episodes, appear in transposition to the fourth semitone (bars 68-82), to the eighth semitone (bars 98-112) and, finally, to the twelfth semitone (bars 128-142), at which point the original tonal arrangement is regained, albeit partly in octave displacement.

The first episode is launched from the same five-note chord built on the perfect fifth that opened all of the refrain's phrases. The shifting of the chord is not by tritones here but by whole steps (see bars 53, 57, 57/ 58, 63, 63/64) and semitones or diminished octaves (see bars 58, 65, 66, 67). The remainder of the components are also related to those heard in the refrain. There is a short upward flourish (in the form of a grace-note upbeat), a *toccata* bar, and a motion in parallel *staccato* fourths (bars 56 and 62) that is reminiscent of the refrain's *staccato, martelé*.[146] Episode 2 develops the refrain's 'convex curve' (first heard in bars 35/36), interspersed with—once again—ascending flourishes and *toccata* patterns. Its final liquidation in *crescendo molto* sets out from the melodic outline of this curve which is, however, retained only in the treble and bass voices (see bar 91) but filled with six voices that exploit the twelve-tone realm while defying parallels. As if in compensation, the second surge, which completes the retransition to the refrain, uses only a single rolled chord (with E/B/(E)/F) for its twentyfold repetition. Both episodes are transposed to the eight semitone (cf. episode 1: bars 113-127 with bars 53-67, and episode 2: bars 158-177 with bars 83-97; the latter transposition contains some internal irregularities and is extended until bar 177).

As I would like to show, this rondo can be read as being inspired by the tapestry. Its principal components seem to attempt musical renditions of that which is depicted in the apocalyptic panel of "Christ on Horseback, Chasing the Beasts." The perfect fifth on which each phrase beginning is based has always been one of the primary means in musical rhetorics to allude to the Divinity. As a result, the sound, in its simplicity and desired *fff* strength, seems to stand for the power of the Divine and of the "Faithful and True." The second component in the refrain, the zigzagged flourish that is pictorially identified through its marking with the words *"comme la foudre,"* as well as the simpler ascending flourishes in the two

---

[146]There seem to be two misprints in these parallels. In bar 56, beat 3, the fourth sixteenth in the left hand is notated as a major third, as is the first sixteenth of the fourth beat in bar 62. These thirds not only interrupt what is otherwise a consistent pattern of perfect fourths, but also fail to recur in the transposition of the episode where the respective bars feature unbroken strings of fourths. It seem thus meaningful to correct this otherwise so carefully proof-read score and substitute, in bar 56, F♯/B, and in bar 62, E♯/A♮.

episodes thus refers to what the composer saw in the tapestry: Jesus wielding His sword inmidst "flashes of lightning." The subsequent broken chords in *staccato, martelé* sound combative, while the ascending *toccata* pattern in the third subphrase and the descending figuration over repeated broken chords in the fourth seem to represent chase and flight. (Interestingly, both the broken chords in bar 37 and the *toccata* attacks in bars 32-34 use the combination of tritone and—clashing—whole tone characteristic of the "lightning," and thus seem to link the arrows in the sky with the energetic powers of the heavenly sword.) The *staccato* parallel fourths in episode 2 and the *toccata* patterns in both episodes take their depictive meaning from the refrain.

Finally, the fact of transposition as well as the interval by which the refrain and its episodes are transposed add yet another dimension. These transpositions to the fourth and eighth semitones can be seen, in context of the entire cycle, as having a connection to the Divine. They recall the central section of *The Spirit of Joy Contemplating the Infant Jesus*," where the hunting song appeared in transposed first to the fourth, then to the eighth semitone (see X, bars 60-63, 84-87, 108-111) and the last section before the coda of *Through Him All Was Made*, where the *Theme of God* was also thus transposed (see the downbeats of bars 161-164, 172-175, and 185-188). Both the hunting song and the *Theme of God* employ mode 2, the mode that exists in only three transpositions. Together with the original (here, in the refrain, duplicated in the transposition to the twelfth semitone), the transpositions thus provide a 'complete' manifestation of the modal symbol of GOD'S LOVE. It seems enlightening, although perhaps for some readers a little far-fetched, to read Messiaen's musical language as declaring the combative acts of Christ on horseback chasing the beasts to be yet another expression of God's Love.

Theologically, the image harkens back to the scripture reference (Hebrews 4:12) of God's Word being sharper than a two-edged sword. In the larger context of the prophets that frame this piece and the related piece XVI, and of the revelations granted them as expressions of God's continuing loving invitation, the apocalyptic sword wielding probably stands for the Word doing battle with whatever evil clouds human cognition and keeps humans from responding freely to God's invitation.

THE WORD

Par Lui tout a été fait (Messiaen, *Vingt regards*, VI)

(Foisonnement des espaces et durées; galaxies, photons, spirales contraires, foudres inverses; par "Lui" [le Verbe] tout a été fait...à un moment, la création nous ouvre l'ombre lumineuse de sa Voix...)

No. VI in the cycle, *Through Him All Was Made*, is dedicated to God's Creation. Messiaen's associations to "all that was made" mention particularly the immensity of time and space ("abundance of spaces and durations"), the unfathomably large and small ("galaxies and photons"). In addition, he draws our attention to some uncommon concepts: "contrary spirals" and "inverted flashes of lightning." If the spiral is the symbol for growth, expanding from a center in ever-growing circular motions, a "contrary spiral" can be understood in two ways: as a process of gradual implosion, in which dispersed matter is attracted closer and closer towards a central point; or (in the sense, possibly implied in this cycle, of Creation climaxing in the Incarnation of the Son of God) as a metaphor for God's all-encompassing, loving embrace focusing on this small planet. And if a flash of lightning is a discharge of energy from a cloud towards the earth (or another cloud), an "inverted flash of lightning" might describe energy emitted by the earth and directed towards the atmosphere—again possibly a metaphor for the salvation of the entire universe that will emanate from the earth with the birth of Christ

Combining all these images, one finds that the message seems to allude to all that is incomprehensible: for our notion (immeasurable space and time), for our senses (the infinitely large and small), and for our logic (inverted motions of growth and energy discharge). This is not so much the Creation of the Book of Genesis, which describes the world in creation very much in terms of what we can see and grasp. The images used here reflect, rather, the account given at the beginning of the Gospel of John, where the Word is referred to as the origin of everything that was to be created. Messiaen's subheading confirms this understanding when he repeats and further specifies the wording of the title: "Through *'Him'* (the Word) all was made."

317

To depict the incomprehensible aspect of the Creation, Messiaen invents a long and very complex form, into which he incorporates almost all musical symbols used elsewhere in the cycle. There is no doubt which structural model the composer had in mind, thanks to both his frequent reference to the form in words and his generous marking with 'subject', 'counter-subject', 'inverted answer', etc.. He seems to have regarded this form as the only apt representation of the immensity of what God's Creation meant. Referring to the coming into being of everything—space, time, stars, and energy particles—he says: "Nobody can speak about this. That is why I have not spoken about it either... I have hidden behind a fugue."

This fugue, however, is in fact unusual in many respects. With regard to the transformation of the thematic material, it is most noticeable that the subject recurs only twice in its original shape; on all other occasions it undergoes many different and very drastic transmutations that, while derived from the basic pitch sequence, generate architectural forms of their own.

Another feature is most unusual: with regard to the overall layout of the piece, Messiaen uses a most striking device, that of an extended mirror effect evoked within the first 129 bars. Among the seven sections that can be distinguished here, the last three constiftute a complete retrograde of the initial three. The unusually extensive retrograde, ending in the single note behind the bar line that matches the single-note upbeat at the beginning of the piece, appears to be a symbol for those incomprehensible, reversed processes: the "contrary spiral" and the "inverted flash of lightning."

The palindrome with its seven structural components is followed by three further sections. Among them, the eighth section is a thirty-bar canon, referred to by Messiaen (in the Author's Note) as a "mysterious stretto." The ninth section quotes the *Thème de Dieu* in *fff*, and juxtaposes it with a new theme, designated as *Thème d'amour*, (Theme of Love). Finally, the tenth section serves as a coda in which, as Messiaen advises us in the score, *La création chante le thème de Dieu*—the Creation itself now sings the theme of God's all-encompassing Love!

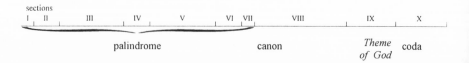

sections									
I	II	III	IV	V	VI	VII	VIII	IX	X

palindrome   canon   *Theme of God*   coda

The graph above gives an overview of the entire piece; proportions follow written note values, not real-time, sounding values (and much less numbers of bars):[147] The fugue is generated from a subject whose pitches (D♯, E, F♮, F♯, A♮, A♯, B, C) represent Messiaen's mode 4 in its fifth transposition. Mode 4, as the previous piece (*The Son Contemplating the Son*) has shown, serves as the musical symbol for the WORD INCARNATE. Just as, at the inception of the Gospel of John, the beginning of all things was manifest in the *Word* and the Creation of the world took its course from there, so it is also in this Creation piece, which is generated from a tonal representation of the *Word*.

The sequence in which the eight pitches of the mode appear in the subject is noticeable for three details, namely their tonal, rhythmic, and registral organization. A surprisingly strong sense of tonality is established through the return, at the end of the phrase, to the initial pitch D♯. In the subject's original shape, heard in the left hand, bars 1-3d, 43-45d, and 59-61d, as well as inverted in the right hand, bars 7-9d and 59-61d, this impression of rootedness is further enhanced in that the phrase is launched from a ninefold repetition of its initial pitch, and in that the return to D♯ falls on the downbeat of the third bar. Furthermore, the sense of tonality is affirmed by the two notes of secondary importance. These two pitches, emphasized both by their ornamentation with grace-notes and by their structurally corresponding placement in a varied sequence (see e.g. bar 2: B and A♯), are clearly perceived as the minor sixth and

[147]The proportion of this palindrome to the entire piece VI is an intriguing one.
* The conventional method of basing any assessment on the number of bars (129 out of a total of 231) would seem rather irrelevant in a work where almost each bar contains a different number of notes. (For an easy and convincing proof, see bar 2, which is 21 times as long as bar 1!)
* A second strategy, based on the number of sixteenth-notes in the respective sections, i.e. on the basic value of the additive rhythm, comes closer to a meaningful answer. This approach yields a seemingly different proportion, whereby the palindrome takes hardly more than half the "space" of the entire piece.
* Finally, in a third step that takes the required tempo changes into account, the proportion is yet different: the approximately 3 minutes and 45 seconds of real playing time for the palindrome constitute much less than half of the total time for this piece, which lasts for at least 8'40" but, depending on how long one pauses on the *fermata lunga* at the end, can easily extend to nine minutes. (This leads to an interesting consideration for performers. Knowing to what extent Messiaen's music is rich in symbolism, the case could be made to plan for a rendition—and thus especially time the *fermata* accordingly—that places the end of the palindrome at the point of the golden section (after roughly two fifth) within the entire piece.

fifth respectively of either a minor or a Phrygian tonality on D♯.[148] As for the rhythm, it is in sixteenth notes, interrupted by sixteenth rests, and creates a distinct metric sense in that all tonally important events fall on stronger beats. Finally, the register is low and the range narrow; the subject's original shape does not include a single octave displacement.

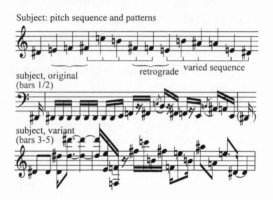

(To show, as a contrast, just one of the many variants: the subject's first transformation, heard in the right-hand part of bars 3-5, uses a rhythm encompassing four different note values and three kinds of syncopation. Furthermore, not only is the initial note dispersed over three octaves, but every consecutive semitone step is also split by octave displacement.)

The counter-subject, introduced against the subject's very first entry, consists of two components: a tritone (D-G♯) and a three-part sequence of a three-note group. The group is devised as a chromatic cluster with octave displacement of the central note. The tritone subsequently takes on a life of its own, outside the counter-subject, serving for the remainder of the first section as a phrase-ending particle; see bars 6 and 12. (It seems interesting that both the tritone and the first three-note group are separated from what follows by considerable rests—as if the two source elements were to be set off clearly and distinctly.) In terms of spiritual symbolism, the tritone often stands for that which is abstract and neutral; it is the only interval that remains "untouched" when stood on its head. The threefold occurrence of a three-note group, on the other hand, has a

---

148 D♯ minor   =   D♯ E♯(=F)F♯ ... A♯ B ...
    D♯ Phrygian =   D♯ E   F♯ ... A♯ B ...
The subject's initial chromatic ascent D♯ E F F♯ is a combination of the two. D♯ minor is, of course, directly related to F♯ major, Messiaen's tonality of GOD'S LOVE.

strong Trinitarian connotation, once again reminding us that Messiaen conceives of the Creation here, in the cycle dedicated to the twenty contemplations of the Infant Jesus, in relation to the birth of the Son of God.

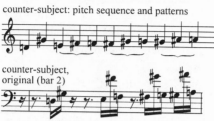

counter-subject: pitch sequence and patterns

counter-subject, original (bar 2)

Of the three sections that recur in retrograde, each is unique in design and material.

The **first section** (bars 1-12) is comprised of two corresponding segments: bars 7-12 repeat bars 1-6 in an intricate combination of inversion, variation and continuation.

- Subject and counter-subject are inverted with regard to both the texture and the outline, and uses the tritone as the interval from which the mirroring takes place; compare bars 1/2 with bars 7/8.
- The subject's rhythmically and registrally distorted first variant, on the other hand, does not partake of the same degree of inversion but recurs in the same voice as it was first heard (the right-hand part). While its interval sequence is literally inverted, the rhythm is very much modified, recognizable more intuitively than on close inspection. (The rudimentary middle voice with its chromatically descending steps, heard in bars 4/5, does not recur.)
- The figure underlying the same bars in the lowest register (cf. left hand, bars 9-12 with bars 3-6) is conceived as a continuing development rather than as an inversion. Like a typical "accompaniment figure" it builds on a one-bar pattern. This particular pattern is, however, a compressed version of the subject's original shape: the twelve sixteenths of bar 3 differ from the preceding statement only in that the note repetition of the initial pitch and the rests are omitted. The process this one-bar pattern undergoes in the course of the section is linear through bars 3, 4, 5, 6, 9, 10, 11 and 12. It is an example of Messiaen's famous 'asymmetric growth': the downbeat note is lowered chromatically (from D♯ in bar 3 to G♯ in

bar 12); the two metrically emphasized notes together with their preceding graces remain stable, while all other notes (i.e. all metrically "light" notes) rise incrementally by a semitone in each bar.

-   The phrase-ending particle is inverted and extended, ascending now through more than one bar of alternating Ds and G♯s.

The **second section** (bars 13-42) also consists of two corresponding segments; the structural processes involved, however, are very different here.

-   Both subsections set out with the subject in three-part stretto canon, accompanied by *ostinato* figures in a fourth layer. The stretto canon in bars 13-20 encompasses three voices that can usefully be considered soprano, tenor, and bass. Their entries follow one another at the distance of an eighth-note, and present the subject from chromatically descending points of departure: from D♯, D and C♯ respectively. The rhythm is defined by three consecutive palindromes, i.e. Messiaen's symbols of THE ETERNAL. The *ostinato* figure, accompanying this first canon in what is heard as the alto voice, consists of ten sixteenth-notes in *legato*, repeated and then shifted in small, irregular steps up and down.

-   In the corresponding stretto canon of bars 26-33, soprano, alto, and tenor enter at a distance of a quarter-note each, and present the subject from D♯, G♯ and D respectively, i.e. from the keynote and the two notes forming the counter-subject's opening tritone. The rhythmic shape of each voice here is that known from piece V of the *Vingt regards sur l'Enfant-Jésus, The Son Contemplating the Son*: four three-note palindromes followed by a vectorial five-note group, i.e. Messiaen's rhythmic symbol of the MANIFESTATION OF THE ETERNAL IN TIME.

-   The two canons, corresponding in their texture (of accompanied three-part stretto) as well as in their position within the section (opening the two similarly designed halves) thus stand symbolically for the two mirroring aspects of the Creation: THE ETERNAL, which initiates the creative process, and THE MANIFESTATION OF THE ETERNAL IN TIME, as which the composer sees Christ's Incarnation in particular, but also the divinity of that which has been created.

- The accompaniment of this second canon comprises two *ostinato* patterns. One consists of six three-note chords in *staccato* (repeated twice, see bars 26-28d and, transposed, bars 30m-32m). The other appears in two-part setting, with a chromatically rising upper voice and small consecutive bifurcations added in the lowest part, creating intervals from the semitone to the perfect fifth.
- Both subsections end with highly unusual superimpositions in volume (and thus, metaphorically speaking, in space). The countersubject, in three-part *unison* and *ff* here, interlocks with homophonic five-chord progressions[149] in *p*. The complete countersubject, in its original pitch sequence but varied with regard to rhythm and register, is heard in bars 21/22/24; the inversion, incomplete, in different rhythm and even more chopped up, appears in bars 34/36/38/39/41. While a mere cursory glance at the score may deceive one into reading this as one element cutting into the other, the hanging ties (see bars 22, 34, 36, 39, 41) show that Messiaen had in mind a tiered texture of what could be described as simultaneously unfolding realities. Significantly, the rhythmic shape of the counter-subject fragments—hardly perceptible owing to the insertions with other material—is once again that of rhythmic palindromes:

bars 21-25:

bars 34-42:

The fugue's **third section** is tripartite; its first and third subsections quote the subject in its original melodic guise with, in addition, one other variant, and thus act as a frame.

[149]Throughout this investigation, I have chosen no to deal with aside Messiaen's *Theme of chords*, which is actually wrapped into this five-chord figure in the two final chords. While it is obvious that these chords, as Messiaen himself has stated and Aloyse Michaely has shown in detail, pervade the entire cycle, it seems to remain unclear what the *Theme of chords* represents on the spiritual level. I have been unable to find any hint for a meaningful interpretation either in the score, or in Messiaen's writings (within the score and elsewhere), or in secondary sources. The reason why I neglect the *Theme of chords* is thus not that suggested by other scholars, viz. the impossibility for these chords to be consciously perceived. The same holds true for many of the other symbols—large-scale retrogrades, extended rhythmic palindromes, complex canons, to name just a few—which nevertheless carry important messages.

- At the beginning of the section, in bars 43/44, we hear the subject in double octaves from D♯, complete with its counter-subject, which also appears in its original shape and tonal frame. The complementing phrase presents the subject's pitches, in almost even rhythmic spacing and each preceded by a chromatic slide, in a large wave that descends through six octaves, rises again and ascends even higher before it levels out. The accompaniment is not derived from the counter-subject but instead from the five-chord sequence that was heard interlocking with it in the previous section,[150] and the following three bars play freely with these same chords.

- At the other end of the section, in bars 59-61, the subject's two versions appear as a hardly perceptible two-part stretto of inversion (as before from the tritone) and original (from G♯ and with fewer note repetitions on the initial pitch).

- The central portion of this section spans bars 50-58; it is laid out in a complex texture of three independent strands:

  * In the lowest strands, a double-octave fragment of the subject (pitches 4-14) appears in the rhythmic guise of two mirrored segments followed by a gradually increasing tail.

    This subject fragment undergoes a gradual process of 'asymmetric growth'—a process irregular in itself here, which is new in this cycle. Throughout the eight transformations, the first, fifth and sixth notes, i.e. F♯, F, and E, remain stable, while the three notes between them rise consecutively and the two notes following the stable ones fall. The three concluding notes, however, change their direction halfway through the segment, and the final note starts as a stable keynote D♯ but later embarks on a chromatic descent.

  * In the uppermost strand, a rhythmically palindromic version of the subject is buffered by shorter free variants, ever more abridged and finally even "eating away" from both sides of the

---

[150]Compare   bar 45, 1st to 4th sixteenth, with bar 23 etc., first chord;
                       bar 45, 5th to 6th sixteenth, with bar 23 etc., second chord;
                       bar 45, 7th to 10th sixteenth, with bar 23 etc., third chord;
                       bar 45, 11th to 13th sixteenth, with bar 23 etc., fourth chord;
                       bar 45, 14th to 17th sixteenth, with bar 23 etc., fifth chord.

statement itself
(see the subject
in bars 50/51,
52/53, 54/55, 55/56, and truncated in bars 56/57).

* The middle layer connects back to the fugue's second section by quoting irregular fragments of the bifurcating *ostinato* figure from the second canon.

Section III is thus closely related to section I, both in that it takes up the original shape of subject and counter-subject that have been abandoned in section II, and in that its central portion recalls the device of 'asymmetric growth' used extensively in the initial section but not in the second. From the preceding second section, two details are retained, which will prove important carriers of meaning throughout this piece: the five-chord motif (introduced in block-chord version in bars 23/24, and taken up in different versions in bars 45/46 and 47-49), and the fact that the subject is conceived as a rhythmic palindrome and thus reminiscent of the palindromes in the canons. Here, however, the entire phrase is captured in one single palindrome, reminding us once again that the Word ("Through Him [the Word] All Was Made") is *eternal*.

Reading only some of the multiple spiritual messages contained in the third section, one finds expressions of the idea of "vertical expansion vs. horizontal shrinking; increasing depth vs. dispersion." Furthermore, its seems intriguing that the nine modified repetitions of the subject fragment in the left hand are out of synchronization with the five repetitions of the palindromic subject statement in the right hand. Without wanting to overstretch the hermeneutic importance of details, it comes to mind that Messiaen wishes to give a musical depiction of an essential trait of all Creation: it is both timeless (sharing in the eternal qualities of its Creator) and time-dependent (as a manifestation in our mortal realm). While there is undoubtedly a higher order, we are likely, when trying to understand the purpose and inner logic of the Creation at any particular moment in time, to perceive these dual aspects as unsynchronized and extremely confusing—as confusing as bars 50-58 of the sixth "Regard" must appear to the unsuspecting listener.

The **fourth section**, marked *Milieu* (middle; a term referring to its position within the large-scale palindrome), contains a musical representation of the very small and the very large, of the "galaxies and photons"

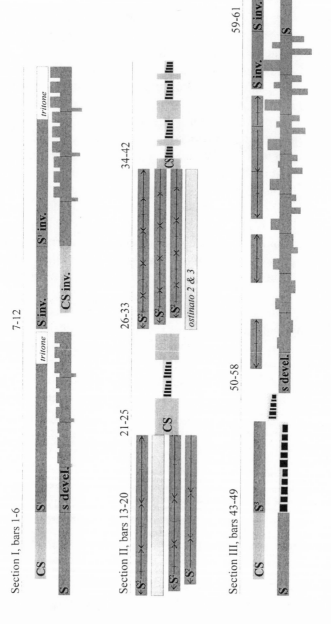

Section I, bars 1-6

7-12

CS   S'   S inv.   *trione*   S' inv.   *trione*

S   s devel.   CS inv.

Section II, bars 13-20

21-25   26-33   34-42

S²   S'   CSI

S²   CS   S'

S²   *ostinato 2 & 3*

Section III, bars 43-49

50-58   59-61

CS   S'   s devel.   S inv.   S inv.

S   S

Section IV, bars 62-68

CS

59-61

Section V, bars 69-88 (retrograde of section III)

Section VI, bars 88-117 (retrograde of section II)

Section VII, bars 118-129 (retrograde of section I)

the composer mentions in his subheading. In terms of the material employed, the seven bars go directly back to the second section whose two halves, as expounded above, end with statements of the counter-subject interrupted by (or overlayered with) the five-chord motif.

The contrast established there is magnified here. What in section II appears as a dynamic juxtaposition of *ff* (for the fragments of the counter-subject) and *p* (for the five-chord motif) becomes *fff* vs. *pp* here; where in section II both components are rhythmically based on sixteenth-notes, section IV presents strictly and consistently opposed values (thirty-second notes for the counter-subject fragments, sixteenth-notes for the five-chord motif). While in section II, the counter-subject is perceived as overlayered or, at worst, temporarily interrupted, continuing its course through and over the soft motif in the other layer without being deterred or thwarted, in section IV the counter-subject is aborted as an effect of the overwhelmingly expansive intrusion, and has to fight its way gradually, in several attempts, until it can finally be heard in its entirety.

The progression to that goal is rich in symbolism.
- The two-part *unison* statement of the counter-subject, six octaves apart (!), is launched in bar 62 with pitches 1-3 (of the total of 11 pitches in the original).

  Bar 63 presents an insertion into this material: a two-part canon in which each hand plays the broken-up version of the five-chord motif introduced in bars 45/46, complemented with a long extension here. The distance between the two entries is one sixteenth, the total length of the sixteenths in bar 31.
- The four bars that follow repeat and modify the dichotomy in two pairs:
  * bar 64 restates pitches 1-5 of the counter-subject; bar 65 interrupts with a slightly shortened version of the canon, now with the left hand entering not one but two sixteenths after the right, in a bar with a total of 29 sixteenths;
  * in bars 66/67, the counter-subject fragment has grown to seven pitches and the five-chord canon is further abridged, to a bar of 23 sixteenths in which the second entry follows the first after three sixteenths.
- Finally in bar 68, the counter-subject's entire eleven-pitch series is completed—and this completion concludes the section.

The numbers used here seem irregular and arbitrary only at first sight. The fact that, regarding the numbers of pitches from the counter-subject, the sequence is 3-5-7-11 (i.e. without the number 9 that would have appeared logical) and, with regard to the number of sixteenths in the five-chord bars, 31-29-23, is meaningful. It is intriguing to realize that all are prime numbers, whereas the omitted figures 9, 27 and 25 as well as all even numbers constitute compound figures, multiples of smaller numbers. Those compound numbers, Messiaen argued at some point, are not "originally created" but derived, whereas prime numbers stand for "genuine creation" (not so much Messiaen's but God's).

The graphic illustration on the preceding pages (pages 326/327) depicts the structural layout of the seven-section palindrome, with some of the components represented as recurring shapes.[151]

Messiaen describes the **eighth section**, i.e. the section following the long and complex palindrome after a *fermata* (bars 130-160), as a "mysterious stretto." Before attempting to approach the mystery, let us take a close look at what happens.

Rhythmically, the section consists exclusively (!) of sixteenth-notes, which pulsate without cessation and longer than we are normally able to follow such temporally unstructured information. In terms of speed, the section is laid out as a kind of broken curve. The first half begins in a slower tempo (Messiaen specifies dotted eighth = 60) and accelerates gradually up to 108, i.e. to almost twice the tempo; the second half begins moderately at 80 but approaches its end via the successive indications *ralentir un peu* (bar 155), *rall.* (bar 158), *rall.* and *rall. molto* (bar 160)—i.e. a very insistent marking for a powerful slowdown. In terms of dynamics, the entire section is held together by a single, very long rise in tension, from *pp* (bar 130), through repeated *crescendo* indications to *più f* (bar 142), followed by further repeated *crescendo* reminders, and leading up to *fff* (bar 161).

With regard to these three external features alone, the section thus encompasses three images:
- the steadiness of the pulsation,
- the vectorial progressiveness of increasing volume, and
- the broken curve of tempo development.

[151] It must be stressed that, in the interest of graphic clarity, the proportions from one section to the other are somewhat distorted. In actual fact, the dimensions of the seven sections that together form the large-scale palindrome are

	I	II	III	IV	V	VI	VII
in sixteenth counts:	120	188	301	96	301	188	120
in playing time circa:	21"	35"	50"	15"	50"	35"	21"

In terms of the tonal organization, this very long stretto is based on the fugue's subject in its various transformations and "asymmetric growth" processes. The first half of the section presents the subject alone, in fifteen beats that represent the pitches

1 1 1, 2 3 4, 5 6 7, 8 9 10, 11 12 13.

The vertical distortion in the subsequent eleven bars lowers the first pitch (in chromatic steps), raises pitches 2-9 (also in chromatic steps) and retains pitches 10-13 unchanged.

The second half of section VIII juxtaposes two different transformations of the subject, one of them in double octaves, the other thickened with inconsistent numbers of additional notes. In the lower register, a double-octave version of the subject repeats asymmetric-growth process in twelve steps witnessed in the first half of the section. In the upper register, a subject inversion of twenty-three beats (with an initial elevenfold repetition of the first pitch; note the prime numbers!) undergoes the same vertical distortion, albeit in inversion: the first pitch ascends and pitches 2-9 descend by chromatic increments, while pitches 10-13 remain stable. From one to three voices accompany this longer, right-hand version, exhibiting various short arrows of chromatic assent or descent. Regarding the interaction of the two strands, the different lengths of the two transformations (23 vs. 15 sixteenth) are responsible for ever different vertical encounters; another result is the fact that the longer version does not get to complete its full (twelve-part) circle of transformations.

The arrival of performance indications requesting a slowdown constitutes a codetta with regard to the shorter left-hand transformation, concluded in bar 153. This codetta now juxtaposes seven seven-beat partial statements in the bass, further subjected to asymmetric growth and thus widely stretched (often across the upper part; see e.g. in bar 156, 158, 160), with gradually diminishing transformations in the upper register (see, in bars 154-160, versions with 16, 15, 14 and 13 beats respectively).

The **ninth section** (bars 161-204) comprises three subsections, laid out almost identically. The thematic material of the fugue seems pushed to the background in favor of the *Thème de Dieu*, the five-chord motif, and a new theme, called *Theme d'amour*.

The initial phrase of the *Theme of God*, in the original tonal context of F♯ major but now in *fff* and enveloped in toccata passages, appears in half-notes on the downbeats of bars 161-164. The final F♯-major chord, which one expects to complete the phrase, is substituted by the first chord of the *Theme of Love* on the downbeat of bar 170. The chords surrounding each of the *Theme-of-God* chords, in toccata-like fashion and with dramatic *crescendo molto* and *pressez* (i.e. a powerful increase in volume along with an increase in tempo), derive from the by now familiar five-chord motif. As in all instances before, this motif is overlaid over an ongoing thematic process; but while it was first heard (in bars 23/24 etc.) in a very high register, and later (bars 63 etc.) in a large wave across the keyboard, it recurs here in very low register.

At this point, Messiaen gives us—for the first time in this piece—an opportunity to relate the overlay of different material with the five-chord motif to a symbolic message. Under the heading for this section, which reads *Victorieux et agité*, the composer reveals *"La face de Dieu derrière la flamme et le bouillonnement"* as his spiritual image. The vision of God's face "behind the flame," or His presence perceived through boiling waters, is reminiscent of the theophanies of the Old Testament, where God appears mostly through a consuming fire or flame[152] or amidst churning water.[153] These elements, violently consuming and engulfing from the human perspective, represent God's chosen way to mark His communication with His creatures. By extension, the chords that Messiaen uses to depict these images may thus stand, in the piece describing God's Creation, for God's continued but veiled presence on earth.

The chords following the *Theme-of-God* climax in bars 165-169 play around the fifth chord and its distortions and lead to a second symbol important in this context: a short theme named *Theme of Love*. Back in tempo after this slightly slower gesture, Messiaen concludes the subsection with a bar featuring in the bass the first twelve pitches of the subject in regular sixteenth-notes, in accented *ff* and octave displacements that stretch each of the original semitones to a distorted octave.

The pitch content of the *Theme of Love* does not stem from any of the modes but presents an example of bilateral symmetry:

F♯ G♯AA♯B|CC♯DD♯ E♯

This *Theme of Love* shares with the *Theme of God* two essential traits: the melodic beginning on A♯ in the top voice over A♯ in the lowest voice, and the conclusion on the F♯ major chord with added sixth. These

---

[152]See Deut. 4, 24 (cf. Heb 12,29) and 4,36; psalms 18,8ff, 68,8-9, 77,18-19, 97, 3-5.

[153]See Hab. 3, 15: "You tread the sea with your steeds amid the churning of the deep waters."

shared features, together with the allusion to the concept of "bilaterality", invites an interpretation of Messiaen's *Theme of Love* as a symbol for the human LOVE OF GOD, as well as the love of one another. Compare the two groups of symbols:

A♯

1: attribute	symbol	musical category	appearance
GOD'S LOVE	*Theme of God*	*thematic phrase*	*horizontal*
	F♯ major+sixth	*chord*	*vertical*
	F♯ major	*tonal context*	*overall*
	mode 2	*pitch content*	*overall*
	A♯	*predominant pitch*	*at the beginning and the end of the Theme of God; at the begin ning and the end of the piece*

2: attribute	symbol	musical category	appearance
LOVE OF GOD	*Theme of Love*	*thematic phrase*	*horizontal*
	F♯ major + sixth	*chord*	*vertical*
	A♯ melodic focus	*pitch*	*top voice*

Since the melodic beginning with A♯ and the conclusion in an F♯-major chord with added sixth characterize both attributes, these symbols will from here onwards simply be referred to as the "note of love" and "chord of love" respectively. (For the same spiritual context in yet different thematic surroundings, we may also refer back to the use of the pitch A♯ and the F♯-major chord with added sixth in IV, *The Virgin's Contemplation*.)

The entire subsection—the original *Theme-of-God* phrase with its overlaid "flame-and-churning-water" chords, the *Theme of Love* and the subject statement in the bass—is sequenced twice. The *Theme of God* thus appears in the other two transpositions of mode 2 (see the downbeats of bars 172-175 [+183] and 185-188 [+196]), providing a 'complete' manifestation of the modal symbol of GOD'S LOVE. Extensions happen in the chords veiling the climax (see the additional bars 176/177 and 169-195) as well as, towards the end of the section, in the threefold, rhythmically augmented statement of the *Theme of Love* and the subsequent fivefold subject statement.

Attempting to read the composer's underlying theology for this section, one can observe the following: the Creation is not only an act of the Word. GOD'S LOVE, communicated to humans through flames and churning water in a threefold (and modally 'complete') way, in turn generates the human potential for love, particularly the potential for the LOVE OF GOD, and thus fulfills the message of the Word.

The final, **tenth section** (bars 205-231) is conceived as a coda to the entire fugue. It is set off from the preceding section by a quarter-note rest, visually emphasized in that the rest occupies a bar all of its own. This, as Messiaen's pedal marking makes very clear, is not a pause or suspension on a overhanging sound but a bit of empty space. The new section is further set apart by the introduction of the F♯-major key signature, one of the tonal symbols of GOD'S LOVE.

The coda encompasses several subsections; these seem to give a summary glance back over the material most prominent in this piece. Messiaen's labeling in the score is again very explicit here.

Bars 205-210 carry, underneath the left-hand staff, the sentence *La création chante le thème de Dieu*—the Creation sings the *Theme of God*; in the "Note de l'Auteur," the wording appears expanded to *La création reprend et chante le thème de Dieu*—the Creation begins anew and sings the *Theme of God*. One is reminded here of the last of Messiaen's subheading sentences: "... all of a sudden, the creation reveals to us the luminous shadow of his Voice." Slowed down to about two-thirds of the previous "victorious" tempo, the two hands each present the chords of the initial phrase from the *Theme of God*, in regular sixteenth values and in stretto canon. The first four-chord quotation in each hand comes with an expressive *crescendo* towards an accented climax; after that, the chords just play along and finally even give up their thematic sequence:

```
bars           205                        206
r. h.  1 2 3 4, 1  2 3 4 1 2 3 4 1 2 3 1 2 3 2 3
l. h.     1 2 3  4, 1  2 3 4 1 2 3 4 1 2 3 1 2 3 2
```

The stretto phrase is rounded off with a six-beat bar that continues both the rhythmic (sixteenth) pulse and the (*ff*) level of intensity, but contrasts the imitative texture with homophonic chords, the (unmarked) transparent *portato* articulation with accented *staccato* attacks under a whole-bar pedal, and the register in the two octaves above middle C with a shift and expansion into frequencies up to an octave higher.

The entire phrase—the stretto canon of the *Theme-of-God* chords and its homophonic conclusion—recurs then in varied format. The canon is transposed down a whole tone, while the third and fourth chords in the right-hand part and the third chord alone in the left-hand part, previously simple (albeit in part enharmonically notated) major triads, are expanded to seventh chords. The complementing homophonic bar is not transposed or altered, but appears in retrograde. This subsection of the coda thus takes up the quotation of the first *Theme-of-God* phrase from the preceding ninth section, subjects it to the "mysterious stretto" from the eighth section, and in the treatment of the complementary bar recalls the device of the retrograde from the larger palindrome contained in the seven initial sections of the piece.

Bars 211-220 are based on a reminiscence of the *Theme of Love* which, like the *Theme of God* before, is rhythmically simplified to even sixteenth-notes. The four chords appear, in its original tonal frame, in the left hand (see bar 211), and are then repeated twenty-five times. The fifteenth appearance (bar 214) shows the first irregularity with a repetition of the third chord; components 20, 23 and 25 further expand the internal and external repetitions within the quotation. In all these cases, the chord that represented the climax within the *Theme of Love* is enhanced with an accent. Meanwhile in the right-hand part, small bifurcating figures recall one of the *ostinato* patterns in the second section; but while both voices move there (cf. bars 28-33), only one of the parts descends chromatically here, leaving the other to establish an almost continuous pedal-note on C♯. But as if that was not enough, those pitches that mark the interruptions of this pedal in the uppermost register create a melodic line of their own, in metric independence from both the *Theme-of-Love* variation in the lower part and the bifurcating figures in the middle of the texture. While the rhythm of these treble notes is intriguing in itself, the pitches confirm the general spiritual message towards which this piece is heading. With repeated but exclusive use of D♯, F♯, A♯, and C♯, they present the seventh-chord version of the F♯-major chord with added sixth, i.e. of the *chord of love*—the chord that was first heard in *The Father's Contemplation* (particularly as the protracted final chord of the initial piece in the cycle) and found to figure also prominently in the *Theme of Love*.

Theme of Love

This subsection concludes, *Plus lent*, with a bar featuring the fifth and fourth chords of the five-chord motif (i.e. Messiaen's *Theme of chords* in its most concentrated form) with transpositions on the intervals of the augmented triad. The nature of these transpositions, which Messiaen uses most prominently only for themes built on his mode 2 (compare, above all, the hunting song in X, *The Spirit of Joy Contemplating the Infant Jesus*), relates this bar to the spiritual message of GOD'S LOVE, while the chords themselves, as we have learned from the composer's verbal clue in the preceding section, stand for the "flame and churning water" behind which God is hidden when speaking directly to humans, and by extension for His communication with His creatures.

The second subsection (bars 222-228) is rhythmically a direct replica of section IV, the *"Milieu"* that forms the center of the large-scale palindrome. Bars with increasing number of thirty-second notes (3, 5, 7, 11) alternate with bars with decreasing numbers of sixteenth-notes (31, 29, 23). Material and texture, however, are different. The three initial chords of the *Theme of God* in *ff* are interspersed with long repetitions of the fifth chord from the five-chord motif, attacked in *ff* but then lingering in protracted *pp*.

After another quarter-note rest, once again emphasized by its notation in a bar of its own and thus creating the visual impression of announcing a coda within the coda, the subject is heard for the last time. The extent (twelve pitches only), the rhythmic regularity (all eighth-notes here), and the nature of the octave displacement link this version to the one introduced in the ninth section; the two-part stretto canon (audibly different from the three-part stretto canon usually employed for the subject) recalls the two-part stretto canon of the five-chord variation in the fourth (*milieu*) section—the texture that, in the preceding bars, is substituted for a simple, homophonic chord repetition. The coda closes with a bar in explicit *accelerando*: very moderate - hurry - very lively. The effect (though not the physical reality) of the arpeggiated ascent that begins with an F♯-major chord but eventually encompasses all twelve pitches, is that of "F♯ with overtones." This chord hangs under a *fermata lunga*—possibly until the sounds dies away.

The spiritual messages included in the three sections following the palindrome are manifold; again, only some can be mentioned here.

The "mystery" Messiaen referred to when writing about the eighth section seems to expose, musically one after the other, the two dimensions of all that God has created. By introducing a rhythmically extremely regular version of the subject (in sixteenth-notes, grouped in five batches of three) Messiaen concentrates our attention once more on the creative power of the *Word.* The absolute orderliness of the transformative process that the subject undergoes in the first stretto canon symbolizes the lawfulness of the Creation. The three-part stretto with its metrically logical entries, its (asymmetric but utterly foreseeable) vertical growth, and its unrelenting, gradual increase of volume seems to remind us of the inevitability of (spiritual) growth. The following, irregular stretto seems to view the same truth from another angle. The known, lawful, fifteen-beat version of the subject that coincides with the length of the chosen bar and undergoes the same growth process as in the preceding stretto, is juxtaposed with the aspect of uniqueness (expressed in the prime-number extension of 23 beats in the treble-register subject). All the while, the volume continues to increase. However, at the very moment when the completion of the twelfth transformation of the regular version reveals the incongruence of lawfulness with uniqueness—determination and freedom, so to speak—the SEVEN-fold transformation of a SEVEN-beat version in the bass, juxtaposed with decreasing extension in the treble version and powerfully decreasing tempo, reminds us of the possible sinfulness that might result from the tension between obeisance and realization of uniqueness.

The ninth section appears, in many ways, as a reaction to this dilemma. Both Messiaen's wording "God's face behind the flame and the churning water" and his musical depiction with the *Theme of God* leading to the *Theme of Love* speak of communication between the Creator and His creatures. The completion achieved in the appearance of the material in all three transpositions of mode 2 (the tonal symbol for GOD'S LOVE), in conjunction with the version of the subject in exactly TWELVE beats, the numerical symbol for completeness, expresses the composer's conviction that regardless of human shortcomings, God's love will fulfill the design of His Creation.

The tenth section can then be seen as presenting a summary of these two aspects on yet a higher level. GOD'S LOVE, as expressed in the *Theme-of-God* excerpt, sounds in stretto canon, reminiscent of the "mysterious stretto" of the eighth section that exposed the human dilemma between lawfulness and uniqueness. The human LOVE OF GOD, represented as multiple repetitions of the *Theme of Love* in a horizontally expanding pattern, is topped with GOD's LOVE as symbolized by the melodic rendition of the *chord of love* in the treble. We are once again reminded that GOD's LOVE embraces "galaxies and photons" when the overlay of that which has been created very small with that which has been made very large sounds in the musical form of the *Theme of God* behind flame and water. The final bars link the *Word* by whom all has been made, in its entirely regular and (with twelve beats) "complete" version, to F♯ major, the tonality of GOD's LOVE.

La parole toute-puissante   (Messiaen, *Vingt regards*, XII)

(Cet enfant est le Verbe qui soutient toutes choses par la puissance de sa parole.)

Best known for its *ostinato* bass pattern that repeats the same chromatic three-note cluster in a pattern of a rhythmic palindrome, this piece is actually unusual on all levels.

To begin with, the title itself is only seemingly self-evident. While anybody brought up in the Christian tradition believes to have some understanding of what the phrase *the Almighty Word* means, the subheading immediately gives us pause. In a distinction that is so much easier in French than in English, Messiaen reflects on the various religious connotations of the term "word". When he writes, in the first half of the sentence, "This Child is the Word that sustains all things," he speaks in the language of the Gospel of John, and repeats what he says in many other places of his work: Jesus is, first of all, the Word Incarnate. In this sense, however, "the Word" is by no means an easy concept; it is neither open to sensual experience nor accessible through reason, but transcends all that we can grasp and, literally, precedes all that we think we can know. In the second half of the same subheading sentence, the composer avows that the Child sustains all things "through the power of His word." In this usage (French *parole*), the "word" has strong connotations of a commitment, a covenant, of "standing by one's word." A third meaning, suggested particularly in the mention of "power" and "sustains all things," points to the Creation as explained in Genesis I, a text that puts particular emphasis that it is God's "word" (in the sense of directed thought rather than in that of articulated sound), and not an act of the divine master sculpturer that causes things to come into being.

In this last sense, the piece is related to Messiaen's Creation piece, no. VI. Messiaen himself, whenever he mentions his fondness for number play, reminds us that TWELVE is two times SIX; thus XII, *The Almighty Word* is linked to VI, *Through Him All Was Made*. Since a thorough analysis will show that the play with numbers, and especially the varying play with the number 12, is indeed a crucial structural feature in this piece, it is worth remembering here that two other notions connected with it concern the concept of completion and the image of the Christ's twelve disciples. The first, the abstract notion of completion, can be seen as relating to the Incarnation of the Word in Jesus, in which God's Love finds its most complete and radical expression. The more concrete image of the twelve apostles supports the meaning of the "word" as commitment and covenant.

Musically, this piece does not employ any of the Messiaen's modes or any of the cyclical themes. Its link to the cycle's religious symbols consists in a tone cluster and a rhythm. The tone cluster, encompassing the three lowest notes on the keyboard (A♮/A♯/B), was first introduced (albeit in its four-note version with an additional C) at the boundary between the two halves of Mary's lullaby in *The Virgin's Contemplation* (see IV, bar 62), where it was interpreted as a symbol of awe—her awe when she begins to comprehend what fate God has laid out for His Son. It was heard again (this time in the three-note version) at the end of the *Virgin and Infant* quotation in *First Communion of the Virgin* (see XI, bar 20). Immediately after the *Almighty Word,* the cluster also features prominently in the refrain of XIII, *Christmas*.

The significant rhythmic pattern consists of a palindrome—in fact: *the* most perfect palindrome, as will be shown shortly—that, in conjunction with the rest that precedes it, recurs 21 times in absolute regularity.[154] As all rhythmic palindromes, it stands spiritually for timelessness or, as we said earlier, for THE ETERNAL, an obvious quality of God's Word. The particular five-part mirror-symmetrical rhythm is the same as that which constituted the initial segment of the first stretto canon in the Creation

---

[154]To be quite accurate: after twenty identical occurrences of the pattern (rest + rhythmic palindrome), the twenty-first is slightly irregular in that the final note breaks off after one sixteenth instead of its predetermined three-sixteenth value. While there is undoubtedly a practical reason, given the momentous final *crescendo* and the intended *secco* effect, one wonders whether Messiaen, so extremely conscientious in matters of symbolic messages, did not also wish to convey an abrupt ending here. In so doing he creates a reminder of the aspect that he so often renders with the French word *terrible*, and that, as in "awesome," is actually very much related to the main notion expressed in this piece.

piece (see VI, bars 13-15). Composed of 3+5+8+5+3 sixteenths, this pattern uses three numbers distinctly recognizable as stemming from the Fibonacci series—another reminder of perfect proportion. An additional aspect of these numbers is that they could be read as 8 (3+5) + 8 + 8 (5+3) = 24, a reading that reveals their connection to the number 12!

The rest that precedes the palindrome and forms part of the faithfully recurring larger unit counts seven sixteenths. This number is reminiscent of the other famous book given us by the apostle who has everything begin with "the Word," i.e. the revelation, or apocalypse, of Saint John. The emphasis is on what might be seen as the opposite to perfection, the failure of humankind in the face of God's act of love (the beast with seven horns, the seven vessels of God's wrath, the book with seven seals). The number also refers specifically to sins, as in "the seven mortal sins" and Mary Magdalene's "seven demons" that Jesus exorcises.

In the *Vingt regards*, Messiaen uses the number seven prominently in another piece dedicated to a very abstract notion, *The Exchange*. As is particularly evident in that earlier piece, Messiaen perceives the spiritual meaning of the 7 as composed of 3 + 4, or the Trinitarian and the human (earthly, material) components. This further stresses the relationship—given even in the case of wrath—between God and His often flawed children. In this context it is interesting that Messiaen allows the compound *ostinato* unit to recur exactly 21 times (3 x SEVEN), combining once again the aspect of divine perfection with that of human imperfection.

On the tonal level, the *Almighty Word* uses the TWELVE tones in the form of FOURTEEN (2 x SEVEN) "pitch personalities," distributed over THREE tonal layers and appearing in THREE distinct shapes. While there is no definite tonality, Messiaen centers the piece around TWO pitches, each of which is highlighted by appearing in TWO registers[155] and by being linked to the two tonal layers superimposed over the bass *ostinato* (see Ex. a in the annotated score excerpts on the next two facing pages). These features, and the inherent number play, deserve further investigation.

All twelve pitches appear throughout the piece, although not in any serial order. Ten of them appear only in one unchangeable form: as a double octave in a fixed register. The other two notes are devised with two forms each. D is heard not only in the lower register in which it opens the piece (see bars 1/2 and 10/11), but also an octave higher; in that position it is often preceded by a descending flourish (see bars 5, 8, 13, 18 etc.). A is employed not only melodically, as a double octave in the

---

[155]The *octava bassa* indication under the D in bar 36 is no doubt an error or misprint.

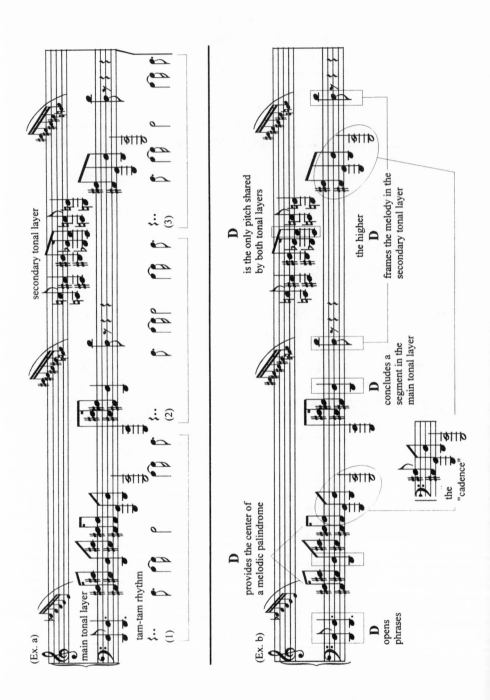

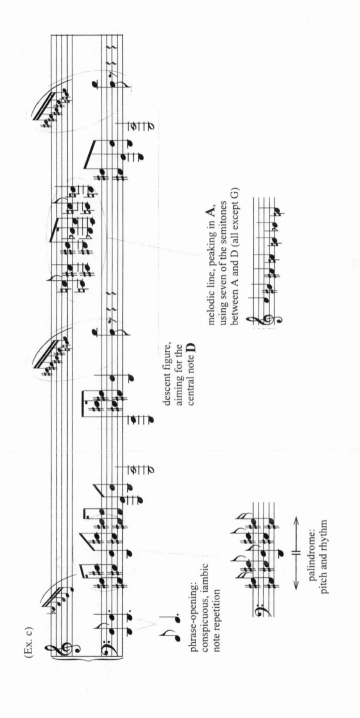

(Ex. c)

phrase-opening:
conspicuous, iambic
note repetition

descent figure,
aiming for the
central note **D**

melodic line, peaking in **A**,
using seven of the semitones
between A and D (all except G)

palindrome:
pitch and rhythm

treble-clef register (see bars 6, 14 etc.), but also as the root of the bass cluster.[156] The fourteen "pitch personalities" are thus the twelve pitches in their double-octave placement plus the higher D and the lower A.

The symbolic aspect of duality (here probably referring to the divine juxtaposed to the human, rather than to the dual nature of Christ) is expressed most visibly (and audibly) in the two preferred notes D and A. Messiaen highlights both not only by allowing each to generate two different shapes, but also by granting them command of different aspects of the piece.

- D is, in its iambic note repetition, very noticeable as the opening particle of the piece (see Ex. b). It is rendered even more conspicuous in that the initial octave, perceived as an anacrusis, is invariably granted a bar of its own. Any interpreter who took the initial octave as an upbeat in an incomplete bar will stand corrected at the discovery that the exact rhythmic pattern (1/8 + 3/8) recurs in bars 10/ 11, 16/17, 27/28 and 44/45. The composer distinguishes these section beginnings through the idiosyncratic use of his bar lines and thus establishes yet another tie to no. VI, in which the initial note of the fugue subject was similarly always given a bar of its own.

- D is also a regular appearance within the sequence of large leaps introduced in bars 2-5 and developed on several occasions later in the piece. Not surprisingly, the conclusion of this sequence is provided by the same lower octave D (see also in Ex. b).

- A, as was already mentioned, is the representative note in the bass cluster, and in that capacity the symbol of *awe*. The pitch gains structural importance when it replaces D in the opening iambus of the ("development") fourth section (see bars 27/28. Note that only the third section forgoes the note repetition in the characteristic opening component, and quotes the rhythm instead with a whole-tone step; see bars 16/17).

- The higher A is, however, most significantly distinguished through its melodic importance (cf. Ex. c). SEVEN times it is heard as the climax of a development that, in contrast to the large leaps mentioned earlier, moves predominantly in stepwise motion and

[156] I consider the chromatic cluster as something akin to a "noise on A" rather than as three distinct pitches. The following analysis corroborates the view that A♯ and B, although literally also notes in that cluster and thus used in double function in this piece, do not have a role that would justify such distinction.

small intervals (see the peaking A in bars 6, 14, 17, 28/29, 34, 41/42, 49). On THREE additional occasions, we hear this A as the resolution to an appoggiatura B (see the rhythmically identical note pairs in the middle of bar 30, towards the beginning of bar 48, and towards the end of the extremely long bar 49).

- The only pitch shared by the 'passages in large leaps' and the 'passages in small melodic intervals' is again the note D. Whenever it forms part of the tonal layer around the melodically leading A, it appears in its higher octave; whenever it serves additionally as a structurally significant component, it characteristically comes emphasized with the grace-note descent referred to above. (In this form it frames the melodic passage within the first section —see the score excerpt for details; it serves as a *caesura* in bars 15 and 29, as a conclusion of the secondary-layer melody in bars 18, 37 and 43.) The common meeaning associated with symbols of descent in the Christian context is that of God's coming down to earth, His entering the human realm.

- Back in the 'large leaps' on the tonal first layer, D is the original center of a pitch/rhythm palindrome in bars 2/3 (cf. Ex. c), and forms part of the "cadential" pattern introduced at the conclusion of the first phrase.

  * An identical repetition of the palindrome recurs in the second section (see bars 11/12) and in the (recap-like) fifth section (see bars 45/46); a developed form of the palindrome that integrates the cadential pitches is heard in the third section (see bars 18-26).

  * Identical recurrences of the cadential pattern can be found throughout the piece; the only significant variation is the switching of the second and third pitches (see e.g. in bars 35/36 where the sequence is A♯-D-G-C instead of A♯-G-D-C).

On THREE occasions, the cadential pattern in leaps unites with the structurally conclusive component on the secondary tonal layer, the grace-note descent leading to the higher octave D, to form a kind of double cadence. This occurs at the end of section I (bars 7-9), towards the middle of the long fourth section (bars 32/33) and, in multiple repetitions, at the end of the piece (bars 51-57).

The THREE different shapes of the pitch personalities can be detected at first glance: there are clusters, octaves, and descending grace-note groups. The fact, however, that the piece contains THREE tonal layers requires the observations expounded above to become evident. The main tonal layer is that grouped around the central D; it encompasses the palindrome (with A♯, C♯, and D) and the cadential pattern (with A♯, D, G, and C). The secondary tonal layer occupies the slightly more elevated register between the higher D and the melodically climactic A; it comprises SEVEN pitches (i.e. all semitones except for G. The additional B is exclusively used in pairing with A and thus serves to strengthen that note, rather than counting as an independent eighth pitch.) The third layer is, of course, taken up by the tam-tam cluster.

As I have attempted to show, the *Almighty Word* is densely symbolic. In terms of the allusions the piece evokes as part of the Messiaen's cycle, there are multiple references (verbal as well as musical through the unusual one-note bars) to piece VI, *Through Him All Was Made*; these reexamine, so to speak, the concept of God's Creation from the central tenet of the Almighty Word. The bass cluster infuses the piece with connotations established earlier in the cycle in the context of the "creation" of the child in Mary's womb, and stands for *awe*. The symbolism attached to the perfect rhythmic palindrome, that based on the golden-section sequence 3-5-8, speaks of the ETERNAL, with particular reference to things 'being in proportion'.

The two tonal layers may be read to stand for the divine (around the primary central note D) and the worldly (around the secondary tonal center A). The predominance on the main tonal layer of interval leaps that are large enough to be perceived as "daunting," combined with the conclusive cadence and the abstract palindrome, point further to symbolic representations of the divine, while the prevalence of small steps, widely known particularly since Bach to represent alternatively human humility, sinfulness and shame, or suffering, corroborates the link between the secondary tonal layer and the transient realm into which the Word is born. This secondary layer in its first appearance is framed by the D that is so characteristically highlighted by a grace-note descent. This further identifies the human realm: the central note of the objective, divine sphere "plunges" into the world of subjectivity.

In terms of the number play, the complete and the Trinitarian are pitted against the fallible. TWELVE tones, 2 x 12 = 24 rhythmic units in the palindrome, and the place in the cycle as no. XII (along with THREE tonal layers employing THREE distinct shapes of pitch personalities, THREE double cadences, etc.) stand against SEVEN pitches on the secondary tonal layer 14 = 2 x SEVEN pitch personalities, 21 = 3 x SEVEN manifestations of the *ostinato* pattern in the bass. The dualism of the divine and the human is expressed in the dual tonal center of D and A. In this dialectic, Messiaen stresses that what matters about the Almighty Word is not its abstract form and supreme power, but the way in which it touches us—in that it "sustains all things," acting not only as an original generating power, but also as a word given us, a promise in which we can trust.

Regard des Anges   (Messiaen, *Vingt regards*, XIV)

(Scintillements, percussions; souffle puissant dans d'immenses trombones; tes serviteurs sont des flammes de feu...- puis le chant des oiseaux qui avale du bleu, - et la stupeur des anges s'agrandit: car ce n'est pas à eux mais à la race humaine que Dieu s'est uni...)

A third perspective of the Word becoming flesh is given in the angels' contemplation of the Infant Jesus. While *Through Him* (the Word) *All Was Made* posited the coming into this world of the Word in the act of Creation itself, and *The Almighty Word* also emphasized the relationship between the generating power and humankind more than it reflected on the Incarnate One, *The Angels' Contemplation* questions the Incarnation itself. To appreciate the angle from which they view the new-born Child, we must forget much of what Christian art (not to speak of devotional objects) of the past 700 years have wanted us to believe. The angels here are far from those gentle, effeminate, jubilant creatures that praise and do not criticize. Quite on the contrary: these angels are, according to Messiaen, those depicted in Michelangelo's *Last Judgment*. Trombones, not harps are their instruments—instruments we associate not with praise but with the distinction between right and wrong, good and bad.

Throughout his work, Messiaen has depicted angels in various lights, from the pure, luminous beings symbolizing life after resurrection in *Les Corps glorieux* to the terrifying angel from the apocalypse. In the prefacing remarks to his *Quartet for the End of Time* he writes that he will never forget that principal person in his life (*ce personnage principal dans ma vie*), that mighty and luminous angel who announces the end of time, and he directs us to the tapestries of the apocalypse at the Castle of Angers for a visual depiction of such an angel.

The Bible speaks on several occasions (see Heb., Eph., 1 Peter) of the possibility that the angels may not have known of God's plan to send

His Son to earth, although Augustine and Thomas Aquinas believed differently. The distinction, however, is an important one, since it contrasts self-determined, critical and potentially insubordinate beings with subservient, largely decorative creatures.

How very seriously the composer takes God's angels becomes evident from another source. When pondering the concept of "communicable language," Messiaen calls angels the only beings who have the privilege of communicating among themselves without language and without any consideration of time and place (cf. his preface to the *Méditations sur le Mystère de la Sainte Trinité*.) Therein, he says, is a power that surpasses us completely, a faculty of transmission almost frightening. And, remembering the first and second of Rilke's *Duino Elegies*, he asserts that the German poet is justified in saying 'Tout ange est terrible!' (Every angel is awesome). The composer further quotes St. Thomas Aquinas's *Summa Theologiae* on the Language of the Angels (question 107): "If the angel, through his will, directs his mental concept in order to communicate it to another, immediately the latter perceives it: in this way the angel speaks to another angel." And, a little later, "the angelic idiom consists in one intellectual operation. Now the intellectual operation of the angel disregards time and place. That is why the diversity of time or the distance of place have not any function where both time and place are disregarded."

It is in light of this respect for the autonomy of the angels that this piece should be understood. These terrible, powerful beings, recognizing that God has chosen the human realm to incarnate His Son, are perplexed. As Messiaen had read in Marmion, they feel profoundly humiliated by the insight that they have been passed over. "Sparkles, percussion effects, powerful breath into immense trombones; your servants are flames of fire... then the song of birds that engulfs the blue—and the astonishment of the angels grows: for it is not with them but with the human race that God has united Himself..."

The piece is laid out in six stanzas followed by a coda; the stanzas are grouped into three longer and three slightly shorter ones, but the two groups are closely interrelated. The three initial stanzas can be viewed as consisting of three segments each that undergo different processes of growth. Of these, the first segment consists in itself of three components. What these three components have in common (and what prompts me to treat them as segments of a single larger idea) is that, unlike the other two components, they each remain unchanged throughout the piece, and together they seem to present a characterization of the angels rather than a reflection or action.

The first figure, component *a1*, appears as the immediate musical rendering of Messiaen's initial word: sparkles. Arpeggiated figures of five white keys in the right-hand part and five black keys in the left-hand part, occupying the same register and overlapping in contrary motion sound wild and puzzling. What we seem to hear are four identical bars with two rudimentary melodic lines, built by the outer voices, around an irregularly scintillating cluster in the center.

Component *a2*, spanning only two bars but sounding almost as long as *a1* owing to a greater number of beats and a much slower tempo, is launched by Messiaen's very abstract *Theme of Chords*. Interestingly, this theme, throughout the cycle heard in myriad transmutations, sounds here in the register and vertical arrangement that Messiaen's "Author's Note" gives as the original! What is more, this is the first appearance in the *Vingt regards* of the form in which the composer claims to have conceived the theme, i.e. as four four-note chords.[157] Messiaen seems to use the *Theme of Chords* in a way that points to the intermediate realm, the level between the divine and the human realms, to manifestations of God's power that are neither the Word itself nor humankind for whom the word is intended. The role of the angels is here being emancipated from mere onlookers at the manger to beings who have a say in the matter of the Incarnation of the Word.

The way in which this representation of the imposing angelic gaze progresses into the four chords that round out component *a2* is intriguing particularly from a rhythmic point of view. The strongly syncopated pattern in which the *Theme of Chords* is presented—each chord pair consists of a very short, accented first attack followed passively (under a slur) by a double-dotted lingering in the second attack—develops in two directions simultaneously. One can hear a stepwise contraction in the first attack of each pair, from the two written-out thirty-second values in the

---

[157]Many other transmutations split the pitches originally arranged as four four-note chords into six chords, or compress them into two, to name just those variations that are potentially recognizable for a listener. Pieces in the cycle in which the *Theme of Chords* appears in a form close to its supposed original are XV, *The Kiss of the Jesus-Child* (bars 73 and 78), and XVII, *Silence's Contemplation* (bars 41ff and 76ff). Note that the *Theme of Chords* does not appear at all in the first five pieces. It enters the cycle, albeit in a contorted form, in the Creation piece VI.

Theme of chords through the two *acciaccatura* attacks to the block appearance of the two final chords (ex. 1). At the same time, the two

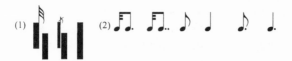

halves of bar 6 can also he heard as a progressive augmentation (or slackening) of the tight syncopations before (ex. 2). It is as though the angels were at the same time "pulling themselves together" and broadening their perspective (and acceptance) of the event. Dynamically, this process is appropriately expressed through gradual softening, indicated both by the transition from accents to the gentler emphasis of dashes and by a *diminuendo* marking.

After this highly articulated component in the central register of the keyboard, the two bars that follow could hardly present a more poignant contrast. A *tremolo* using two adjacent tritones in the highest ranges and *staccato* tritones in the lowest octave convey an effect of what Messiaen announced in his subheading as "percussion effects." In its repetitiveness these bars seem related to the "sparkles" of bars 1-4. At the same time, the *crescendo molto* launched from an initial *pp* makes this component *a3* sound utterly dramatic. Messiaen thus establishes a musical link between verbal terms: the seemingly innocently descriptive ideas of "sparkling" and "percussive," and the imposing declaration "Your servants are flames of fire."

If the *Theme of Chords* may be read as standing for the sagacity of the majestic angels (and thus for their interior attributes), the representations surrounding it of something sparkling and percussive probably allude more to their autonomy and imposing appearance (and thus to external traits).

As was mentioned earlier, these three segments of component *a* remain unchanged in themselves in the otherwise highly evolutionary stanzas 2 and 3. What happens, though, is that they are enriched by insertions, in such a way that the segment as a whole does, indeed, grow! Wedged between segments *a1* on one side and *a2/a3* on the other, we find an insertion in stanza 2 (2 x 5/8, see bars 23/24). This insertion recurs but is preceded by a second one, also ten eighth-notes long, in stanza 3 (see bars 49/50 for the reiterated insertion, preceded now by the material in bar 48). The contents of these insertions gives two messages. The only message in insert 1 and the more obvious one also in insert 2 is that of bird song—the expression of nature's joy over the birth of Christ (an admonishment to the angels or a manifestation of their generous feelings?) The other, somewhat hidden in the third voice of insert 2 (see the additional stems in the left hand of bar 48) contains, in its circling motion around the note C♯, a reminiscence of what our analysis of IV, *The Virgin's Contemplation*, revealed as Mary's apprehension of the suffering awaiting her son (compare this figure's pitch sequence C♯-D♯-C♮-C♯-D♯ with IV, bars 35/36 etc.: C♯-C♮-D♯-E-D♮-D♯-C♯).

The second segment in the original stanza (see bars 9-13) is based on a rhythm heard twice before in the cycle. Messiaen introduced the sequence, consisting of four palindromic groups of three values each followed by a tail in unidirectionally increasing values, in V, *The Son Contemplating the Son*. Sounding there in contrapuntal juxtaposition both with its augmentation by 150% and with the *The Father's Contemplation*, the characteristic rhythmic pattern was interpreted as a symbol for an aspect of Jesus in His two natures, as the MANIFESTATION OF THE ETERNAL IN TIME. In the immediately following VI, *Through Him All Was Made*, the same rhythm was heard stripped of its chordal richness and in a melodic shape very much leveled in comparison to the zigzag in V. This rhythmic pattern, which formed the second three-part canon (see VI, bars 26-33), introduces the concept of that which is eternal but manifests in time into Messiaen's interpretation of the Creation as a result of the generating powers of the Word.

Here, seen from the angel's perspective, the three-part canon is retained; each voice comes in the (very abstract) interval of a tritone, and all melodic (emotional) inflection has been abandoned. It is as though the composer sought to paint a musical image of angels, with eyes deformed by the inordinate strain,[158] reflecting the incomprehensible mystery of this Incarnation of the Eternal Word into the realm of mortality and time.

[158]See Claude Samuel, *Entretiens avec Olivier Messiaen* (Paris: Leduc, 1967), p. 17.

That they do indeed have difficulty grasping the full truth is also made musically evident. In stanza 1, the canon breaks off before any of the voices have completed the pattern. What we hear, then, is an acknowledgement of the *eternal* aspect, but an inability to fathom its *manifestation in time*.

By the time segment *b* recurs in stanza 2, however, the angels have apparently grown in understanding: all three voices get to complete the full pattern, and they even continue until the lowest has presented another instance of the initial palindrome (see bars 29-37). Finally in stanza 3, as if wanting to make up for their original lack of comprehension, the angels contemplate the mystery of the MANIFESTATION OF THE ETERNAL IN TIME long enough to allow two complete statements of the pattern in each voice (see bars 55-68).

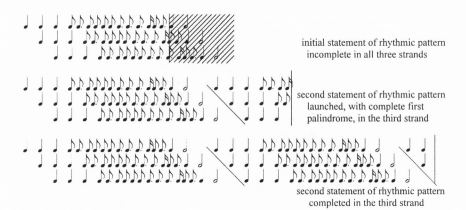

initial statement of rhythmic pattern
incomplete in all three strands

second statement of rhythmic pattern
launched, with complete first
palindrome, in the third strand

second statement of rhythmic pattern
completed in the third strand

Segment *c* is clearly the most striking among them all. The bass leads with a two-bar motif in *fff* double octaves that Messiaen marked as "trombones." Accompanied by accented *staccato* attacks in the high register that derive six of their ten different pitch combinations from the *Theme of Chords*,[159] the motif is followed by one full and one partial sequence. In the course of these sequences, the intervallic gap between

[159]Were one to number the chords and thus trace their recurrences, one would find the following sequence, whereby chords 5-10 constitute a transmutation of the *Theme of Chords*:

bars	14						15							16					
chords -	1	2	3	4	1	5	6 -	5	6	5	6	7	8	9 -	5	6	7 -	8	9 10

bars	17						18					
chords -	1	2	9	10	8	9	10 -	2	3	4	1 5

the lowest and highest notes widens increasingly. Messiaen employs this process of asymmetric growth on many occasions both within the *Vingt regards* and elsewhere. Like all growth processes, its wider symbolic meaning is that of *transformation*. In this cycle, the vertical spreading was introduced in III, *The Exchange*, and was identified as standing for spiritual growth. In XIV, Messiaen's subheading explains, the majestic angels sound the instruments with which they are fated to summon us at the "end of time." They play their trombones here to express their increasing astonishment, "for it is not with them but with the human race that God has united Himself." The further enlargement in stanzas 2 and 3, realized both vertically and finally also horizontally with regard to rhythm, underscores the angels' increasing puzzlement. Despite their growing willingness to contemplate the implications of the MANIFESTATION OF THE ETERNAL IN TIME, they remain nevertheless perplexed that God should have chosen the earthly realm to incarnate His Word.

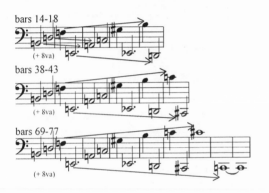

The three initial longer stanzas, built entirely of the three segments described above, are followed by three shorter stanzas in which the imposing trombone motif is suspended, and one gets the impression that joy gradually overrides perplexity. Segment *a* is represented here only by a simplified version of its first component—a significant excerpt of the original pitches is retained but reduced to mere descending arpeggiated chords—and accompanied by bird song (see bars 78-83). In segment *b*, the highest of the three canonic strands abandons the characteristic rhythmic pattern to give expression to more of the same gaiety (see bars 84-88). Both segments undergo a horizontal enlargement similar to the one observed in stanzas 1-3, so that stanzas 4-6 sound like a prolonged, jubilant celebration, "bird song that engulfs the blue." (See the illustration below.)

Only one little detail mars this impression of rising comprehension and acceptance on the part of the angels. The third statement of the segment *b* is two bars shorter in stanza 6 than it was in stanza 3. The result is that neither of the two remaining canonic voices is allowed to complete

351

a₁	a₂	a₃	b	c
bars 1-4	5/6	7/8	9-13	14-18

a₁	x	a₂	a₃	b + extension	c+ extension
bars 19-22	23/24	25/26	27/28	29-37	38-43

a₁	y	x	a₂	a₃	b + extension (even longer)	c+ extension (longer)
bars 44-47	48	49/50	51/52	53/54	55-68	69-77

a var.	b var.
bars 78-83	84-88

a var. + extension	b var.+ extension
bars 89-96	97-105

a var.+ extension (longer)	b var.+extension (longer)
bars 106-114	115-127

transition	coda(from c)
bars 128-131	132-156

the tail of the rhythmic pattern that speaks to the *manifestation in time* (see the abrupt hush and cut-off in bar 127). All is thus not well for Gods fire-flaming servants, and the coda confirms this. After four bars of a new kind of "sparkle," the trombone motif recurs in full *fff* force (bars 132-133). The piece concludes with a powerful demonstration of what Messiaen marks explicitly as "the angels' growing astonishment." Discarding the accompanying chords that brought with them the moderating objectivity of the *Theme of Chords*, the trombone octaves now sound in *unison* texture. Moreover, the tempo is now almost four times as fast as before, and the monumental asymmetric growth emphasized with a *crescendo* from *pp* to a level beyond *fff*. Far from being placated, these angels are forces for humans to reckon with, Messiaen seems to say, terrible in their reprimand if we do not live up to the gift granted us through Christ's Incarnation among us.

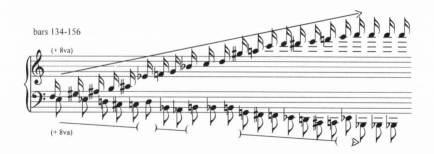

bars 134-156

THE EXCHANGE OF NATURES
AND THE NATURE(S) OF
TIME AND SILENCE

L'échange (Messiaen, *Vingt regards*, III)

(Descente en gerbe, montée en spirale; terrible commerce humano-divin. Dieu se fait homme pour nous rendre dieux...)

In this powerful piece, the concept of *The Exchange* both serves as the theological stimulus of manifold implications and determines the musical development on various levels.

Messiaen guides our understanding of the spiritual complexities inherent in the theological usage of the word "Exchange" with several verbal clues. The first words of his subheading, "Descent in a shower of sparks, ascent in a spiral," refer to Christ's coming down to earth and rising back up to heaven, His Incarnation (God becoming Man) and Ascension (Man becoming God). The word *gerbe*, literally denoting a sheaf of flowers but also used for the flower-like creations in fireworks, connotes beauty and abundance, an affectionate present, but also a limited life span; cut flowers in a vase will delight for only a few days, those created of colorful lights in the sky enchant for but a few seconds. In a secondary usage, the word *gerbe* also designates the tail of a comet, and in Christian images thus refers to the Star of Bethlehem. The spiral is a frequent symbol for spiritual purification, denoting growth, life, and development, both within Christianity and beyond (one thinks of the spiral as the neo-Platonist symbol for prayer and contemplation, circling around a subject and ascending at the same time, and as a Buddhist symbol for the gradual process on the Path to Enlightenment).[160]

[160]For readers interested in the exact understanding of these symbols, it might help to recall that a spiral differs from a helix—with which it is often confounded in less careful everyday language—in that a helix screws around an assumed center pole at equal distance, while a spiral departs from a central point in widening circular motion. Both contain the element of progression (usually depicted as ascending, though that is not a necessary condition). But while a helix is repetitive, a spiral expands and thus epitomizes growth—conceptually *ad infinitum*.

The wording Messiaen chooses for the second clause of his prefacing text, "terrible human-divine commerce," is reminiscent, for many musicians, of the hauntingly beautiful motet *O admirabile commercium* by Renaissance composer Josquin Desprez. Its lyrics, in translation, are "O admirable exchange. The Creator of human-kind, taking on a living body, was worthy to be born of a Virgin, and, coming forth as a human, without seed [semen], has given us His Deity in abundance."[161] This text thus carries a message very close to the one Messiaen is expressing.

The adjective in Messiaen's sentence, however, is not *admirable* but *terrible*—a word the composer uses again in piece XVIII of the cycle, *Regard de l'Onction terrible*. In the latter instance, the intended connotation is clearly that of "awesome," exceeding the grasp of humans, and possibly also undeserved by them. It helps to rephrase the sentence under consideration here with this meaning in mind: "awesome human-divine exchange."

The final line in Messiaen's subheading, "God becomes Man to make us gods..." or, more literally, "God turns Himself into Man so as to make us gods," is close to Josquin's "has given us His Deity in abundance." The concept of Man being given "a share in the divine nature" reflects a basic idea in Greek theologies after the third century: God becomes a human being so that humans can become God.

Musically, the concept of exchange and two-way "commerce" of essences is depicted in a most intriguing twelve-step transformation of a two-bar unit. The unit consists of four components made up of several smaller segments, all of which express different aspects of the awesome exchange. The transformation from bars 1/2 to bars 23/24 is very simple

---

[161]The motet, in four parts, appears in *Josquin Desprez: Werken* (ed. A. Smijers and others, Amsterdam 1921-) Book *Motetten i:2*. The complete text reads: *"O admirabile commercium. Creator generis humani, animatum corpus sumens, de virgine nasci dignatus est, et procedens homo, sine semine, largitus est nobis suam deitatem."* Messiaen identifies the text as stemming from the antiphon for January 1. He may have been inspired by Marmion who dedicates an entire chapter to the topic of the Admirable Exchange (see Marmion, *Le Christ dans ses Mystères*, chapter VII).

Also important for an understanding of the wording, and especially the music based on it, is the Christmas antiphon *Mirabile mysterium*. The full text *(Mirabile mysterium declaratur hodie: innovantur naturae, Deus homo factus est; id quod fuit permansit, et quod non erat assumpsit, non commixtionem passus neque divisionem.)* translates as: "A wonderful secret is being revealed today: natures are being renewed, God has become Man; that which He was, He remains, and that which He was not, He assumes, suffering neither mixture nor division." There is a direct musical depiction here of "that what He was, He remains."

—listeners perceive above all the steady, protracted *crescendo* and slightly changed pitches in unchanging rhythm. At the same time, it is utterly complex, as I will show in detail below.

Component *a* (bar 1, upper and middle staves) consists of two segments: a swift descent in five double thirds and, after considerable suspension, a much slower repetitive pulsation in pitches that derive (in octave displacement) from the chromatic cluster E♭-E-F-G♭. The first segment denotes motion, both rhythmically and in its pitch range, which spans almost three octaves; the second segment stands for motionlessness or stability, along with increasing intensity (a

component *a*
comprises ten semitones, with a central cluster E♭ E F G♭; all pitches remain unchanged throughout the piece.

crescendo that seems to propel energy into the rest that follows). In its entirety, component *a* can further be read as depicting, by its rhythmically unfathomable entry and its metrically inconclusive ending, notions of something "with neither beginning nor end."

This component is the only one to remain unchanged throughout the twelve transformations of the two-bar unit. In his "Author's note," Messiaen explains as follows: "God, that is the line in alternating thirds: that which does not move, that which is very small. Man, that is the other fragments which grow, grow and become enormous, according to a process that I call 'asymmetric growth'."[162] Elsewhere, the composer adds to this interpretation of the motionless, thus spaceless, timeless God, by declaring that eternity, as a quality pertaining to God's being, is symbolized by the point or the blink of the eye—so that any notion of time and space may be suspended.[163]

Component *b* presents a three-note group, accented and in double octaves, launched from E and expanding from there by chromatic steps to

[162]Dieu, c'est le trait en tierces alternées: ce qui ne bouge pas, ce qui est tout petit. L'homme, ce sont les autres fragments qui grandissent, grandissent et deviennent énormes, selon un procédé de développement que j'appelle: "agrandissement asymétrique". *Vingt Regards sur l'Enfant-Jésus* (Paris: Durand, 1944), p. II.

[163]Michèle Reverdy, *L'oeuvre pour piano d'Olivier Messiaen* (Paris: Alphonse Leduc, 1978), p. 37

both sides (see bar 1, lower staff). The widening initiated within the three-note group itself continues throughout the subsequent eleven trans-formations, culminating in an immensely powerful two-octave leap E-E (see bar 23).

component *b*
begins on E—the note that provides the invisible center for the following gradual interval growth.

The pitch development consists of gradual chromatic spreading, expanding up to a two-octave leap E—E.

Component *c* consists of two segments that are rhythmically bound together in a nonuplet (which concludes in syncopation) but distinguished by the different transformational processes the composer has them undergo. The first six pitches, constituting a seemingly irregular ascent (B♭-C-D-F♯-B-C♯), are united in that they rise, throughout the transforma-tions, by chromatic increments. The second segment, consisting of the three-note group that concludes the nonuplet, expands in both directions.

component *c*
commences with 9 semitones from a single cluster:
F♯ G A♭ A B♭ B C C♯ D.

Throughout the piece, the first 6 pitches rise chromatically; the remaining 3 pitches expand their intervals (thus mirro-ring component b) and conclude in a dramatic crossover— a true "exchange."

A closer look reveals that both segments of component *c* are conceived in intriguing sequence and relationship to the two preceding components.

- Five of the six pitches in the ascending first segment of component *c* can be read as a cluster with octave displacement (B♭-B♮-C♮-C♯-D). They are thus directly related to the second seg-ment of component *a,* which also constitutes a cluster with octave displacement.

356

- The remaining pitch F♯ serves as a logical extension—a further chromatic step upwards—of the rising leg of the fork in component *b* (see, in the pitches of the original unit in bars 1/2: E-F...F♯; in the first transformation of bars 3/4: F-F♯...G).
- Finally, the second segment of *c*, the expanding three-note group, is a mirror image of component *b*. (Compare bar 1: E-D♯-F, a concave curve later transformed with the first and last notes rising, and the middle note falling, with the convex curve in bar 2: A♭-A-G that is later transformed in that the first and last notes descend and the middle note ascends.)

Component *d* is conceived in contrary motion of two homorhythmic figures. When first heard at the end of bar 2, they appear as a kind of distorted vertical mirror-image. Further transformations, however, occur according to very unusual rules. In the right-hand part, the first and third notes descend throughout the twelve variants of the unit, while the two final notes along with all five notes in the left-hand part rise chromatically. The right hand's second note E, however, remains unchanged throughout the piece, confirming the pitch E as the tonal center. This static pitch E adds a further dimension to the concept of "center" established in component *b*. There, the center is depicted as, on the one hand, the hinge and starting point (bar 1) and, on the other hand, as the point of final attraction (bar 23). Component *b* thus addresses the process from E to E—the gesture of God's covenant, to which the Unchanging One invites humankind with His descent unto earth (see bar 1) and from which He emerges, after manifold, seemingly arbitrary distortions, greater than ever yet still the same (see bar 23). In component *d*, by contrast, E is a modest,

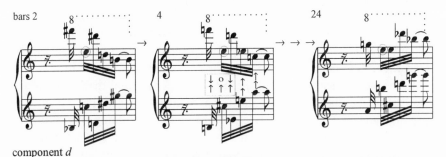

component *d* is a homorhythmic component that begins in (not-quite-exact) mirroring movements.

The pitch development includes an unwavering E (thus confirming the central note of component *b*), a "collapse" at the beginning (i.e. in the first three note pairs), and a final victory of the rising motion.

easily underrated but utterly reliable presence. Meanwhile, the texture around this humble repeated E collapses, while the "conclusion" of the component (and, for that matter, of the entire basic unit upon which this piece is built) presents an unquenchable ascent.

Component d is again related to the component preceding it in that the first three pitches of the left-hand part (in bar 2: B♭-C-D) repeat the initial pitches of component c, albeit in octave transposition and with a distorting octave displacement.

The strange transformational procedure employed in the first twenty-four bars of this piece is rich in metaphorical message. Messiaen verbally (in the "Author's Note") draws our attention to the fact that "God is that which does not move" (or, that which does not change). Musically, he shows us two additional ways in which God is present through Jesus, as well as the complex reaction by which humans attempt to imitate the exemplary Son of Man in the effort to accept God's invitation to "become God."

The first is the way in which God enters our world, the descent in a shower of sparks (component $a)$, an entry whose initial moment is metrically and rhythmically incomprehensible and whose target is depicted as dynamically growing beyond what we are given to hear. The second way in which God is manifest is epitomized in the constant, almost imperceptible presence of the single unchanging pitch E.

The growth necessary for Man's transformation is aptly portrayed in the two mirror-image expansion processes. With all due caution and awareness of possible over-interpretation, one may try to see the first (component b) as the example given by Jesus—whose human development begins and ends in the unchanging, eternal and by implication divine center (the central note E). The mirroring segment, i.e. the latter part of component c, could (with equal caution) be read as Man's striving to imitate Christ and thus experience spiritual growth of his own. The larger portions of both components c and d embody a rise in complex patterns, very possibly an attempt to picture the spiritual rise "in a spiral". Towards the end of Man's effort, in the vicinity of the Divine presence of the unchanging E, Messiaen's choice of suddenly folding the texture in might signify his conviction that the "commerce" is in fact an extended process—a protracted give and take that comprises further "lowering" motions of God as he acknowledges human endeavors and meets us in our efforts.

If one can accept this interpretation as the composer's possible spiritual message, one can further say that the first bar of the unit that undergoes all these transformations stands for God's gesture initiating the exchange, while the second bar is dedicated to Man's response—and eventually God's acknowledgment of Man's effort. The hidden numbers with which Messiaen no doubt played here as much as he is known to have done in other compositions, include *seven* beats for *three* segments in bar 1, *four* beats for *four* segments in bar 2. The number 3 as the symbol for the Trinity is thus combined with the number 7, which plays an important role in the revelation of St. John and points to mankind not yet fit to be redeemed; see the beast with seven horns, the seven vessels of God's wrath, the book with seven seals, as well as the gothic symbol of the "seven mortal sins" and Mary Magdalene's "seven demons" that Jesus exorcises after his resurrection. The number four, by contrast, can be associated with human nature. In the Western tradition, the figure 4 is best known in relation to Aristotle's four elements (fire, water, earth, and air), denoting the components of which all matter consists. This number play thus supports an interpretation by which the first bar represents the divine and the second bar the human part of the "exchange."

The coda of the piece (see bars 25-31) bears out much of this interpretation. After the twelve-part consummation of the transformative process completed in bars 23/24, the powerful dynamic increase extends further through a threefold repetition of bar 1, thus reinforcing God's "descent in a shower of sparks" (component *a*) and Jesus' beginnings on earth (component *b* in its original pitches). The number of repetitions, three, also governs the subsequent bar with its threefold reiteration of the still unchanged component *b* (see bar 28), as well as the three-beat rest in bar 29. Then, for the first time in this piece, we are witness to an expansion process not in space but in time. Component *b*, requested yet louder than ever before, is being stretched to roughly six times its previous speed. After this final dimension of the transformative process, completion is attained in wholeness: bar 31, recalling the "collapsing" texture of the "commerce," sounds the entire twelve-tone aggregate. It may hardly come as a surprise that the piece closes with an accented, syncopated E in the treble, assuring us once more of God's eternal presence.

Regard du temps   (Messiaen, *Vingt regards*, IX)

(Mystère de la plénitude des temps; le temps voit naître en lui Celui qui est éternel...)

In order to understand the many shades of meaning embedded in the title of this piece, one might do well to translate it in several different ways. *Time's Contemplation* and *Time Looking Upon the Infant Jesus* both presume Time as one of those "immaterial or symbolic creatures" whom Messiaen mentions in the very first paragraph of his "Author's Note." At the same time, the wording also rings with insinuations of the "perspective of time."

Messiaen's subheading leads us closer to both his intended message and the sources on which he draws. It contains two components which shed light on how one might usefully interpret this deceivingly simple piece. The initial "Mystery of the fullness of time" derives its wording from the New Testament. In Gal 4, 4 we read: "But when the fullness of time had come, God sent his Son"; and in Ep. 1, 8-10: "In all wisdom and insight, He has made known to us the mystery of His will in accord with His favor that He set forth in Him as a plan for the fullness of times, to sum up all things in Christ, in Heaven and on Earth."

The mystery of time was a favorite theme of Greek and Latin theologians from the fourth century onwards, and Augustine, especially, struggled with it. Augustine's "liberation from time," which he saw ushered in by the incarnation of the Eternal, is one of Messiaen's paramount concerns (*"mon désir de cessation du temps"*)—a concern to which he dedicated above all his *Quartet for the End of Time* (1940/41).

"Fullness of time" thus comprises two shades of meaning. From God's assumed perspective it denotes the moment in which time is "ripe" for the incarnation of the Christ; from a human perspective it stands for an obliteration of the one-dimensional notion of Time in favor of one that accommodates the Eternal. Messiaen's second sentence, "within time is born He who is eternal..." expresses this juxtaposition of time with eternity and provides, as I shall show, the basis for the musical depiction.

Before we take a look at the composition itself, a further comment of Messiaen's should be investigated. In the "Author's Note" he speaks of "a short theme" which he characterizes as "cold and strange" and which he likens to "Chirico's egg-shaped heads." This remark is intriguing for various reasons, the most obvious being that the piece actually contains *two* themes that are equally important, recur with equal frequency, and undergo an equal number of modifications. While the very general reference "short theme" directs an unsuspecting reader almost automatically to that which is first heard, the further attributes—cold and strange—point to the second thematic component rather than to the first. With this tentative clue in mind, it may be worth exploring the likeness to which Messiaen alludes.

Giorgio de Chirico was an Italian painter of Greek descent, twenty years the composer's senior. In the period between 1917 and 1940—just prior to the composition of the *Vingt regards* in 1944—Chirico developed, together with Carlo Carrà, what has become known as "pittura metafisica" (metaphysical painting). While this style combines elements of early Renaissance art with strong classical tendencies, Chirico's paintings of that time characteristically involve surreal interpretations of the world: roads or squares without surrounding buildings, peopled with puppet-like humans often shown with heads depicted as blank ovals, empty and bleak. Art critics commented on the cold, harsh light and eerie shadows in Chirico's paintings. His art is perceived as conveying an immense calm, reminding some viewers of visions antiquity had of the realm of the dead.

Such a reading of Chirico's art in turn sheds some light on Messiaen's own understanding of what his themes—and the words he chose to preface the music—stand for. Imagining the plenitude of Time is like looking into one of Chirico's empty faces. Our conception of the fullness of Time translates into a feeling that we are lost, blank, humbled: we cannot conceive either the beginning or the end of Time, nor its nature.

Messiaen's piece IX, 44 bars and slightly over three minutes long, uses nothing but two short themes and a single closing chord. The structural layout is utterly simple:

section I:		b		$b_{var.1}$		$b_{var.2}$
	a		$a_{var.}$		$a_{dev.}$	

section II:			b	$b_{var.1}$	$b_{var.2}$
	a	$a_{var.}$			

section III:			b	
	a	$a_{var.}$	$a_{dev.}$	

	Coda:	twelve-tone
	$a_{dev. (tail)}$	chord

The two themes differ from one another in virtually every respect—a fact that corroborates the dualism of the second phrase of the subheading remark and that invites an interpretation of the various musical parameters in the light of "Time" and "Eternity" respectively.

Theme *a* (see bars 7/8)

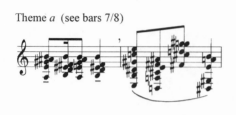

Theme *a* is laid out as a homorhythmic phrase. The chordal texture is generally in five parts but expands for two attacks to six parts and thus clearly does not invite us to read voices horizontally. The setting is morphologically that of an organic entity. The parts are so close that division for a pianist's two hands is arbitrary. (Consequently, the theme is given here in single-staff notation.)

The register is confined to a total of two and a half octaves, with the widest six-note chord (see the downbeat of bar 2) spanning exactly two octaves. The pitch range expands almost equally on both sides of the center of the keyboard. While there is no pulse and therefore, in the strictest sense, no meter, phrasing within the theme is unambiguous and coincides with the bar line, thus giving this theme a sense of metric order not actually supported in the rhythmic design.

The rhythm is both restricted and complex. On the one hand, the phrase employs only three different note values, a simplicity one might associate with folk tunes—tunes known by and representing "the people." On the other hand, the version given in the example (which is actually a variation, but one that is slightly simpler than the original of bars 1/2), allows to detect two rhythmic palindromes. The inherent complexity of these horizontally mirrored rhythmic sequences lies in the fact that they cut across the clearly perceived phrasing, and thus speak of an underlying order not "realized" on the surface.

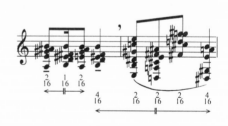

In terms of tonal organization, theme *a* features two clearly audible central notes. B is the main melodic pitch which anchors the treble; all three versions of the theme begin and end with B in the upper voice. E, though mostly hidden in the middle of the texture, is equally important; it forms part of most chords and acts as a general tonal mooring. The predominant interval, as the reduction shows, is the perfect fifth—one of those intervals whose simple frequency relation (2:3) has been perceived throughout the ages as particularly agreeable to humans.

tonal centers and perfect fifths in *a*

Before considering the remaining parameters as well as the variations this theme undergoes, let us pause here and compare all that we have found so far with corresponding aspects of theme *b* which is shown, in the following example, in its essence.

Theme *b*

- Where theme *a* is strongly based on superimposed perfect fifths, theme *b* features the tritone as its most prominent interval, and the augmented and diminished octaves respectively as frames for its three-note chords. The tritone, the arithmetic bisection of the octave, has long been considered an interval unsuitable for "proper" music. (One is reminded of Bach's struggles with his church board on just this issue.) Like the diminished and augmented distortion of the octave, it is regarded as fundamentally beyond the grasp, and the pleasure, of the human ear.

- Where theme *a* acts as an organic entity—with independent and largely unpredictable movements within its chords, varying numbers of parts, and a highly idiosyncratic overall shape—theme *b* appears as an entity created according to objective laws. Its three strands (consisting of two three-note chords in strands 1 and 2 and a single tritone dyad in strand 3) move with utmost regularity and order, strand 1 descending in whole-tone steps, strand 2 ascending in whole-tone steps, and strand 3 in a curve of ascent followed by descent.

- Where theme *a* creates a sense of "knowing-where-we-are"
through the use of its two central tones B and E, and includes
pitch repetition both horizontally and vertically, theme *b* meticulously avoids any predominance of a particular tonal detail.
Each vertical collection contains eight different pitches, and each
strand progresses without a single horizontal repetition of even
the pitch class. Theme *b* is thus tonally devised in such a way as
to counteract any tonal hierarchy, epitomizing an almost frightening equality of all components, an absence of purpose,
emotion, even of aliveness. (This was the theme that reminded
Messiaen of Chirico's blank faces!)

The way in which Messiaen actually employs the theme-*b* material
allows us to extend the comparison to a number of further parameters.

- Where theme *a* displays a rhythm that is "human" both in its
limitation to few note values and in the unruliness of a palindrome that cuts across phrasing, theme *b* contains a rhythmic
pattern of utmost regularity. The three-chord thematic unit is organized as a palindrome of half-note / quarter-note / half-note,
followed by a repetition in which the rhythm is diminished to
exactly a fourth of the original size (i.e. eighth-note / sixteenth-
note / eighth-note).
- Where theme *a* is designed in a chordal, homorhythmic setting,
theme *b* is laid out as a rhythmic canon. This canon evolves in
obedience to simple, powerful laws. The second and third strands
enter each at a distance of an eighth-note. Yet there is an odd
detail. In a canonic texture employing additive rhythms and heard
without any context of a pre-established regular meter, bar lines

Theme *b* (see bars 2-6)

are, of course, exclusively visual aids. The intriguing fact that Messiaen has written his bar lines (here only given in dotted lines) in such a way as to place all chords a sixteenth value "off beat" is certainly not a mere perverse oddity. Instead, one might take it as an expression of the notion that this theme actually happens "beside" time—not without any time, but transcending any preconceived order.

Finally, there is the question of pitch expansion.

- Where theme *a* was compact and securely anchored in the keyboard's central register, theme *b* spans seven octaves; while the pitch range of theme *a* falls easily within that of human singing voices, the range of the outer strands of theme *b* is extreme and "out of this world."

What is left for the analyst to do, in the process of reading the musical language as a message with regard to the theological concepts that gave rise to it, is to trace the evolution of each theme. As was mentioned earlier, each theme appears in three versions. Comparing the performance-related parameters as well as the nature of the modification in both themes, we find that the contrast established so far is further reinforced.

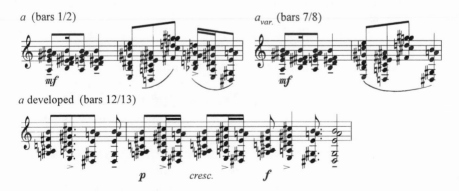

The performance indications for theme *a* request *mf* (a middle, mean, "human" degree of loudness). Strategically placed dashes enhance the deceptive metric impression, while slurs and accents serve as indicators of emotional involvement and—once again—hierarchy. (The first chord under a slur is more active than any event following it; the accented chord at the beginning of the second slur has even more weight than the unaccented initial attack under the first slur; etc.) The corresponding indications for theme *b*, by contrast, demand a simple *pp*. In connection with the extreme registers, this soft hue creates an almost unworldly color. In its absence of any inflection, it embodies perfect emotional detachment.

Regarding the extent and nature of the modification undergone by each theme in the course of the piece, the original theme *a* and its variation differ only at the very end where the original features a short-short-long group instead of the simple quarter-note chord in the variation. The difference is one of surface embellishment only and does not touch structure. (This is the reason why the previous discussion was entirely based on the simpler version.)

The development of theme *a*, while close to the original and variation in all aspects of texture and tonal organization as well as with regard to the main characteristics of its phrase structure, behaves very independently in all other respects. The long phrase comprises only three different chords: the closing harmony of theme *a* preceded by one of the embellishing chords from the original phrase, and a new chord as an opening. The chord structure is no longer determined by superimposed fifths but shows a prevalence of perfect fourths.

Rhythmically, the development of theme *a* builds on the original only indirectly and only in its first component. The three-chord unit is laid out as a palindrome in which the central value is a sixteenth longer than the those surrounding it. (In the corresponding palindrome that opens the original phrase of theme *a* as well as its variation, the central value is a sixteenth shorter than the flanking chords.) From there, the three-chord group proceeds through a strongly metric pattern and its exact repetition into a tail displaying again an organic type of growth.

In terms of performance indications, the entire second subphrase is marked as a powerful *crescendo*. The elevated emotionality, epitomized in this strong dynamic increase but also in the shifted accent (see the first subphrase) and in the unprecedented, very insistent inner repetition, enhances the feeling that this theme represents time as we humans know it. Time is depicted here as subjectively perceived; one moment seemingly stretched, the next moment as if rushing; with an appearance of repetitiveness that, rather than a necessity, is—as in Messiaen's development of theme *a* with its mere three chords—a result of our choice to see ourselves as trapped in a framework of limited options.

The modifications undergone by theme *b* are of an entirely different nature. They follow the same set of objective laws that governs every other aspect of this theme, and can thus be described in a single sentence. While the second subphrase, the faster-paced repetition of the three-chord palindrome, remains completely unchanged throughout the composition, the first, slow-paced palindrome exhibits two utterly regular changes. This rhythmic unit is diminished to three fourths of its former size in the first variation, and augmented to five fourths of the original in the second variation.

The rhythmic palindromes in theme *b* and its variations:

$$\frac{8}{16} \quad \frac{4}{16} \quad \frac{8}{16} \quad \frac{2}{16} \quad \frac{1}{16} \quad \frac{2}{16}$$

$$\frac{6}{16} \quad \frac{3}{16} \quad \frac{6}{16} \quad \frac{2}{16} \quad \frac{1}{16} \quad \frac{2}{16} \quad \text{(one quarter subtracted from each value in the first three-chord group)}$$

$$\frac{10}{16} \quad \frac{5}{16} \quad \frac{10}{16} \quad \frac{2}{16} \quad \frac{1}{16} \quad \frac{2}{16} \quad \text{(one quarter added to each value in the first three-chord group)}$$

This is all that happens: objective, lawful growth; no alteration whatsoever with regard to tonal organization, register, structure, dynamic level, phrasing, articulation!

"Mystery of the fullness of time. Within time is born He who is eternal." Messiaen's musical interpretation makes use of all conceivable compositional parameters to depict the two extreme aspects within the "fullness": human, subjectively and emotionally perceived, measured time and divine, all-encompassing, objective, unhierarchical eternity.

Regard du silence   (Messiaen, *Vingt regards*, XVII)

(Silence dans la main, arc-en-ciel renversé...chaque silence de la crèche révèle musiques et couleurs qui sont les mystères de Jésus-Christ...)

When the title of a piece of music refers to silence, this always gives us pause. In other circumstances we ask ourselves, self-consciously, "Are we making too much noise?" Yet as a preface to a musical composition, this question seems odd at first. And yet: the silence of which we often speak wistfully does not necessarily mean the absence of any sound. What we are more likely to mean is the absence of mechanical or motor-driven noises, thoughtless chatter, and mind-numbing entertainment. This kind of silence, rather than being completely void, can be surprisingly filled with the softer voices around us, as well as allowing the gentler notes within us, often drowned out by superficial busy clatter, to be heard.

Silence is intrinsically linked to the concepts of respect, piety, and awe. The way in which the Infant Jesus is seen from the perspective of silence, then, is free from any audible expressions of affection, praise, or hope, allowing instead the unfathomable event to speak to the onlookers. "Each silence of the manger reveals music and colors that are the mysteries of Jesus Christ," Messiaen concludes his subheading.

There are three instances in the cycle where silence is evoked; each contributes a shade of meaning. In XI, *First Communion of the Virgin,* Messiaen has Mary address the child in her womb as "my love without the noise of words." In this sense, silence comes to stand for the ineffable, that which is beyond comprehension and expression through words.

In XIX, *I Sleep But My Heart Wakes*, the word silence appears not in the title or in the subheading but in the additional explanation contained in the preface. There Messiaen declares the piece to be a "dialogue of mystical love" and adds: "The *silences* play and important role here" (emphasis Messiaen's). In this case, the plural "silences" denotes, of course, the practical aspect of the respite from sound: musical rests. However, the fact that Messiaen should have highlighted the word *silences* in print seems significant and establishes an internal link between the word and the theme of mystical love also evoked in *First Communion of the Virgin.*

Finally and most prominently, Messiaen uses the word "silence" in V, *The Son Contemplating the Son*, where he speaks of a "refraction of joy" elicited by the "birds of silence." As the analysis will reveal, the composer created a particularly strong musical connection between this piece and the *Silence's Contemplation*. Both subheadings also share the references to unusual forms of light and to the mystery of Christ (cf. V: "Mystery, rays of light in the night"; XVII: "inverted rainbows... music and colors that are the mysteries of Jesus Christ.")

The musical connections between the two pieces are certainly striking. Having seen how *The Son Contemplating the Son* develops *The*

Father's Contemplation vertically, in that it quotes the entire musical argument of the opening piece in its third strand, adding two entirely new and idiosyncratic strands above it, *Silence's Contemplation* can be viewed as developing *The Son Contemplating the Son* horizontally, in that it quotes the idiosyncratic two-strand rhythmic pattern in its entirety, adding a two-segment middle section with contrasting material.

The way in which Messiaen both clearly quotes and equally clearly redefines the opening section is most intriguing. Bars 1-19 of this piece correspond with the two uppermost strands in bars 1-19 of V. The upper strand quotes the original rhythmic sequence—consisting of four different palindromes followed by a unidirectional tail in increasing note values—that was identified as a symbol for the MANIFESTATION OF THE ETERNAL IN TIME; the lower strand presents the augmentation of the same rhythm by 150%, as did the middle strand in the fifth piece. The upper-strand sequence is heard three times, the lower-strand sequence twice; hence the two aspects of Jesus end by falling together. (Very strictly speaking, Messiaen cuts the concluding statements in both strands short by one quarter value.)

In *The Son Contemplating the Son*, the modes employed are mode 6 (THE SUFFERING ON THE CROSS) for the upper strand, mode 4 (THE INCARNATION OF THE WORD) for the middle strand. The symbolic representation of the suffering Son of God is rendered exclusively in three-note chords, while that of the just-born Child of Man appears in four-note chords, where 3 epitomizes the Trinitarian and 4 the human perspective. In *Silence's Contemplation*, the lower strand retains the modal definition as the INCARNATION OF THE WORD (i.e. mode 4^4, as in V), whereas the upper strand is tonally defined by mode 3.

The symbolic meaning of this mode has to be derived more indirectly than, say, that of modes 2 and 7, which were introduced in the context of a theme. The determining feature is the rhythmic relationship of the juxtaposition of modes in this and in the fifth piece, which prompts us to interpret each pair as representing two aspects of Jesus. By the time listeners come to the *Silence's Contemplation*, they have been exposed to extensive passages of mode 3 in the long second episode of XIII, *Christmas*. As has been shown, Messiaen's *Christmas* does not deal with abstract concepts of Jesus' Incarnation and destiny, but above all with the very concrete event of the birth of a child—albeit a special one. An interpretation of mode 3 as a symbol of the CHILD IN THE MANGER probably comes very close to what the composer must have intended. If we accept this reading, we state that both textural strands in *Silence's Contemplation* refer with their modal symbolism to the Child, and both (therefore, one is tempted to say) are clad in the four-note chords of the human sphere.

At the same time, the intervallic structure in the chords and the way in which Messiaen orders the chord types to form patterns with or against the palindromes is quite extraordinary. We may best be able to appreciate the significant differences if we compare the two parameters in the two pieces.

chord patterns:

palindrome	1			2			3			4		
V, strand 1	a	b	a'	c	c	d	a	b	a'	c	c	d
V, strand 2	g	g'	h	h	i	i'	g	g'	h	h	i	i'
XVII, strand 1	a	a	a'	a"	a"	a'''	a"	b	c	a'''	d	b
XVII, strand 2	h	i	h	k	k'	l	h	i	h	k	k'	l

In V, strand 1, the Suffering on the Cross is set up in chord patterns whose boundaries coincide with those of the rhythmic groups; in strand 2, the Word Incarnate is given the larger framework of two consecutive palindromes to complete its series. Moreover, the third and fourth palindromes in both strands repeat the chord patterns of the first and second groups, thus projecting an impression of non-developmental timelessness in this part of the phrase. In XVII, the Word Incarnate has taken on a structure almost identical with that associated with the Suffering on the Cross—as if the distinction between two views of Jesus explored here is not that between the Christ at death and the Christ at birth, but rather that between the newly-born Son of God and the newly-born son of Mary. With this tentative interpretation in mind, it then does not come as much of a surprise that the chordal representation of the Child in the Manger is not designed to honor the timelessness of rhythmic mirroring at all, but clearly laid out as a developmental phrase!

characteristic intervals:

chord	1	2	3	4
V, strand 1	P5/P4	P4+M3	P5/trit	dim. 8/m6
V, strand 2	—— all chords built with a tritone inside a diminished octave			
XVII, strand 1	—— all chords built on one or mostly two major thirds[164]			
XVII, strand 2	P5/trit	trit/dim.8	P5/trit	P4+M3/trit

[164]The basic chord species here, marked as "species a" in the graphic representation on the following page, is an augmented triad to which varying intervals are added, some below, some above.

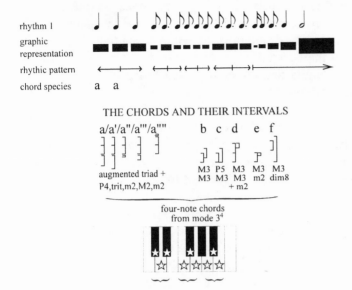

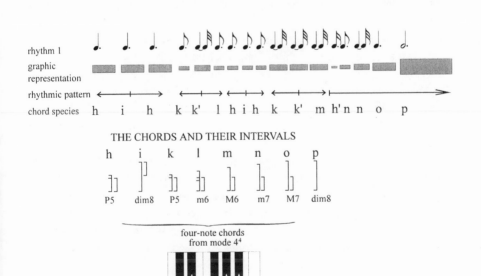

In V, strand 1, the chord sequence symbolizing the SUFFERING ON THE CROSS presents itself as encompassing a great number of intervals; the chords in strand 2, by contrast, all have two intervals in common that appear in various positions of interlocking with one another. In XVII, the strand representing the CHILD IN THE MANGER builds all its manifestations from a single core, while that epitomizing the WORD INCARNATE is now complex and multi-facetted.

This redefinition of the two aspects of the Child continues all the more poignantly in the unidirectional "tails" following the four palindromes. While the temporally determined segment of Mary's son develops mostly already known constellations (three of the tail's five chords were heard before), the time-determined aspect of the Son of Man moves Him to different grounds (all but the tail's first chord are new).

The overview on the preceding page shows both complete strands in their rhythmic patterning, chord species and mode, in a format that is comparable to that used in the chapter dealing with V.

Between this opening section and the closing section (bars 88-109) we find two sections that are closely related among themselves (cf. bars 20-52 and bars 53-87); furthermore, each is structurally laid out to describe an arch. There are three segments, each of which consists in itself of three components.

- Component *a1* comprises seven bars (bars 20-26) that play with the idea of chord pairs. The first pair is in *f* and articulated with dashes, the second one is accented and in *ff*; the third, a contraction of the *Theme of chords*, comes in *p* but still with clearly separated chords; the fourth, back in *f*, contracts the chord pair rhythmically, de-emphasizing the first to the length of an *acciaccatura*. Finally, the fifth, which is repeated twice, groups the two chords under initial accents and slurs in *mf*.

  Component *a2* (bars 27-29) sets out with a slurred chord pair in *mf* followed by two superimposed chords in *p*; the same group is then transposed twice, each time by a major third, while increasing in loudness to *più f*. (While the initial seven bars of segment *a* use all twelve tones, the second component is derived from mode 3^3, recalling the CHILD IN THE MANGER.)

  Component *a3* (see bars 30-36) concludes this segment with seven bars in mode 2—the mode of GOD'S LOVE.

- Segment *b* is indicated as roughly one-and-a-half times as fast as the two segments that surround it; at the same time, its components are much more concise.
Components *b1/b2* share a single bar (see bar 37). Both are tonally derived from mode 4^4, the mode of the WORD INCARNATE. The entire left-hand part and the beginning in the right hand can best be understood as two superimposed four-note chords (of which the one in the upper stand is broken up into 3+1 notes, the one in the lower strand into 2+2 notes) whose eight voices move down stepwise through the pitches of the given mode. The right-hand part follows this pattern for six chords and one rest (i.e. 7 sixteenths), after which the remainder of the bar in this strand presents material not connected to what precedes and accompanies it. Instead we hear three groups of three sixteenths each, distinguished by the "color" effect of its grace-note chords.
Component *b3* covers three bars (see bars 38-40). The first comes as an arpeggiation of three-note chords above four-note chords around the three pedal notes A♭/D♭/G♭; the second is a transposition by a major third downwards; and the third bar displays three layers: two superimposed, largely sweeping chords, C major over A♭^{7}, over a protracted bass pedal E♭.
- Segment *c* returns to the play with chord pairs in the slower tempo. In the first four bars (component *c1*), Messiaen has created a highly complex structure, based on the original four-part version of the *Theme of chords* and the extension by four six-part chords which that was given in the *The Angels' Contemplation*. If we refer back to XIV, bars 5/6, we find that the composer uses here, on the downbeats of bars 41-44, the complete, extended chord sequence in the form of four chords each preceded by a grace-note chord. Simultaneously on the second and third beats of these bars Messiaen exposed the same chord progression in retrograde. (He explicitly marks these four bars "rainbow"!)
The next four bars (component *c2*) feature more play with chord pairs (bars 45, 48) and a literal image of an "inverted rainbow" (bars 46/47). The segment—and the section as a whole—concludes, in component *c3*, with a reaffirmation of GOD'S LOVE (mode 2^2 in bars 49-52).

What may have caught our attention in the description above is the play with the Trinitarian vs. human numbers, 3 vs. 7. There are THREE segments. The first consists of SEVEN plus THREE plus SEVEN bars; the second encompasses units of SEVEN sixteenths, THREE times THREE sixteenths, and THREE bars based each on THREE constant elements. The third segment, too, encompasses THREE components.

As the entire section is repeated, these groupings are further emphasized.

- In segment *a*, the initial seven bars remain unchanged, while the three-bar component *a2* appears in retrograde motion and the seven-bar component *a3* transposed a tritone upwards and with a tripartite version of the original penultimate bar (cf. bar 35 with bars 68, 69, 70).
- In the second segment, the broken four-note chords of component *b1* move in contrary motion, component *b2* is insignificantly varied, and component *b3* appears transposed a fifth upwards.
- In segment *c*, the first two components recur unchanged (except for an extension by one chord-pair in bar 83), while the third component, still in mode 2, is transposed up a minor third and slightly varied.

The closing section of the piece (bars 88-109) relates to the opening section on first hearing by the fact that it takes approximately the same playing time;[165] it also picks up both the extremely soft hues of the opening and the two-tiered, modally determined chord progression. At the same time, Messiaen integrates here the idea of the arch (or rainbow) introduced in the repeated middle section.

Comparing the closing section with the opening we find that texture, rhythm and development procedures are very different indeed. For the first fifteen bars, the section presents itself in *toccata*-style with regular attacks in alternating hands—a more drastic contrast to the complexly polyphonic rhythmic sequences of the first section can hardly be imagined. Only in the final seven bars does Messiaen add chordal graces, thus softening the uniformity of the motion.

[165] The tempo of the closing section is with ♪ = 144 more than twice as fast as the ♪ = 66 in the opening section. At the same time, however, the first fifteen bars (bars 88-102) are implicitly in four-four time, while bars 1-19 only contain two quarter-values each. Moreover, bars 103-109, back in the original two-four, slow down considerably. Both sections thus take approximately 1 minute and 10 seconds performance time.

The way in which Messiaen uses the chord progressions and their modes is, again, both related to and very different from what we observed in the opening section. As before, the two strands derive their tonal material entirely from modes 3^4 and 4^4 respectively, and the structure of the individual chords is identical with that heard at the beginning of the piece. In the upper strand, we hear three complete statements of the mode-3 chord progression that, in the opening section, was associated with the rhythmic sequence symbolizing the MANIFESTATION OF THE ETERNAL IN TIME (see right-hand part, bars 88-90 [first chord], 90-92 [second chord], 92-94 [third chord]). A fourth statement follows after some interpolated development in bars 97-99d. During all the bars pertaining to the regular and complete progression, the lower strand presents an "accompaniment" using the three initial chords of the mode-4 sequence in a pattern that reads 1-2-3-2, 1-2-3-2 | etc.; it is almost as though the WORD INCARNATE supported the CHILD IN THE MANGER in a way similar to that by which GOD'S LOVE sustained the difficult duality of the Son in V.

Just as there are three + one statements of the complete chord progression, the development of this final section consists of one + three segments. The first segment presents a stepwise ascent and descent of four-part parallels in the respective modes; the second quotes only the ascending portion.[166] The third segment shows the same modal four-part parallels generating large leaps in the upper strand against—and this catches our eye—three consecutively growing arches of palindromically arranged chords in the second strand; one may feel reminded of the rainbows the composer mentions in the subheading. Finally in the fourth segment of the development (see bars 103-109), Messiaen gives us seven identical bars—diminishing in loudness and in tempo—in which the idea of rainbows is explored in both strands, sevenfold, with the pinnacle of each arch marked not by its on-beat notes but in its beautiful graces.

In several of his interviews, Messiaen described this composition as a multi-colored and immaterial, many-hued and unfathomable music, a music of confetti, of buoyant gemstones, of jangling reflections, a music that cannot be perceived with the senses, but can only be understood through an act of faith. It seems as though he attempted to capture the impenetrable mystery in highly symbolic musical tropes—a mystery that, when using words, he found best described by the allusion to silence.

---

[166] Cf., in the right-hand part,   in the left-hand part,
         bars 94 [fourth chord] to 96,   bars 94 [fifth chord] to 96,
         bars 99 to 100 [second chords]   bars 99 [third chord] to 100 [third chord].

Appendix I: Les tierces alternées

(Debussy, *Préludes*, vol. II, no. 11)

The caption of this prelude sounds somewhat foreign in the company of Debussy's wording which is generally so much more poetic. "Alternating thirds" could very well be imagined as the title of one of the composer's études. But then again, Debussy's études are by no means merely what their title suggests: studies written for the purpose of improving keyboard technique. Following a tradition of which Chopin's opp. 10 and 25 are arguably the most remarkable examples, Debussy conceived his etudes as pieces that, despite their definite technical assignments, are each a distinct musical vignette of often lyrically inspired character. In this context, and in the close relationship that the composer thus seems to perceive between pieces with pictorial titles and those with a more technical designation, "Les tierces alternées" finds its place within this collection of preludes.

Having said this, it nevertheless remains interesting that Debussy had originally planned for a prelude with a caption like the others, a piece to be called, after the story in Rudyard Kipling's *Jungle Book*, "Toomai des Eléphants." It is not known why the composer changed his mind on the issue. A prelude stimulated by Indian images might have provided a good match for *La terrace des audiences du clair de lune*.

In the absence, then, of an extra-musical source, and within the self-imposed constraints of basing an entire composition on nothing but a single interval appearing in alternating hands, it is particularly challenging to discern the features that shape this prelude into a highly eloquent work of art. These are, above all, the structural layout, the rhythm, the play with dynamics, the texture, and hidden melodic lines.

The design of the prelude can be described as a free rondo. Here is the skeleton:

A	represents the original refrain section (bars 11-33). It is followed by a first episode,
B	which, as in classical rondos, is fairly close to the refrain in character and tonality (bars 34-64). The refrain then recurs as
A'	with interesting variations and new ideas (bars 65-86). The second episode
C	constitutes a distinct contrast to the refrain in all parameters (bars 103-116), while the second recurrence of the refrain
A	is an almost identical recapitulation of the original (bars 125-148), and
B	recurs as a reminiscence with its four initial bars in the coda.

The overall design is completed by

In1	a first introduction in bars 1-10, clearly marked off from the main body by double bar lines;
In2	a second introduction in bars 91 (or 90?)-102, evolving from what precedes (a four-bar extension or codetta of the A' section) and into what follows (the second episode C) in an almost imperceptible manner;
T1,T2	transitions (bars 117-124, bars 149-153); and a
Coda	with B material plus extension (bars 154-165).

Another, rather subtle structural feature is hidden in the particular use of the *toccata* pattern of the two alternating hands. Note how the sections are distinguished:

In1	right-hand thirds on strong beats
A	left-hand thirds on strong beats
B	beginning with left-hand thirds on strong beats, but changing "focus" in bar 46 and thus dividing the episode
A'	changing back to left-hand thirds on strong beats
Intr 2 + C	another change, with two aspects: technically, hands alternate irregularly on the strong beats; practically (see e.g. bars 91/92 etc.), this organization no longer corresponds with audible patterns of "higher" and "lower" thirds.
T1	left-hand thirds on strong beats (with, as a result of the tie, an ambiguous beginning)
A, T2 + coda	left-hand thirds on strong beats

In terms of rhythmic strategy, the predominant pattern of uninterrupted sixteenth-note motion in sections A/B/A' is preceded by longer and much more varied rhythms in the initial introductory phrase; it is again contrasted in the second introduction and in section C. Furthermore, smaller deviations from the prevailing pattern occur in the bars leading up to the second introduction (see the sudden longer note values in bars 87-89) as well as in the transitions and the coda (see the syncopations in bars 122 and 124, the rest in bar 151, and the spaced writing in the final bars 162-165.)

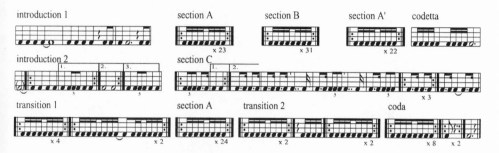

While the second episode (section C) and its introduction afford the most noticeable rhythmic contrast, the first episode (section B) brings the greatest dynamic surprises. After a prevailing tone color of *pp*, hardly disturbed in its tranquillity by two short swells, section B features *crescendo* motions hushed by downbeat returns to *p* or even *pp subito*, a six-bar *poco a poco crescendo* from *p* to *f*, as well as the decidedly jerky *f crescendo / p diminuendo* contrasts in bars 57-60.

Furthermore, there are changes in *tessitura* worth exploring. After an introduction that is widely spanned across four octaves, bars 11-33 appear as a very much centered, gentle curve, setting out in the region around middle C from where both melody and "background" ascend into the treble register before they fall back to the central register. Bars 34-45 are rooted much higher on the keyboard, and they are surpassed by a further climb in bars 46-52. There follows a spectacular plunge over three octaves that leads into the low-registered passage in bars 58-64. The varied refrain (bars 65-86), while beginning in the original middle-C range, describes a concave curve, i.e. one that is a rough mirror image of that heard in the corresponding bars 11-33. Bars 87-102 span the widest local range within the piece, covering more than two octaves in each small unit. Bars 103-116 give a even more wide-ranged impression by different means, positing treble-register material of a similar two-octave span above a contra-octave pedal-note B♭, explicit in bars 108 and 110 and implicitly perceived through six further bars. A transition centered on the C below middle C and an even lower coda round off the play with tessitura in this prelude.

As for the subtle textural colors created within the pattern of alternating thirds, the following observations regarding the longest passage in regular semiquavers may give an idea in which direction performers could deepen their explorations:

Bars 11-22   are conceived with a double-note melodic line in the lower register before a background of written-out double-note mordents (or trills with interruptions, whichever way one wants to hear this). Most of the melodic notes are followed by what amounts to an echo repetition. The representation in terms of local dynamic means thus distinguishes three "colors."

bars 11-14, 15-18

Bars 23-33   continue the pattern of melody, background mordents, and echoes. The echoing repetitions, however, are now all in the higher octave.

Bars 34-39, 42/43   give up the previous distinction of foreground and background, of melody and accompanying trills. Instead, the *toccata* pattern proceeds in bitonal strands (white keys only for the left hand, black keys for the right) that join in basically the same motion. All notes are thus equally important here.

Bars 40/41, 44/45   feature an after-beat melody (presented in the form of a double-note line passing, in portato, through the inversions of an augmented chord, and accompanied by a pedal.

Bars 46-57   present a treble melody with what appears as only rhythmically varied chordal support; one hears a progression in parallel four-three chords.

bars 46-47, 48-49

Bars 58-64   contain several layers; these, however, are designed not with melodic but with dramatic effects in mind. An (afterbeat) "background" transmutes gradually from A♭/C through A♮/C to B♭/D♭. The on-beat double-notes either blend with the background in octaves, in very low register and *p diminuendo* (as in bars 58 and 60), or they contrast in an interspersed bar by means of a second layer that creates a seventh chord and urges in *f crescendo.*

During the final four-bar *diminuendo* that serves as a retransition to the A' section, the seventh-chord impression is further expanded in that the upper part includes an anticipation (albeit on "wrong" beats) of the upcoming mordent figures. Finally, the last sixteenth-note in bar 64 is undoubtedly conceived as a melodic upbeat.

A final comment regards the tonal language Debussy employs in this prelude. It is intriguing to discover that, in addition to the various means listed above, he also distinguishes the various structural sections by using different tonal material.

- Both introductions are based on the two whole-tone scales. In the first introduction, what could be read as tetrachordal excerpts are heard, alternating between the two scales. In the second introduction, the two initial subphrases derive their pitches from the whole-tone scale on C♯, while the third subphrase (bars 99-102m) stems from the scale on C (see example next page).
- Section A is basically diatonic. The "background" double-note trills employ only white keys, and the melody could cautiously be interpreted as representing the Lydian mode on F, with G♯ the artificial leading-note to the third (see bars 11-18) and coloring by means of chromatic neighbors (see bars 22-26 and bar 31).

Introduction 1

Introduction 2

C♯/D♭- D♯/E♭- F - G - A - B

A♭- B♭- C - D - E

- Section B is more varied in itself. It begins with a bitonal passage (see bars 34-45) that consists of six bars with the left hand playing exclusively on the white and the right hand exclusively on the black keys. The pitch content of the left hand throughout the passage is that of the chord C-E-G-B-D-F, while the right hand begins taking its notes from the diatonic chord D♯-F♯-A♯-C♯ but changes then (see bar 40) to the augmented chord A♭-C-E, adding for neighbors its whole-tone relatives F♯-B♭. The second passage with its four-three chords was mentioned earlier; it is followed in bars 52-56 by sequences in parallel seventh chords from the E♭-major scale (with F♯ the artificial leading-note to the third). The final bars have already been referred to in detail.

- Section A' begins like section A in the Lydian mode on F. Bars 71-80 can be heard as the Lydian mode on A♭, bars 81-89 as the Lydian mode on A.

- Section C is again based on A♭. All metric accents support this central pitch (see the downbeats in bars 103-107 and 108, 110, 112), and in bar 108 the key signature is explicitly changed to establish the three flats as integral parts of the tonality. The scale suggests the Lydian mode—were it not for the F♯ that adds a sharpened sixth degree and thus throws the mode into doubt. While F♯ could be heard as an (albeit very unusual) leading-note to G, the entire tonal framework is soon weakened, and the section ends on the repeated chord C-E-G♭-B♭.

- After a *fermata*, this chord serves as the basis for the whole-tone scale on which the initial bars of the first transition are built (see in bars 117-120: A♭-B♭-C-D-E-F♯/G♭-A♭).

  The four bars that complement the transition, on the other hand, use a diminished triad with minor seventh (see bar 121: C-E♭-G♭-B♭) that is moved in parallel shifts through minor thirds (see bars 121/123) or a chromatic ascent (see bars 122/124).

- The second transition exhibits yet another pattern. For the first time in this piece, neither the scale context (which is chromatic here) nor the chordal structure of the four-note ensemble built by left-hand third and right-hand third is at issue, neither bitonality nor "melody + background." Instead, we hear a protracted chromatic descent in "zigzag" motion.

- The coda begins with a reminiscence from section B and extends the bitonal effect established there throughout a liquidation process during which first the pitches, then the rhythm get locked. No new tonal scheme is established, and the prelude closes on the isolated third C-E.

Appendix II:
Messiaen's Musical Language

As Messiaen expounds in his treatise *The Technique of My Musical Language*, he was fascinated by the idea of choosing pitch content in such a way that it would both create a distinct color and allow reference to various "tonal" areas. He found a systematic solution in modes based on strictly repetitive interval groups. These modes—created from a repetition of a small basic unit—allow far fewer than the twelve transpositions possible for the Greek modes on which traditional Western music is based. Owing to their inner repetition, transposition by certain intervals will cause the pitch content to run into itself.

A useful way of understanding Messiaen's "Modes of limited transposition" is to regard them as derived from the phenomenon of equidistance in pitch content, and to observe that the number of transpositions possible increases with the size of the interval from which the inner repetition is generated. (Note that Messiaen includes the original version when counting the number of transpositions.) Here is, as a reminder, the catalog of equidistant organization within the octave:

equidistance	*result*	*repetition after*	*no. of transpositions (incl. original)*
in scales	*chromatic scale*	*1 semitone*	*1*
	whole-tone scale	*2 semitones*	*2, on C+C♯*
in chords	*diminished seventh*	*3 semitones*	*3, on C, C♯ and D*
	augmented triad	*4 semitones*	*4, on C, C♯, D, D♯*
in interval	*tritone*	*6 semitones*	*6, on C, C♯, D, D♯, E, F*

Various composers (including Rimsky-Korsakov, Ravel, and Stravinsky in his octatonic scale) are credited with having experimented with symmetric modes. Probably the first to base a series of works on his own, artificial mode was Skryabin (see e.g. his piano sonatas nos. 6 to 10).

Messiaen adopts the "Skryabin scale" as his mode 2 (following the whole-tone scale as mode 1) and adds five new patterns. Although he does not offer this explanation, these modes can usefully be remembered in their relationship to the above-mentioned equidistant phenomena within the octave.

mode 1 =   *whole tones only, two transpositions*
mode 2 =   *1 semitone + 1 whole tone*
             repeated on the notes of the diminished seventh chord,
             three transpositions;
mode 3 =   *1 whole tone + 2 semitones*
             repeated on the notes of the augmented triad,
             four transpositions;
mode 4 =   *2 semitones + 1 minor third + 1 semitone,*
             repeated on the notes of the tritone, six transpositions;
mode 5 =   *1 semitone + 1 major third + 1 semitone*
             repeated on the notes of the tritone, six transpositions;
mode 6 =   *2 whole tones + 2 semitones*
             repeated on the notes of the tritone, six transpositions;
mode 7 =   *3 semitones + 1 whole tone + 1 semitone*
             repeated on the notes of the tritone, six transpositions.

The table on the next page shows, in the format of letter-names over the note C,

     (a) the equidistant phenomena mentioned before, and
     (b) Messiaen's modes as described above.

While Messiaen uses his modes both vertically and horizontally, so that they inform the melodic as well as the harmonic parameters of his music, there are a few instances where the idea of a diatonic scale, and of a chord defined more by its relation to that scale than by the modal transposition on which it is based, gains significance. This is particularly true for the F♯ major scale and the F♯ major chord with added sixth.

More often than not in Messiaen's music (both within the *Vingt Regards sur l'Enfant-Jésus* and in other compositions), we find local accidentals instead of a designated key signature. A notable exception, however, is the signature indicating an F♯ major context. Although those of Messiaen's pieces that are notated in this key signature are by no means tonal—and thus require a wealth of additional accidentals—the composer seems to make a specific point by deliberately providing the general key signature. This fact thus invites further investigation.

APPENDIX II: MESSSIAEN'S MUSICAL LANGUAGE

(a) Equidistant pitch groups

The chromatic scale

```
C D♭ D E♭ E F G♭ G A♭ A B♭ B
C D♭ D E♭ E F G♭ G A♭ A B♭ B
```

The whole-tone scale

```
C   D   E   F♯   G♯   A♯
  D♭   E♭   F   G   A   B
C   D   E   F♯   G♯   A♯
  D♭   E♭   F   G   A   B
```

The dimished-seventh chord

```
C       E♭       G♭       A
  C♯       E       G       B♭
    D       F       A♭       B
C       E♭       G♭       A
  C♯       E       G       B♭
    D       F       A♭       B
```

The augmented triad

```
C       E       G♯
  D♭       F       A
    D       F♯       A♯
      E♭       G       B
C       E       G♯
  D♭       F       A
    D       F♯       A♯
      E♭       G       B
```

The tritone

```
C           F♯
  D♭           G
    D           G♯
      E♭           A
        E           B♭
          F           B
C           F♯
  D♭           G
    D           G♯
      E♭           A
        E           B♭
          F           B
```

(b) Messiaen's modes

Mode 2 (1:2, three transpo.)

```
2¹  C D♭    E♭ E    G♭ G    A B♭
2²     D♭ D    E F    G A♭    B♭ B
2³  C    D E♭    F G♭    A♭ A    B
2¹  C D♭    E♭ E    G♭ G    A B♭
```

Mode 3 (2:1:1, four transpo.)

```
3¹  C    D E♭ E    G♭ G A♭    B♭ B
3²  C D♭    E♭ E F    G A♭ A    B
3³  C D♭ D    E F G♭    A♭ A B♭
3⁴     D♭ D E♭    F G♭ G    A B♭ B
3¹  C    D E♭ E    G♭ G A♭    B♭ B
```

Mode 4 (1:1:3:1, six transpo.)

```
4¹  C D♭ D        F G♭ G A♭        B
4²  C D♭ D E♭        G♭ G A♭ A
4³     D♭ D E♭ E        G A♭ A B♭
4⁴        D E♭ E F        A♭ A B♭ B
4⁵  C        E♭ E F G♭        A B♭ B
4⁶  C D♭        E F G♭ G        B♭ B
4¹  C D♭ D        F G♭ G A♭        B
```

Mode 5 (1:4:1, six transpo.)

```
5¹  C D♭        F G♭ G        B
5²  C D♭ D        G♭ G A♭
5³     D♭ D E♭        G A♭ A
5⁴        D E♭ E        A♭ A B♭
5⁵           E♭ E F        A B♭ B
5⁶  C           E F G♭        B♭ B
5¹  C D♭        F G♭ G        B
```

Mode 6 (2:2:1:1, six transpo.)

```
6¹  C    D    E F G♭    A♭    B♭
6²  C D♭    E♭    F G♭ G    A    B
6³  C D♭ D    E    G♭ G A♭    B♭
6⁴     D♭ D E♭    F    G A♭ A    B
6⁵  C    D E♭ E    G♭    A♭ A B♭
6⁶     D♭    E♭ E F    G    A B♭ B
6¹  C    D    E F G♭    A♭    B♭ B
```

Mode 7 (1:1:1:2:1, six transpo.)

```
7¹  C D♭ D E♭    F G♭ G A♭ A    B
7²  C D♭ D E♭ E    G♭ G A♭ A B♭
7³     D♭ D E♭ E F    G A♭ A B♭ B
7⁴  C    D E♭ E F G♭    A♭ A B♭ B
7⁵  C D♭    E♭ E F G♭ G    A B♭ B
7⁶  C D♭ D    E F G♭ G A♭    B♭ B
7¹  C D♭ D E♭    F G♭ G A♭ A    B
```

Two features immediately connected to Messiaen's use of the F♯ major context assist in discerning the composer's likely criterion for the choice of just this key. One is the fact that he prefers the F♯ major chord, in the overwhelming majority of cases, in the first inversion. This is the most "symmetrical" of the possible chord positions, featuring a central perfect-fourth interval flanked by thirds on either side (albeit necessarily one major and one minor third). The second feature is the tonic chord with added sixth that, again, Messiaen employs almost exclusively in the first inversion. Within the simple four-part chord, the notes of this chord —A♯C♯D♯F♯—accomplish a perfect symmetry: a central major second is framed by minor thirds on either side.

Proceeding one step further and placing the chord onto the keyboard, in the position clearly preferred by Messiaen, one recognizes that there is a striking visual symmetry anchored in the keyboard's central D—and this visual symmetry applies equally to the entire F♯ major scale whose pitch content presents itself in perfect bilateral symmetry on a keyboard instrument.

Visual symmetry on the keyboard:

The F♯ major scale and the inverted F♯ major chord with added sixth.[167]

 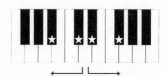

In his treatment of rhythm, Messiaen referred to Beethoven as the master of the rhythm of "masculine" character: a rhythm that is heard in relation to, and often in conflict with, a regular metric order. By contrast, Messiaen described Debussy as someone who had listened to the irregularly flowing movements of wind and waves. Allegedly in extension of what he heard prepared in Debussy's music, Messiaen developed his concept of rhythm as the multiplication of a smallest unit. In the realm of "additive rhythm," regular pulsation of larger entities is abandoned. We witness an emancipation of the indefinitely variable, individual figuration that places music into a temporal continuum that is not prestructured and could extend indefinitely.

---

[167] The seventh chord D♯-F♯-A♯-C♯ appears regularly over A♯ as a root and could thus usefully be described as a four-three chord. However, owing to the symbolic significance of the key of F♯ in Messiaen's work, the chord is here read as a major chord with added sixth. This notation should not be mistaken for figured-bass writing.

Seemingly opposed to this musical allusion to infinity, the "charm of limited possibilities" to which Messiaen referred so frequently also manifests in his organization of time. In the temporal realm as in the realms of structure and tonal material, symmetry and symmetry breaking constitute devices that carry essential spiritual messages. Messiaen's "non-retrogradable rhythms"—those rhythms with two symmetrical wings that read backwards the same as forewards—are by now famous. Their occurrence throughout Messiaen's work allows to distinguish three subcategories.

The first contains rhythmic patterns that, in their entirety, present a palindromic series of time values. (The concomitant spiritual aspect that comes to mind is that of timelessness or, as it will be referred to here, the *Eternal*.) A second category of rhythmic patterns based on the concept of the palindrome comprises phrases made up of several rhythmic groups each of which is *in itself* mirror-symmetrical. (As a tentative translation for this musical symbol into a concept of larger reality one might here think of pluralistic notions of time).

Finally, as a further development of the previous two cases, there are phrases consisting of several palindromic rhythm groups followed by a tail in vectorial time organization. This dissymmetric form, more complex than the others, is clearly Messiaen's favorite. The composer seems to employ this rhythm to symbolize the alliance of timeless, eternal qualities with time-determined, i.e. earthly concerns. (This third category of rhythmic organization will therefore here be referred to as the *Manifestation of the Eternal in Time*.)

A further step from here leads to symmetric and asymmetric growth processes in time and space. Messiaen has dedicated substantial portions of his treatise *The Technique of My Musical Language* to musical phenomena symbolizing the concept of gradual augmentation. Summing up his many examples one can identify mainly three areas where such processes apply: time (gradually growing or diminishing note values), register (gradually increasing or contracting intervals), and phrase structure (expansions or abbreviations on the horizontal plane).

In the realm of time, there are three closely related ways in which growth occurs. The first and simplest option comprises cases where the number of smallest time units in consecutive rhythmic attacks is steadily augmented, usually by one increment at a time (either by continually adding the same value, as in a row like 2, 3, 4, 5, etc. units, or through a more complex process as that known from the Fibonacci series where each consecutive value equals the sum of the two preceding ones: 2, 3, 5, 8, 13 etc.). In a second case, key strokes of increasing duration alternate with strokes of fixed value (e.g. 4, 2, 5, 2, 6, 2, 7, 2 etc. units) Finally, in a third setting, development of time values takes place on two simultaneous levels—growing on one layer, diminishing on the other. These may either run simultaneously or alternate in interlocking bars:

12 11 10 9 8 7 6 5 4 3

3 4 5 6 7 8 9 10 11 12

or

12 ₃ 11 ₄ 10 ₅ 9 6 8 7 7 etc. units).

In the realm of register, the most noteworthy phenomena are Messiaen's famous "asymmetric expansions" *(augmentations asymétriques)*: An original pitch outline is stretched and oddly distorted as if reflected in a mirror with an undulating surface.

Structural growth occurs when recurring statements of a phrase or motive are expanded by external extensions at either side, by internal extension or inserts, or by a gradually growing tail or transition.

While growth processes occurring in the realm of time clearly represent irreversible developments, those in register can take all forms—from fairly symmetrical distortions resembling those generated by regularly curved mirrors through strongly dissymmetric ones to "collapsing" and partly overshadowing processes. (The examples of structural growth appearing in Messiaen's *Vingt Regards sur l'Enfant-Jésus* include both symmetric and vectorial processes.)

Appendix III: Brief Overview of Messiaen's Piano Cycle *Vingt Regards sur l'Enfant-Jésus*

For performers and analysts, it is intriguing to try and find the correlation between, on the one hand, characteristic features of rhythm, harmony and mode, melody and structure and, on the other hand, the contents and images provided in Messiaen's theological reflections that preface the music. When asked what he thought of the relationship between the contents of the music and the compositional details, the composer (who claimed that he despised the term "program music") replied, "They are inseparable."[168] What importance the composer attached to the subheading remarks can be gleaned from the fact that, on occasion of the first performance, he read each of them aloud immediately before the respective piece was played.

To facilitate the usage of the following analysis for readers who wish to concentrate on individual pieces rather than proceeding from chapter to chapter through the entire work, here is a short overview of the spiritual context and its connection to the various musical symbols. The way in which Messiaen employs his modes within the present cycle is very consistent. Mode 1, the whole-tone scale, is the only mode not distinctly used as a symbol. Mode 2 provides the most important tonal realm of the work, while modes 3-7 appear only in the context of particular theological concepts. Introduced as the single occurring mode in the opening piece of the cycle, mode 2 may usefully be regarded as the modal equivalent to a "home key." Thus inextricably linked to the *Theme of God*, this mode is —and remains throughout the cycle—a musical representative of God, the Father, and *God's Love*.

---

[168]Messiaen, "Die Vögel erwachen und improvisieren" (conversation with Almut Rößler), in: *Neue Musikzeitung* 6/7, 1979.

Three modes are spiritually linked with the immediate birth of the Holy Child. Mode 5 is heard in only one of the pieces, namely in XVI, *The Prophets, the Shepherds, and the Magi Contemplating the Infant Jesus*. Mode 3 can be read as a symbol for the *Child in the Manger*. This mode appears prominently in the second episode of the piece *Christmas* (XIII). Mode 7 appears prominently in no. II *The Star's Contemplation* where it underlies the unison statement of the *Theme of the Star and of the Cross*. It is quoted in the same meaning in VII, *The Cross's Contemplation*, and as a short reminder in XI *First Communion of the Virgin*.

Of particular interest are the combinations and juxtapositions of modes whose reference to specific spiritual attributes can only be entirely understood when taking other pieces of the cycle into account. When mode 3 occurs in juxtaposition with mode 4 (as e.g. in bars 1-19 of XVII *Silence's Contemplation* where the manger is mentioned in Messiaen's prefacing remark), an additional aspect is added to the event of the Nativity, beyond that of the *Child in the Manger*. The hermeneutic background of mode 4 can be identified as the *Word Incarnate*. This interpretation provides a meaningful link to the interpolations of mode-4 material into the *Theme of God* in *First Communion of the Virgin*. Here, the use of mode 4 may be read as a way of underlining the aspect of divine Incarnation in the Annunciation.

The joint appearance of modes 6 and 4 seems to point to another duality in Jesus: on the one hand His mission on earth, which ends with Him taking upon Himself the sins of the world in His *Suffering on the Cross* (mode 6), on the other hand His birth full of hope and promise, as the *Word Incarnate* (mode 4). Messiaen uses this combination twice. In *The Son Contemplating the Son* (V), the chord progression in the first textural strand is drawn from mode 6^3 while that in the second strand represents the pitch content of mode 4^4, thus depicting that Jesus' divine mission was, from the very beginning, the overshadowed by the reality of his suffering. Significantly then in *The Cross's Contemplation*, a piece that is otherwise not modal (see below), the middleground chords at phrase endings recall this duality by taking their pitches from mode 6^3 in the right hand and from mode 4^6 in the left hand, again pointing to the fact that the end is part of the beginning, the suffering is an aspect of grace, and the promise is at the same time still present at the moment of Crucifixion.

piece no./ title		mode	symbol
I	*The Father's Contemplation*	2	God's Love
II	*The Star's Contemplation"*	7	Star and Cross
V	*The Son Contemplating the Son*	6	Suffering on the Cross
		4	Word Incarnate
		2	God's Love
VII	*The Cross's Contemplation*	7	Star and Cross
		6	Suffering on the Cross
		4	Word Incarnate
X	*The Spirit of Joy Contemplating*	4	Word Incarnate
		2	God's Love
XI	*First Communion of the Virgin*	2	God's Love
		4	Word Incarnate
		7	Star and Cross
XIII	*Christmas*	3	Child in the Manger
XV	*The Kiss of the Jesus-Child*	2	God's Love
XVI	*The Prophets ... Contemplating*	5	The Prophesied One
XVII	*Silence's Contemplation*	3	Child in the Manger
		4	Word Incarnate
XX	*The Church of Love Contemplating*	2	God's Love

Where modes, which order tonal material, may be read as denoting something akin to an innate quality, growth processes signify development and directionality. Messiaen uses three kinds of growth processes: those expanding in time, in register, and in terms of structure. The attribute to which all three kinds of growth processes seem to relate is perhaps best captured in the word *Transformation*. Aspects of this concept include the realms of the Word becoming flesh (in the exchange of divine and human nature in Jesus), the Word engendering reality (in the Creation), and the Word spawning a living faith (in the Church). There is also an element of transformation by rapture (in the Spirit of Joy, Mary's perception of the God within her womb, and the reaction of the angels).

As these introductory remarks have tried to show, Messiaen's musical language can indeed be read as symbolic, containing representations of divine attributes and other transcendental concepts. It is intriguing although by no means surprising to notice that superior order, regularity and symmetry reign in all musical symbols referring to divine properties as such; see, among others, the symmetric properties of tonality, mode and chord chosen for *God's Love* as well as the symmetric organization of time values in the symbols of the *Eternal*. Figurative expression of organic development and dissymmetry, on the other hand, occurs where

393

the composer portrays the intersection of the infinite with the finite realm; see e.g. the vectorial conclusions in the rhythmic symbols of the *Manifestation of the Eternal in Time* and the manifold growth processes representing the idea of *Transformation*.

As for the cyclical themes and the group of attributes they represents, the most important one is the *Theme of God.* Throughout the cycle, it recurs in various forms and degrees of extensiveness—quoted in the entirety of its two stanzas with coda as presented in the opening piece of the cycle, or only alluded to through details of tonal organization or one of its characteristic tonal symbols. In two instances, the complete musical message of the initial piece recurs intact. The fifth piece of the cycle, *The Son Contemplating the Son*, is conceived as a variation of *The Father's Contemplation*. It literally quotes the entire thematic argument of the *Theme of God*, which appears in a supporting position, as the lowest of three clearly distinct strands within a texture that could be described as three homophonically singing choruses. The second variation of *The Father's Contemplation*. is heard at the very end of the cycle, in the final section of the final piece, *The Church of Love Contemplating the Infant Jesus*.

Beyond these striking recurrences in its entirety of the piece that epitomizes God's Love, there are further suggestive allusions created by one or more of the symbols subsumed within the first group. Piece XI, *First Communion of the Virgin*, portrays Mary's love of the child growing in her womb, whose divine nature has been revealed to her in the Annunciation. God's Love is powerfully evoked here by a repeated quotation of the initial phrase of the *Thème de Dieu*, in a version very close to the original thematic material. Interestingly, the concomitant mode 2, dominating bars 1-20, is here countered by material in mode 4. As will be shown in more detail below, this is the mode Messiaen uses repeatedly to point to the aspect of Incarnation of the Divine Word in Jesus.

The initial phrase of the *Thème de Dieu*, in the original tonal context of F♯ major but now enveloped in toccata passages, appears also in the tenth section (bars 161-204) of piece VI, *Through Him All Was Made*. Here, the *Thème-de-Dieu* phrase is followed by two sequences in the other two transpositions of mode 2, thus providing what could be called a complete statement of the modal symbol of God's Love. Moreover, it is in this piece that Messiaen introduces, immediately prior to the conclusion of the embellished *Theme-of-God* phrase, his *Thème d'amour* which, as we shall see, stands for the human Love of God. The composer's underlying theology could thus be rendered as follows: the creation is not only an expression of God's Love; the manifestation of God's (complete) Love in His creation in turn generates the human potential of love, particularly of the Love of God.

Another piece that restates all three transpositions of mode 2 is no.X *The Spirit of Joy Contemplating the Infant Jesus*. This time, no melodic connection with the *Thème de Dieu* exists. Messiaen's particular use of tonal spheres, however, clearly places this quotation of mode 2 in the immediate context of the symbol group representing God's Love: In the fourth section of the piece, the three transpositions of mode 2 appear in sequential phrases following each other very much like those in *Through Him All Was Made*. Interestingly, Messiaen describes the thematic context for this indirect allusion to God's Love with the words "like a hunting song". The fifth section contains a close reference to the *Thème de Dieu*, in which the original chords, characteristic melodic intervals and strict use of mode 2 are retained, while rhythm, meter and phrase length are freely modified.

That God's Love is ever-present even in his *Almighty Word* is musically acknowledged in piece XII of the cycle. It contains three recurring motives that, while thematically entirely unrelated to the *Thème de Dieu*, draw very obviously on the pitch content of mode 2.

XV, *The Kiss of the Jesus-Child*, also contains many of the symbols epitomizing God's Love. The key signature is F♯ major, every two-bar phrase in the refrain leads to the F♯ major chord with added sixth, and the identical codettas in bars 60/61 and 135/136 complete the reference with further statements of the "chord of love." The *Thème de Dieu*, quoted in the refrain in a modification that transcends any mode, is returned to its original format in the central episode (bars 64-73), thus combining the F♯ major context with mode 2^1. The nineteenth piece of the cycle, *I Sleep, But My Heart Wakes* which, according to Messiaen's subtitle, refers to the "sleeping Jesus who loves us", contains a similarly multi-layered allusion to God's Love. F♯ major here is not only indicated in the key signature but actually appears, in the main section as well as in the final bars of the piece, in completely untainted chords, thus bathing the listener, as it were, in pure love for what in the extremely slow tempo of this piece lasts more than a minute. In-between, mode 2 dominates section B as well as the first half of the Coda, and the "chord of love" is prominently stated at structurally crucial points.

Appendix IV:
French Performance Indications

1. CLAUDE DEBUSSY: *PRÉLUDES*

I/1 ...   ... Danseuses de Delphes

lent et grave	slow and solemn
doux et soutenu	soft and sustained [in tone color]
doux mais en dehors	soft but enhanced

I/2 ...   ... Voiles

modéré	moderate
dans un rythme sans rigeur et caressant	in a rhythm without rigidity and caressing
très doux	very soft
expressif	expressive
toujours pp	always *pp*, i.e. no strong-beat accents
très souple	very relaxed
cédez - - // a tempo	"give way" [slow down] to // resume tempo
serrez	"contract", i.e. speed up slightly
en animant [169]	enlivening / quickening
rapide	swift
emporté	carried away
très retenu	very much held back [in tempo]
au movement	in the [original] tempo
comme un très léger glissando	like a very light *glissando*

---

[169] Note the difference between the present and the past participles, which is crucial for a full understanding of the composer's expressive intention: *en retenant* (slow**ing** down) and *en animant* (enliven**ing**) designate a gradual process, whereas *plus retenu* (in a slower tempo) and *plus animé* (in a more lively tempo) indicate that a tempo slower or faster than the preceding **has been reached**. Throughout his work, Debussy distinguishes meticulously between the two aspects of "ongoing development" and "new state attained."

doucement en dehors	gently enhanced
très apaisé et très atténué	very much appeased and soothed
jusqu'à la fin	to the end

I/3 ...   ... Le vent dans la plaine

animé	lively
aussi légèrement que possible	as lightly as possible
cédez - - // a tempo	"give way" [slow down] to // resume tempo
laisser vibrer	allow to ring (i.e. let the sound fade)

I/4 ...   ... "Les sons et les parfums tournent dans l'air du soir"

modéré	moderate
harmonieux et souple	harmonious and supple
en animant un peu	enlivening a little (i.e. picking up some speed)
en retenant	slowing down
égal et doux	even and soft
en dehors	enhanced
serrez un peu	"tighten", i.e. speed up, a bit
retenu	held back [in tempo]
plus lent	slower
cédez	"give way", i.e. slow down
la basse un peu appuyée et soutenue	the bass somewhat heavy and sustained
tranquille[170] *et flottant*	calm and floating
en retenant	holding back, i.e. slowing down
léger	light
plus retenu	in a slower tempo
comme une lointaine sonnerie de cors	like a faraway sounding of horns
encore plus lointain et plus retenu	even further away and slower

I/5 ...   ... Les collines d'Anacapri

très modéré	very moderate
quittez, en laissant vibrer	leave [the keyboard with your hands] while allowing [the sound] to ring
vif	vivacious
léger et lointain	lightly and far away

---

[170]This indication is perhaps slightly ambiguous: *tranquille*, as in English "tranquil", does not necessarily signify a slower tempo but more often just a composed attitude. The subsequent *tempo*, however, defines the term in bar 41 in retrospect as denoting also reduced motion.

en serrant	"tightening", i.e. speeding up
joyeux et léger	joyous and light
cédez - - // a tempo	"give way" [slow down] to // resume tempo
un peu en dehors	somewhat enhanced
avec la liberté d'une chanson populaire	with the freedom of a folk song
un peu marqué	somewhat accented
plus modéré	more moderate, i.e. slower still
retenu	held back [= slower tempo]
presque lent	almost slow
lumineux	luminous
très retenu	very slow

I/6 . . .   . . . Des pas sur la neige[171]

triste et lent	sad and slow
Ce rythme doit avoir la valeur sonore d'unfond de paysage triste et glacé	this rhythm should have the sound value [coloristic effect] of a sad and icy landscape
expressif et douloureux	expressive and sorrowful
en animant surtout dans l'expression	enlivening particularly in terms of expression [i.e. by increasing not so much the tempo but rather the intensity]
p expressif et tendre	in a soft hue that is expressive and tender
comme un tendre regret	like a tender regret
plus lent / très lent	slower / very slow

I/7 . . .   . . . Ce qu'a vu le vent d'ouest

animé et tumultueux	spirited and tumultuous
plaintif et lointain	lamenting and far-away
un peu marqué	somewhat accented
commencer un peu au-dessous du mouvement	begin somewhat below the [original] tempo
revenir progressivement au mvmt. animé	return gradually to the lively tempo
strident	piercing
un peu retenu	somewhat held back [in tempo]
p mais en dehors et angoissé	soft but enhanced and anguished
en serrant et augmentant beaucoup	getting much faster and louder
très en dehors	very much enhanced

---

[171]The word *cédez*, where not followed by - - //, indicates a small and gradual lessening of tempo followed by a passage in a distinctly slower pace; *retenu* refers to a tempo that is slower (as opposed to gradually getting slower).

peu à peu crescendo en serrant	gradually louder while getting faster
incisif	incisive
furieux et rapide	furious and rapid
serrez et augmentez	contract and augment [= faster and louder]
retenu	held back, i.e. slower tempo
au mouvement	back in tempo

I/8 . . .   . . . La fille aux cheveux de lin[172]

très calme et doucement expressif	very calm and softly expressive
sans rigeur	without rigidity
cédez - - - //mouvement	"give way" [slow down] to // resume tempo
très peu [crescendo]	increasing very little
un peu animé	somewhat livened
sans lourdeur	without heaviness
très doux	very soft
murmuré et en retenant peu à peu	murmured and gradually slowing down

I/9 . . .   . . . La sérénade interrompue

modérément animé	moderately lively
comme en préludant	as if improvising an introduction
les deux pédales	[use] both pedals
expressif et un peu suppliant	expressive and somewhat pleading
estompé et en suivant l'expression	blurred and freely emotional
cédez - - - // a tempo	"give way" [slow down] to // resume tempo
très vif	very fast
retenu - - - // a tempo	held back [slower] up to // resume tempo
librement	freely [in terms of rhythm]
modéré	moderate
lointain	far away
rageur	furious
revenir au mouvement	return to the [original] tempo
doux et harmonieux	soft and harmonious
en s'éloignant	moving away

I/10 . . .   . . . La cathédrale engloutie

profondément calme,dans	profoundly calm,
* une brume doucement sonore*	in a softly resonant haze
doux et fluide	soft and fluid

[172]The expressive indications in this piece, together with the dynamic markings which remain in the *p-pp* range with the exception of a single bar in *mf*, point to the delicate nature of the girl depicted in the poem; the simplicity of the melodic material and the harmonic layout emphasise her candour. The result is a musical miniature of truly impressionistic coloring—in the best sense of that often-misused word.

sans nuances	without nuances [of tone color/dynamics]
peu à peu sortant de la brume	gradually emerging from the haze
marqué	accented
augmentez progressivement, sans presser	increase gradually, without rushing
sonore sans dureté	resonant without harshness
un peu moins lent, dans une expression allant grandissant	somewhat less slow, with growing feeling
expressif et concentré	expressive and concentrated
flottant et sourd	floating and muffled
comme un écho de la phrase entendue précédemment	like an echo of the phrase heard previously
dans la sonorité du début	in the resonance [color, intensity] of the beginning

I/11 ...   ... La danse de Puck

capricieux et léger	capricious and light
retenu - - - // mouvement	slower up to // then back to tempo
pressez	hurry, i.e. get faster
aérien	airy, celestial
doucement soutenu	softly sustained
un peu en dehors	somewhat enhanced
en cédant	in "giving way", i.e. slowing down
dans le mouvement	in the [original] tempo
plus retenu	[even] slower
marqué	accented
rapide et fuyant	swift and fleeting

I/12 ...   ... Minstrels

modéré, nerveux et avec humour	moderate, pithy and humorous
les "gruppetti" sur le temps	the note-groups *on* the beats
cédez - - - // mouvement	"give way" [slow down] to // resume tempo
un peu plus allant	a little more forward-moving
très détaché	very much detached
en cédant	giving way = slowing down
moqueur	mocking
expressif	expressive
en dehors	enhanced
mouvement plus allant	tempo more forward-moving
serrez - - - //	"tighten," i.e. speed up
sec et retenu	dry and held back

II/1 . . .   . . . Brouillards

modéré	moderate
extrêmement égal et léger	extremely even and light
la main gauche un peu en valeur	the left hand somewhat more
sur la main droite	emphasized than the right hand
cédez - - - // mouvement	slow down up to // [back in] tempo
un peu en dehors	somewhat enhanced [here probably
	refering to the tenor]
un peu retenu	somewhat held back, i.e. slower
un peu marqué	somewhat accented
en retenant et en s'effaçant	slowing down and vanishing
presque plus rien	almost nothing left [this may refer to
	both sound and motion: "fading into
	nothingness"/"no more animation"]

II/2 . . .   . . . Feuilles mortes

lent et mélancholique	slow and melancholy
doucement soutenu et très expressif	softly sustained and very expressive
un peu plus allant	a little more forward-moving
et plus gravement expressif	and more solemnly expressive
un peu en dehors	somewhat enhanced
plus lent	slower
marqué	accented
cédez - - - // mouvement	slow down up to // [back in] tempo
dans le sentiment du début	in the feeling of the beginning
lointain	far away

II/3 . . .   . . . La Puerta del Vino

mouvement de Habanera	in the tempo of a Cuban *tango*
avec de brusques oppositions	with brusque contrasts of extreme
d'extrême violence et de	violence and passionate sweetness
passionnée douceur	
âpre	rude
très expressif	very expressive
marqué	accented
au mouvement	in [the original] tempo
passionnément	passionately
ironique	ironical
gracieux	gracious
en retenant	gradually slowing down
un peu retardé	somewhat delayed
lointain	far away

II/4 ...   ... "Les fées sont d'exquises danseuses"

rapide et léger	swift and light
marqué	accented
au mouvement	in [the original] tempo
cédez - - - //	"give way", i.e. slow down, up to //
sans rigeur	without rigidity
expressif	expressive
retenu - - - //1er mouvement	"held back", i.e. slower, up to // first tempo
caressant	caressing
en retenant	gradually slowing down
doux et rêveur	soft and dream-like
un peu en dehors	somewhat enhanced
serrez	"tighten", i.e. speed up
au mouvement (en retenant)	in [the original] tempo, then gradually slowing down

II/5 ...   ... Bruyères

calme - doucement expressif	calm - softly expressive
doux et léger	soft and light
un peu animé	somewhat lively
joyeux	joyous
expressif	expressive
doux	soft
cédez - - - // au mouvement	"give way" [slow down] to // resume tempo
en retenant	holding back, i.e. slowing down
doucement soutenu	softly sustained
sans lourdeur	without heaviness

II/6 ...   ... "General Lavine" - eccentric

Dans le style et le Mouvement d'un Cake-Walk	in the style and tempo of a cake-walk
strident	piercing
spirituel et discret	witty and cool
sec	dry
traîné	sluggish, dawdling
mouvement	tempo; or: back to tempo
très retenu	very much held back, i.e. slowed down
animez	enliven, i.e. speed up

II/7 ...   ... La terrasse des audiences du clair de lune

lent	slow
un peu en dehors	somewhat enhanced

403

marqué	accented
un peu animé	somewhat lively
au mouvement	[back] in tempo
en animant peu à peu	gradually more and more lively
cédez - - - // mouvement du début	"give way," i.e. slow down up to // [in the] tempo of the beginning
plus lent	slower
timbrez légèrement la petite note	give the small note a light sound color

II/8 . . .   . . . Ondine

retenu - - - // au mouvement	slower up to // [back in] tempo
scintillant	sparkling
doux	soft
à l'aise	at ease
léger	light, weightless
en dehors	enhanced
expressif	expressive
le double plus lent	twice as slow
un peu au-dessous du mouvement	somewhat below tempo
doucement marqué	gently accented
aussi léger que possible	as light as possible[173]

II/9 . . .   . . . Hommage à S. Pickwick Esq. P. P. M. P. C.

grave	stately
sonore	resonant
aimable	amiable
expressif	expressive
peu à peu animé	gradually picking up tempo
léger	light
retenu	held back, i.e. slower
mouvement	[back in] tempo
animez peu à peu	increase the tempo little by little
lointain et léger	far away and light
mouvement retenu	reduced tempo[174]

II/10 . . .   . . . Canope

très calme et doucement triste	very calm and sad in a soft way
cédez - - - // mouvement	"give way" [slow down] to // resume tempo

[173]The Italian indication in bar 44, *murmurando* (murmuring), gives a good idea of the color Debussy imagined for these broken-chord figures.

[174]Note that *même mouvement* (bar 44) explicitly specifies "same tempo," thus indicating a rather fast pace for the "whistled tune."

404

animez un peu	increase the tempo somewhat
marqué	accented
1er [premier] mouvement	first tempo
retenu	"held back," i.e. slowed down
plus lent	slower
très doux et très expressif	very soft and very expressive
très lent	very slow
encore plus doux	even softer

II/11 . . .   . . . Les tierces alternées

modérément animé	moderately lively
cédez	"give way," i.e. slow down
un peu plus animé	somewhat more lively
légèrement détaché sans sécheresse	lightly detached without dryness
les notes marquées du signe -	the notes marked with a dash
doucement timbrées	softly resonant
doux et lié	soft and linked
retenu	"held back," i.e. slowed down
gracieux	gracious
au mouvement	in [the original] tempo

II/12 . . .   . . . Feux d'Artifice

modérément animé	moderately lively
léger, égal et lointain	light, even and far away
marqué	accented
en se rapprochant peu à peu	gradually drawing nearer
très en dehors	very much emphasized
laisser vibrer	allow to vibrate
strident	piercing
retenu - - - //	"held back," i.e. slowed down, up to //
mouvement(plus à'laise)	[back in]tempo (more at ease [i.e. not so strictly metrical, not hurried])
volubile	undulating
les basses légères et harmonieuses	the bass-notes light and harmonious
doux et harmonieux	soft and harmonious
incisif et rapide	harsh and swift
mouvement élargi	broadened tempo
éclatant	bursting out
plus lent	slower
très retenu	very much "held back" = slowed down
encore plus lent	still slower
aussi léger et pp que possible	as lightly and softly as possible
de très loin	from very far

2. MAURICE RAVEL: *MIROIRS*

Noctuelles

très léger	very light
pas trop lent	not too slow
sombre et expressif	gloomy and expressive
très expressif	very expressive [here: slowing down]
revenez au premier mouvement	return to the first tempo
en dehors	enhanced
presque lent	almost slow
lointain	far away

Oiseaux tristes

très lent	very slow
très doux	very soft
lointain	far away
pressez	"contract", i.e. speed up
revenez au mouvement	return to the [original] tempo
lent	slow
presque ad lib.	almost without stable pulse
pressez légèrement	"tighten", i.e. speed up slightly
encore plus lent	even slower
sombre et lointain	gloomy and far away

Une barque sur l'océan

d'un rythme souple	in a supple rhythm
très enveloppé de pédales	very much immersed in pedals
en dehors	enhanced
un peu en dehors	somewhat enhanced
très expressif	very expressive
sans nuances	without nuances [of tone color, dynamics]
augmentez peu a peu	increase gradually [in loudness]
le trémolo très fondu	the tremolo very much fused

Alborada del gracioso

assez vif	rather fast
sec les arpèges très serrés	dry, the rolled chords very brisk
plus lent	slower
1er (premier) mouvement	first tempo
très mesuré	very metrical
enlevez la sourdine	lift the soft pedal
le chant mf très expressif	the chant in *mf* and very expressive

très rythmé	very rhtythmical
ralentir	slow down
même mouvement	[in the] same tempo
cédez légèrement	slightly "give way", i.e. slow down
gardez la pédale jusqu'à *	keep the pedal down up to *
sans ralentir	without slowing down
très sec et bien rythmé	very dry and very rhythmical
cédez très peu	"give way", i.e. slow down, very little
revenez au mouvement	return to [the earlier] tempo
très marquè	very much emphasized

La vallée des cloches

très lent	very slow
très doux et sans accentuation	very soft and without any accents
p un peu marqué	soft, a bit emphasized
très calme	very calm
largement chanté	chanted in a grand gesture

* * *

3. MAURICE RAVEL: *GASPARD DE LA NUIT*

Ondine

lent	slow
très doux et très expressif	very soft and very expressive
cédez légèrement	give way, slow down slightly
un peu retenu	somewhat "held back", i.e. slower
au mouvement	back in [the original] tempo
le chant bien soutenu et expressif	the chant very sustained and expressive
augmentez peu à peu	augment gradually [loudness and speed]
retenez	hold back, i.e. slow down
un peu plus lent	somewhat slower
encore plus lent	even slower
le plus p possible	as p soft as possible
un peu plus lent qu'au début	somewhat slower than at the beginning
un peu en dehors	somewhat enhanced
très lent	very slow
rapide et brillant	swift and brilliant
retenez peu à peu	hold back, i.e. slow down gradually
au mouvement du début	in the tempo of the beginning
bien égal de sonorité	very even in tone color
sans ralentir	without slowing down

Le Gibet

très lent	very slow
sans presser ni ralentir jusqu'à la fin	from here to the end without hurrying or slowing down
sourdine durant toute la pièce	soft pedal for the entire piece
un peu marqué	somewhat emphasized
expressif	expressive
très lié	very much linked
un peu en dehors	somewhat enhanced
toujours ppp	always (continuing) ppp
un peu en dehors, mais sans expression	somewhat enhanced, but without expression

Scarbo

modéré	moderate
sourdine	soft pedal
très fondu, en trémolo	very much faded, like a tremolo
très long	very long
en accélérant	getting faster
vif	fast
au mouvement	in [the old] tempo
sans ralentir	without slowing down
un peu marqué	somewhat emphasized
ppp très fondu et bien égal de sonorité	ppp, very faded and very even in tone color
sans arrêt	without stopping
un peu retenu	somewhat slowed down
x = y *du mouvement précédent*	note value x (in the passage to come) equals value y in the preceding tempo
toujours pp	always (= continuing) pp
toujours en accélérant	getting still faster
1er (= premier) mouvement	[back to the] first tempo
en retenant un peu	slowing down somewhat
un peu moins vif	somewhat less fast
très peu retenu	slowed down very very little

4. OLIVIER MESSIAEN: *VINGT REGARDS SUR L'ENFANT-JÉSUS*

I   Regard du Père

extrêmement lent	extremely slow
mystérieux, avec amour	mysterious, with love
thème de Dieu	theme of God

II   Regard de l'étoile

modéré	moderate
comme des cloches	like bells
accords de carillon	carillon chords
modéré, un peu lent	moderate, somewhat slow
thème de l'étoile et de la croix	theme of the Star and the Cross

III   L'échange

bien modéré	very moderate
agrandissement asymétrique	asymmetric growth

IV   Regard de la Vièrge

bien modéré	very moderate
tendre et naïf	tender and naive
la pureté	the purity
plus vif	faster
sans Ped	without pedal
modéré	moderate
percuté, comme un xylophone	percussive, like a xylophone
oiseau	bird
très modéré, très tendre	very moderate, very tender

V   Regard du Fils sur le Fils

très lent	very slow
polymodalité et canon rythmique par ajout du point	polymodality and rhythmic canon by lengthening each value by half
doux et mystérieux	soft and mysterious
thème de Dieu	theme of God
lumineux et solennel	luminous and solemn
pressez un peu	speed up a little
un peu plus vif	somewhat faster
comme un chant d'oiseau	like bird song
1er mouvement	[back in] first tempo

6 (pour 4)	sextuplet
beaucoup plus lent	much slower

VI Par Lui tout a été fait

modéré, presque vif	moderate, almost fast
sujet, contre-sujet	subject, counter-subject
sujet changé de rythme et de régistres	subject in different rhythm and registers
réponse contraire	inverted answer
contre-sujet contraire	inverted counter-subject
stretto du sujet, canon de rythmes non-rétrogradables	subject in stretto, canon of non-retrograd-able [i.e. palindromic] rhythms
thème d'accords concentré	concentrated theme of chords
sujet, canon à 3 voix	subject in three-part canon
fractionnement des accords de la 23ᵉ mesure	break-up of the chords from bar 23
un peu moins vif	somewhat less fast
fragment du sujet	fragment of the subject
agrandissement asymétrique	asymmetric growth
éliminé à gauche / à droite	[notes] eliminated at the left / the right
milieu	center
voir 45ᵉ mesure	see bar 45
groupes formant des valeurs très brèves et très longues	groups of very short and very long values
très brouillé de pédale	very much muddied by pedal
reprise rétrogradé	recapitulation in retrograde motion
1er mouvement	[back in] first tempo
court	brief [halt, for the fermata]
moins vif	less fast
pressez peu à peu jusqu'à environ 108 à la ¹/8	increase the tempo gradually up to approximately 108 for the ¹/8
ralentir un peu	slowing down somewhat
dessus	[hand turned] over
victorieux et agité	victorious and restless
la face de Dieu derrière la flamme et le bouillonnement	God's face behind the flame and the churning water
un peu plus lent	somewhat slower
thème d'amour	theme of love
au mouvement	[back] in tempo
la création chante le thème de Dieu	the Creation sings the theme of God
lent	slow
très modéré	very moderate
très vif	very fast

VII Regard de la Croix

bien modéré	very moderate
expressif et douloureux	expressive and sorrowful
thème de l'étoile et de la croix	theme of the Star and the Cross

VIII Regard des hauteurs

vif fast	
modéré	moderate
un peu vif	somewhat fast
le rossignol	the nightingale
l'alouette	the lark
le merle et tous les oiseaux	the blackbird / robin and all the birds
très vif	very fast
brouillé de pédale	muddied in pedal
un peu vif	somewhat fast
pressez	speed up
sec dry	

IX Regard du temps

modéré	moderate
canon rythmique	rhythmic canon

X Regard de l'Esprit de joie

preque vif	almost fast
thème de danse orientale et plain-chantesque	oriental dance theme in the style of plain chant
violent	violent
court	brief
modéré	moderate
expressif	expressive
thème de joie	theme of joy
un peu plus vif	somewhat faster
brouillé de pédale	muddied in pedal
agrandissement asymétrique	asymmetric growth
au mouvement plus vif	[back] in the faster tempo
bien modéré (mais de plus en plus véhément)	very moderate (but increasingly more vehement)
comme un air de chasse, comme des cors	like a hunting song, like horns
cette mesure un peu plus lente; id. aux passages similaires	this bar somewhat slower; the same in the similar passages
cuivré	brassy
très modéré	very moderate
dans un grand transport de joie	in a great ecstasy of joy

411

encore plus modéré	even more moderate
expressif	expressive
thème de Dieu	theme of God
pressez	speed up
pressez beaucoup	speed up very much
plus lent	slower
très lent	very slow
les petites notes: lentes	take the grace-notes slow

XI Première communion de la Vierge

très lent	very slow
intérieur	intimate
thème de Dieu	theme of God
un peu plus vif	somewhat faster
oiseau	bird
premier mouvement	first tempo
plus lent	slower
rappel de "la Vierge et l'Enfant"	reminiscence of "The Virgin and theInfant"
très rapide	very swift
modéré, un peu vif	moderate, somewhat fast
Magnificat - enthusiasme haletant	Magnificat—breathless enthusiasm
rapide	swift
au mouvement	[back] in tempo
pressez	speed up
modéré	moderate
battement du coeur de l'Enfant	heartbeat of the Infant
les petites notes: (encore) plus lentes	the grace-notes (even) slower
embrassement intérieur	intimate kiss
tendre	tender

XII La parole toute-puissante

un peu vif	somewhat fast
tam-tam; pédale rythmique sur un rythme non-rétrogradable	tam-tam; rhythmic pedal on a non-retro-gradable (palindromic) rhythm
roulement de tambour	drum roll

XIII Noël

très vif, joyeux	very fast, joyous
comme des cloches	like bells
modéré, un peu vif	moderate, somewhat fast
comme un xylophone	like a xylophone
fractionnement des accords de la 6ᵉ mesure	break-up of the chords from bar 6

412

au mouvement	[back] in tempo
sans attendre	without waiting
très modéré	very moderate
tendre	tender

XIV   Regard des Anges

très vif	very fast
modéré	moderate
thème d'accords	theme of chords
canon rythmique	rhythmic canon
trombones	trombones
fractionnement du thème d'accords	break-up of the theme of chords
même mouvement	same tempo
comme un oiseau	like a bird
bien modéré	very moderate
la stupeur des anges s'agrandit	the angel's amazement grows

XV   Le baiser de l'Enfant-Jésus

très lent, calme	very slow, calm
thème de Dieu en berceuse	theme of God in the style of a lullaby
un peu plus lent	somewhat slower
au mouvement	[back] in tempo
peu à peu mf	gradually [up to] mf
expressif	expressive
un peu ralenti	somewhat slowed down
ralentir la dernière croche de la mesure, ralentir les derniers battements du trill; un court point d'orgue sur la triple croche; la pédale pendant la virgule	slow down the bar's last eighth-note, slow down the last shakes of the trill; a brief pedal-point on the thirty-second-note; [sustain] the pedal during the caesura
id. *aux passages similaires*	equally in similar passages
la petite note lente	[take] the grace-note slow
pressez... pressez encore	speed up ... speed up even more
vif	fast
au mouvement très lent	in a very slow tempo
modéré	moderate
le jardin	the garden
léger	light
thème d'accords	theme of chords
accords de carillon	carillon chords
presque vif, avec passion	almost fast, with passion
les bras tendus vers l'amour	arms extended towards love

très intense d'expression	of very intense expression
reprenez le mouvement peu à peu	gradually resume the tempo
marquez beaucoup des accents	stress the accents very much
pressez un peu	speed up a little
très ralenti	in a very much slower tempo
encore plus ralenti	slowed down even more
le baiser	the kiss
avec amour	with love
chantant, très lié	singing, very smoothly linked
court	brief
très modéré	very moderate
l'ombre du baiser	the shadow of the kiss
doux et suave	sweet and pleasant
un peu ralenti	in a somewhat slower tempo
extrêmement lent	extremely slow

XVI   Regard des prophètes, des bergers et des Mages

modéré	moderate
comme un tam-tam	like a tam-tam
laisser résonner	allow to reverberate
valeurs progressivement accélérées	progressively faster note values
hautbois	oboe
un peu criard	somewhat shrill
énergique	forceful
sourd et lointain	muffled and far away
valeurs progressivement ralenties	progressively slower note values

XVII   Regard du silence

très modéré	very moderate
canon rythmique par	rhythmic canon by adding a point
ajout du point	[i.e. lengthening each value by half]
impalpable	impalpable
bien modéré	very moderate
thème d'accords	theme of chords
au movement	[back] in tempo
modéré, presque vif	moderate, almost fast
thème d'accords, rétrogradé	theme of chords, in retrograde and
et droit	straight motion
en arc-en-ciel	in the style of a rainbow
même mouvement	same tempo
pédale jusqu'à la fin	pedal all through to the end
laisser vibrer	allow to reverberate

XVIII Regard de l'Onction terrible

modéré	moderate
valeurs progressivement ralenties	progressively slower note values
valeurs progressivement accélérées	progressively faster note values
vif	fast
bien modéré	very moderate
arraché	snatched
solennel, mais un peu vif	solemn, but somewhat fast
comme la foudre	like lightning
martelé	hammered
au movement	[back] in tempo
thème d'accords	theme of chords

XIX Je dors, mais mon coeur veille

lent	slow
souple et suave	supple and sweet
un peu lent	somewhat slow
avec charme	with charm
thème d'amour	theme of love
berceur	rocking
un peu plus vif	somewhat faster
très modéré	very moderate
expressif	expressive
extatique	ecstatic
thème d'accords concentré	concentrated theme of chords

XX Regard de l'Eglise d'amour

en gerbe rapide	in a swift spray
1er thème non-rétrogradable	first palindromic theme
amplifié à gauche... et à droite	broadened at the left.... and the right
thème de Dieu	theme of God
brouillé de pédale, confus et menaçant	muddied in pedal, confused and threatening
agrandissement asymétrique	asymmetric growth
bien modéré	very moderate
vif	fast
presque lent	almost slow
presque vif	almost fast
thème d'amour	theme of love
passionné	passionate
un peu moins vif	somewhat less fast
avec un sentiment de joie intense	with a feeling of intense joy
très modéré	very moderate

415

comme des cloches	like bells
accords de carillon	carillon chords
un peu plus lent	somewhat slower
valeurs progressivement ralenties	progressively slower note values
très lent, solennel	very slow, solemn
glorification du thème de Dieu	glorification of the theme of God
plus vif	faster
pressez	speed up
au mouvement	[back] in tempo
oiseau	bird
triomphe d'amour et de joie	triumph of love and joy
partir en dessous du mouvement et le reprendre peu à peu	begin under tempo and pick up gradually
sec	dry

416

Further Reading

On the hermeneutic approach to music:

Cone, Edward T., *Musical Form and Musical Performance*, New York: W. W. Norton, 1968

Dahlhaus, Carl, *Systematische Musikwissenschaft,* Laaber: Laaber-Verlag, 1982

Dahlhaus, Carl, *Beiträge zur musikalischen Hermeneutik,* Regensburg: G. Bosse, 1975

Kivy, Peter, *Sound Sentiment: An Essay on the Musical Emotions,* Philadelphia: Temple University Press, 1989

Kramer, Lawrence, *Music as Cultural Practice, 1800-1900*, Berkeley: University of California Press, 1990

Kramer, Lawrence, *Music and Poetry: The Nineteenth Century and After,* Berkeley: University of California Press, 1984

Langer, Suzanne, *Feeling and Form: A Theory of Art,* New York:: Scribner, 1953

Lippman, Edward, "The Problem of Musical Hermeneutics: A Protest and Analysis" in *Art and Philosophy: A Symposium,* New York: New York University Press, 1966

Meyer, Leonard, *Music, the Arts, and Ideas; Patterns and Predictions in Twentieth-Century Culture,* Chicago: University of Chicago Press, 1967

Meyer, Leonard, *Emotion and Meaning in Music,* Chicago: University of Chicago Press, 1956

Treitler, Leo, *Music and the Historical Imagination,* Cambridge, Mas- sachusetts: Harvard University Press, 1989

Tomlinson, Gary, *Music in Renaissance Magic: Toward a Historiography of others*; Chicago: University of Chicago Press, 1992

On Debussy:

Barraque, Jean, *Debussy,* Paris: Seuil, 1962/1979

Briscoe, James R., *Claude Debussy: A Guide to Research*, New York: Garland, 1990

Debussy, Claude, *Letters,* London, Boston: Faber and Faber, 1987 and Cambridge, Mass: Harvard University Press, 1987

Debussy, Claude, *Debussy on Music: The Critical Writings of the Great French Composer Claude Debussy*, New York: A. A. Knopf, 1977

Dumesnil, Maurice, *Claude Debussy, Master of Dreams,* Westport, Conn: Greenwood Press, 1979

Hirsbrunner, Theo, *Debussy und seine Zeit,* Laaber: Laaber-Verlag, 1981

Howat, Roy, *Debussy in Proportion: A Musical Analysis,* Cambridge, New York: Cambridge University Press, 1983

Jarocinski, Stefan, *Debussy: Impressionism and Symbolism,* London: Eulenberg Books, 1976

Jankélevitch, Vladimir, *Debussy et le mystère,* Neuchatel: Barconnière, 1949

Jean-Aubry, Georges, *La musique française d'aujourdhui,* Paris: Perrin, 1916

Koechlin, Charles, *Debussy,* Paris: H. Laurens, 1027

Laloy, Louis, *Debussy,* Paris: Aux Armes de France, 1944

Lesure, François, *Debussy avant Pelléas,* Paris: Klincksieck, 1992

Lockspeiser, Edward, *Debussy,* London: Dent / New York: Pellegrini & Cudahy, 1951; New York: McGraw-Hill, 1963/1972

Lockspeiser, Edward, *Debussy: His Life and Mind,* London: Cassell, and New York: Macmillan, 1962-65

Lockspeiser, Edward, *Debussy et Edgar Allan Poe,* Monaco: Editions du Rocher, 1962

Metzger/Riehn (ed), *Claude Debussy,* Munich: edition text und kritik, 1977

Myers, Rollo, *Debussy,* London: G. Duckworth, 1948

Nichols, Roger, *Debussy*, London: Oxford University Press, 1973

Nichols, Roger, *Debussy Remembered*, London: Faber and Faber, 1992; Portland, Or: Amadeus Press, 1992

Seraphin, Hellmut, *Debussys Kammermusikwerke der mittleren Schaffenszeit: Analytische und historische Untersuchung im Rahmen des Gesamtschaffrens unter besonderer Berücksichtigung des Ganztonge-schlechts*, Munichen, 1962

Séroff, Victor Ilyitch, *Debussy, Musician of France*, London: J. Calder, 1957

Thompson, Oscar, *Debussy, Man and Artist*, New York: Dover Publications, 1967

Vallas, Leon, *Claude Debussy, His Life and Work*, London: Oxford University Press, 1933

Vuillermoz, Emile, *Claude Debussy*, Geneve: R. Kister, 1957

Wenk, Arthur B., *Claude Debussy and the Poets*, Berkeley: University of California Press, 1976

Wenk, Arthur B., *Claude Debussy and Twentieth-ceetury Music*, Boston, MA: Twayne Publishers, 1983

Winzer, Dieter, *Claude Debussy und die französische musikalische Tradition*, Wiesbaden: Breitkopf und Härtel, 1981

On Ravel:

Brook, Donald, *Five Great French Composers—Berlioz, César Franck, Saint-Saëns, Debussy, Ravel: Their Lives and Works*, London: Rockliff, 1946

Bruyr, José, *Maurice Ravel ou Le Lyrisme et les Sortilèges*, Paris: Editions Le Bon Plaisir, Libraire Plon, 1950

Calza, Renato, *Maurice Ravel nella storia della critica: poetiche decadenti raveliane e interpretazioni novecentesche in Francia, Italia, Inghilterra e Stati Uniti*, Padova: G. Zanibon, 1980

Colette et al., *Maurice Ravel, par quelques-uns de ces familiers*, Paris: Editions du Tambourinaire, 1939

Demuth, Norman, *Ravel*, New York: Collier Books, 1962

Hirsbrunner, Theo, *Maurice Ravel, sein Leben, sein Werk*, Laaber: Laaber-Verlag, 1989

James, Burnett, *Ravel: His Life and Times*, Tunbridge Wells, Kent: Midas Books, and New York: Hippocrene Books, 1983

Jankélevitch, Vladimir, *Maurice Ravel*, Paris: Editions du Seuil, 1956 (English: New York: Grove Press, 1959)

Jean-Aubry, Georges, *La musique française d'aujourdhui*, Paris: Perrin, 1916

Landowski, W.-L., *Maurice Ravel, sa vie, son œuvre*, Paris: Les Editions Ouvrières, 1950

Lesure, François, *Maurice Ravel*, Paris: La Bibliothèque nationale, 1975

Machabey, Armand, *Maurice Ravel*, Paris: Richard-Masse, 1947

Marnat, Marcel, *Maurice Ravel*, Paris: Fayard, 1986

Myers, Rollo, *Ravel, Life and Works*, London: G. Duckworth, 1960

Nichols, Roger, *Ravel*, London: J.M. Dent & Sons, 1977

Nichols, Roger, *Ravel Remembered*, London: Faber, 1987

Onnen, Frank, *Maurice Ravel*, Stockholm: Continental Book Cp., 1947

Orenstein, Arbie, *Ravel, Man and Musician*, New York: Columbia University Press, 1975

Ravel, Maurice, *Ravel According to Ravel*, London: Kahn & Averill, 1988

Ravel, Maurice, *Ravel au miroir de ses lettres*, Paris: R. Laffont, 1956

Roland-Manuel, *Maurice Ravel et son œuvre*, Paris: Durand, 1914/1926

Roland-Manuel, *Maurice Ravel*, Paris: Gallimard, 1948; New York: Dover Publications, 1972

Perlemuter, Vlado, *Ravel d'après Ravel*, Lausanne: Editions du Cervin, 1953

Stuckenschmidt, Hans H., *Maurice Ravel: Variationen über Person und Werk*, Frankfurt: Suhrkamp, 1966 (English: *Maurice Ravel: Variations on His Life and Work*, Philadelphia: Chilton Book Co., 1968)

van Ackere, Jules, *Maurice Ravel*, Bruxelles: Elsevier, 1957

van der Veen, J., *Problèmes structuraux chez Maurice Ravel*; Bericht über den 7. internationalen musikwissenschaftlichen Kongress Köln 1958; Kassel, 1959

On Messiaen:

Ahrens, Sieglinde, *Das Orgelwerk Messiaens*, Duisburg: Gilles und Francke, 1976

Bell, Carla, *Olivier Messiaen*, Boston: Twayne, 1984

Flynn, George W., "Olivier Messiaen: Mystical Composer," *The Christian Century* 109: 652-4 (Jul 1-8 '92)

Forster, Max, *Technik modaler Komposition bei Olivier Messiaen*, Neuhausen-Stuttgart: Hannsler, 1976

Gavoty, Bernard, *Musique et mystique: le 'cas' Messiaen*, Paris: 1945

Griffiths, Paul, *Olivier Messiaen and the Music of Time*, London/Boston: Faber and Faber, 1985

Halbreich, Harry, *Olivier Messiaen*, Paris/Fayard: Fondation SACEM, 1980

Hill, Peter, *The Messiaen Companion*, London: Faber and Faber, 1995

Hirsbrunner, Theo, *Olivier Messiaen: Leben und Werk*, Laaber: Laaber Verlag, 1988

Hohlfeld-Ufer, Ingrid, *Die musikalische Sprache Olivier Messiaens: dargestellt an dem Orgelzyklus 'Die Pfingstmesse'*, Duisburg: Gilles und Francke, 1978

Lee, Hyeweon, *Olivier Messiaen's 'Vingt regard sur l'Enfant-Jésus': A Study of Sonority, Color, and Symbol*, University of Cincinnati, Dissertation 1992

Mari, Pierette, *Olivier Messiaen: l'homme et son œuvre*, Paris: Editions Seghers, 1965

Massin, Brigitte, *Olivier Messiaen: une poétique du merveilleux*, Aix-en-Provence: Alinéa, 1989

Messiaen, Olivier, *La technique de mon langage musical*, Paris: Alphonse Leduc: 1956 [1944]

Metzger, Heinz-Klaus et al (eds.), *Olivier Messiaen*, Munich: edition text + kritik, 1982

Michaely, Aloyse, *Die Musik Olivier Messiaens: Untersuchungen zum Gesamtschaffen;* Hamburger Beiträge zur Musikwissenschaft (Sonderband), Hamburg: Verlag der Musikalienhandlung K. D. Wagner, 1987

Michaely, Aloyse, "L'abîme: Das Bild des Abgrunds bei Olivier Messiaen"; *Musik-Konzepte*, vol. 28, Munich: edition text + kritik, 1982

Michaely, Aloyse, "Verbum Caro - die Darstellung des Mysteriums der Inkarnation in Olivier Messiaens 'Vingt regards sur l'Enfant-Jésus'," in *Hamburger Jahrbuch für Musikwissenschaft*, vol. 6, Hamburg: 1984

Morris, David, "A semiotic investigation of Messiaen's 'Abîme des oiseaux'," *Music Analysis*, viii (1989): 125-158

Nichols, Roger, *Messiaen*, London/New York: Oxford University Press, 1975

Reverdy, Michele, *L'œuvre pour piano d'Olivier Messiaen*, Paris: Alphonse Leduc, 1978

Rößler, Almut, *Contributions to the Spiritual World of Olivier Messiaen*, Duisburg: Gilles und Francke, 1986

Samuel, Claude, *Entretiens avec Olivier Messiaen*, Paris: Editions Pierre Belfond, 1967

Samuel, Claude, *Musique et couleur: nouveaux entretiens avec Olivier Messiaen*, Paris: Ed. P. Belfond, 1986

Sherlaw Johnson, Robert, *Messiaen*, London: J. M. Dent & Sons, 1974 and Berkeley, CA: University of California Press, 1989; now Oxford: Oxford University Press.

INDEX OF COMPOSITIONS

The Author

Siglind Bruhn, born in Hamburg, Germany, is a musicologist, concert pianist, and interdisciplinary scholar. An independent researcher in music analysis/musicology, she is presently affiliated with the University of Michigan as a Research Associate in Music and Humanities.

Prior to coming to the United States, she was the Director of Studies for Music in the School for Professional and Continuing Education at The University of Hong Kong (1987-1994), and the Founding Director of the Pianisten-Akademie in Ansbach, Germany (1984-87). Internationally, she has been a Guest Professor for 20th-century Music at the Central Conservatory in Beijing, and a visiting artist and/or visiting lecturer to universities and conservatories in several European countries as well as in China, Taiwan, Australia, South Africa, Namibia, Lebanon and Ecuador.

She holds three post-graduate degrees: an M.M. in piano performance and piano pedagogy (Stuttgart), an M.A. in literature and philosophy (Munich), and an interdisciplinary Ph.D. in music analysis/musicology/ psychology (Vienna). As a performing pianist, she has given solo and chamber music recitals in twenty-two countries on all five continents. As a researcher she has published eight monographs, contributed numerous articles to scholarly journals in Europe and the United States, edited three collections of research essays, and translated one music-theoretical work from English into German. Major book publications include *Die musikalische Darstellung psychologischer Wirklichkeit in Alban Bergs Wozzeck* (Bern: Peter Lang, 1986), *J.S. Bach's Well-tempered Clavier: In-depth Analysis and Interpretation* (Hong Kong: Mainer International, 1993; 4 volumes), *Musikalische Symbolik in Olivier Messiaens Weihnachtsvignetten* (Frankfurt: Peter Lang, 1997), *Alban Berg's Music as Encrypted Speech* (New York: Garland, 1997; contrib. ed.), *Messiaen's Language of Mystical Love* (New York: Garland, 1998; contrib. ed.), *The Temptation of Paul Hindemith: Mathis der Maler as a Spiritual Testimony* (Stuyvesant, NY: 1998/99).

425